VOLUME X:
The T.U.E.L. – 1925-1929

HISTORY OF THE LABOR MOVEMENT IN THE UNITED STATES

VOLUME X:
The T.U.E.L. – 1925-1929

BY PHILIP S. FONER

INTERNATIONAL PUBLISHERS, New York

LIBRARY OF CONGRESS CATALOGING-IN-PUBLICATION DATA

(Revised for volume 10)

Foner, Philip Sheldon, 1910-
    History of the labor movement in the United States.

    Includes bibliographical references and indexes.
    Contents: -- v. 2. From the founding of the
American Federation of Labor to the emergence of
American imperialism --   -- v. 5. The AFL in the
progressive era, 1910-1915 --   -- v. 10. The T.U.E.L.,
1925-1929.
    1. Trade-unions--United States--History. 2. Labor
movement--United States--History. I. Title. II. Series.
HD6508.F57   1975   331.88'0973   75-315606
ISBN 0-7178-0092-X
vol. 10 ISBN 0-7178-0690-1 cl.   -0691-X pbk

Contents

Preface

This is the tenth volume of my *History of the Labor Movement in the United States*. It is also the second volume dealing with the Trade Union Educational League. The preceding volume covered the TUEL from its founding in 1920 to the end of the Gompers Era in 1924. The present volume carries the history of the Trade Union Educational League from 1924 to its end in 1929 and its replacement by the Trade Union Unity League, whose history we will deal with in the next volume.

In the previous volume I criticized most labor historians for virtually ignoring the activities of the Trade Union Educational League during the early years of its existence. Nearly all labor historians view the TUEL as virtually dead by 1925. But, as we shall see in the present volume, the Trade Union Educational League continued to hold aloft the banner of labor militancy, of industrial unionism, of labor solidarity, and other progressive issues in the years that followed the inauguration of William Green as the successor to Samuel Gompers as president of the American Federation of Labor. Moreover, this in a period that the standard interpretation sees as deprived of labor militancy, a period of lean years not only for organized labor, but also for the radical movement in general. The Trade Union Educational League waged some of the most militant labor struggles in American history. During a time of unabashed class collaboration by the established trade union leadership, the TUEL kept alive militant working class traditions and an active core of the Left in the labor movement.

As in the case of previous volumes of the *History of the Labor Movement in the United States*, in writing volume 10 I have received help from many institutions and people. I am again grateful for the cooperation of libraries, librarians, and archivists. I particularly thank Dorothy Swanson of the Tamiment Institute Library of New York University who has been so helpful in this and previous volumes. I wish also to thank the University of Pennsylvania Library, especially its splendid interlibrary loan department, the State Historical Society of Wisconsin, the Library of Congress, New York Public Library, the Chicago Historical Society, YIVO Institute for Jewish Study Archives, New York City, the libraries of the University of Wisconsin, Indiana University, Princeton University, Columbia University, Temple University, Harvard University, Rutgers University, University of California (Los Angeles), University of California (Berkeley), State University of New York at Binghamton, Syracuse

University, University of Oregon, University of Rochester, Pennsylvania State University, Ohio State University. I am, as in the past, grateful to my brother Henry Foner who read the entire manuscript and made valuable suggestions

Philip S. Foner
Emeritus Professor of History,
Lincoln University, Pennsylvania

VOLUME X:
The T.U.E.L. – 1925-1929

CHAPTER 1

ENTER WILLIAM GREEN

At the 1924 convention of the American Federation of Labor, a few weeks before the death of Samuel Gompers, its long-time president, Morris Sigman, Socialist president of the International Garment Workers' Union, presented the "old man" with a bust of himself. At the 1925 convention, Socialist Max Zaritsky, on behalf of the needle trades' right-wing officials,* presented a bust of Gompers as a gift to the convention. President William Green, formerly secretary-treasurer of the United Mine Workers, who had assumed the AFL presidency after Gompers' death in 1924, announced that the bust would be turned over to a leading museum, and that a Memorial Fund had been launched to honor the name of the AFL leader.[1]

But two years after Gompers' death, J. Louis Engdahl wrote in the *Workers Monthly*:

> When the Forty-Sixth Convention of the American Federation of Labor met at Detroit, Michigan, October 4-14 (1926), the memory of Samuel Gompers, so fresh the year before at Atlantic City, had become faint indeed. It was not until the afternoon of the third day that the name of Gompers was even mentioned....

Noting that after nearly two years' effort, only $98.50 had been collected by the Gompers' Memorial Fund, Engdahl concluded that "Gompers is gone; even as a memory. Yet," he went on, "the loosening of Gompers' dead hand upon the American labor movement has unleashed no latent force of progress. Instead reaction still sits in the saddle and drives toward even greater conservatism. Class collabora-

---

* All except the Amalgamated Clothing Workers of America, which was kept out of the American Federation of Labor until 1932. Even if the Amalgamated had been part of the AFL, it would probably not have joined in the tribute.

1

tion offers an opportunity to surrender much, with the flag of truce raised high by the labor officialdom in the industrial class struggle."[2]

The position of president of the American Federation of Labor gave William Green a full opportunity to carry out his "religiously inspired dream of labor-management cooperation."* Craig Phelan, Green's biographer, points out that "by the 1920s and 1930s... as industrial relations became increasingly complex and depersonalized and as society became more secular, the ideal of Christian cooperation waned. Yet Green was so strongly wedded to these values that he proved incapable of abandoning them even after years of failure. Under his guidance the evangelical labor tradition... became ... a hindrance to working-class organization, a handmaiden to craft unionists, and a contributor to the division of the labor movement."[3]

At the time Green became AFL president, the federation was in decline, and the opposition to it by open shop employers was increasing week by week. Under Green the AFL reacted to these developments by endeavoring to "sell" itself to industry. "In the hope that employers voluntarily could allow their workers to organize and bargain collectively, the AFL's high command abandoned whatever vestigial militancy it retained and advertised all the virtues of trade unionism."[4] So Craig Phelan puts it.

The AFL's "high command" received considerable aid in selling "the virtues of trade unionism" from Ralph M. Easley, founder of the Na-

---

* For the emergence of such religious influences in the labor movement, especially of the Catholic Church, see Philip S. Foner, *History of the Labor Movement in the United States* 3 (New York, 1960): 113-36.

** In a previous volume we described the formation of the National Civic Federation at the turn of the twentieth century, the active participation of the AFL leaders, headed by Samuel Gompers, in the work of the NCF, and how this was used by a section of the most important industrial and financial leaders in the United States—most of whom were open shop employers who bitterly fought unionism in their own industries—joined in promoting the concept of harmony between capital and labor through the Civic Federation. They were willing to sit down with labor leaders at sumptuous dinners and other gatherings and deal with them, but not in their own industries, as long as the union leaders rejected socialism, independent political action, industrial unionism and any form of radicalism. From the beginning, militant trade unionists and Socialists condemned the labor bureaucrats for associating with Morgan, Rockefeller, Harriman, and other wealthy monopoly capitalists while these men were viciously exploiting their own workers and maintaining the open shop in their industries. Gradually, large sections of the rank and file joined in this criticism, so that by the end of World War I, the NCF was dormant.

In the 1920s some AFL leaders tried to inject new life into the National Civic Federation, particularly Matthew Woll, a member of the AFL Executive Council and president of the Photo-Engravers' Union. Woll was elected NCF vice-president in January, 1926, and in June of that year, became acting president. James O. Morris points out that in the AFL-NCF alliance of the 1920s, "many of the employing group [in the

tional Civic Federation and chairman of its Executive Council.** What Easley, Green and most of the top AFL leaders had in mind when they spoke of "the virtues of trade unionism" was spelled out by Easley in a pamphlet mailed to businessmen in 1924. Easley pointed out that the labor movement of every industrial country except the United States was in the hands of Communists or radical Socialists who were "harassing their governments." In contrast, at its convention at El Paso in 1924, the AFL had discussed a working arrangement with the Citizens' Military Training camps, had voted overwhelmingly against the diplomatic recognition of Soviet Russia by the United States, against the formation of a labor political party, and had reaffirmed its traditional opposition to government "interference in industry." "In the light of such a record," Easley asked, "why should any good American be opposed to the trade union movement?"

Easley noted, however, that a number of employers did not appreciate the AFL's "worthy record" or what the Federation was doing in keeping radical unionism in check, and unfortunately, oblivious to their own interests, were extremely anti-union in outlook. This at a time when labor and capital "should be working together against common foes whose philosophy spells the taking over of all their property and the government as well." He finally asked: "Can a *modus vivendi* be established?"[5]

The AFL under William Green's leadership was eager to achieve this *modus vivendi* by any means possible. This was made clear by the proceedings of the 1926 AFL convention in Detroit. In his opening address Green took the occasion to notify open shop employers, especially those in Detroit, that the AFL delegates were not dangerous men and women. He said:

> Perhaps they still entertain the idea that the representatives of labor are vicious backwoodsmen who know little about cultured life, but as a refutation of that impression, I invite them to come here; I invite them to come among us during the deliberations of this convention, sit with us, look and listen, and when they depart I will leave it to their judgment and

National Civic Federation] were representatives of open-shop or company-union industries." These included Nicholas F. Brady, president of the New York Edison Company; Samuel Insull, president of the Commonwealth Edison Company; Nathan M. Miller, general counsel for United States Steel; and E.K. Hall, vice-president of American Telephone and Telegraph. (James O. Morris, "The AFL in the 1920's: A Strategy of Defense," *Industrial and Labor Relations Review* 11 [July, 1958]: 578-79). For the formation and ideology of the National Civic Federation, *see* Philip S. Foner, *History of the Labor Movement in the United States* 3 [New York, 1960]:78-111.

to their conscience as to whether or not the representative men and women of labor assembled here in this city do not compare favorably with any other group in society.... But, my friends, I am sure that much of this apprehension expressed is due to a lack of understanding of the motives, the principles and the policies of our great American labor movement.[6]

As if further to assure the open shoppers that they had nothing to fear from the AFL, Green continued Gompers' bitter anti-Soviet policy. At the first convention over which he had presided, he made this clear. The International Labor News Service reported: "In order that his own personal position might be thoroughly understood by all, President Green took the floor of the American Federation of Labor convention and discussed the committee report on the resolution asking recognition of the Soviets. He came emphatically to the support of the committee which reported against the resolution. He said in part:

This subject seems to come before each succeeding convention of the American Federation of Labor, and, for some reason or other, those who are behind this propaganda that has for its purpose the recognition of Soviet Russia by the American Government refuse to accept the decisions of the convention from time to time as final. And I suppose, like Banquo's ghost, it will not down, it will always be here at the convention of the American Federation of Labor; but I sincerely hope that the vote of the delegates at this convention will be so decisive and overwhelming as to leave no doubt as to the attitude of this great economic force in America's life....

We have a little evidence of Russian propaganda here in America now. Through their agencies here they are carrying on that propaganda. They publish dirty, filthy sheets, and anyone who has read these sheets must form their own opinion of a government that would stand for such publications.

And we know from a mass of data and information gathered—and I have it in my personal possession—that those who are circulating this propaganda receive their instructions from the very roots of the Moscow government.*

We are not going to embrace this destructive force and for that reason you are going, I believe, to register your opposition to this government that would use the opportunity, if it is given it through recognition to undermine our free institutions and destroy all the traditions of America.[7]

---

* Although Green did not spell it out, the delegates knew he was refering to the Trade Union Educational League and the Communist Party.

Green's hope that the vote at the 1925 AFL convention would bury the issue of recognition of Soviet Russia was doomed to disappointment. It appeared again at the 1926 convention, and once again Green spoke out against recognition and any other form of relations between the United States and the Soviet Union. Speaking in reply to the fraternal greetings of the British delegates, Green said:

> At the moment there stands an impregnable barrier between the working people of the government of that country (the Soviet Union) and the American Federation of Labor.... There must be a psychological change, a change in the viewpoint of those who embrace the philosophy followed by the peoples in that great country before we can ever think of establishing cooperative relations between them and the American Federation of Labor.... When they (the workers of the Soviet Union) embrace a philosophy that is so antagonistic to the philosophy embraced and followed by the American Federation of Labor, then it would be a waste of time and effort to reconcile our conditions.[8]

The rebuff to the Soviet workers was not the only effort made by Green to prove to the open shop employers they had nothing to fear from the AFL. Although graciously greeting the fraternal delegates from the British Trade Union Congress, Green assured American industrialists that the AFL would give no support to the British general strike of that year, and, under no circumstances, would ever consider breaking a trade agreement once it had been concluded:

> We realize of course, that the trade union movement in each country must be governed by circumstances and conditions prevailing within their own respective jurisdictions. They know what is best for them.
>
> And so we say to our British brethren that what you think is best for you, you may inaugurate and put into effect. We have confidence in your judgment, in your intelligence and in your experience.
>
> We are committed here (in the United States) irrevocably to the principles of collective bargaining and trade agreements.... As we believe in collective bargaining, in the making of wage agreements, so we here in America are religiously committed to the observance of any contract we make anywhere in any place.[9]

At the 1925 AFL Convention the issue of wages caused an unusual stir. "A fair day's pay for a fair day's work" had always been the AFL slogan, and the initial report on wages by the Executive Council revealed no intention to change it. The report dealt exclusively with wage reductions in the textile industry, where repeated slashes in the pay envelope had taken place since the last convention. The report pleaded with the employers that "wage reductions diminish purchasing power of the group of workers in the textile industry which is reflected in the business of the whole community and extends out into the industrial fabric of the whole nation." Instead of wage reductions, the Executive Council offered as their solution to the problem the elimination of waste through more efficient management to be achieved through intelligent cooperation between the employer and the wage worker.

At this point John P. Frey, who, as editor of the *Molders' Journal*, had fashioned a reputation as the ideologist of the AFL, offered an amendment to the Executive Council report, declaring that "Social inequality, industrial instability, and injustice must increase unless the workers' real wages, the purchasing power of their wages, is increased in proportion to man's increasing power of production."

Frey declared that "we never could discover what the fair wage was or what the fair day's work might be, because we differed with our employers. Only within recent years many of our representatives adopted a still more unsound statement of the basis on which wages should be computed—a living wage. I don't know what a living wage is. It is unfair that we should base our wages on our own conception of our cost of living rather than upon the value of what we are creating."[10] Frey boasted that he had had Karl Marx's *Capital* in his library for the last twenty-five years, and his point about the value labor created indicated that even if incompletely, some of it had rubbed off on him.

Delegate Lynch of the printers supported Frey in part. "The productive power in this super-age in which we live, this abundance which we are enjoying, is due to a very great extent to labor-saving machinery and the effect of labor-saving machinery will not be regulated entirely by the wage. This definition should include not only increases in wages, but also be accompanied by further reduction in the hours that wage earners work."

The resolutions committee, headed by Matthew Woll and James Duncan, suggested that the question of "wages" be referred back to it. This was endorsed by the delegates, and the committee returned with a revised report accepting the Frey-Lynch modification, which was then unanimously adopted by the delegates.[11]

Little, however, was said at the 1926 convention about the "new wage theory" enunciated at and adopted by the 1925 convention, All that Green said on this issue was that "American labor suggests that as the productivity of the individual worker is increased and as his efficiency is raised higher and higher throughout the operation of these economic forces, his wages, first of all, must increase in proportion with his productivity and his efficiency."[12] Just how to achieve even this was not discussed.

The 1926 convention met just as Henry Ford announced that the five-day week would go into effect in his plants. It came on the heels of the strike of the New York Fur Workers in which, as we shall see, labor in the fur industry of that city, through its own power, won the five-day, forty hour week. At the AFL convention, one of the printers' delegates urged adoption of the four-day week in American industry to give time for recuperation from the heavy exactions of human energy by modern industry. But all the convention came up with was for the progressive shortening of the work-week, with no mention of any specific number of hours as the immediate goal, nor of any way which "the shortening of the work-week" was to be achieved.[13]

The only reference at the convention to organizing the unorganized came in the speech by Rabbi Dr. Stephen S. Wise, who had become deeply involved in the strike of the Passaic textile workers, which we will discuss below. He told the delegates:

> Remember this: Organize the textile industry of America, basic and fundamental to the life of America. Give your help to the Passaic strikers; organize the textile industry of America, and may you always bear yourself with the courage and dignity ... with which the strikers of Passaic have borne themselves....

Sarah Conboy, secretary of the United Textile Workers of America, took up a collection among the delegates which netted more than a thousand dollars. The international officials of the major unions met and pledged $25,000 for the immediate relief of the Passaic strikers. With this, the issue of organizing the unorganized was laid to rest.[14]

The resolution adopted on company unions exuded Green's philosophy. It read: "To accomplish the substitution of union-management cooperation for company unions and to substitute voluntary trade unions for employer controlled unions will be a service not only to American workers, but to American industry in all its branches and to the American public in general."[15] However, James O. Morris has noted that while publicly "in its official pronouncements in the 1920s, the AFL took a firm stand against company unions and considered union-management [cooperation] to be the substitute for and not the complement to company unions," at the same time not so publicly, Green and other top AFL leaders sought to achieve "a compromise between company unions and trade unionism."[16]

Much time was devoted at the convention to prove that the AFL should be known and accepted as a loyal, patriotic organization. A resolution was adopted approving in superlative terms of the militarist centers known as the Citizens' Military Training Camps. From 1919 until his death in 1924, Samuel Gompers lectured annually at the Army War College in Washington, and the Naval War College in Newport. For many years after 1924, John P. Frey was also a frequent lecturer at the Army War College and the Army Industrial College.[17]

William Green contributed to this jingoistic tradition, addressing the Army War College in 1925. He fervently assured his listeners that

> Labor is intensely patriotic and conscientiously devoted to American ideals, to American institutions and to the American form of government.... I can say with certainty...that ... labor ...will offer itself when the Republic is assailed in defense of the Homeland, our Glorious Flag and the United States of America.[18]

In 1926 the AFL endorsed the Citizens' Military Training Camps, which had been set up as a result of the postwar National Defense Act.* In August, 1926, the AFL Executive Council, headed by Green, journeyed to Plattsburgh for a three-day inspection tour of the camp there. They were feted by local Elks and Rotary clubs during their stay and, after winding up their visit with "a colorful review of the 1,600 infantrymen" announced approval of what they had seen. Green was convinced that there was "a wrong impression in some quarters as to the work, training, purposes and objectives of the military training camps."[19]

The Executive Council reported to the October 1926 convention of the AFL that military training "occupied the small part of the day at Plattsburgh" and that "athletic events took up most of the trainees' time." "This kind of training," the Council continued, "is building up the mind and the body of the American youth. It stimulates the patriotic spirit of the youth. He is taught citizenship...we believe it would be advantageous to all the boys in our country to take advantage of the opportunities afforded to them in the camps."

The Cloth Hat, Cap and Millinery Workers' International Union, the International Ladies' Garment Workers' Union, and the Pennsylvania Federation of Labor sharply condemned the Executive Council's bid for endorsement of the CMTC, and contended that the camps not only encouraged the cult of militarism but also that the

---

* The National Defense Act became law in 1920, and in 1921 the first Citizens' Military Training Camps were established. By 1926 there were forty-seven of such camps. (The Military Training Camps Association of the United States, *The Military Training Camps*, Chicago, 1925, p. 34.)

Military Training Camp Association, the directing agency of the camps, derived its chief support from open-shop employers who were using it to inculcate anti-unionism among the trainees and to turning out scabs. The Amalgamated Clothing Workers, still outside of the AFL, also vigorously condemned CMTC.[20]

Speaking as secretary of the Resolutions Committee, Matthew Woll emphatically denied the interpretation that the AFL wished to encourage militarism but, on the other hand, he boasted that the AFL had never opposed the building up of "strong bodies, healthy minds and patriotic souls." The convention voted to concur in the Council's report and the AFL endorsed the Citizens' Military Training Camps. Not even the Cloth Hat, Cap and Millinery Workers' and International Ladies' Garment Workers' delegates, or those of the Pennsylvania State Federation of Labor, voted in the negative.[21]

This unanimity of opinion at the convention was not surprising. There were no Communist delegates at the convention. That had been settled to the satisfaction of the AFL and industrial leaders at the Portland Convention in 1924, when William F. Dunne, the delegate from Montana, was refused accreditation on the sole ground that he was a member of the Communist Party.* Delegate Max S. Hayes, a long-time member of the International Typographical Union and editor of the Socialist *Cleveland Citizen*, was farthest to the left of any delegate. He was on the floor repeatedly speaking for a labor party, recognition of Soviet Russia, and support for the Passaic strikers. But when it came to voting, Hayes voted with the rest of the delegates, enabling President Green to declare Hayes' proposals defeated "unanimously." When the committee on resolutions reported against recognition of Soviet Russia, Green called for "such a decisive vote that there will be no doubt in the minds of the American people and the people throughout the world where the American Federation of Labor stands." The vote was unanimous for the resolution; not even Max Hayes dared to vote against it.[22]

Thus Green adjourned the 1926 convention glorying in the declaration; "It is significant that in this convention no point of order was raised by any delegate or upon any question, and no roll call was demanded by the convention except the one just taken upon the convention city."[23] In short, no new ideas or debate over pressing

---

* *See* Philip S. Foner, *History of the Labor Movement in the United States* 9 (New York, 1990):167-68.

problems facing the labor movement disturbed this gathering of the American Federation of Labor. All of labor's problems could be solved through the magic of labor-management cooperation.

In his biography of William Green, an expansion of his essay we have referred to and quoted from, Craig Phelan concludes that Green "did not address realistically the issues confronting organized labor in the 1930s," and that his conservative moralism led him to become "a hindrance to working-class organization and a contributor to the division of the labor movement."

This, shorn of Green's conservative moralism and religiosity, could be applied to nearly the entire leadership of the AFL. Indeed, Green's view that capital and labor were equal partners, and should work together to achieve capital-labor accord and to jointly oppose rank-and-file insurgencies pervaded the entire American Federation of Labor top leadership from the Executive Council to the International unions and many of the state and local federations. Perhaps the most glaring example of this policy was the action of the Detroit Federation of Labor, an umbrella organization of AFL unions in that city, in asking the Detroit auto employers to make regular financial contributions to the Federation. In 1926 a General Manager of the Maxwell Motor Company asked advice of Hudson's Ray Chapin about the visit of "a representative of the Detroit Federation of Labor" and "represented that all of the leading motor manufacturers of Detroit made annual contributions to the Federation and that the money was used, in part at least, to combat radicalism in union ranks."[24]

Thus it appears that labor "radicalism" as represented by the Trade Union Educational League, which was in the midst of trying to organize the auto industry of Detroit, united the open shop employers and the AFL of that city at the expense of both the organized and unorganized workers.

CHAPTER 2

THE MINERS

In *Political Affairs* of August 1980, Daniel Mason asked the question: "John L. Lewis—Hero or Villain?"[1] In the period covered by the previous and present volume, it is easy to answer that question in one word: "Villain!"

Lewis's life-style separated him completely from the members of the United Mine Workers, who were forced to struggle continuously for a bare living. He began to live like a millionaire. His departure for a six-week vacation in Great Britain on the *S.S. Celtic* in 1925 was reported in the society column of the *New York Times.* On his passport, he described himself, not as a labor leader, but as an executive. According to Melvyn Dubofsky and Warren Van Tyne in their biography of Lewis:*

> He followed his own rules of social etiquette religiously. He kept fellow officers of the UMW at a distance, practiced regal aloofness and acted in the union as a king to his court. Lewis reserved his friendship for business executives. high public officials, and members of the hereditary American elite. They dined with Lewis on a reciprocal basis, and he charmed them with well-told stories and stimulating conversation. The Herbert Hoovers, the Gardner Jacksons, the Harrimans, the Cyrus Chings, corporation executives in general—they were the type of people John L. Lewis cultivated.[2]

Cusling's Survey, a business newsletter, reported that Lewis was "one of the wisest small traders that ever takes a flyer in the stock market. His success...shows that he knows economics far better than

---

* The biography is the most complete record of John L. Lewis's life, but it is marred by a bitter anti-communism which belittles and distorts the Communists' role in the United Mine Workers, especially during the decade of the 1920s.

nine out of ten coal operators. And he is making more money for himself today than are ninety-five out of a hundred operators."[3]

By 1920, Lewis had already taken the step toward an alliance with the coal mine operators, against the interests of the workers he supposedly represented. By 1924 this had become a regular pattern of his leadership, along with his having become either the foremost, or next to William L. Hutcheson of the Carpenters, the leading union tyrant in the American labor movement. As we have made clear in the preceding volume, Lewis consolidated his power by fraud, bribery, and corruption. He took from the districts the right to elect their officers and appointed his henchmen as officers. He created an army of gunmen and gangsters as well as a spy system designed to finger his opponents, especially Communists. The 1920 national convention put the finishing touches on his dictatorship. The convention gave him authority to expel union members, revoke charters of subdistricts and local unions and set up his own organizations in their place.

But Lewis's brutal consolidation of power and his indifference to the interests of the UMW membership met with resistance. The rank-and-file tried again and again after 1920 to repudiate his leadership and policies. Although not the only one to protest, the Trade Union Educational League was in the forefront of the struggle. An indication of this resistance was the UMW election of 1924 when George Voyzey, a little known Communist and TUEL activist, received one third of the vote for president in opposition to Lewis, in a count supervised by Lewis's henchmen.[*]

Reviewing the 1924 UMW convention for the *Daily Worker,* Scott Nearing noted that there was no issue more important to the American labor movement than "the disorganization of the American mine workers." Citing the report of the U.S. Coal Commission of September 22, 1923, Nearing pointed out that in Alabama, Colorado, and New Mexico, the union had been "practically wiped out"; in Washington, it had been "reduced to a fifth of its 1921 strength,"; in Arkansas, Oklahoma, and Texas, "cut in half," and in Illinois and Ohio, "severely reduced." Out of the 17 districts, "only three show gains." He concluded:

[*] *See* Philip S. Foner, *History of the Labor Movement in the United States* 9 (New York, 1990):268.

This is a matter of vital concern to every man who mines coal, and to every man and woman who is working to build up the American labor movement.

The miners must gain back their lost membership. They must organize the outlying nonunion fields. The health and strength of the American labor movement are both seriously involved.[4]

Unfortunately, the situation only grew worse.

JACKSONVILLE AGREEMENT

The agreement concluded after the strike of 1922 was due to expire in the bituminous industry on April 1, 1924.* In January, 1924, the UMW convention authorized Lewis "to secure the best agreement obtainable from the operators in the Central Competitive Field on the basis of no reduction in wages" for a four-year period (April 1, 1924, to March 31, 1928). On February 19, 1924, the so-called "Jacksonville agreement" to last until 1927, was drawn up between the operators and miners of the Central Competitive Field. The operators agreed to continue paying $7.50 per day, the same rate as that of 1922.[5]

This wage was considerably above the prevailing one in the non-union fields, and inroads on the union operators by those who were producing coal in nonunion mines grew rapidly. When the Jacksonville agreement was signed, the output of the organized fields was 60 percent of the total. During the following year, however, they produced only 40 percent of the coal tonnage and their position was becoming increasingly unfavorable. This was precisely what Lewis had anticipated. The Jacksonville agreement, he believed, would drive 200,000 miners out of the industry since they would become surplus as hundreds of mines closed down, unable to compete with the nonunion mines.[6]**

---

* On September 7, 1923, after a strike that lasted only five-and-a-half days, a new two-year anthracite agreement was reached which included a ten percent wage increase for day and tonnage miners and a voluntary system of dues check-off in which union delegates, not management, collected the money. Despite the ten percent wage increase, anthracite miners earned less than those in the bituminous fields. Moreover, the operators still rejected he idea of a closed shop and continued to run many of their mines as non-union. (*New York Times*, Sept. 8, 1923.)

** Lewis personally preferred a total reorganization of the soft-coal industry. Throughout the '20s, he and his economic adviser, W. Jet Lanca, corresponded about and discussed privately their plans to stabilize the coal industry by consolidating production into fewer, more efficient units; restricting competition in marketing and pricing; and liberating the coal industry from the anti-trust laws. (Melvyn Dubofsky and Warren

When the operators in the union mines asked the UMW for a renegotiation of the Jacksonville scale, Lewis refused on the ground that the industry was undergoing a needed adjustment which, when completed, would result in many fewer miners, fewer mines and a stable, more prosperous industry. The response of the operators was varied. Union operators in West Virginia simply repudiated the Jacksonville scale and returned to the one in force in 1919. In many cases, they set out to destroy the union.

Although the struggle, which began in 1925, raged throughout most of the nation's coal fields, its most serious impact was in western Pennsylvania, especially in the Pittsburgh district. It was there that Lewis's refusal to support the drive for including the nonunion fields was most severely felt. In August, 1925, the Pittsburgh Coal Company, largest in the district and the world's largest commercial producer of bituminous coal, rejected the Jacksonville agreement and reopened on a nonunion basis. It was soon joined by other big coal corporations, including the Pittsburgh Terminal Coal Corporation, the second largest producer in western Pennsylvania, and the Bethlehem Steel Corporation, third largest producer in the Pittsburgh district. In all, some 110 mines in Pennsylvania changed from union to nonunion operations during 1925. Nor was this all. The largest mines in the tri-state area of western Pennsylvania, eastern Ohio, and northern West Virginia were all operating nonunion. Eight months after the Jacksonville agreement was signed, a drop of 118, 017 had taken place in the paid-up membership of the UMW in the bituminous districts.7

As the union losses multiplied, the opposition to Lewis within the UMW rallied its forces. In the spring of 1925, the Miners' Progressive Committee of the UMWA, headed by George Voyzey, proposed the following program to meet "the immediate needs of the miners" and halt the collapse of the union:

A fight against wage cuts, for a wage increase
A six-hour day and a five-day week.
Unemployment insurance to be taken out of the entire profits of the
    industry and administered by a committee of miners

Van Tyne, *John L. Lewis*, New York, 1977, p. 106.) John Brophy considered this policy simply an application of "the businessman's *laissez-faire* philosophy, which ignored the plight of the individual miner and the real need for reforming the whole economic order." (Sister M. Camilla Mulloy, O. P., "John Brophy: Militant Labor Leader and Reformer: The CIO Years," unpublished Ph.D. dissertation, Catholic University of America, 1966, p. 30.)

A national agreement to cover the entire industry.
Nationalization of the mines, to be administered by the Miners' Union.

Since it was clear that unless all miners were unionized and received the same scale, low-wage mines would continue to threaten
the viability of operators with union contracts, the program called for
a major unionizing campaign. It demanded that "all paid officials
[organizers, etc.] be taken out of organized districts and placed in
nonunion fields; that each district be instructed to elect a specified
corps of organizers to be sent into nonunion fields; that an intensive
organizational campaign be immediately started, and that our international officers be instructed to negotiate with the railroad unions
for the purpose of forming a strike alliance."[8]

Lewis's response came in his book, *The Miners' Fight for American
Standards*, published in the early summer of 1925. In it he declared
that the union would "take no backward step" and would refuse to
revise downward the wage rates set by the Jacksonville agreement as
many of the operators had demanded. He assured businessmen of
the UMW's conservatism, writing:

> The policy of the United Mine Workers of America is neither new nor
> revolutionary. It does not command the admiration of visionaries and
> utopians. It ought to have the support of every thinking business man in
> the United States, because it proposes to allow natural economic laws
> free play in the production and distribution of coal....[9]

To achieve total unionization of the industry so that the same
scale would prevail everywhere, Lewis appealed to the federal government to help the United Mine Workers organize the nonunion
operators, especially in West Virginia, Kentucky, Alabama, and western Pennsylvania, and thus guarantee the integrity of the Jacksonville
agreement. Nothing, however, came of this plea.[10]

On September 1, 1925, the two-year agreement with the operators
in the anthracite industry expired. One hundred and fifty thousand
miners in anthracite struck for a ten percent increase in wages for
tonnage miners and a dollar per day increase for draymen, plus the
check-off of union dues at the company offices. As a result of the
strike, 828 mines belonging to 135 companies were shut down.[11]

The operators locked out the strikers and obtained state and federal injunctions to prevent the union from picketing companies that
had violated the Jacksonville agreement.[12] On November 22, Lewis
publicly requested that President Coolidge support the union and
compel the mine owners to abide by the Jacksonville agreement. In
his reply, drafted by Secretary of Commerce Herbert Hoover and

Secretary of Labor James J. Davis, Coolidge deplored any breach of contract by operators but noted that the Coolidge Administration had not signed the Jacksonville agreement and that "the government not being a party to contracts has no status in enforcement." Lewis was advised to take his grievance to the courts.[13] In short, Lewis's belief that the Republican Administration, for which he had rendered such faithful service, would save the union before the Jacksonville agreement went down the drain proved to be an illusion. Meanwhile, the Miners' Progressive Committee, led by the Communists and others in the anti-Lewis coalition, condemned the policy of relying on the Republican Administration to solve the miners' problems. The Committee called for a general strike of all the coal miners, unity of the railroad workers with the anthracite strikers, and no settlement without an increase in wages.[14]

"SAVE-THE-UNION" MOVEMENT

With the support of Lewis and his agents, meetings of the Miners' Progressive Committee in the anthracite districts were broken up and their speakers arrested. Patrick Toohey and Alex Reed, two leading Communists and activists in the Committee, were sent to prison for six months as vagrants. Members of the Lewis machine actually appeared in court and testified against the radical miners and urged that they be jailed as agents of a foreign power seeking to disrupt the UMW. After Toohey and Reed were sent to prison, Rinaldo Cappelini, president of District 1, the largest district of the UMW in anthracite, and as we have seen, a former militant who had sold out to Lewis in return for a lucrative union appointment, wrote to the Scranton Chief of Police, congratulating him on having arrested the progressive miners.[15]

On February 12, 1926, Lewis signed a new contract with the anthracite operators. It said nothing about any of the demands that had led to the strike, offering the strikers only a promise of five years of fixed wages for the anthracite miners.

The Miners' Progressive Committee published an open letter to the miners criticizing the agreement and urging them to carry on the struggle to victory:

> We the rank-and-file miners, we're ready to fight to the end—to victory.
> We put up the longest battle in the history of the anthracite.
> We are fighting to save our union and prevent our becoming virtual slaves.[16]

The miners went back to work on February 18, 1926, without gaining any concessions from the operators. The union managed to fight off compulsory arbitration during the 170-day strike, and the *American Federationist* declared that as a result, "unionism was more firmly rooted in the anthracite industry than ever before...."[17] But the strike settlement did not halt the loss of union territory and the breakdown of the Jacksonville agreement. Anthracite production steadily declined, replaced more and more by oil, gas, and electricity, while bituminous coal was increasingly being produced in nonunion mines. By the end of 1926, 61.3 percent of all miners were working without a union contract.[18]

Wage reductions on top of union losses caused a wave of indignation among the union membership, and created a large group of dissidents ready to do battle with the Lewis Administration. In the summer of 1926, Brophy met with Communists and others who opposed the Lewis machine. (Among those who attended were Powers Hapgood; Albert Coyle, left-wing editor of the *Locomotive Engineers Journal;* and Art Shields, a Communist journalist.) They discussed a plan to defeat Lewis in the December UMW election.[19]

In a meeting with Communist leaders, including William Z. Foster, Hapgood obtained agreement for the withdrawal of Communist candidates if Brophy were to seek the UMW presidency. In August, Brophy issued an open letter announcing his candidacy, criticizing Lewis's administration of the UMW and promising to organize the nonunion fields. A "Save-the-Union" Committee was organized to nominate candidates in the international and district elections of 1926, with Brophy as its candidate for international president.[20]* The "Save-the-Union" movement, an alliance of progressive non-Communists and Communists opposed to Lewis's rule and policies, had an official publication, the *Coal Miner,* published in Springfield, Illinois, with Frank Keeny of West Virginia as editor. One of the movement's

---

* In a review of Howard Closer's *The American Communist Party* in 1958, Foster wrote, in reference to the "Save-the-Union Committee": "This movement was organized completely by the TUEL with the full support of the Communist Party, and it operated on this basis throughout its several years of existence." (*The Worker,* Sunday, Dec. 14, 1958.)

The records of the Central Executive Committee of the Trade Union Educational League for February 17, 1926, read: "...Foster moved that the 'Save the Union' slogan not be put out at this time, and that the CP first organize a committee of the progressives and let them to put up the slogan; if the committee does not then put up the slogan, the CP should do so itself." (Daniel Bell Papers, Tamiment Institute Library, New York University.)

leading spokespersons was Alex Howat, the deposed president of the Kansas district. Howat toured the mining fields on behalf of the anti-Lewis forces.[21]

In a "Save-the-Union" pamphlet distributed among the miners, Brophy discussed the loss in membership suffered by the UMW, analyzed the causes for the decline and presented a program for remedying the situation. He pointed out that since the 1922 strike, the union had lost more than 200,000 members and that entire districts were dead and dying because of the mistaken policies of the union's leadership. Brophy pointed to Lewis's failure to uphold the rule that no operator could sign with the union for only part of the mines under his control. Had he adhered rigidly to this rule, Brophy insisted, the union would not be in so precarious a position.[22]

Brophy further contended that Lewis's policies could not solve the basic problem of overdevelopment and unemployment. The proud slogan, "No Backward Step," was nothing but an inducement for operators to transfer production from their union to their nonunion mines. While the policy prevailed on paper, miners were working for next to nothing, and the union was collapsing.[23]

Brophy proposed a concrete program to restore the UMW to its former prosperity and influence; (1) no wage cuts; (2) organization of the nonunion fields; (3) an active campaign of education among the membership for nationalization of the mines, and establishment of the six-hour day and five-day week; (4) formation of a Labor Party in an effort to establish a government sympathetic to the miner; (5) reinstatement of all members of the union unjustly expelled; (6) expiration of the bituminous and anthracite agreements at the same time; (7) honest elections; (8) democracy in the union.[24]

Lewis's response was typical. He refused to meet Brophy on the issues. Instead, he resorted "to time-tested tactics." He had the union journal make no mention of the Brophy campaign; union officials appointed by Lewis and paid from the international treasury campaigned for the incumbent president. Above all, he red-baited. Lewis pointed out that Brophy's program was almost identical to that adopted by the Pittsburgh Conference called by William Z. Foster in 1923. At the AFL convention in October 1926, Lewis read from correspondence between Albert Coyle and Powers Hapgood, stolen by one of Lewis's agents, which discussed several prominent Communists. Lewis pointed his finger at the convention gallery where William Z. Foster was seated and called him "the arch priest of communism in the United States" who made annual visits to Russia to make his reports and receive his orders.[25] The *New York Times* was jubilant.

"Never has a convention of the American Federation of Labor," it reported on its front page, "witnessed such an excoriating attack on Communist policy to 'bore from within and seize, control, and wreck the American labor movement' as marked today's session." But when Brophy denied that he and Hapgood had ever received the Coyle letter and stated that Lewis was using immoral methods, the *Times* buried the statement on page seven "under a microscopic head-line."[26]

On November 14, 1926, the anti-Lewis forces held a mass meeting at the Imperial Theater in New Kensington, Pennsylvania to secure the endorsement of Brophy's candidacy for the office of international president. Lewis's supporters at the meeting made a determined attack upon Powers Hapgood, the main speaker, charging him with being an ally of large West Virginia non-union coal interests in a campaign to destroy the United Mine Workers. When Hapgood denied the charge and challenged his accusers to offer proof, Lewis's supporters proceeded to break up the meeting.[27]

On the eve of the election, William Z. Foster issued a public appeal on behalf of Brophy's candidacy. It began:

> The United Mine Workers of America is falling to pieces. The whole organization is in serious danger of destruction. It is collapsing under the attacks of the coal operators and through the misleadership of the corrupt Lewis administration. The entire American labor movement is passing through a crisis, but, in no section of it is the crisis so intense as amongst the miners. Their union actually faces destruction unless there is a radical change in policy by the leadership. The loss of the Miners' Union would break the backbone of the American labor movement, reducing it almost entirely to skilled workers and enormously accelerating the present disastrous drift into intensified class collaboration. The reverberations would be felt throughout the trade union movement of the world. The most important struggle now in the labor organizations of this country is to save the Miners' Union.

Foster listed a number of demands which the UMW had to champion, such as higher wages and shorter hours and for the organization of the unorganized, the nationalization of the coal mines, establishment of a Labor Party, for an offensive and defensive alliance with the railroad workers. Yet still more was needed:

> It must set up an inner democracy, permit free expression of opinion, and abolish the unparalleled terrorism against the left wing and progressive fighters in the union. This is a program which will save the union and put it again in a fighting position.

Foster continued:

The accomplishment of this vitally necessary program requires the sweeping away of the corrupt Lewis administration. Fortunately an opportunity to do this presents itself in the union elections now approaching....

In the present elections John Brophy, president of District No. 2, a man long associated with various progressive movements in the Miners' Union, has announced himself as a candidate against Lewis.... The struggle between the Brophy forces and Lewis will be a fight between the forces of progress and those of destruction in the union. Upon the outcome depends the very existence of the organization. Notwithstanding differences of opinion upon many subjects, the body of progressives, radicals, and revolutionaries in the union must make common cause against the corrupt Lewis machine in this election. The victory of Lewis would be the death of the Miners' Union. The great masses of honest rank and filers will support the slate headed by Brophy.[28]

In an election that was said to have been the most corrupt in the history of the union, Lewis again triumphed. Soon after the balloting for officers took place, it was announced that the slate headed by Lewis had triumphed by 173,323 votes to 60,661.[29] The outcome was announced, but the details were suppressed, and a breakdown of the vote cast by each local was withheld. Brophy and his supporters claimed that, as in the past, Lewis's triumph was stolen at the ballot box.[30]

In 1926, Lewis also eliminated Frank Farrington as a union rival, although in this case, it was no loss to the cause of progressive trade unionism. While Farrington was in Europe, Lewis discovered a secret contract his rival had signed with the Peabody Coal Company under which Farrington was to be paid $25,000 a year for three years as the company's "labor relations expert" while serving as an officer of District 12 in Illinois. On August 25, 1926, Lewis revealed this information to District 12's executive board and demanded that either Farrington resign as district president or the board dismiss him. Farrington resigned his district presidency and went to work for the Peabody Coal Company as a labor consultant.[31]

Shortly after the 1926 elections, Powers Hapgood observed that Lewis's anti-Communist drive was ruining the United Mine Workers. He asked a pertinent question: "Must they [the Communists] always be told to go to hell and their cooperation refused in certain things in which every honest progressive believes merely because we differ from them in ultimate revolutionary ideology?"[32] To Lewis, the answer was simple. The Communists, in alliance with Brophy, had seriously threatened to replace him as president. To maintain his domination, the Communists had to be expelled.

When the National Committee of the Trade Union Educational League met on January 17, 1927, Foster reported that "left wing delegates are being removed in all parts of the coal districts and replaced by reactionaries." He added that "[Jack] Johnstone and others [are] going to the convention to organize the left wing and put our program into effect."[33] But so effective was the purge that few of Lewis's opponents attended the convention, and any hope the left wing had of "putting our program into effect" quickly faded. In fact, Lewis had eliminated so many opponents through expulsions that the opposition was not able to muster the numbers needed to obtain roll call votes on crucial resolutions.[34]

The convention lasted only a week, but in those seven days, the Lewis machine raised the president's salary from $8,000 to $12,000 annually; amended the constitution to provide for the expulsion of "any member who espoused Communist tendencies," eliminated from the constitution's preamble the phrase that miners were entitled to the "full social value of their product," substituting instead the words "an equitable share of the fruits of their labor"; ceded to the International Executive Board the right to levy assessments on union members without a time limit; repudiated the policy of supporting the nationalization of the coal mines; voted against recognition of the Soviet Union because of "its desire to subvert American trade unions and the American government"; endorsed the AFL's nonpartisan policy of rewarding labor's friends and punishing its enemies, and passed a rule denying delegates the right to amend a report or resolution until after it had been voted on.[35]

Lewis's arrogance reached new heights at the 1927 convention. To delegates who dared to question him about Howat, he replied: "It does not make any difference what you think. The chair has ruled." When Howat himself asked for the right to speak, Lewis responded: "You will not, and you will sit down." When several delegates asked why the union had never released the complete tabulation in the 1926 election, Lewis simply answered that he did "not feel like spending $10,000 just to please one Communist [John Watt]." In the same speech, he referred to "John Brophy and all his slimy friends." Lewis accused Brophy of "having committed treason by providing the operators with information detrimental to the coal miners"—all because Brophy had dared to challenge Lewis for the union presidency and to declare publicly that as a result of Lewis's policies, the union had lost power and members. Brophy, Lewis charged, was "nothing more nor less than a traitor." To Brophy's demand for a full tabulation of the 1926 election results, Lewis responded that in making this request, Brophy was simply "pursuing the policy set by William Z. Foster and the Communists."[36]

Powers Hapgood was sent as a delegate by his local union, but he was not even reported on by the Credentials Committee because, it was alleged, he was not a member of the union. His name appeared neither on the list of delegates nor on the list of those contested before the Committee. When Hapgood asserted his right to be seated and speak as a delegate, Lewis ruled that he was not a member of the union. He added: "Anyone who thinks he can abuse the privilege of the convention and come here and defy the chairman... or the convention rules is merely a fool." Then turning directly to Hapgood, Lewis shouted: "If I hear another word from you, you will be ejected from the convention and conducted to the streets." Later Hapgood was waylaid by Lewis's goons, who entered his hotel room and beat him severely.[37]

Following the convention, which he called "the most reactionary in the history of the U.M.W.A.," Foster reported to the Executive Committee of the TUEL on "The Immediate Tasks of the Left Wing in the Coal Mining Industry." He concluded that "the 'Save the Union' slogan is basically correct," and that the slogan "must be maintained and all our work in the coal industry must be carried on with a keen realization that the U.M.W.A. is in great danger." He also insisted that "our election campaign proved a success."

> The left wing gained invaluable experience; it improved its organization; it demonstrated the effectiveness of the united front policy and set up valuable contacts with progressives; and the left wing progressive ticket undoubtedly polled a majority of the votes cast in the election. Lewis could hide this majority only by a steal of more than 100,000 votes. In District 5 and in various sub-districts, the left-progressive ticket undoubtedly polled a majority of the votes cast in the respective elections.

Foster, however, conceded that "the fight of the 'Save the Union' progressivism at the (UMW) convention ... was not so successful." Apart from the arbitrary undemocratic conduct of the Lewis machine, "the lack of a strong organ for the opposition movement was a tremendous handicap at all stages of the fight." At the same time, Foster accused the left delegates at the convention (37 Communists and a group of progressives varying "from one-fifth to one-third of the total delegates") of "lacking in aggressiveness." "They failed to make an effective reply to Lewis's tactics by a sustained and scathing criticism of his disruptive policies and a militant insistence on the 'Save the Union' program. They failed to bring the program squarely before the convention and to make it the central issue of struggle."

But this was no time to lament past mistakes. The Jackson agreement in the bituminous fields expired on March 31st. In addition to fighting the Lewis machine

> the left wing must take the lead in mobilizing ideologically and organizationally the great mass of miners, in spite of official sabotage, for open conflict with the coal operators. Throughout the entire coal industry, organized and unorganized districts included, we must popularize the demands of the "Save the Union" program (no wage reductions, wage increases for unorganized miners, one agreement for all bituminous miners, 6-hour day, 5-day week, all agreements to include all mines of a given company, organize the unorganized, etc.) Far and wide we must raise the slogan, "Miners, Get Ready to Strike!"
> Together with these economic slogans shall be advocated inner union slogans leading directly to the building, democratizing, cleansing and educating of the union, and for the mobilization of the masses against the Lewis machine, including Democratization of the Union; Tabulated Returns of the Election Vote; Condemnation of Fraudulent Convention Practices; Repudiation of Restrictions Against Foreign-Born Workers Holding Union Offices; Against the Unrestricted Power of the International Board to Levy Assessments; Against the Appointive Power; For a Labor Party; Nationalization of Coal Mines....
> The whole left wing press shall take up the miners' situation and strive to impress its importance upon the entire labor movement and to rally the organized masses behind the miners. This agitation shall be carried on in the general sense of "Save the Miners' Union," with appropriate solidarity slogans.[38]

1927-28 STRIKE

On April 1, 1927, 175,000 miners in the bituminous fields of eight states (Illinois, Pennsylvania, Ohio, Indiana, Arkansas, Kansas, Iowa and West Virginia) went on strike protesting wage cuts and demanding the continuation, unchanged, of the Jacksonville agreement. Anthracite miners who were operating under an agreement signed the year before were prevented from walking off their jobs in support of the bituminous strikers.[39]

Meeting on April 12, 1927, the Central Executive Committee of the Workers' Party discussed the miners' strike and made it clear that Communists were expected to do all in their power to aid the strike, and that hostility to Lewis did not mean abandoning the rank-and-file miners in their battle. Foster urged "that all our comrades in these districts who are striking miners, should be categorically instructed not to leave the districts, but to remain in the places where they are on strike"; that "wires shall be sent to our language bureaus immediately urging them to put men in the field in the Pittsburgh district"; that "wherever we pull masses of miners out on strike they shall immediately enter into negotiations with the UMWA so as to set up a situation where these officials cannot attack the strike successfully, but our comrades to retain a firm grasp over the situation"; that "we instruct our comrades generally throughout the mining section to carry on mass picketing wherever any attempts are made to scab, and that they stimulate the development of marches of the miners to pull out these scabbing men. They shall also strive to have left-wing speakers at all possible mass meetings of miners." Foster also proposed that "on the question of settlements, our comrades shall express an active opposition and fight against all individual settlements as well as district settlements." Finally, Foster proposed that "in the anthracite district we begin to lay the basis for agitation for the eventual calling out of the anthracite miners in support of the bituminous miners." All of these proposals were carried unanimously. After this, Pat Toohey was instructed to "devote his major attention to field strike work," and the *Daily Worker* staff was instructed to devote "more space and more prominent space for the miners' strike," and to feature on its front page "facts in the mining struggle, particularly the question of Organizing the Unorganized." A special committee was then appointed "to take up the problem of relief in the miners' strike" and to seek international assistance to help the miners.[40]

While supporting the union's struggle in the strike, the Communists did not abandon the battle against the corrupt and dictatorial Lewis Administration. At a meeting of the Mining Sub-Committee of the Party's Central Executive Committee, held on May 25, 1927, major attention was paid to mapping out details for an investigation of "the corrupt elections in the last general election of the UMWA." The Communist leaders proposed establishing a new miners' paper, to be called the *Coal Digger* (although they did "not insist on any particular name") to be edited by John Brophy, and with Alex Howat as business manager. They also proposed that "the paper be launched under the auspices of a voluntary association to investigate the corruption shown in the last general election of the UMWA and to prove the claims of B[rophy] that he was duly elected to promote the Save-the-Union program to build and revive the old fighting traditions of the Miners Union." It was also proposed that the paper, "while contesting the election and claiming the presidency for B[rophy], shall carry on a vigorous campaign for a militant strike struggle, linking up the anthracite grievances with the demands of the bituminous miners, for intensifying the campaign to organize the non-union territory, the setting up of relief committees with the

UMWA as a basis, thus laying the basis for the calling of a general strike through out the coal industry and for a national agreement. The paper shall also carry on a propaganda campaign for the nationalization of the mines and the other planks of the Save the Union program."[41]

From the outset, the striking miners endured intense hardships. In addition to using strikebreakers, including Blacks from Tennessee and Alabama, private police, and injunctions to break the strike, the operators evicted striking miners from their company homes and cut off credit at the company stores. In Pennsylvania alone, some 8,000 to 10,000 families were housed in crude, union-built barracks. Relief was minimal. Few families received as much as five dollars per week, with the average well below that amount. Lowell Limpus, a reporter for the New York *Daily News,* wrote:

> I have just returned from a visit to "Hell-in-Pennsylvania." I have seen horrible things there; things which I almost hesitate to enumerate and describe. I can scarcely expect my story to be believed. I did not believe it myself when the situation was first outlined to me. Then I went into the coal camps of western and central Pennsylvania and saw for myself.
>
> ...Many times it seemed impossible to think that we were in modern, civilized America.
>
> We saw thousands of women and children, literally starving to death. We found hundreds of destitute families living in crudely constructed bare-board shacks. They had been evicted from their homes by the coal companies. We unearthed a system of despotic tyranny reminiscent of Czar-ridden Siberia at its worst. We found police brutality and industrial slavery. We discovered the weirdest flock of injunctions that ever emanated from American temples of justice....[42]

At Lewis's urging, a special convention was convened in Pittsburgh by President William Green to assist the UMW. Attended by over 300 AFL representatives, it adopted resolutions calling upon all international unions to send money, materials and organizers to assist the strikers. The conference also urged the AFL Executive Council to confer with President Coolidge about the "intolerable situation" in Pennsylvania. The delegates pleaded with the mine operators to observe the law "and to pay no heed to power assumed by those who are unauthorized under the law to limit, circumscribe, or repress their rights as citizens."[43]

While the UMW and AFL leaders were begging the coal operators to obey the law, the Ohio and Pennsylvania Miners' Relief Committee sponsored by the TUEL called for a wide fund-raising campaign to help the strikers defeat the unprecedented opposition of the coal operators. Meanwhile, the wives and daughters of the strikers, organized into UMW women's auxiliaries, were conducting relief activities and joining their male relatives in mass picketing, braving the Coal and Iron Police, the state troopers and the company thugs. One reporter wrote from the coal fields: "The women are right in the front-line of the struggle—in many places coming out on the picket line, battling with the Coal and Iron Police and the troopers, daring merciless clubbing and coming back to the fight with cool courage again and again after they have been beaten up.[44]

Black coal miners were special targets of Coal and Iron Police brutality. A Report of a Committee appointed by Black workers of the non-union Pittsburgh Coal Company told a gruesome story, noting that "men employed by the Coal Company and known as Coal and Iron Police,"

> have terrorized and intimidated the colored people and have trans-gressed upon their rights, to such a degree that great concern is felt in some quarters for their future welfare, and it is quite possible in the very near future they will be compelled to band together for mutual protection.
>
> During the course of our investigation, we found numerous instances of ferocious brutality, too numerous to mention, but well known to the coal miners who live in these communities....
>
> However, we are glad to know that there is still some spirit left which we hope will eventually bring about a change for the better, which can only be accomplished by the combined effort of all colored coal miners....[45]

There was no point complaining to the company or to the Coal and Iron Police whom they hired. As Peter Gottlieb points out: "The Coal and Iron Police supplanted local law enforcement authorities to become the sole power in and around open-shop mines. To their rules and harsh actions, there was no appeal for strikers or strike-breakers.[46]

It is understandable that even the Black strikebreakers turned to the UMW for protection. The *Pittsburgh Courier*, the national circulation Black newspaper, reported that "black miners were joining the UMW in significant numbers."[47]

In September, 1927, Lewis gave up the battle and instructed each district to sign up a separate agreement, making the best deal it could, and return to work.[48] With this capitulation, the "Save-the-Union" movement again became active. It denounced the sellout and called upon the miners to continue the struggle for a centralized wage policy.[49] In January, 1928, a "Save-the-Union" conference adopted the slogan "Lewis Must Go."[50]

On February 18, 1928, Foster reported to the TUEL National Committee: "The left wing, not officially known as TUEL but the Save the Union Committee, is waging war against the Lewis machine under the slogan: 'Lewis Must Go.' This has been adopted and used in Ohio effectively. Conferences held in Illinois were very good, although little preliminary organization work was done .... Conferences were being held in Kansas, Wyoming, Ohio and Pennsylvania. *The Coal Digger* is being received enthusiastically in all parts of the industry."*

Supplementing Foster's report, William F. Dunne informed the National Committee "that the anthracite situation is almost one of civil war, particularly in District 22. Pressure of unemployment, speed-up and violation of contract are bringing things to a head. Our organization is not keeping pace with the sentiment of the rank and file."[51]

In March 1928, the women of District 5 met in conference in Pittsburgh. The delegates, coming from all coal centers of the district, voted to organize a Mine Women's Progressive Committee, adopted resolutions in favor of the "Save-the-Union" program, and urged all women to support the continuing miners' struggles. They also elected representatives to the National Miners' "Save-the-Union" Conference to be held in Pittsburgh on April 1.[52]

The call for the April Conference, issued from Pittsburgh on March 1, 1928, was signed by John Brophy, Pat Toohey, and Powers Hapgood, and was addressed "To all local unions and members of the United Mine Workers of America and the miners of the unorganized districts." It read in part:

> The purpose of this conference will be to work out a program to meet the deep crisis which has been brought upon the union by the incompetence and corruption of the Lewis machine....
>
> The "Save the Union Committee" calls upon the members of the United Mine Workers and the miners in the unorganized districts to unite to smash the conspiracy against the miners' union and living and working conditions in the mining industry.
>
> The miners must unite. The strike can and must be won. We must mobilize our full forces to spread the strike and to beat back the open shop attacks of the employers.

---

* On March 17, 1928, Foster predicted that *The Coal Digger*, organ of the "Save the Union" Committee, "should have 100,000 circulation soon." (National Committee, Trade Union Educational League, Daniel Bell Papers, Tamiment Library, New York University.)

The Lewis machine and its ruinous policies must go. Miners, take control of the local unions! Take the union into your own hands!...

The National "Save the Union" Conference will take definite steps:

2. To mobilize the full forces of the miners—organized and un-organized—to win the Pennsylvania and Ohio strike.*

3. To organize the great mass of unorganized miners and to weld them into one powerful union.

4. To advance the general program of the "Save the Union Committee": for a six-hour day and five-day week, for nationalization of the mines, for a labor party, for state insurance and relief of unemployment and for equal division of work, a national agreement for all coal miners, against arbitration and speed-up agreements, no wage cuts, for the Jacksonville scale, for an honest and aggressive leadership, the re-establishment of democracy in the union and abolition of company control....

Miners everywhere; Come to the National Conference of the "Save the Union Committee." If your local union does not elect delegates, then form groups to send representatives. Disregard all intimidation and ignore all rumors of postponement of the conference.

The National "Save the Union" Conference will put a halt to the offensive of the operators and will mark the beginning of a new period of growth and success for the miners' union.[53]

On April 1, 1928, delegates representing 100,000 miners from all over the country met in conference in Pittsburgh. They passed resolutions for continuation of the strike, organization of the unorganized, equal jobs and equal pay for Black miners, nationalization of the coal industry, and for the extension of the strike to the anthracite miners. The conference also issued a call to the wives and daughters of miners to organize their forces and stand shoulder-to-shoulder with the men in the fight to win the strike.[54]

On April 16, 1928, the "Save-the-Union" Committee formally issued a call for continuation of the strike until victory. Thereupon, several thousand additional miners joined the walkout.

In May 1928, a U.S. Senate Committee appointed to investigate the situation in the coal industry in Pennsylvania, West Virginia, and Ohio submitted its report. Senator Frank Gooding of Idaho reported that "conditions which exist in the strike-torn regions of the Pittsburgh District are a blotch upon American civilization .... The committee found men, women and children living in hovels which are more unsanitary than a modern swinepen."** Another senator ob-

---

* This is the enumeration in the original.

** In the Hocking and Sunday Creek Valleys of southeastern Ohio the miners' conditions were so terrible during the strike that the Cleveland *News* sent Dan Gallagher, a reporter, to tour the area. Gallagher traveled into the hills and visited small mining towns where he saw many homes with children and adults who were so lacking in clothing that they could not even get to the relief stations to secure aid. The response

served that "had I not seen it myself I would not have believed that in the United States there are areas where civil government was supplanted by a system that can only be compared with ancient feudalism." The investigation confirmed that there was a reign of terror incited by the operators, that private police were beating defenseless people, that miners' families were being evicted from their homes, and that the courts were issuing injunctions wholesale and violating civil liberties.[55]

DECLINE OF THE UMW

On July 18, 1928, the fifteen-month old strike came to an end. The operators succeeded in rolling back wages and working conditions that it had taken over three decades to win. The UMW was virtually eliminated from western Pennsylvania, eastern Ohio, and northern West Virginia.[56]

In 1921 when John L. Lewis was elected president of the United Mine Workers, the union was the largest and most powerful industrial union in the United States. Within seven years of Lewis's election, the UMW was prostrate and with only its leadership and administration intact.

The Central Executive Committee of the Trade Union Educational League viewed the settlements of the 1927 strike as constituting "a direct betrayal of the miners," and as confirming "that our analysis of the mining situation is correct, that the union is being gradually disintegrated, and is in danger of destruction. The 'Save the Union' slogan is basically correct."[57]

The Communists were the most active and influential group of the "Save-the-Union" campaign which rallied around Brophy after the disastrous end of the coal strike. They were not, however, the only ones to feel the wrath of the Lewis machine. Any union members sympathetic to Brophy or the "Save-the-Union" campaign found themselves labelled as "Red" and expelled from the UMW as dual unionists. John Brophy and Pat Toohey, president and secretary-treasurer respectively of the "Save-the-Union" Committee, were ex-

---

to his articles produced contributions from Cleveland of goods for the miners, and the Ohio National Guard was called out solely to aid in the collection and distribution of relief donations. The Guard established kitchens that fed children one meal a day. (Richard Straw, "An Act of Faith: Southeastern Ohio Miners in the Coal Strike of 1927," *Labor History* 21 [Spring,1980]: 234-35.)

pelled from the union as dual unionists by presidential order. William Boyce, Black leader of the Committee, was suspended from the union "for a period of 99 years." Powers Hapgood was deprived of the opportunity to work as a union miner. Unwilling to work in a nonunion mine, he was denied, at Lewis's order, a union card wherever he went.[59]

Wherever the "Save-the-Union" Committee went, its members came under physical attack from Lewis's goons. In Pittsburgh, in September 1928, Committee members were denied access to their meeting hall as two hundred UMW goons attacked them in the streets. One Committee member was killed and five injured. The police then arrested over 122 men, nearly all Committee members.

Every union member who failed to follow "the Lewis line" faced expulsion. One local after another was placed under presidential jurisdiction, giving Lewis control of the entire organization and subjecting it to one-man dictatorship. And while all this was occurring, UMW membership kept declining—dropping from 600,000 in the mid-1920s to between 60,000 and 150,000 in mid-1928.[60]

The "Save-the-Union" movement of the miners wrote significant pages in the history of the American labor movement. It represented a coalition of Communists and non-Communists united in a common objective—to defeat the Lewis "rule-or-ruin" policy and restore the United Mine Workers to the status of the vanguard of working class militancy in the United States. The miners faced physical attacks, expulsion and other reprisals. But they knew that they were not fighting just for themselves. As the Trade Union Educational League pointed out:

> The struggle of the miners to save their union, to organize the unorganized, to beat back the attempts to destroy the living standards built up after decades, is the struggle of the entire labor movement. The issue of the fight against class collaboration, against cringingly accepting lower wages and longer hours, vitally concerns every craft and every section of America's army of labor. The outcome of the struggle conducted by the "Save the Union" Committee, backed up by the overwhelming mass of the rank and file, will affect the course of the future development of the labor movement.[61]

CHAPTER 3

MACHINISTS AND CARPENTERS

In the years before 1924, as we have seen in our previous volume,* the entrenched, reactionary leadership of the International Association of Machinists, headed by President William A. Johnston, launched continuous attacks on the Trade Union Educational League. These intensified after 1924, as Johnston initiated an expulsion policy against groups of local unionists accused of belonging to the TUEL and the Workers' (Communist) Party.

In this situation, William Z. Foster was forced to explore ways of attuning the League to the more moderate opposition to Johnston, gathered around J.F. Anderson.[1] This had not been an easy decision for Foster since Anderson, though reluctantly, had supported the settlement of the 1922 railroad shopmen's strike.[2]** For Foster the agreements arising out of the strike had symbolized the beginning of the decline of unionism during the 1920s into "class collaboration."[3]

While Anderson, like Foster, had deplored the lack of unity exhibited by the shop crafts during the 1922 strike, he, unlike Foster, saw industrial unionism as a matter of gradual "evolution," with its achievement in the far distant future. On the issue of amalgamation, Anderson was skeptical. In late 1923, he noted that "there are plenty of examples of trades banded together in amalgamated units having the same hard struggle to advance the interests of their members as so-called independent unions." As an example, he cited the United Mine Workers, an industrial union, that had "almost complete control of their industry." Still, "they are obliged to strike, and their

---

* *See* Philip S. Foner *History of the Labor Movement in the United States* 9 (New York, 1990): pp. 194-200
** *See ibid.*, pp. 174-182

31

strikes are not always successful."[4] He said nothing about the corrupt Lewis machine and Lewis's continual concessions to the operators.

Despite all this, the TUEL, as we saw in the last volume, supported Anderson and his ticket, at the same time making it clear that this was not so much an endorsement of all he stood for, as it was a determination to eliminate the Johnston leadership.[5*]

After one of the bitterest campaigns in the history of the union, during which Anderson predicted that all the votes might not be counted, the results were published in June, 1925. According to the official announcement, Johnston received 18,021 votes and Anderson 17,076. William Hannan, the only candidate on Anderson's ticket to defeat his opponent, was elected vice-president, having received 17,338 votes.[6] In "The Situation in the Machinists Union and the Immediate Tasks of the Left Wing," Foster boldly declared that the TUEL campaign in supporting Anderson "was a success."

> It gave the Party and the TUEL new contacts in the union and tended to break the isolation generally of the left wing in the labor movement; it resulted in an overwhelming defeat of the expulsion policy and enabled the left wing to work openly in the Machinists organization; it brought forward the Communists as practical and effective leaders; it caused the elimination of that outstanding symbol of class collaboration, Wm. H. Johnston; it gave the left wing extensive experience in the application of the united front policy in American trade unions...."

The campaign, Foster observed, had also revealed "many outstanding weaknesses." There had been no systematic recruitment of party members, and the TUEL did not work diligently enough to establish left-wing and progressive groupings or party fractions within the IAM. Foster then proposed a "minimum program ... to build the Party and left wing forces in the IAM." This included launching "a campaign to recruit Party members among organized and unorganized machinists"; "concentration of Party forces in the IAM around the campaign to organize the unorganized"; "condemnation of the B&O Plan";** "immediate amalgamation of all metal trades"; "immediate campaign for a Labor Party; a fight against company unionism"; and a special campaign for the re-

---

* *See ibid.*, pp. 200.

** For a discussion of the "B&O Plan" in the Machinists' Union, *see* Philip S. Foner, *History of the Labor Movement in the United States* 9 (New York, 1990): pp. 183-86, 197-98.

moval of the radical bar in the Constitution and for the organization of Negroes into the union.[7]*

As Foster was making his assessment, the situation in the Machinists' Union was developing rapidly. After the election, Anderson published and sent to all IAM lodges, and to officers of other unions, a circular entitled "The Story of the Big Steal," in which he accused Johnston of fraud in the ballot counting. Anderson was suspended from membership in the union by President Johnston for having committed a "subversive act." He would remain suspended "until such time as he would file a satisfactory apology and retraction with the General Executive Council ... together with his pledge and promise that he would never thereafter violate its Constitution or be disloyal to its principles and to the purpose for which it was organized."

Anderson appealed his suspension to the General Executive Council which sustained the order of suspension. After negotiating with a special committee established to reconcile the opposing Johnston and Anderson factions, the latter withdrew his appeal from the decision of the Executive Council suspending him from membership. Thereupon the Executive Council by unanimous vote restored him to full membership. An appeal, signed by the Executive Council and Anderson, was sent to the union membership, urging them "to forget all partisan differences."[8]

In the midst of the factional Johnston-Anderson fight, Johnston essentially outlawed Communists by ukase, as Mark Perlman, an authority on the union, puts it.[9]

In July 1925, the General Executive Council issued an order to the effect that members of the union must quit the Workers' (Communist) Party and the Trade Union Educational League by October 15, 1925, or be expelled from the IAM. Moreover, the logic employed in the expulsion campaign was broad enough so that every IAM member who endorsed progressive measures was subject to the action of the International. This was made explicit in an article in the *Machinists' Journal* entitled, "The Communist Plague in Our Union," which stated:

> Each Communist, whether he belongs officially to the TUEL or not, is bound by party discipline to act in all union matters by party discipline, to act in all union matters, not as the interests of the organization would dictate, but in accordance with the order of the secret Communist Cen-

---

* For a discussion of the constitutional ban against Black workers in the IAM, *see ibid.*, p. 368.

tral Committee. It is clear, therefore, that anyone who openly supports in any manner Communist activity aids thereby our bitterest enemy in fighting our union, and must therefore be regarded as an enemy of the Union.

After lengthy extracts from the "Theses" of the *Communist International* and other Communist sources which, it concluded, "conclusively proved that the destructive activity of the Workers Party and the Trade Union Educational League had but one objective—to destroy the entire American labor movement if it could not control it." Hence:

> Our local unions must not permit any member of this so-called Workers Party, or any of its followers to hold any paid or unpaid offices in our organization. Our organization must not allow any of its officers, elected by our members, to receive orders from an outside enemy organization, from a political clique which constantly engages in conspiring against our organization. We must have discipline in our ranks. No organization can exist without discipline and any one of our members who places the discipline of the Workers Party above the discipline of his own union and aids thereby our enemies to plot against and injure our organization, is himself an enemy of the union and must not be permitted to hold membership in it.[10]

At the same time that this ukase was issued, a change appeared in the *Machinists' Monthly Journal*. From 1914 on a statement of aims appearing at the front of each issue of the *Journal*, had put the union on record in favoring "amalgamation." In 1925, following the expulsion of TUEL and other progressive members, the statement of aims on the *Journal* favoring amalgamation was modified. A codicil was added which held that "This shall not be construed to favor the theory of industrial unionism."[11] After all, who but Communists and/or TUELers and their "dupes" would favor industrial unionism? Thus espousal of industrial unionism risked immediate expulsion.

In response to the expulsion edict, the National Committee of the TUEL met on September 10, 1925 to develop a policy on this critical matter. A letter was drawn up, signed by William Z. Foster, and sent to District Organizers which urged the necessity of developing "a skillful and intransigent resistance to the order issued by President Johnston of the Machinists' Union... The following is our general line of policy. You should make all comrades acquainted with it but do not let this communication get out of your hands."

The first phase of the fight against the expulsion order was to prevent the local unions from putting it into effect. Every device had to be used to this end. When the order came before the locals, TUEL members should move to table it, or to file it, or to find other ways to bury it, and keep the locals from acting upon it. In the event Johnston should instruct local secretaries to refuse to accept dues from specified members, it was necessary to do everything possible to get them to ignore those instructions. Threatened members in certain cases "can stave off expulsion by paying dues in advance for several months, by which time the expulsion order may be defeated."

> In the event we cannot block the enforcement of the expulsion order, we must fight militantly in the local unions for regular trials and oppose the policy of expulsion without trial. The securing of trials will open up a whole vista of possibilities of delaying and preventing the expulsion order from going into effect. We should insist upon the application of the two-thirds rule in the question of expulsions. In all these maneuvers against the application of the expulsion policy we should carry on the most militant campaign to win the support of the rank and file. Our fight against expulsion should be linked up with the general fight against the reactionary policies of the Johnston machine....

An important aspect of the fight against the expulsion policy, Foster stressed, would be to line up the Anderson group against it, "and enlist them as far as possible in our general fight against the expulsion policy." When actually confronted with certainty of expulsion, the policy should be:

> (a) Members who are not definitely known as party members shall deny their membership in the Party and the T.U.E.L.
> (b) Members who have been quite definitely known as Party members shall state that they were no longer members.
> (c) Outstanding leaders who are widely known as Party members shall refuse to obey Johnston's order and shall fight against expulsion on the basis of their right to belong to the Party and the League.... In all cases, however, where comrades deny their party membership, they shall, nevertheless, continue to maintain their membership and to carry on all Party activities.

Recognizing that this policy was fraught with danger, the letter to the District Organizers added:

> The necessity of denying membership shall be explained to our membership and to the rank and file of the unions so that our militants may not be discredited.[12]

At the same time that this letter was dispatched to District Organizers, the Central Committee of the Workers' (Communist) Party distributed a resolution to all party members in the Machinists Union. Basically it repeated what had been set forth in the letter, but it added the following:

> Under present conditions, in order to mobilize the widest possible support of non-party workers in carrying on the fight in the trade unions

against the expulsion of the Communists, the basis of this fight shall not be the right of the union members to be members of the Communist Party only, but the struggle must be carried on the broader basis for the right of members of the trade unions to hold membership in any political organization they see fit. The fight against the expulsion policy must be tied up with the general fight of progressives against the reactionaries.[13]

The letter to the District Organizers had concluded with the assurance that if the program outlined in it was "applied with judgment according to the various situations throughout the Union," Johnston's attack on the left-wing "can be broken up and very few of our militants will be victimized."[14] This seems to have been whistling in the dark, since it most certainly did not happen. The hope of rallying the supporters of Anderson against the expulsion policy proved to be just that—only a hope.* In early 1926, Anderson's membership was restored, and the Anderson and Johnston factions in the IAM reached an understanding which isolated the members of the Trade Union Educational League. Both sides agreed to support a compromise president for the International machinists union, Arthur G. Wharton, who was elected in 1927 without opposition.[15]

Foster acknowledged that the election of Wharton posed many difficulties in opposing the expulsion policy. "Wharton is a powerful leader," he wrote. "He has many warm friends in the union, including outstanding leaders in the fight against Johnston, and because of the tradition that he was a progressive a dozen years ago, and because of his minority role in the hated Railroad Labor Board.** The fight against him will be difficult, especially in the early stages.[16]

Just how difficult soon became clear. In an introductory circular, the new president of the IAM wrote: "If we are coarse [sic] we will be

___

* In his doctoral dissertation, "William Z. Foster: Labor Organizer and Communist, 1910-1926," Edward P. Johanningsmeier puts part of the blame for the failure to win Anderson and his followers on Foster. While Foster had been willing to compromise on a number of issues in order to build this coalition, he argues, Foster was "uncompromising on the B&O Plan." This, in fact, Johanningsmeier insists, made it difficult for the TUEL to establish "united fronts" in the unions during the 1920s. For Foster's "unalterable opposition to the B&O Plan created significant dissension among progressive unionists, many of whom favored the plan as a way to save their weakened unions." (University of Pennsylvania, 1988, p. 625.)

This may have been true at first, but soon enough even those who fervently supported the B&O plan in the hope it would halt the decline of the union movement learned the truth of the prediction Foster had made of the havoc the plan would create among unions which adopted it. In fact, both Foster's and the TUEL's prestige mounted when these predictions were, unfortunately, realized.

** See Philip S. Foner, *History of the Labor Movement in the United States* 9 (New York, 1990): 14, 174-75, 184.

less visionary and more practical in continuing our efforts in the direction of securing immediate and material benefits."[17] Following an ardent campaign to end the expulsion policy, TUEL members who had been suspended or expelled by Johnston were reinstated only under the condition that they swear that they had given up membership in the Workers' (Communist) Party and the Trade Union Educational League. So as to make certain that they did not swear falsely, they were also forced to swear that they would never publicly espouse any of the principles of either organization.[18] Forced to keep silent on the pressing issues facing the IAM and the entire labor movement, they could do little to advance their cause. David M. Schneider observed in 1927 that "At present they [the Workers' (Communist) Party and the Trade Union Educational League] exert little influence in the International Association of Machinists."[19]

The same conclusion could have been reached about the influence of the Workers' (Communist) Party and the Trade Union Educational League in the United Brotherhood of the Carpenters and Joiners, headed by John L. Lewis's rival as a corrupt, despotic union leader—William L. Hutcheson.*

When Hutcheson won re-election in 1924, protests arose throughout the entire union over the counting of the vote. The most important protests came into union headquarters from Pittsburgh, Peoria, and St. Paul. Hutcheson thereupon launched a new policy to handle these protests. He established a procedure of allowing dissenters to voice their outrage, and then either expelling them outright from the union, or "demanding contrite and self-debasing apologies which permitted them to remain in the union only on tenure of good behavior. Hutcheson was the final arbiter of what did and did not constitute good behavior."[20] A typical act of contrition was that of L. F. Kringle, the St. Paul dissenter, who had charged that in Hutcheson's re-election, the ballots of 900 local unions had been arbitrarily thrown out. Faced with expulsion from the union, he said: "I am more than willing to admit that it [the protest] was an error of mine for which I owe you an apology, and am glad to do so, hoping that you may be able to overlook an error on my part...." He was then reprimanded, and forced to promise never again to protest any action by the leadership.[21]

---

* For the earlier activities of the TUEL in the United Brotherhood of Carpenters and Joiners, see Foner, op. cit., 9: pp. 201-207.

Hutcheson then appointed a series of Executive Board committees and sub-committees which travelled from local to local to investigate Communist and TUEL influence. He sent them out with the notice that "there are two 'isms' that should enter our organization—that is unionism and Americanism, and all other 'isms' or advocates should be kicked out and kicked out quickly."[22]

Morris Rosen, a TUEL activist in New York, who had dared to run against Hutcheson for president, had to answer the following questions:

First Vice President Cosgrove:
"Do you believe in Industrial Unionism?
Morris Rosen: "I believe in amalgamation."

Cosgrove repeats the above question several times and Rosen gives the same answer. Cosgrove then gets angry and says: "That means yes."

W.T. Allen: "Are you a Communist?"
Rosen: "I refuse to answer that question. I believe it is unconstitutional to ask it."

Rosen was expelled from the union.[23]

The battle in Detroit began on January 9, 1925 when Hutcheson ordered William "Bud" Reynolds expelled. "The ostensible crime," notes Robert A. Christie, "was membership in the Trade Union Educational League. The real crime: Detroit went for Rosen by forty-one votes in the election."[24]* Despite the fact that Hutcheson had campaigned vigorously against him, Reynolds had managed to capture the vice-presidency of the District, the presidency of his own local Union 240, and "strong rank and file support."[25] All this carried not the slightest weight with the Hutcheson machine.

On January 10, 1925, Frank Duffy, a Hutcheson henchman, informed the members of Local 240 by mail that they were to expel Reynolds. When they refused, the union lawyer obtained an injunc-

* Christie makes clear the utter degradation of the Carpenters' leadership, but he does this as if he is writing about a lark, and treats the people who were victims of Hutcheson's viciousness as men who deserved what they got. He describes the TUEL as the "Brotherhood's opera bouffe left wing." Charging them with daring to "infiltrate" the Carpenters' Union, he completely forgets that they were *bona fide* members of the union. (Robert A. Christie, "Empire in Wood: A History of the United Brotherhood of Carpenters and Joiners of America," Ph.D. dissertation, Cornell University, 1954, p. 487.)

tion against Reynolds' participation in union affairs. However, Reynolds defied the injunction, was attacked and beaten by Hutcheson's goons, and was arrested by the police for disturbing the peace.

Hutcheson then led an investigating subcommittee out to Detroit. To no one's surprise, the committee recommended lifting Local Union 240's charter if the members did not expel Reynolds, and have Hutcheson take over the District Council.[26]

On May 16, 1924 the National Committee of the Trade Union Educational League met to discuss the District situation. They had before them a letter from Reynolds reporting that a pledge had been submitted to Local 420 which every member was required to sign. It read:

> I, the undersigned, do hereby promise and agree that I will observe and comply with all the laws, rules and regulations of the United Brotherhood of Carpenters and Joiners of America, and that I will in no way affiliate with or give support, assistance or comfort to the Trade Union Educational League, or any similar or kindred organization.
>
> In subscribing to the above, I do so of my own free will and accord, and agree that if I should violate said agreement, or pledge, it is understood that my membership in the United Brotherhood of Carpenters and Joiners of America be forfeited without complaint by me.[27]

Reynolds reported that "about fifty members of local 420 had signed the pledge, but many had refused. The two Mullen brothers, old and influential members...stated that they would not sign and would carry it to the Supreme Court if necessary. The members of the Jewish local and the local itself by a motion point-blank refused to sign it.... It is safe to assume that we can get anything from 600 to 1000 (in my local union) to refuse to sign this pledge. At least three prominent members of as many locals will carry the case to court if necessary and I will be powerless to stop it.... A serious building slump is settling in in Detroit and the town is flooded with carpenters from everywhere looking for work. This situation is bound to produce unrest and strengthen our position of opposition."[28]

Foster proposed that the TUEL National Committee endorse the policy advocated by Reynolds, not to sign the pledge, to work out detailed means to continue the fight within the scope of the union constitution, to fight against dual union tendencies among the workers, to give no support, direct or indirect, to those who wished to take the case to court, and to censure those who signed the pledge without consulting the TUEL.[29] The proposals were immediately adopted, and immediately telegraphed to Reynolds.[30]

Once aware that the TUEL members in Detroit would not take the issue of the pledge to court, the Hutcheson machine expelled every single member who refused to sign it.

This ended the protest in Local 140 and eliminated Reynolds as a threat to the machine.[31] In this connection, Daniel Bell, who collected the record quoted above, commented: "One interesting aspect of this was this decision not to go into court. Actually the union would have been most effective if it did go into court since it could probably stop Hutcheson at this point, but the left-wing prejudice against using the capitalist courts was probably too strong at that time. This is an illustration, perhaps, of the weakness of the TUEL, created by the nature of left-wing ideology."[32] Actually, it was an ideology that Foster and other leaders of the TUEL inherited from their IWW and Syndicalist years.*

The scene next shifted to Chicago. As we have seen in our previous volume, the arbitration award handed down in 1920 by Judge Kenesaw Mountain Landis to settle a building trades strike in Chicago was widely regarded as "an open shop instrument which stripped the unions of many of their gains and much of their power."** Although the other building trades unions signed the award and agreed to abide by it, the Carpenters refused. Harry Jensen, president of the Carpenters Chicago District Council, asked permission of the membership to sign with the employers on the best terms possible. They refused him, fearing that he would capitulate and sign the Landis award. Jensen then called on Hutcheson to negotiate with the employers. The morning after the negotiations ended, the Chicago papers headlined the news that the Carpenters had thrown aside the Landis Plan and obtained the closed shop. A day later, Jensen was elected to head the District Council for another term. Then a month later, the terms of the contract Hutcheson had negotiated leaked out. In all important respects, it was a repetition of the Landis award.[33]

The TUEL militants denounced Jensen and Hutcheson for having pulled off a "sellout." Winning control of Local 181, they sent a resolution, replete with anger and rage, to the 1924 convention. It was pigeonholed in the usual Hutcheson manner. Then after the

---

* *See* Philip S. Foner, *History of the Labor Movement in the United States* 4 (New York, 1965).

** *See ibid.,* 9 (New York, 1990):201.

convention adjourned, Hutcheson immediately informed the leaders of Local 181 that the signers of the resolution must be expelled. The five dissidents were tried by local leaders who were members of the Hutcheson machine, and the trial was denounced as "a Star Chamber affair." The expulsion charge was dissemination of "scurrilous literature." The men on trial provided the photostat of a notarized affidavit of one of the members of the local trial board in which he swore that the report of the trial was tampered with after it left the local, so as to make the recommended penalty more severe. It was ignored, and the signers of the resolution were expelled while the other members of the local were warned that they would receive the same treatment if they protested the action.[34] In the end, the expulsion of the five men was lifted, after each had signed a statement pledging to sever connections with the Trade Union Educational League and after they had apologizing publicly for insulting Hutcheson. They were reinstated on probation with the understanding that they would again be expelled if they uttered or published any statements advocating principles and issues associated with the Trade Union Educational League.[35]

In early 1926 Hutcheson took on the New York carpenters led by Morris Rosen, TUEL activist. In 1923 Rosen had entered the Brotherhood, and within a year, led a progressive slate in Local 376, which wrested control of the union from the "old gang that was loyal to Hutcheson." When Rosen engaged accountants to look into the records of the previous treasurer, Meyer Rudinsky, it became evident that at least $1,200 was missing and had been stolen. After the local expelled him, Rudinsky went to Hutcheson, who sent a henchman to take possession of the local's books. Rosen refused to turn them over, fearing, as had often happened before under Hutcheson, that they would disappear and with them the evidence. He based his action on a clause in the Brotherhood's constitution which allowed the International officers to examine local union's books, but only within the local's jurisdiction. Rosen interpreted this to mean that the books had to be examined in the local offices, and Hutcheson's agent received no books.

In June 1926, a committee appointed by Hutcheson and headed by Frank Duffy reported that Rosen refused to surrender the books to conceal the fact that the local's funds had been given to the Trade Union Educational League. Although no evidence was produced to back up the charge, Rosen and a number of his followers were expelled, and local 376 was suspended—all subject to convention appeal.[36]

A few members of Local 376 were reinstated before the convention met, but they had first to sign the pledge not to associate in any shape or form with the TUEL, not to support in speech or writing any issue associated with the League, and they were barred from any office in the union for five years.[37]

As a grand gesture, Hutcheson allowed Rosen to appear at the 1928 convention, even inviting him to the platform to state his case. "Please come here," he told Rosen, "and stand here beside the flag, the one you don't think so much of." When Rosen requested a fair chance to speak, Hutcheson told him ominously: "I will take care of [you]... [afterwards]. Go as far as you like."

Rosen then proceeded to deliver a long attack on Hutcheson, calling him a dictator and a traitor to the best interests of the carpenters. Thereupon Duffy, who was presiding, pointed an accusing finger at Rosen, and told the delegates: "There are two of us here on the platform today—Morris Rosen and myself. The organization is not big enough for both of us. Either he goes out or I go out, and I'm not going out." Only by the narrowest of margins was Rosen able to escape violence. This is made clear in the following dialogue:

Hutcheson: "Please get out of this building and off the Brotherhood's property as quickly as possible.
A Delegate: "Mr. President and Delegates—As a member of the United Brotherhood I would make one request on behalf of the man we have expelled, and that is that we grant him a safe conduct until he has left the city of Lakeland."
Hutcheson: "That will be done. I am going to ask every member of the Brotherhood in this room to do this—just show that you are real men and do not lay your hands on the likes of him until he gets out of our sight."[38]

Then a mass purge followed:

Delegate Flynn: "That is the only one, Mr. Chairman?"
Hutcheson: "Let us deal with the rest of them tomorrow morning."
Delegate Flynn: "Are the names of the destructionists available, those who are seated in the hall? If they are let's deal with them the same as we have with Rosen."
Hutcheson: "It is in order, and the secretary will give the names of the members you refer to."
Duffy: "Robert Golden, 1164."
Hutcheson: "Please rise, you are accused of being a communist."
A Delegate: "I move ... that Robert Golden be expelled from the Brotherhood."
The motion was seconded and carried unanimously.
When Golden attempted to resist, President Hutcheson shouted:
"Get out...and do not make it necessary to put you out."

Duffy: "Nathan Rosen, 1164..."

Hutcheson: "He is not present, but we can take the same action."

Duffy: "Thomas Schneider ... 2090."

Hutcheson: "He is present as a delegate. What is your pleasure."

A delegate: "I move that Thomas Schneider...be expelled from the Brotherhood."

By this time it was late in the afternoon, and the delegates adjourned for dinner. A special committee was given the rest of the alleged Communists to handle as it saw fit. The committee heard from eleven men in all, three of whom were ousted as Communists. Eight of them supplied affidavits of non-communism. Of these, two were given a "clean bill of health," and six were put on probation because a "disturbing element has been...active lately in Chicago."

One of the men put on probation, pleading against the action, said: "We have been trying to...put new blood in the organization ... for ... without opposition you [the United Brotherhood] would be stagnant and dead." To which Hutcheson's spokesperson, John Halkitt replied: ."That is fine up to a certain point...but...when the majority has spoken you must desist from opposition to the organization."

In short, dissenters would not be tolerated, and the men being expelled, suspended, or put on probation were being so treated "primarily because they were dissenters, whatever else they may or may not have done."[39]

As the letter of the National Executive Committee of the Trade Union Educational League in the case of the expulsion of its members from the International Association of Machinists had predicted, once the Communists were expelled or suspended, it would not be long before any member who opposed the leadership would share the same fate. And since any expelled or suspended member in a closed shop local* lost any opportunity to work at his trade, the purge was very effective. Even in the case where a closed shop did not exist, collusion between the employers and the dictatorial union leaders produced the same result.

In the case of the Carpenters' Union, Hutcheson made it clear that any one who was suspected of left leanings, or even just opposition to the leadership, had to take an oath similar to the one used in Detroit or face expulsion and loss of a job.

---

* In a closed shop only union members in good standing can work in the place of employment.

For all practical purposes the activity of the Trade Union Educational League in the United Brotherhood of Carpenters and Joiners was at an end. On August 5, 1926, Foster reported to the TUEL Executive Committee. He conceded that great difficulties stood in the way of making any headway in the battle for progressive trade unionism in the Carpenters' Union. But he insisted that the proper way to deal with the situation was "to start an organization to build the union," pointing out that membership in the union had either stood still or declined since 1920. The report continued:

> Foster proposed that the organization committee be used as an instrument to build the carpenters union and eventually to capture the district council, and that a left-wing bloc be built within the organization.[*]

But the advice proved to be impossible to carry out—at least for the time being.

*TUEL Minutes, Daniel Bell Collection

CHAPTER 4

THE LADIES' GARMENT WORKERS

The expulsion policy practiced in the Miners', Machinists', and Carpenters' Unions was also present in the needle trades' unions. But basically the expulsion strategy in the garment trades backfired. In the Ladies' Garment Workers' Union, despite the aggressive campaign of expulsions that began early in 1923,* the Trade Union Educational League was able to score a number of sensational victories.

The 1924 ILGWU convention was a complete rout for the left. The convention rejected all official appeals against expulsions, suspensions, and reorganizations that had taken place since the previous convention. The membership learned just how little democracy there was in the ILGWU under right-wing (Socialist) leadership, and what they learned made them more sympathetic to the left wing.

At the same time conditions in the trade were also deteriorating. The union had recently lost a long general strike in Philadelphia, and the left wing charged sabotage. The attempt to organize Chicago's dress market involved a very costly strike that ended in failure in June of 1924. In New York things were ripe for a major strike, but the administration settled on the appointment of a Governor's Commission to study the situation, feeling that a strike was too costly. Here, too, the left wing found willing ears for its charges of collaboration with the employers.[1]

Up to this point the Trade Union Educational League was still mainly educational in nature, even though it engaged in election

---

* *See* Philip S. Foner, *History of the Labor Movement in the United States* 9 (New York, 1990): 272-73, 278-80

campaigns. There was no way to continue along that path. The League had either to quit or fight for control of the union. There was little question as to which way the TUEL would go. Foster made it official in September 1924, when he proclaimed in the *Labor Herald*:

> The next task of the Trade Union Educational League is to crack the hard shell of official opposition against the progressive movements now surging amongst the rank and file. The usurping bureaucrats must not be allowed to get away with the present outrageous flouting of the workers' interests. The league must bring direct pressure to bear against them and whenever possible, drive them from office, or where this is not achieved, teach them obedience.
>
> The era of passing resolutions only to have them thrown into the waste basket by sneering and stupid officials is past; the era for action is at hand.[2]

With the local ILGWU elections in the fall of 1924 and spring of 1925, the left wing was ready, and turned them into referenda on union democracy. They ran on a platform that stressed militancy, but their main demands were reinstatement of expelled members, and the end of barring candidates from the ballot. The new constitution required all candidates to sign an anti-TUEL loyalty pledge to get on the ballot, and the candidates of the left went ahead and signed. The left was allowed on the ballot, and the result was that the left wing won control of the executive boards of Locals 2, 9, and 22 in New York (with some 70 percent of the membership), and made major gains in Boston, Chicago and Philadelphia.

Through this series of stunning victories, the radicals gained control of the Executive Board of Local 2, which had only recently been created by joining together Local 1, one of the focal points of radical opposition, with Local 17, a major conservative bulwark. The union administration had expected that the conservatives would dominate the merged organization. Then the conservative Executive Board of Local 22 lost to an insurgent slate, and Local 9, the finishers, reelected Louis Hyman and a left-wing Executive Board. The radicals also succeeded in defeating a referendum proposal drawn up by the New York Joint Board to raise the weekly dues from 35 to 50 cents. The National Committee of the Needle Trades' Section of the Trade Union Educational League campaigned against the proposal and was so successful that even the conservative-controlled Locals 12 and 35 defeated the board's recommendation.[3]

The administration looked around desperately for an excuse to step in and soon found it. As the 1925 May Day demonstrations approached, the administration suggested that "this May Day in particular should be utilized as a great protest against the contemporary autocrats in Russia who had squelched every trace of independent thought...and crowded their jails with thousands of Socialists, trade unionists and anarchists."* The large locals rejected this advice and included Moissaye J. Olgin, editor of the Yiddish language Communist daily, *Freiheit,* in their speakers list for a joint May Day meeting of Locals 2, 9 and 22. The meeting endorsed a wide-ranging resolution to fight the open shop and the use of child labor and to work toward the amalgamation of craft unions. It also demanded that the United States establish diplomatic relations with the Soviet Union.[4]

MORE EXPULSIONS

Using the May Day meeting as a justification, the New York Joint Board suspended and placed on trial seventy-seven members of the Executive Board of the left-wing Locals 2, 9 and 22, which, taken together, constituted more than half of the union's membership. The suspension of the majority of the Executive Boards simply because these locals had been addressed by a Communist speaker was an indication of how dictatorial the conservative leadership had become.** One night, right-wing emissaries seized the headquarters of Locals 2 and 9, but when they attempted to gain control of Local 22's property, they were "beaten off," the *New York Times* reported, by two hundred young women. Indeed, the *Times* reported that most of the expelled members of the Executive Boards were women and that they were replaced by men.[5]

At a mass meeting held on June 15, 1925, the three locals established a Joint Action Committee to fight the expulsions and reinstate those on trial.*** The committee drew up a program suggested by the

---

* However, to make the action appear less arbitrary, a further charge was added that the executive board of Local 22 had acted improperly in allowing bonds owned by the local to be used as security for a loan for a left-wing summer camp near New York City. Thus the legal basis for the suspension was made to appear as misuse of funds, but the financial aspect is scarcely mentioned in the pro-administration accounts of the actions, or even in the GEB report itself. (*Report of the General Executive Board to the 18th Convention of the International Ladies' Garment Workers' Union, 1925,* pp. 45-46; Stanley Nadel, "The Communists and the Needle Trades, from 1920 to 1928," MA thesis, Columbia University, 1973, p. 28.)

** The GEB noted that "the simple act" of inviting a Communist to address the meeting "amounted in itself to little," but that "the circumstances under which it was done" were significant since they "showed clearly the trend of their minds." (*Proceedings of the ILGWU Convention, 1925,* p. 45.)

*** The formal name was the Joint Committee of Action, but it became known as the Joint Action Committee.

TUEL, condemning all dual union tendencies and warning that a split would prove "ultimately disastrous" and cause the return of sweatshop conditions. The JAC pressed for a "militant defense of the workers in their day-to-day grievances" by demanding higher wages, shorter hours, better working conditions, greater union democracy, more open accounting procedures and a strengthening of the union's ideological and organizational base.[6]

The left wing set out to forge a united front among all workers opposed to the ILGWU leadership. As William Z. Foster explained: "It will...be possible for us, by the systematic and intelligent application of our united front slogans and tactics," to "unite masses [of workers] into struggles against the powerful and firmly entrenched reactionaries."[7] In order to achieve this goal, the JAC drew up a program that dealt with the most important issues for the rank-and-file workers. The program was not only the result of the influence of the Communists and the TUEL members in the JAC, but was proposed by workers of varying political beliefs. It was not, despite the conservatives' claim, in any way a "Communist" program. As David Gurowsky points out: "Unlike the entrenched union officialdom, the [Joint Action] Committee did not isolate itself from the masses, but operated as working members of the union themselves, to attract those garment workers unhappy with the incumbent leadership, for whatever reason, to its side."[8]

Not surprisingly, the Joint Board trial committee found all seventy-seven defendants guilty and suspended them for three years, despite the fact that the only specific act the trial committee mentioned was the May Day meeting.[9] While the administration went through the formalities of a trial, the JAC took its fight into the shops and streets. The radicals held their first demonstration on July 9, 1925, when about thirty thousand cloakmakers and dressmakers poured into Yankee Stadium. The organizers allowed only those workers with up-to-date union cards inside, and thousands were turned away. Characterized by the left wing as the "largest mass meeting ever held by members of the International," the rally adopted a resolution supporting the demands for a forty-hour week, a guaranteed thirty-six-week work year and control of the sub-manufacturers. It also condemned the recent increases in the dues rate, claiming that the receipts were being wasted on useless projects. In addition, the left wing demanded the resignation of Sigman, Israel Feinberg and Perlstein. The JAC declared that it would not recognize any agreements made by the conservatives with the employers during the dispute. Finally, the JAC set up a defense fund to help those workers who needed legal aid because of their struggle for progressive union. ism.[9]

The Joint Action Committee decided next to hold a two-hour work stoppage on the afternoon of August 20, to "demonstrate once more that the vast membership of the union stands with us in this fight."[10] President Sigman issued an "Appeal and a Warning" to the membership, and the cloak manufacturers announced that "in the event of employees leaving their work .. it will practically be optional with the employers whether the employees shall be allowed to return to work." Thus, the manufacturers lined up with a union leadership in opposition to its own membership. Despite these pleas and warnings, twenty to thirty thousand garment workers walked off their jobs on August 20.[11] It is clear, even to scholars who are bitterly anti-Communist and totally uncritical of the ILGWU administration, that in the struggle against the Sigman administration, the TUEL enjoyed the support of most of New York's garment workers.[12]

With the members supporting the Joint Action Committee, the administration came under increasing pressure to compromise. Morris Hillquit, chairman of the Socialist Party, strongly urged a settlement, and even the *Forward* Association (a center for anti-Communist agitation) favored one. Unable to hold out, the administration agreed to a truce with the Joint Action Committee.

"I am aware of the danger lurking in the peace settlement," Sigman lamented, "but what can I do? The *Forward* is threatening to cut off my support. Besides, I do not want people to accuse me later of being the cause of the ruin of the ILGWU."[13]

The agreement was called a "peace without victors or vanquished" by the administration.[14] But it was in reality a victory for the left wing. In addition to winning reinstatement, the left now had an opportunity to gain reforms that might well result in their winning control of the union. The settlement included acceptance by the GEB of the right of all members to express their political beliefs freely, the lifting of all the suspensions imposed in July, and the establishment of committees (open to all members of the three locals) to supervise new elections. The troublesome issue of proportional representation was resolved by the agreement to hold a special "harmony" convention five months early—on November 23, 1925—to deal with the question and submit its proposals on the subject to a membership referendum, with both majority and minority viewpoints to be submitted for consideration.[15]

1925 ILGWU CONVENTION

The new elections which were held in Locals 2, 9 and 22 and in the New York Joint Board resulted in sweeping victories for the left wing. The left also did very well in the elections for convention delegates in the big locals across the country. The administration won the support of all the small locals, which would lose their power in the union if the convention went in favor of proportional representation.[16]

The left went to Philadelphia, seat of the convention, with the votes of nearly 70 percent of the membership, mostly from the large locals. But because of the inequitable representation system, the smaller right-wing locals were able to control over half the delegates. For example, eight small locals, with a total dues-paying membership of 197, were represented by 17 delegates, while Locals 2, 9, 22 and 35, with 39,000 workers, received only 49 seats. The 114 delegates supporting the left wing at the convention represented 44,762 workers, while the 148 delegates supporting the administration represented only 15,832 workers.[17] Because each of the small locals, some of which existed mainly on paper, was guaranteed at least two votes by the constitution, the right wing was able to control a majority of the delegates.[18]

The key debate at the convention occurred when the committee on officers' reports endorsed the administration's policies. The left wing submitted a counter report, pointing to the decline in union membership and insisting that the employers, taking advantage of the ILGWU's preoccupation with internal disputes, had been able to undermine working conditions and drive the union out of many shops. The administration defended the expulsions and blamed "Communism and Communist tactics" for many of the union's difficulties. By a roll-call vote of 150 to 112, the convention upheld the expulsion policy.[19]

The recommendation in the report presented by the constitution committee fell far short of proportional representation and, more important, made no mention of any membership referendum. As Louis Hyman came to realize that the administration had no intention of allowing a referendum on proportional representation, he called for a walkout of "everybody ... in sympathy with the people who have been fighting with the Joint Action Committee." Hyman thereupon left, followed by most of the other left-wing delegates.[20]

William F. Dunne, a member of the Central Executive Committee of the Communist Party, who was in Philadelphia as an observer for the *Daily Worker*, met with the left-wing delegates at a nearby hotel, convinced them that "a secessionist policy" would bring "disaster" for "the entire left wing," and urged them to return to the convention. The next morning the left-wing delegates were back, and the right wing agreed to seek a solution to the problem. Finally, it was agreed that a referendum would be held on the representation issue and that the radicals would be granted four or five seats on the General Executive Board. The conservatives assured themselves of overall control of the union by holding eleven of the fifteen seats on the GEB.[21]

On the final day of the convention, the Appeals Committee recommended that all members who had been deprived of the right to hold office because of membership in the TUEL, but who had not been charged with any overt acts against the union, should have their rights restored. The committee further recommended that all other disciplined members have their union membership restored, but that any further return of rights (such as the right to hold office) be left to the local union. Over the objection of the left wing, which demanded the return of all rights to its members, the convention approved it. In the elections, however, Hyman and three other left-wingers were elected to the new GEB, over the objection of many conservatives.[22]

With the end of the "harmony" convention, the focus of the struggle shifted back to New York City. New elections held in Locals 2, 9, 22 and 35 resulted in sweeping victories for the left wing. The radicals won a majority on the New York Joint Board. Louis Hyman was elected general manager and Charles (Sascha) Zimmerman manager of the Dress Division. Especially important was the victory of the radical "Progressive Cloak and Dressmakers" slate in the election for business agents. The business agent, the direct link between the shop worker and the union hierarchy, was responsible to see that the employers complied with the union contract. He visited shops, listened to workers' complaints, and met with the owners to resolve grievances. The left wing charged, however, that the agent and the employer often maintained a collusive relationship detrimental to the interests of the membership, because the business agent frequently overlooked contract violations in return for bribes from the owners. This was known by so many workers from their own experience that they overwhelmingly elected all candidates of the "Progressive Cloak and Dressmakers" slate to office.[23]

1926 STRIKE IN NEW YORK

Once in control of the New York Joint Board, the left wing set out on an organizing drive in the dress industry. While wages had dropped for nearly all workers since 1924, the decline had been most severe for the women in the dress industry.[24] The new organizing campaign, launched in January 1926, quickly brought many additional members into the union. Local 22, for example, grew from seven thousand to eleven thousand members. The dressmakers rallied enthusiastically to the Joint Board, and the union brought many former union shops back into the fold, with wage increases for the workers.[25]

But the Joint Board's main interest was in signing an effective new cloak contract with the employers following the expiration of the existing agreement at the end of June 1926. In 1924, Governor Alfred E. Smith had appointed a commission to study the garment industry. While the union awaited its report, expected in the spring of 1926, the Joint Board held a referendum on a special strike fund under which every worker was assessed $20. The assessment was approved by the membership.[26]

On May 20, 1926, the Governor's Advisory Commission issued its "Final Recommendations." The report proposed that the jobbers be limited in the number of contractors with whom they could do business, but it failed to recommend (as the union had demanded) that they be held responsible for conditions in their contractors' shops. It suggested pay raises ranging from $2.50 to $6 a week for the inside shops, improvements in the unemployment insurance fund and the establishment of an employment office. However, it ignored the union's demand for thirty-six weeks' guaranteed employment and a forty-hour week. Worst of all from the workers' point of view was the recommendation that the larger employers (shops with thirty-five or more workers) be allowed to replace up to 10 percent of their workers once a year. This right of "reorganization" would allow employers to fire the most militant workers in the shops without regard to seniority and without cause.

In its desire to avoid a strike, the ILGWU leadership had hoped that the commission's report would recommend measures to curb the power of the jobbers in the industry, and a shorter work week. When the report was made public, however, the Sigman administration did not dare to support it openly. The left wing organized against it, and on June 1, the Joint Board rejected the "Final Recommendations." A week later, two thousand shop chairman did the same, unanimously.[27]

On June 29, 1926, 25,000 cloakmakers gathered in Madison Square Garden and unanimously voted to strike. Speakers at the meeting included Morris Sigman, Hugh Frayne of the AFL, Ben Gold, left-wing leader of the furriers, Sidney Hillman, president of the Amalgamated Clothing Workers, and Louis Hyman, general manager of the New York Joint Board. All spoke in favor of a strike, and Sigman urged:

> In order to win this fight, it is imperative that, without exception, we should all—no matter what social ideas and theories we may cherish—in this general strike be united wholeheartedly and inspired by one central objective, to secure as speedily and as completely as possible the winning of the vital demands for which it is fought.[28]

A nine-point program was adopted, demanding a limitation on jobbers, higher wages, a thirty-six-week year based on the forty-hour week, the right of union representatives to examine employers' books to check for compliance with the contract, the unionization of designers and examiners, the establishment of a labor bureau that would try to equalize work among the contractors' shops, a limit to the use of labor-saving machines, and no reorganization rights for the employers. In an unprecedented move, the cloakmakers defeated Sigman for the post of chairman of the General Strike Committee and elected Louis Hyman—the first time someone other than the International president assumed that position.[29]

Hyman told the press:

> The strike is inevitable. The jobbers who control most of the trade, and the manufacturers who are half jobbers, have made it unavoidable. The misery of the cloakmakers, their inability to make a living in the shops, their intolerably long periods of unemployment, and the general demoralization in the industry fostered by the jobber system of production, have left for the cloakmakers no other avenue of relief but to strike for their demands.[30]

On July 1, the strike of forty thousand cloakmakers began, almost one-quarter of them women, and it completely closed down the industry. On July 7, headlines in a New York newspaper read: "Garment Walkout 100 Percent Perfect." The article went on: "In past strikes, strike leaders of the International Ladies' Garment Workers' Union point out, it was necessary to send out committees to cover weak spots here and there, but this time such a procedure is unnecessary. Both of the trade dailies—the *Daily News Record* and *Women's Wear Daily*—reported a one hundred percent strike."[31]

The strikers showed their militancy by mass picketing demonstrations, and their morale remained high. On July 16, the International reported that the strike was "in excellent shape." With as many as twenty thousand workers engaged in mass picketing, the New York Police Department's Industrial Squad began arresting thousands of strikers on charges of "blocking traffic." In addition, the strikers had to fight gunmen hired by the employers. Citing the fact that many of those injured by the gangsters were women, the *Daily Worker* declared that the "women strikers are proving their determination to drive out the terrorism of the gangsters and continue the struggle to victory."[32]

In mid-September, the employers secured an injunction against the union that banned all picketing. The union, with Hyman and Sigman in agreement, ignored the injunction, and the number of arrests soared, reaching six hundred on a single day. Seventy percent of those arrested were women strikers.[33]

On October 8, in response to an appeal from the Cloakmakers' Union, a trade union conference was held that brought together representatives of 800,000 workers in virtually every union throughout the metropolitan area. The appeal declared that the industry was again threatened with the return of the sweatshop system; it cited the wholesale arrests of pickets and the use of gangsters by employers against strikers, and an injunction against the union "so sweeping in scope, drastic in effect and reckless in its provisions as to make it unique in the history of labor jurisprudence." It urged labor solidarity in support of the strikers, noting that the "employers pin their whole hope on their ability to starve the workers into submission."[34] The unionists adopted a program to help the striking garment workers, condemned the injunction, pledged $1 a week from each union member as long as the strike continued. Funds for the strike came in from other sources as well. The Amalgamated Clothing Workers donated over $250,000, while the Workmen's Circle contributed $50,000 and the American Fund for Public Service presented the strikers with a six-month loan of $100,000. "The American labor movement is rallying like one person to the support of the strikers from one end of the country to the other," exulted *Justice*. The strike also won international support in the form of messages from the Bureau of Amsterdam International Alliance of Clothing Workers' Unions and the All-Union Needle Trades Workers' Union of the Soviet Union.[35]

From early July on, many small independent manufacturers began to settle with the union, but the three major manufacturers' associations refused to budge. According to Benjamin Gitlow, then a leading Communist, the manufacturers were ready to settle the strike in September on the basis of a forty-hour week, an increase in wages, and a modified form of reorganization, but the strike leaders could not accept the settlement because the Communist Party leaders (William Z. Foster and Jay Lovestone) opposed it as inadequate.[36] Most historians have accepted Gitlow's accusation as true, and anti-Communist historians have used it to accuse the Communist Party leadership of having forced the garment workers to "suffer for years to come."* However, the evidence for Gitlow's statement that such an offer was made is not at all clear-cut, and there is no reference to it in the contemporary press.

On November 13, an agreement was reached with the inside manufacturers' Protective Association, covering about one-third of the workers. The contract was for three years, and in it the union conceded the employers' main demand—10 percent reorganization rights for the manufacturers who employed a minimum of thirty-five workers (raised to forty in June, 1928) for thirty-two weeks a year. In return, the employers agreed to reduce the workweek to forty-two hours immediately and to forty in June, 1928; to raise wages by 10 percent over the amounts proposed by the Governor's Commission, and to limit the number of submanufacturers per jobber.[38] Noone was happy with the agreement, especially with the reorganization clause, but both the left-wing officials and the membership realized that "while a better agreement might have been reached, the long strike had depleted their treasury, exhausted them, and left them to face a bleak winter."[39] The shop chairmen voted to accept the agreement by almost four to one.[40]

The settlement left the radicals in a weakened position within the union, and *Women's Wear* predicted that the right wing would provoke a "bitter internal fight."[41]

---

* In "Reds Versus Pinks: A Civil War in the International Ladies' Garment Workers' Union (*New York History* 66 [January, 1985]: 66-67), Stanley Nadel does not go this far, but he accepts Sascha Zimmerman's conclusion (in an interview with him) that "there can be no more striking example of what Party domination means to a union." Nadel calls the comment "apt" but he offers no evidence for this statement apart from Zimmerman's remark, and fails to note how hostile to the Communist Party Zimmerman had become at the time he was interviewed.

LEFT-WING CONDUCT OF
1926 STRIKE ATTACKED

It was an accurate prediction. The administration followed a two-pronged approach. After the strike failed, the right wing claimed to have opposed it from the beginning, even though Sigman had rejected the Governor's Advisory Commission Report and right-wing leaders Salvatore Ninfo and David Dubinsky led the crucial strike settlement committee. Only after the poor settlement in November did the right wing begin to criticize the strike publicly. As Stanley Nadel points out: "There was nearly unanimous public support for a strike call...and the cloakmakers would have been very displeased with any group that had opposed the strike."[42] The second and more immediate approach of the right-wing leadership was revealed in a statement issued by the administration on December 1. It accused the strike leaders of allowing the Communist Party to direct the strike, of allowing possible opportunities for a good settlement to pass unexplored, and of mismanaging strike funds.* The General Executive Board further charged that the settlement agreed to was a disaster for the workers and that the few gains could have been won without a strike. The statement concluded:

> It is the sacred duty of the labor movement to rid itself of this pestilence The Communist leadership of the Cloakmakers Union has all but ruined the organization. The great task before the cloak-makers of the New York Joint Board at this time is to rid themselves of their irresponsible and ruinous leadership.[43]

At a rally called by the right wing the following day, Sigman and Dubinsky demanded that the incumbent General Strike Committee resign. The demand was rejected, and the committee chairperson denounced Sigman and Dubinsky for conspiring to break the strike. The *Daily Worker* declared angrily: "Never in the history of the American labor movement has such a treacherous and dastardly move been undertaken against thousands of militant and courageous workers."[44]

The split in the union leadership did not go unnoticed by the employers. Those who had settled earlier on the union's terms now demanded new terms equivalent to those won by the Protective Asso-

---

* After a careful study of the issue of strike finances, Gurowsky concludes that there was no evidence of widespread misuse of funds. (David Gurowski, "Factional Disputes within the ILGWU, 1919-1928," Ph.D. dissertation, SUNY at Binghamton, 1978, p. 76.)

ciation. Seeing their chance, the independent manufacturers and the members of the Sub-Manufacturers' Association pressed for a similar agreement. Then, on December 9, the submanufacturers locked out their workers. The same day, representatives of thirty-five unions met at the Rand School of Social Science, the educational institution of the Socialist Party, and formed the Committee for the Preservation of the Trade Unions in order to wage war on the Communists.[45]

On December 11, President Sigman published a scathing denunciation of the left wing in the *Forward* and promised that the GEB would intervene in the strike. The next day he called an emergency meeting of the board, which accused the left-wing strike leaders of wrongly permitting the submanufacturers to enjoy the same reorganization rights granted the inside manufacturers and of improper use of union funds. The left-wing representatives denied these charges, but the conservatives voted, with only three left-wing members dissenting, to assume control of the strike. The GEB then issued a statement proclaiming its direction of the strike and the lockout.[46]

Once back in power, the conservative strike leaders immediately agreed to arbitrate the differences with the contractors. Within three days, the arbitrators rendered a decision granting the submanufacturers the right to reorganize their shops if they employed a minimum of thirty-five workers (to become forty in June, 1928) for at least thirty-two weeks a year, provided that they had been in business for at least two years. The settlement brought wage scales and hours into line with those agreed to by employers in the rest of the cloak industry.[47]

The left wing responded with street demonstrations and called a mass meeting at Madison Square Garden for December 18. The Committee to Save the Trade Unions (headed by Abraham Beckerman of the Amalgamated Clothing Workers, who had a reputation for strong-arm methods) threatened to take over or break up the meeting. In an atmosphere of tight security, eighteen thousand workers entered the Garden and encouraged the left-wing leadership to carry on the fight. In order to raise money for the struggle, they decided to sell bonds with the slogan "Save the Cloakmakers' Union." The meeting passed resolutions condemning President Sigman and demanding his resignation.[48]

PURGE OF THE LEFT WING

The General Executive Board retaliated the next day by revoking the charters of Cloakmakers' Locals 2, 9 and 35 and ordering the members of these locals to re-register with the new committees set up by the GEB or be considered out of the union. Three days later, the GEB did the same to Dressmakers' Local 22. The purge of the left wing was extended to all the other cities where the ILGWU had branches, except Chicago, where the left wing controlled the Joint Board and was too strongly entrenched to be attacked immediately.[49]

On January 18, 1927, the last of the three major agreements was signed. The new contract with the Merchant Ladies' Garment Association (the jobbers) ended the twenty-eight week strike on the same terms as those that had been rejected in the original decision to walk out on July 1. It called for work to be done in union shops, made the jobber part of the impartial machinery, permitted the impartial chairman to investigate the owners' books, and established a joint committee to wipe out all sub-standard and nonunion shops. President Sigman defended the settlement as having been concluded "under an emergency."[50] Sigman also launched a bitter attack on the entire 1926 strike. He charged that the strike was "illegal," had been called for political purposes by "Communists," was led by "Communists," and was thoroughly "mismanaged."[51] The left wing replied with a detailed refutation of each of these charges. It quoted from an affidavit sworn to by Sigman on September 20, 1926, in response to the attempts of the employers to obtain an injunction against picketing. To the employers' charge that the strike was illegal, Sigman had then replied:

> I hereby deny all allegations to the effect that the general strike now pending in the cloak and suit industry in the City of New York is an unlawful strike, or that the defendants are engaged in a conspiracy to injure or ruin the plaintiff corporation or any of the members of the same, or any illegitimate motives in the conduct of said strike.
>
> On the contrary I aver that the said strike was forced upon the workers in the industry; that it is being conducted by them for the protection of their vital economic interests, and that their struggle is not only legitimate but highly meritorious, and one that should commend itself to the sympathies of all right thinking men.

Sigman also refuted the charges of the employers that the strike was led by "Communists." He said in the affidavit:

> The moving papers [to secure the injunction] seek to represent the present strike as something different from the ordinary labor struggle; as a

sort of sinister movement against law and order led by Communists for political purposes. I absolutely deny the said statements. The defendants are not, as alleged, "Communists recently from Russia." They are workers of many original races and nationalities, residents and citizens of the United States who are not concerned in this struggle about anything but an opportunity to earn an honest and modest living for themselves and their families .... Whatever the individual political persuasions of any Union official may be, they do not and cannot enter into the present controversy or influence the conduct of the workers in any way. The pending strike of the cloakmakers of the City of New York is solely and exclusively an economic trade union struggle.

As for the strike having been "mismanaged," the left wing noted that the settlements with the independent shops were negotiated by the Settlement Committee, which was headed by Salvatore Ninfo, chairman, and David Dubinsky, secretary, both right-wingers, and received the approval of the General Strike Committee of which Sigman was a member. The settlement with the inside manufacturers' association was worked out in conferences at which President Sigman, Ninfo, Dubinsky, Morris Hillquit—as well as Louis Hyman and other left-wingers—acted as spokespersons for the union. The new agreement was signed by Sigman and Hillquit for the International, and by Louis Hyman on behalf of the Joint Board. While the agreement fell short of what the strikers needed and wanted, it did obtain "far better terms than those proposed by the Governor's Commission." The forty-hour week was won; increases in wages of from four to eight dollars were won in every craft while the Commission had recommended increases of from two to three dollars; unionization of the examiners, which the Commission had denied, was won; most important of all, the right of the employers to reorganize their shops up to ten percent was greatly restricted. The Commission had restricted such reorganization to firms employing thirty-five workers, but the settlement further restricted it by the addition of clauses stipulating that employers must also guarantee thirty-two weeks of work a year and that they must pay an additional week's wages to workers discharged under its provisions. Thus, an employer could not take on extra workers he did not need for the last few weeks in the season so as to fraudulently claim the privilege of reorganization, but had to employ at least thirty-five workers for at least thirty-two weeks before he could qualify.[52]

In February 1927, Joseph S. Zack, secretary of the National Needle Trades Committee, reported to the National Committee of the TUEL on the situation in the International Ladies' Garment Workers Union. This was accompanied by a "Resolution on the ILGWU strike." The Resolution noted that the cloakmakers' strike began under exceedingly difficult circumstances. There existed something of a crisis on all sides. The position of the union in the industry was poor because of the growth of the jobber evil, the spread of the out-of-town shops, the loss in membership, and the compromising of the union's demands by the Governor's Commission. The internal situation of the union was also critical. The organization had just passed through the great battle led by the Joint Action Committee. The morale of the membership was low. The discredited leaders still held many powerful positions in the union, which they used effectively to demoralize the rank and file and to injure the strike. Finally, in the Party fraction itself, considerable friction existed because of the long struggle of the Party to eliminate rightist tendencies from the leadership of the fraction.

Because of all this, the strike needed "a powerful, militant, fighting Communist strike leadership which could have cut the Gordian knot of all these troubles by throwing the union with maximum force against the employers, smash the power of the sabotaging reactionary officials and unite the Party fraction solidly behind our strike leaders." But the strike especially lacked the Communist militancy it so badly needed. "It lacked dynamic fighting spirit. It has been properly called a 'soulless' strike."

Then followed an analysis of "wrong policies by the left wing leaders (which) contributed to deprive the strike of its needed militancy and effectiveness." One was the failure to fight the right wing. The report attributed this to "the prevalence of an incorrect theory...that the left wing cannot fight on two fronts simultaneously—that is, against the bosses and the bureaucrats at the same time.... The false notion existed that in the name of unity in the strike it was necessary to stop the open fight against Sigman and Company. The effect was to give these misleaders a free hand. Failure to fight the right wing, despite the Party's insistence that it be done, did much to weaken the strikers' fighting capacities and morale."

The report went on to note that the united front relations between the Party leaders and Louis Hyman were seriously deficient. "Hyman was against the strike. He was forced into it. All through it his attitude was pessimistic and defeatist.... Hyman maintained himself much as the *actual* strike leader and largely inflicted his colorless and defeatist policies in the strike. Thus the left wing carried the full responsibility for the strike but did not have the real direction of it. The failure to take actual leadership in the hands of the left wing, as the Party directed many times, weakened the strike substantially. The whole fight was kept on the defensive."

A key reason for the outcome of the strike was the underestimation of the leading role of the Party. "This manifested itself in a variety of ways, including a failure to maintain close relations with leading Party Committees in critical situations, failure to build a thoroughgoing system of Party fractions, and failure to execute Party decisions promptly and fully."[53]

So much for the right-wing charge that the strike was lost because the Communist Party completely directed it from beginning to end. Indeed, on several occasions during the strike, the records of the National Committee reveal anger on the Committee's part over the refusal of the strike leaders to follow the advice of the Party.[54]

What about the future? It is interesting, in view of the fact that the formation a year later of the Trade Union Unity league, which abandoned the "boring-from-within" strategy in large measure to organizing independently, has been attributed solely to a change in the trade union line of the Communist International. However, on February 2, 1927, Joseph Zack, secretary of the Needle Trades Committee, wrote in his report to the TUEL National Committee:

> As to the prospects of maintaining a union under our control at this time outside the A.F. of L., if there is such a possibility anywhere, it is in the needle trades. It can be done, but it will require a long, persistent struggle, and surely no guarantee can be given, the greatest drawback being the fact that we have not sufficient strength amongst the Italian workers whom the right wing can use with the support of the bosses as its mass base. The only way in the long run of maintaining a union outside the AF of L is to force the bosses to recognize it, which cannot be done without strikes, and perhaps a general strike.[55]

CHAPTER 5

THE LADIES' GARMENT WORKERS: II

At this stage, two groups emerged which sought to halt the internal conflict and achieve peace between the right and left wings before the ILGWU was destroyed. One was the Tolerance Group, made up of rank-and-file members of conservative locals, and the other was the Committee of Fifty, established by one thousand moderate and left-wing shop chairmen. Both groups worked for readmittance of the Communists and other barred workers to the union. They demanded the reinstatement of all expelled members, of the ousted Joint Board officials and of the four reorganized locals to their former positions, which was to be followed by new, impartially supervised general elections. Their program also called for proportional representation, amalgamation of needle trades' unions, tolerance of all political beliefs and the organization of the unorganized.[1] Meanwhile, many manufacturers, especially those with predominantly left-wing shops, continued to deal with the radical leadership. But the conservatives pressured the impartial chairman, Raymond V. Ingersoll, to declare that the employers must deal only with the Sigman-controlled organizations.[2] Following this victory, the conservative General Executive Board moved to entirely eliminate the left wing from the union. On February 14, 1927, the GEB revoked the charters of the four left-wing locals (2, 9, 22 and 35), declaring that they had not paid their *per capita* assessments. The Board demanded that the radicals surrender all books, funds, assets and property. The insurgents refused to comply, and the GEB expelled the four locals.[3]

The radicals disregarded the expulsion order, claiming that they were the official union They had held elections on February 5 (which had been originally scheduled for December but had been postponed because of the strike) in which the left-wing managers of Locals 2, 9 and 35 (Joseph Boruchowitz, Abe Zirlen, and Joseph Goretzky) had been returned to office with almost unanimous support.[4]

The left wing strengthened its ties with both the Committee of Fifty and the Tolerance Group. It also forged an alliance with the radical fur workers, who, as we shall see, were fighting a similar reactionary leadership in their union. Together the two left-wing needle trades' groups founded the Joint Board of Cloak and Dressmakers and Furriers. In January, 1927, the radical ladies' garment workers and fur workers sponsored a Left Wing Needle Trades Conference. The delegates condemned the divisive policies of the incumbent leaders of both unions, called for the reinstatement of all those who had been expelled, demanded greater union democracy, and discussed the need to amalgamate the workers of the various needle trades unions. The conference voted to support the cloakmakers "with greatest enthusiasm." Two months later, the radicals formed the Needle Trades Unity Committee devoted to fighting "gangsterism," and corruption in the ladies' garment and fur workers' unions, and to gather support for a united, industrially-based union.[5]

In May, 1927, the Committee of Fifty started a drive to bring peace to the ILGWU and to seek new elections under the control of neutral observers. But the ILGWU leadership refused to work with the committee calling it a "Communist subterfuge," set up to do the bidding of the Workers' Party.[6] Responding to a report "that peace between International and its local unions with Communist factions is near," Sigman wrote:

I absolutely deny that such a movement exists. Furthermore, I state there is no possibility for... peace. [It] will never take place. Our position and the position of the American Federation of Labor is very definite and clear and no local union or International union can remain part of the organized American trade union movement if it will make up with Communists or Communism....[7]

This approach angered Reverend John Haynes Holmes, liberal director of the American Civil Liberties Union. "He [Sigman]," Holmes wrote, "says that everyone who disagreed with him is a Communist. He and his union have been brutal and cruel in their treatment of their opponents who disagree with their policies."[8] Holmes was referring not only to the expulsion policy but to the hiring of gangsters to force garment workers to register with the right-wing locals and Joint Boards. When the gangsters did not succeed, the aid of the employers was enlisted. The manufacturers refused to hire anyone who did not register with the GEB-organized locals. In fact, the worker was required to sign a loyalty oath swearing that he or she was not a member of a "dual union." As garment workers—dressmakers and cloakmakers alike—explained, they were "psychologically forced to go to the right wing because of their bread and butter .... The bosses were a great help [to the right-wingers] without whom they could never have had the union."[9] Nevertheless, while the right wing retained control of the ILGWU machinery, it never really won the support of the membership. On November 14, 1927, the Committee of Fifty called a meeting at Mecca Temple which was attended by about four thousand workers. In a report to the Joint Board of Locals 2, 3, 9, 22, 35 and 82, all expelled by the General Executive, Louis Hyman emphasized: "The meeting was an indicator of the strong sentiment among the cloak and dressmakers in favor of making an end to the fight by giving the right to the members to decide on the issues involved in the struggle.... In view of this sentiment there may be a possibility for the Committee of Fifty Movement to develop into a real factor in the present struggle."[10]

On December 18, 1927, the New York Yiddish paper *The Day* carried an editorial in which it called a blatant lie Sigman's contention that the fight in the ILGWU was at an end, and that the International "has control over the workers." *The Day* then made a proposal that the AFL should intervene for the purpose of ending the civil war in the Cloak and Dressmakers' Union, and requested an answer from the contending factions. The Joint Board of the Cloak and Dressmakers' Union immediately replied on behalf of the left wing:

> We have not begun the struggle; it was forced upon us by Sigman and his General Executive Board. The struggle which we are carrying on and have carried on in our Union was aimed at the improvement of the conditions of the workers and at establishing and standardizing Union conditions in the cloak and dress trade. We have struggled at all times as we are doing today for the elementary, democratic rights of our membership as guaranteed by the constitution of the International. The Policy of the Joint Board is that the Union must include all workers of the trade, regardless of their political convictions. We were at all times opposed to discrimination against any members of the Union. We have fought and are still fighting today against the policy of expulsion and persecution of members and locals for difference of opinion.... The Joint Board has at all times welcomed and will welcome everyone who is earnestly interested in helping to bring the civil war to an end on a basis that will help to unite the ranks in re-building the Union and will give the membership the right to choose its representatives.

As for the proposed role of the American Federation of Labor, the Joint Board pointed out that the AFL had "actively assisted Sigman in the present conflict, and has thus helped to bring about the present chaotic conditions in the cloak and dress industry."*

> nevertheless we say that if the A.F. of L. is ready to see to it that the civil war in the Cloak & Dressmakers' Union shall come to an end on the basis that the cloak and dressmakers shall administer their own affairs in a democratic manner without any discrimination, we have no objection to the proposal.[11]

Following the publication of the Joint Board's statement, the editor of *The Day* sent a letter to the Board, through Louis Hyman, its chairman, asking "for a short and concise answer to just one specific point, and that is whether you would welcome the coming in of the A.F.L. to work out terms of peace, in a manner satisfactory to most of the members of the ILGWU?"[12] Replying for the Joint Board, Hyman declared: "...we are willing to have the Federation come into the present situation and begin negotiations at once with the object of bringing the internal struggle in our Union to an end, in the interests of all the workers in the industry." Hyman spelled out the basis of a settlement: the abolition of all discrimination and the restoration of full constitutional rights to all the members of the union. "The settlement arrived at is to be approved by the majority of the members of our Union."[13]

Sigman not only ignored *The Day*'s invitation, but he launched a bitter attack on the Joint Board in the *Forward*, repeating the familiar charge that it acted only as the Communist Party dictated.[14] At a meeting of the General Executive Board in January, 1927, the committees representing both the Tolerance Group and the Committee of Fifty, who came with proposals for peace, were not admitted. Their communications, however, were read, and it was decided that "no peace will be made with the Communists."[15] Thereafter, the slogan "No peace with the Communists" was headlined day after day in the *Forward*.[16]

---

* The letter of the Joint Board to *The Day* also pointed out that "the A.F. of L. has also been active in the civil war in the Furriers' Union, which has contributed to the complete demoralization of the entire needle industry...." (Statement of Joint Board of Cloak & Dressmakers' Union in Answer to the Editorial which appeared in "*The Day*,' on Sunday, December 18, 1927, "Minutes of the Joint Board Cloak and Dressmakers Union," original in possession of Henry Foner, microfilm copy in Tamiment Institute Library, New York University.)

On February 4, 1928, the Committee of Fifty, now composed entirely of non-Communist cloak and dressmakers, wrote to AFL President William Green, deploring the situation in the ILGWU:

> It is enough to state that the horrors and chaos which existed in this industry prior to 1910 are gradually coming back. Unscrupulous employers, glad to take advantage of the situation, are pitting one faction of the workers against the other. Union standards are disappearing. The sweatshop is again thriving.

The right-wing administration, the Committee of Fifty informed Green, "exists by virtue of the fact" that the employers

> ...are discharging all workers who refuse to join the newly-organized locals. It is conceded on all hands that the present administration cannot survive one day without that support. This means that the Union has not become a labor organization, but an employers' organization.... Such an employers' union can only breed corruption inside and chaos all around.

DECLINE OF THE ILGWU

At the time this was written, the ILGWU's position in the industry had reached its lowest point. By mid-1928, the union was, in Fannia Cohn's words, in a "lamentable position."[17] The fully organized cloak shops had declined from over 80 percent in 1926 to 7 percent, with another 43 percent nominally organized by the union but, in effect, working in contravention of the union contract. The remaining 50 percent were completely nonunion establishments, The Joint Board of Sanitary Control reported in March, 1928, that there were twenty-eight non-union shops in the industry, twice as many as in 1925. The dress industry, once three-quarters unionized, was now only one-third organized. The average workweek, for those who could find work, climbed to six and seven days and more than fifty hours, while wage rates dropped by 30 percent. By 1928, the ILGWU reported a membership of only 30,300 workers—a far cry from the more than 90,000 members it had had in 1926. Most workers, disgusted by the right-wing policies and collusion with the employers, simply dropped out of the union.[18]

The right wing had won control of the union machinery, but what it had really achieved was the wrecking of the union. The union had lost two-thirds of its membership, and most of the shops were organized only on paper. Between 1925 and 1928, the number of nonunion shops had more than doubled, the union label had been discontinued, the unemployment fund had ceased operating and the job-bers enjoyed free rein.[19]

There was plenty of blame to be shared for this deplorable situation, and the left-wing leadership which had headed the strike in 1926 with such limited success certainly deserved a portion of it. But by far the most important contributing factor was the fact that the right-wing leadership of the International, supported by the AFL, the Socialist Party, the *Jewish Daily Forward* and the employers, was determined to eliminate the Trade Union Educational League by any and all means. It made no difference that the League's program for social and industrial change had attracted many garment workers. To most of these workers, the fact that Communists held positions of importance in the League did not interfere with their belief that the TUEL was a legitimate expression of workers' discontent.

The Committee of Fifty decided that the union's biennial convention scheduled for Boston in the spring of 1928 would provide an excellent opportunity to take steps to reverse the tragic situation of the union, and that the first step was to repudiate the expulsion policy. The Committee recommended that the left wing send a delegation of ten people to the convention to seek peace. A shop delegate's conference, attended by four hundred representatives, endorsed the recommendation. But *Justice*, the administration's official organ, called the proposal "vain and futile" and predicted that no time would be wasted at Boston "in galling and sterile debate" over peace with the Communists.[20]

On May 7, 1928, the day the convention opened, 150 workers representing the locals of the New York and Chicago Joint Boards, the Cutters' Welfare League, the Committee of Fifty, the Tolerance Group, Italian workers and the imprisoned cloakmakers,* marched to the convention hall, seeking admission as delegates. But the right-wing leadership, led by Sigman, Schlesinger, Dubinsky and Ninfo, had called upon the Boston police to prevent the radicals from entering the hall. One hundred policemen met the marchers and denied them entrance. The radicals thereupon left their credentials to be delivered to the Credentials Committee.[21]

---

*These were the cloakmakers who had been imprisoned during and after the strike for assault and causing damage to property. (*New York Times,* Jan. 30, 1927.)

In a letter to the convention, May 8, 1928, the Joint Board Cloak and Dressmakers' Union of New York and the Joint Board of Cloak and Dressmakers' Union of Chicago, wrote angrily:

> If there are any delegates or workers who harbored any illusions that this convention, controlled by Sigman, Dubinsky, Breslau, Ninfo and Schlesinger cliques, will take any steps to make an end to the chaos and demoralization in our Union, the action in unseating our delegates has deprived the so-called convention of every right to call itself a convention that has authority to speak in the name of the workers of our industry, and has converted it into an assembly of hand-picked delegates with whose aid the various cliques who have maintained themselves in power, and their acts will therefore be repudiated by the great mass of cloak and dressmakers.[22]

The few center and left-wing delegates who had been allowed to enter the convention hall, mainly those from Los Angeles, Toronto, and Locals 2 and 9 in New York, presented resolutions asking that "all expelled locals and individuals be reinstated unconditionally, that no expulsions for political reasons shall again be practiced in our union," and that all political views be tolerated. Motions were introduced by some delegates calling for discussion with the left-wing workers outside the hall.[23]

The chairman of the Credentials Committee reported that the Committee refused to recognize the credentials of the men and women who had marched to the hall because they were no longer members of the ILGWU. In its report, the Resolutions Committee indicated that it did not "find it necessary, at present, to give any time" to the resolutions calling for peace and reconciliation.[24] In the police-barricaded hall, William Green urged the ILGWU leadership to stand firm against any proposals for unity and warned that if the Left and its allies "gain control in spite of all we can do, then the last step will be taken. The charter of the union will be revoked."[25] And AFL Vice-President Matthew Woll pledged the Federation's continued aid in the battle against the Left.[26]

Only one gesture was made toward a more flexible policy. After an agreement was reached, following many hours of negotiation, between the forces representing Morris Sigman (made up primarily of out-of-town leaders) and those of Benjamin Schlesinger (composed mainly of those from New York), under which Sigman remained as president and Schlesinger became vice-president in charge of the New York City unions, the convention adopted a General Executive Board proposal to allow Communists into the union but deny them the right to hold office. This was both an acknowledgement of the disastrous effects Sigman's unyielding policies were having on the union and a concession to Schlesinger's desire for some sort of compromise.[27]

The radicals, however, charged that the concession was meaningless, and the *Daily Worker* called it a "fake."[28] Thereupon the Joint Boards of New York and Chicago called upon those who "have been working for Unity of all workers for the purpose of rebuilding the Union and restoring union conditions," to meet at the Hotel Brewster in Boston on May 9th while the convention was proceeding. The call for the conference observed:

> We are calling this conference for the purpose of uniting all honest and sincere workers in the great task of once more re-establishing our Union as the standard bearer of the militant workers of this country. At this conference we will work out plans and lay the basis for a big campaign to organize the thousands of workers who are today working in sweat shops throughout the entire country. We will take steps to re-establish the 40-hour week, the week work system, the minimum wage scales, etc. and work out plans to cope with the many other difficult problems such as the jobbing-contracting system, unemployment, etc. These problems cannot be effectively solved by the workers of our trade alone, but only thru the united efforts of all needle trade workers thru a powerful amalgamated union in the needle industry.[29]

Delegates from Boston, Philadelphia, Chicago, Cleveland, Los Angeles, and New York responded to the call and spent two days at the conference. They reported that "the internal struggle has shattered the Union everywhere, that union control and union standards have been lowered in all centers and that the workers everywhere are in revolt against the misleadership of the International clique."[30] The conference established the National Organization Committee of the ladies' garment workers. The Committee of Fifty officially affiliated with the NOC as a means of restoring "unity to the ranks of the workers," but the Tolerance Group, while present, still remained aloof.[31]

The National Organization Committee adopted a program committed to rebuilding the union "over the heads of the Sigman-Schlesinger clique." The Committee planned to unionize the open shops, establish new shop chairmen's bodies and mount an offensive against the evils of the industry. Its main demands included implementation of the forty-hour week, worker control of the unemployment insurance fund, abolition of the contracting and sweating systems, an end to the speed-up and removal of the standards of production "that reduce us to mere automatons." Louis Hyman was elected chairman and Rose Wortis secretary of the NOC.[32]

On May 28, 1928, the Tolerance Group announced its affiliation with the National Organization Committee. Disillusioned with the right-wing leadership's role at the convention, the Group charged that the ILGWU was not truly independent, and while it accused the left of being controlled by outside forces, the organization was itself under the control of the Socialist Party and the *Jewish Daily Forward*. It charged that the 1926 expulsions had been ordered by the Socialist Party and that the right-wing leadership had been the agents of the Party and of Abraham Cahan of the *Forward*. Therefore, the Tolerance Group decided that the only alternative was to "join with those elements who are in agreement with our program and have made a sincere effort to bring it into being."[33]

The National Organization Committee moved swiftly into action. It held mass meetings in all the major union centers, founded organizing committees in the largest cities to recruit new members, and established shop chairmen's bodies and shop delegates' organizations in New York and Los Angeles to coordinate activity. The New York workers organized an open forum in which the rank-and-file discussed the union's problems, and then formed a volunteer committee of five hundred to police the industry in order to force the employers into compliance with union standards. The Committee set an initiation fee of $3.35, equal to that of the ILGWU in 1910.[34]

On October 25, 1928, Morris Sigman, whose policies of no compromise with the left-wing had reduced the ILGWU to a shell of a union, resigned as president. He was replaced by Benjamin Schlesinger, and in one of his first acts, he proposed an amnesty plan to bring all former members back into the union, regardless of past activities, upon payment of nine months back dues. The union would tolerate all political beliefs as long as the reinstated workers strictly adhered to the ILGWU constitution and did not remain under the influence of any political party. The local elections, scheduled to be held in the next few weeks, would be postponed until February, 1929, so that committees of impartial outsiders could be selected to supervise the voting.[35] The National Organization Committee called Schlesinger's proposals a "fake," and on December 13, 1928, at a mass meeting of their followers, the radicals rejected the amnesty plan. The expulsion policy had not really been altered, they charged, because the union offices would still be controlled by the right wing, and expelled left-wing officials would not be restored to their rightful places. Moreover, it would be easy to charge that anything the Left did in the future would be under the influence of the Communist Party. In addition, the maintenance of the unfair representational system by which small conservative locals gained disproportionate representation meant that the right-wing leadership would continue to control the union undemocratically and continue the disastrous policies that had weakened the organization and destroyed the working standards of its membership.[36]

The truth is that the left wing was now in the process of forming their own organization, a process which was part of a general change in the trade union policy of the Communist Party. The change, as we shall see, was from boring-from-within to independent radical unionism. By the end of 1928 the transition was complete, and the Needle Trades Workers Industrial Union was created out of the remnants of the ILGWU left wing (about 2,500 strong) and the left-controlled Fur Workers' Union.[37]

The right wing of the ILGWU had regained control of the union, but only the wreck remained. The ILGWU was down to half or even one-third of its 1926 membership in New York City, and most of the ladies' garment industry was no longer unionized. Even then, most of the remaining union shops were "only unionized on paper." The union was not only impoverished but heavily in debt.[38]

Stanley Nadel draws an important conclusion from these developments in the ILGWU. He notes that "most striking in these events was the readiness of the Socialist leaders of the ILGWU to sort of stay away from the demands of democratic rules."

> They barred left wing candidates from elections and from office, then they suspended them from membership in the union. When the left wingers were elected in sufficient numbers to control local executive boards, the administration suspended local self-government. In the final battle of 1927, the Socialists allied themselves with employers, the police, even with gangsters to restore their control of the union. In the end, they were even prepared to destroy the ILGWU, all in order to "save" it.[39]

CHAPTER 6

THE FUR WORKERS

In late 1925 the New York Joint Board of the International Fur Workers' Union began preparations for a strike which would show all the needle trades workers what a left-wing administration could do.

The agreement with the New York fur manufacturers' association was due to expire on January 31, 1926. When the leadership of the Joint Board, under Ben Gold, began negotiations with the manufacturers, high on the list of their fourteen demands were the issues of hours of labor and workers' control. Heading the list was a five-day, 40-hour week, and it also included a 32-hour week in slack seasons, the right of union inspection of shops, a 25 percent wage increase, an unemployment insurance fund to which every manufacturer was to contribute 3 percent of his total wage costs, May Day as a paid holiday, and the equal division of work.[1]

EVENTS LEADING TO THE 1926 STRIKE

Several conferences were held between the Associated Fur Manufacturers and the union, but no agreement was reached. The Association's representatives set down one condition and clung to it: if the union was willing to withdraw its three major demands—the 40-hour week, equal division of work and the 3 percent unemployment fund—the Association would try to reach an understanding on the other points. However, if the union refused to withdraw these three demands, the Association would withdraw from the negotiations.[2]

When this position was maintained at a final conference, and the union again refused, Dr. Paul Abelson, the impartial chairman, intervened and asked the union's representatives to state the minimum terms upon which they would consent to sign a new agreement. The union's Conference Committee then retired to one room and the Association representatives to another directly adjoining it.[3]

At the union's Conference Committee caucus, Gold suggested that a final effort be made to break the deadlock and avoid a strike: He proposed that the manufacturers be informed that if they agreed on all other demands, the union would be ready to discuss how far the three-month period of equal division of work then in effect should be extended.[4] Gold then asked each member of the Conference Committee for his opinion. After every member had voted in favor of the proposal,[5] International President Shachtman threw a bombshell into the proceedings by launching a vicious attack on the Joint Board leadership. He suddenly accused Gold and his associates of being "agents of Moscow" and charged that the negotiations were being conducted at the command of the "Communist Party." The Conference Committee sharply criticized Shachtman for echoing the employers' charges.[6]

Gold conveyed to Dr. Abelson the union Conference Committee's compromise offer on the demand for equal division of work, but it was rejected by the Association leaders. The union promptly submitted the issue to a referendum vote of the entire membership of the four locals: "Shall the old agreement as offered by the manufacturers be accepted, or shall the Joint Board be authorized to call a general strike for the enforcement of the new demands presented to the Fur Manufacturers' Association?"

On February 3, as the fur workers prepared to cast their ballots, Association President Samuel N. Samuels published an "Open Letter to the Members of the Furriers' Union," in which he urged the workers to repudiate their leadership in the strike referendum. He was confident that the workers could still defeat the "Communist conspiracy" by voting "against a strike," but if they allowed themselves to continue to be misled by their revolutionary leaders, he warned, the manufacturers would "fight the union to the bitter end."

The fur workers' answer came swiftly. By a vote of 6,702 in favor and only 629 against, the secret ballot referendum authorized the general strike.[7]

The Association then brought matters to a head. Meeting behind closed doors on February 11, it declared a lockout to "protect the workers, the bosses and the shops from these Communist terrorists." Under no circumstances, said the manufacturers, would they "deal with the Furriers' Union" as long as its leaders "insist upon becoming dictators in the fur industry, in order to force upon it new and radical changes in working conditions, which are not economical, are impossible, impractical and which only oppress and destroy the individuality of the workers." Every Association member would pay a sum equal to one-half of the yearly dues for a "special emergency fund ... for whatever purpose may be deemed necessary and proper."[8]

The Association also made public statements suggesting that it would welcome and be willing to negotiate with any group in the union that "wishes to submit other demands to the manufacturers." Immediately, former members of the right-wing machine published a denunciation of the union leadership and charged that the demands presented to the employers were deliberately utopian for the sole purpose of forcing a strike from which only the "Communists" would benefit.[9]

In truth, there *was* a conspiracy on foot, but it was not a "Communist conspiracy." Rather it was a conspiracy between the leaders of the Association and the men who had formerly led the union and had been repudiated by the fur workers. By forcing this battle upon the union, the employers hoped that with the aid of the underworld, the right-wingers and the *Jewish Daily Forward*, the discredited former leaders would come back into power. Once back, they would restore the policy of "hearty cooperation" which had proved so profitable to the manufacturers and so disastrous to the fur workers. As the *Fur Age Weekly*, an employers' organ, predicted confidently:

> The strike cannot endure. The leaders cannot offer the workers anything but hopes. They cannot support their members during a strike. They cannot expect help from other unions because other unions are not in sympathy with the left-wing movement.... *If the leaders of the union do not make swift progress toward the promised goal it will not be long before they are cast aside.*[10]

ORGANIZATION OF THE 1926 STRIKE

On February 1 the union responded by calling out all its members in one of the most militant strikes New York has ever seen. Gold was authorized by the Joint Board to prepare all the details involved in the forthcoming battle. The plan he evolved, unanimously adopted by the General Strike Committee, was one of the most careful and thorough organizations of a strike machinery in American labor history. There was a committee for every phase of the strike: A General Picketing Committee of one thousand fur workers; a law committee, a publicity committee, a control committee, a relief committee, a women's committee, a committee for the Greek strikers,* a grievance committee, a settlement committee and an out-of-town committee. Even the older workers were organized into a special committee. These committees were staffed entirely by rank-and-file workers.

The separate committees were part of the General Strike Committee which was headed by Ben Gold and included, among others, Aaron Gross, Jack Schneider, Fanny Warshafsky and Esther Polansky as well as International President Shachtman. In addition to the committees, there was the powerful body of fifteen hundred shop chairmen who joined with the strike committee in formulating the strike policies. The union was organized in such a manner that nothing could happen in any shop, building or hall without the General Strike Committee being immediately informed.

Gold received visits from "Little Augie," Lepke, Gurrah, and other underworld characters who were looking for an opportunity to reap a harvest, as they had done in previous strikes, but they were told that "there will be no gangsters and no hired men in this strike!"[11]

As soon as the strike machinery was organized, Gold announced the Joint Board's decision that no one would be paid for his work in the strike. Another decision was that for the entire duration of the struggle the officials of the union would not receive their salaries. And if relief would be distributed to the workers to enable them to live, it would be allotted on the basis of need rather than on personal connections with the top leaders.

Confident that the union was thoroughly prepared, the workers waited for the union's answer to the lockout. It came on February 16, 1926. Early that morning the streets in the fur market were flooded with the "red circular" issued by the General Strike Committee. It called on all twelve thousand members of the Furriers' Union to leave their shops at 10 A.M. and begin the battle for "bread, freedom and human living standards."[12]

MASS PICKETING

The moment the strike began, mass picketing demonstrations of almost the entire membership were held through the fur district, fighting the police and the employers' goons. Hundreds of strikers

---

* At this time 90 percent of the Greek fur workers did not understand English. It was necessary to have groups of Greek fur workers who understood English to speak to the Greek strikers. The Greek strikers met in a special hall, and had their own hall chairman, hall committee, finance committee, picket committee, etc.

were arrested during the first few weeks of the strike, and many more were beaten. "THIRTEEN STRIKERS ARRESTED ON THE PICKET LINES!" read a typical headline in the press. Before two weeks had passed, more than two hundred strikers had been arrested while picketing. Many were arrested several times. Barely were they released from jail than they would be back on the picket line. Esteem for the women strikers, including Greek and Black women, mounted by leaps and bounds as the fur workers saw them arrested, thrown in prison, and when released, back on the picket lines. A contemporary report noted:

> The women fur workers were seen in large numbers on the picket lines where many were arrested and beaten by police. During the 17 weeks of struggle, the women fur workers bravely resisted the clubbing of police and the jail sentences. They eagerly participated in the mass meetings called by the Joint Board and in all other strike activities led by the left wing.[13]

On Monday, March 8, ten thousand strikers responded to Gold's call. The police plunged into the mass of workers and beat down hundreds of strikers—men and women alike. The workers fought back. Frail girls leaped up fearlessly and returned blows squarely in the policemen's faces. As the line of strikers continued to forge ahead, police in patrol cars drove with breakneck speed into large numbers of workers on the sidewalks. Still the mass of strikers did not budge. In spite of every new assault by mounted police and motorized squads, the line grew. In the face of this immovable force, the police were powerless. Finally, the great mass of pickets broke through completely and marched triumphantly to the strike halls. Besides the hundreds of strikers beaten up in that single demonstration, one hundred men and twenty-five women were arrested.[14]

Patrolling the fur districts seven days and seven nights a week, the strikers eliminated any scab work in New York City. The manufacturers began to rely more and more on getting work done in out-of-town shops. In overcoming this new problem, the strike committee faced a serious obstacle—the open cooperation between the right-wing leaders of the International and the out-of-town employers who were doing scab work, After Shachtman disappeared, Winnick took over as acting President, and to all demands that the International do something to stop out-of-town scab work, he replied that the strike in New York was a "political maneuver" by the Communists. He added: "Therefore we shirk responsibility of any scab work that is being done outside of New York."[15]

The *Forward* attacked the strike as "Communist" and tried to organize a right-wing campaign against the leadership of the union. It sought to promote the takeover of the strike by the International, and proposed that Abe Beckerman, leader of the strong-arm men in the Amalgamated Clothing Workers, be brought in to run it. Beckerman's gunmen did intervene and tried to take over the strike halls, but they were overpowered by hundreds of strikers.[16]

The solidarity of the strikers in the face of police brutality, arrests and attacks by the gangsters won the admiration and support of broad sections of the labor movement. On March 23, the Central Trades and Labor Council of New York City, composed of delegates from all AFL unions in the city, heartily endorsed "the management and conduct of the Joint Board Furriers' Union...in their strike," and pledged its full support to the union.[17]

PROSPECTS FOR EARLY SETTLEMENT

By this time, many manufacturers were privately conceding that they could not defeat the union, and even though some scab work was being done in out-of-town shops with the connivance of leaders of the International, they knew that they would be forced into bankruptcy if a settlement did not come soon. As the weeks passed, more and more members of the Association pressured their leaders to settle with the union and end the strike.

There were two distinct groups on the Association's Board of Directors. One group, headed by President Samuels, represented the most vociferous anti-union elements. Aggressive and arrogant, they were determined to smash the union as they had in 1920. The second group represented the richer, comparatively "liberal" manufacturers and several of the skin dealers. Their financial losses during the strike were much greater than those of the group headed by Samuels, and they were eager for a settlement. Outstanding among them was Motty Eitingon of Eitingon-Schild Company, the wealthiest fur importer in the trade.

Eitington, with a large investment in fur skins languishing, unused, negotiated with Gold, and after a series of careful discussions, he proposed a compromise on a nearly 50-50 basis on all outstanding issues. Gold agreed to a ten percent wage increase and agreed to bargain on equal distribution of work, but he flatly rejected a 42-hour week. Aware of the importance of setting a precedent of 40 hours for the entire labor movement and sensitive to the religious sensibilities of Jewish workers regarding Saturday work, and recognizing the possibility of using shorter hours as a partial cure for seasonal unemployment and the special health hazards posed by prolonged work in the fur industry, Gold held firmly to the 40-hour standard. Two months after the strike began, Eitington and Gold shook hands on a settlement which led off with the provision for a five-day, 40-hour week, and included equal division of work during four months of the year, no contracting and a ten percent wage increase, with other points to be negotiated.[18]

ALLIANCE TO BREAK THE STRIKE AND ITS DEFEAT

But nothing came of this agreement. Socialist opponents of the union leadership, both inside and outside the International, joined New York AFL organizer Hugh Frayne in persuading AFL president William Green to help settle the strike behind the strikers' backs. The agreement, which the New York fur workers had no part in negotiating, was drawn up in Washington by Green, Samuels Shachtman and Meyer London. It called for a 42-hour week, a ten percent wage increase, and the renewal of most of the work rules in the old agreement.[19]

"The end of the left-wing rule is in sight," the *Fur Age Weekly* predicted happily when the news of the Washington agreement was made public.[20]

At this point the right-wing leaders of the International attempted to get blanket permission to authorize their settling the strike on unspecified terms at an April 15 mass meeting at Carnegie Hall. The fur workers received letters informing them that the terms of the settlement would be made public at the Carnegie Hall meeting. The letters enclosed a ballot to be returned, unsigned, to the International officers indicating if the workers wanted them to "go into conference with the Associated Fur Manufacturers for a settlement of the strike."

"Would be of great help to us if you would address our meeting," Shachtman wired William Green. "We feel that your presence would save the situation." But Green decided it would be unwise for him to appear, and he confined himself to sending a message pledging the Federation's support to the International "in such action as may be taken in negotiating a settlement with the fur manufacturers upon a fair, just and satisfactory basis."[21]

Contrary to the apparent expectations of the right wing, the left wing encouraged the membership to attend the meeting. The strikers turned out en masse, filling the hall and the streets outside. The police manned the doors and, under instructions from the right wing, kept out all known left wingers who tried to attend the meeting, but could hardly keep out the rank-and-file.

The meeting never got under way. Upon hearing that Gold and the others had been denied admission, the strikers began to chant "We want Gold!" Frayne arose to call the meeting to order and to read William Green's telegram of greetings. The workers shouted that they wanted Gold. For more than a half hour Frayne stood there, unable to make himself heard. The workers outside picked up the cry until it reverberated through the packed streets: "Gold! Gold! Gold! We Want Gold!" The strikers kept up the cry until the meeting was finally called off.[22]

The right-wing leaders of the International charged that the demonstration inside Carnegie Hall had been "engineered by communist agitators under Gold's direct supervision." *Women's Wear Daily* promptly labeled this "ridiculous." "If the demonstration was engineered by the left wing," the trade journal declared, "it was executed by a leaderless left wing. Those in charge of arrangements had taken steps to keep out every person whose presence was not welcome to them."[23]

The AFL leaders were now in a dilemma. They either had to denounce the strikers who had so clearly demonstrated their support for the left-wing leaders, or to come to terms with the left-wing Joint Board. Faced with this choice, they gave in momentarily. Less than a week after the ill-conceived Carnegie Hall meeting, the fur workers attended another mass meeting at the 69th Regiment Armory, This meeting was addressed by both William Green and Ben Gold. At the Armory Green endorsed the strike and agreed to assist in negotiations to help the strikers win their original demands. After the cheers and applause for Gold had died down, Gold told the workers that "this meeting proves that the fur strikers are not fighting for themselves alone but for the cause of organized labor in America." He then contrasted the wealth of the employers to the conditions of the fur workers, and concluded: "All this wealth we, the workers, created. We are not going to be cheated out of it. We are going to ask for all we can get, so that our lives may be more human and decent."[24]

On May 17, the General Strike Committee issued an appeal to all labor organizations in New York City to join the drive for a 40-hour, five-day week. Already, the New York section of the International

Ladies' Garment Workers' Union had adopted the demand in principle. The Cap Makers endorsed it. The Amalgamated Clothing workers had accepted it at their recent convention. AFL president Green had given the 40-hour week his endorsement. This, then, was the time for the workers of New York to come to the aid of the striking fur workers and make the demand for the 40-hour week the demand of New York's organized labor.

The call closed with a stirring appeal:

A new era is dawning upon the working class, new vistas open before the laboring masses. Let us all unite in raising the banner of the FORTY-HOUR WEEK. Let us become the battle-cry of labor all over New York, all over the country.
LONG LIVE THE 40-HOUR WEEK!
LONG LIVE THE SOLIDARITY OF THE WORKING CLASS!
LONG LIVE THE WORKERS' STRUGGLE FOR FREEDOM!
ONWARD TO NEW STRUGGLES AND NEW ACHIEVEMENTS!

Along with the call went invitations to all branches of organized labor in New York City to participate in a giant rally at Madison Square Garden on May 22. President Green, Shachtman, John Coughlin of the State Federation of Labor, representatives of the Amalgamated Clothing Workers, ILGWU, Hat and Cap Makers, Teachers Union and other labor organizations were invited to address the meeting.[25]

Madison Square Garden was jammed on the afternoon of May 22, 1926. It was the greatest indoor labor mass meeting ever held in New York City up to that time. "Not Barnum's elephants nor Tex Rickards's leather pushers were the attraction that filled the monster new Madison Square Garden this time," wrote one reporter. "The forty-hour week fight of the striking furriers did it." Cloak and dress makers, shoe workers, food workers, bookkeepers, printers, teachers, building trades workers, waiters and others, joined the striking fur workers in demanding a forty-hour week for all organized labor.

Telegrams of support came from all over the nation: the state federations of Pennsylvania, Minnesota and California, the central labor bodies of Minneapolis, St. Paul, Milwaukee, and St. Louis and the needle trades unions of Pittsburgh, Philadelphia, Boston and New York. "The mound of AFL telegrams," commented a reporter, "was spectacular proof that the furriers' strike was not the outlaw movement that certain groups have tried to represent it, but a bona fide trade union struggle that has inspired New York labor and the labor movement outside as have few strikes."[26]

The packed Garden and the pile of telegrams more than offset the failure of William Green, Oizer Shachtman, Sidney Hillman, and Morris Sigman to come to the rally. Hillman and Sigman sent telegrams declining to attend on the ground that one union alone should not have taken the initiative to call a mass meeting of this character.

John Coughlin brought the official endorsement of the forty-hour campaign from the AFL unions in New York. John Sullivan, president of the New York State Federation of Labor, also heartily endorsed the demand of the fur workers. The manager of the Cloak and Dress Makers' Unions and the president of the Teachers' Union were among other AFL leaders of New York who endorsed the demand and brought greetings.

But Gold in his speech sharply criticized Hillman and Sigman for refusing to attend. He was particularly indignant at Hillman because the meeting had been planned in consultation with the president of the Amalgamated Clothing Workers who had promised to be one of the speakers at the Garden mass meeting.* The importance of the meeting, Gold assured the cheering audience, was not diminished in the slightest by the absence of timid labor leaders. The rally would help the fur workers win their strike. And this, in turn, would spur other workers in the United States to gain the forty-hour week.[27]

On May 27 there was exactly $70 in the strike treasury. At least $50,000 was needed in four days for strike relief. A group of shop chairmen told the General Strike Committee: "The union needs money. Some of us want to lend money to the union. We can get loans from other workers, too." The strike committee told them to do what they could.

Thus a rank-and-file drive for "40-Hour Liberty Loans" was born. When Gold announced at the strike halls that from this day on the strikers themselves had become the bankers and were building a strike fund through loans to the union, there were shouts from every side pledging to bring loans. One striker walked to the platform, and announced: "I have paid fifteen years on my insurance policy. Many times my wife and I have not eaten in order to have the money to make the next payment. But now I know that we have a union that

---

* The Amalgamated had given $25,000 to the fur strikers, and Hillman had promised another $25,000.

will take care of us. So tomorrow I am cashing in my policy and I will bring $1,000 to my union."

At the meeting in Webster Hall alone, $19,000 was pledged as loans to the union. At the Manhattan Lyceum another $9,000 was pledged. The union issued bonds to donors, to mature in six months. On June 1, strike relief was paid out as usual![28]

When over $100,000 of "40-Hour Liberty Loans" was subscribed, the final hope of the employers vanished. Every attack, every maneuver, had failed to break the strike. Now, at the beginning of the fifteenth week. The workers were giving another remarkable demonstration of their determination to achieve victory no matter how many months it would take.

And the mass picketing demonstrations were as large and enthusiastic as they had been during first week of the strike.[29]

VICTORY FOR THE FUR WORKERS!

On June 11, 1926, the strike was finally settled, after seventeen long weeks. The agreement provided for a forty-hour week, no overtime except from September through November, and then only in the form of an additional half day on Saturday at extra pay, a 10 percent wage increase (which, in the words of the *New-York Times,* meant "a considerable wage increase for many workers, especially women fur workers"), an end to subcontracting, ten legal holidays, all but three of them paid, and the discharge of all scabs, with a union committee to rule on their future eligibility for employment in the industry. The collective agreement was to run for three years, retroactive to February 1, 1926, when the old agreement expired. The agreement applied also to the United Fur Manufacturers Association, made up largely of Greek manufacturers, and the Fur Trimming Manufacturers Association.[29]

While the demand for unemployment insurance had been dropped, the agreement represented a major victory. On June 14, the strikers ratified the agreement by an almost unanimous vote. Only forty workers out of all the thousands of strikers, opposed the settlement. When the vote was announced, the workers decided to hold their last demonstration on the following day. They assembled in the strike halls in their best clothes. Many brought their wives and children with them. Banners and signs decorated the walls. With several bands on hand to furnish the music for the festivities, they marched through the streets. For four hours, the twelve thousand furriers paraded. Thousands of cloak and dress makers hurled confetti from the windows, and shouted: "Long live the Furriers' Union! Long live the forty-hour week!"[30]

The workers had won more than a forty-hour, five-day week, wage increases and other important gains. The strike had erased the blot of the 1920 disaster from the union's history. It had given the twelve thousand fur workers of New York a new confidence in themselves. A true unity of the rank-and-file had been created, and it was widely acknowledged that "the women workers had played a prominent part in the victory." A magnificent tradition had been born among the fur workers—the tradition of 1926—that was to inspire them in later struggles and make possible new victories.

For the American working class as a whole the fur workers' general strike of 1926 was an event of the utmost significance. It stood out in a period of labor defeats, "union-management cooperation," wage cuts, blacklistings, company unionism, open-shop drives and reactionary national, state and local politics. At a time when workers were suffering setbacks on all fronts, the fur workers proved that a militant rank and file led by a progressive leadership could win their demands against the most powerful opposition. They proved that conducting a labor struggle by involving the whole membership was infinitely more effective than relying on professional gangsters.

As Bert Cochran, a historian generally critical of Communist union activity, has put it, the Socialist/AFL leaders had "attempted repeatedly to inject themselves into the strike leadership, to wean away the membership, but their maneuvers came to nothing; their standing was poor with the ranks, and they were just running a campaign of ... obstruction." The result of the strike, Cochran continues, was a "spectacular left wing victory ... the first 40-hour, five-day week in the garment industry."[31]*

---

* An utterly ridiculous statement appears in the *Biographical Dictionary of American Labor*, edited by Gary M. Fink. In the biographical sketch of Ben Gold, there is the following: "[He] was one of the leaders of a largely unsuccessful general strike of New York fur workers in 1926...." (Westport, Conn., 1984, p. 253.)

CHAPTER 7

THE FUR WORKERS: II

During the 1926 strike, James O'Leary, reporter for the New York *World*, asked Ben Gold whether the reports that he was a Communist were true. "Sure, since 1919," came Gold's reply.[1] This was "sensational" news, but when the right wing used it in the elections that followed the 1926 victory, it discovered that the outcome of the strike had only served to increase the respect the workers had for a Communist trade union leader. The election of left-wingers to positions of leadership in many of the out-of-town locals made it clear that the days of the right-wing officials were numbered. The fur workers were now in a position to sweep the right-wing leaders of the International out of office at the convention scheduled for May, 1927.[2] In a letter to a right-wing fur union leader on August 23, 1929, William Green noted:

> It is clearly evident that the American Federation of Labor saved your organization from the Communists. At the time we took charge of the situation in New York, the membership of your International Union was about to elect Communists as officers of your International organization. The influence of Communism and Communist leaders was very great. They had practically captured your International Union.[3]

AFL INTERVENES TO SAVE RIGHT WING

The intervention of the American Federation of Labor began only a few weeks after the 1926 victory. On July 19, 1926, Ben Gold, manager of the New York Joint Board, received a notice from Green that the Executive Council of the AFL had

> ...authorized and instructed the President of the American Federation of Labor to appoint a committee representing the Executive Council for the

purpose of making an investigation into the internal affairs of the International Fur Workers Union, the recent strike of the New York membership of that Union, the developments which took place in the working out of a new wage agreement and the general policy pursued by the Strike Committee which directed the strike in New York City.

"The Executive Council desires to know," the communication continued, "whether those in charge of the recent strike in New York City were conforming to the laws, usages and administrative policies of the American Federation of Labor in their management and conduct of the strike."

The committee to investigate the conduct of the 1926 strike was chaired by Matthew Woll, vice-president of the AFL, and consisted of Hugh Frayne and Edward F. McGrady, general organizers of the Federation; John Sullivan, president of the New York State Federation of Labor; and Joseph Ryan, president of the New York City Central Trades and Labor Council. All of them were well known for their bitter opposition to Communists and left-wingers in general.[4]

INVESTIGATION OF THE 1926 STRIKE

"Please give the committee access to all books, records and accounts of the local strike committee of which you were chairman, and the books, records and accounts of any subcommittee created by the local strike committee," Green notified Gold. To give the investigation an air of impartiality, the AFL president sent a similar letter to Shachtman, asking him to give the committee access to all books, records and accounts of the International Union which the committee might consider pertinent to its investigation. But in a private letter to Shachtman on July 23, 1926, conspicuously marked "confidential," Hugh Frayne secretly reassured Shachtman that the committee had already met and drawn up its plan of operation. It was essential that Shachtman be present when the committee met, he wrote, to "enlighten us with such information as will be helpful in the work."[5]

In the weeks to come, the investigation committee issued statement after statement to the press, announcing that it was conducting an impartial inquiry and that it was neutral in the conflict between the International and the Joint Board.[6] Nor is this surprising since it was clear that the AFL was anything but neutral. It all became evident months later. On March 14, 1927, Green wrote: "The International Fur Workers Union appealed to the American Federation of Labor to make an investigation of the 1926 strike of the Fur Workers of New York City which was originated, directed and administered by the Joint Board of the International Union." "What are we accused of?" Gold asked. Green had neither stated the grounds upon which the investigation had been ordered, nor disclosed upon whose initiative it was being undertaken, he pointed out. "This is an unusual procedure indeed," Gold continued. "Is the AFL in the habit of ordering special investigations of strikes simply because it is generally interested in the welfare of the organizations concerned? We think not. On the contrary, the AFL policy has always been to grant the affiliated organizations great latitude in the conduct of their strikes. Such an investigation as the one proposed is almost, if not altogether, without parallel in American trade union practice. Our Joint Board requests from you a definite statement of the specific reasons for the proposed investigation."

"We are proud of our long, hard-fought and successful strike," Gold's letter concluded. "We have no objection to its being investigated by a fair and properly authorized committee. The Joint Board is a loyal and disciplined section of the AFL. But we insist upon knowing why the investigation is being undertaken and upon whose initiative. We also propose that our Joint Board be allowed three members upon any such committee and that it conduct its hearings publicly in a hall which will permit the attendance of the largest possible number of trade unionists and the press."[6]

But all requests for a specific statement of charges and for open hearings were denied. Protesting that the investigation was in violation of the International Constitution and the laws of the AFL, the Joint Board nevertheless finally agreed to make its books and records available to the committee, so that "the American labor movement might learn how to conduct a strike."[7] Throughout August and September, 1926, the investigating committee met in secret session. It inspected the books of the Joint Board and took personal testimony. The testimony of the witnesses was kept secret. Had it been made public, the record would have revealed very plainly the difference in treatment accorded to the spokespersons of the Joint Board and those of the International. The former were repeatedly asked if they were members of the Communist Party, if they supported and endorsed the *Freiheit*, and other questions intended to give the impression that the leaders of the strike were "Moscow agents" and that the strike itself was a "Communist plot." On the other hand, spokespersons for the International were not asked if they were members of the Socialist Party, if they endorsed the *Forward*, of if they had held any meetings with other right-wing trade union leaders during the strike to betray the strikers.

The right-wing leaders of the International accused the strike leaders of squandering the union's money, of bribing the police, of forcing strikers to join the Communist Party, of terrorizing workers who refused to continue on strike, of prolonging the strike at the order of the Communist Party, and even of placing "Communist agents" in the offices of New York newspapers—including the *New York Times*—to report the strike in a manner favorable to the Communists.[8]

These accusations were readily accepted without question by the investigation committee. All requests by representatives of the Joint Board for the right to cross-examine witnesses were rejected. Likewise rejected was the Joint Board's request for an opportunity to cross-examine some fifty-eight signers of affidavits who claimed they had been victims of beatings during the strike.[9]

On January 13, 1927, the committee reported to the AFL Executive Council that it had found the Joint Board guilty of "bribery, debauchery, and flagrant dishonesty" and announced that "a most serious state of affairs" existed in the International Fur Workers' Union, "due to the fact that a communist leadership had gained the ascendancy in the New York locals." Unless drastic defense measures were resorted to at once, this same leadership would gain control of "the whole of the International Fur Workers Union." "This must not come to pass!" the committee proclaimed, and it called for strong measures to end the "communistic ... ascendancy in the New York locals." The International Fur Workers Union was therefore urged to "expel from its membership all who admitted affiliation to the Communist or Workers' Party; or the Trade Union Educational League, or those who may be found to have such affiliation." Should this prove to be insufficient to meet the crisis, the International was asked to revoke the charter of the New York Joint Board and of all local unions which refused to comply with this directive.[10]

On January 8, 1927, a week before the report was made public, Shachtman had already assured Green of the International's decision "to reorganize the Joint Board." He appealed to the AFL's Executive Council to appoint a committee "to give the International Union assistance and advice as well as active support" in carrying through the expulsion of the Joint Board. The Executive Council approved the report of the investigation committee and authorized Green to appoint a special committee to cooperate with the International Fur Workers Union "to rid this organization of its communistic leadership."[11]

EXPULSION OF THE JOINT BOARD

The AFL soon appointed a special committee to "rid the Furriers' Union of its communist leadership and destructive influence." On February 8, 1927, the special committee met with the "Committee for Preservation of the Trade Unions," to discuss plans for expulsion of the New York Joint Board of the Furriers Union. The Committee for Preservation of Trade Unions had been organized in December, 1926 by right-wing Socialist union officials, including Morris Sigman and Julius Hochman of the ILGWU, Abraham Beckerman of the Amalgamated Clothing Workers, Morris Feinstone of the United Hebrew Trades, Abraham I. Shiplacoff of the International Pocket Book Workers, and Alex Rose of the Millinery Workers. The committee declared war on the left-wing forces in the needle trades unions, and called for the expulsion of all Communists from the labor movement. The National Executive Committee of the Socialist Party hailed the organization of the committee and endorsed its program.[12]

After the meeting with the Committee for Preservation of the Trade Unions, Woll, Frayne, and McGrady wrote to Green: "It was pointed out by everybody at this meeting that the communists in the fur industry were much better entrenched than they were in all of the other needle trades and that consequently the fight would be more bitter and costly." "The International Fur Workers Union," they continued, "was not only bankrupt, but owed considerable money and could give no financial assistance." The money, then, would have to come from outside sources. Fortunately, the Committee for Preservation of the Trade Unions pledged "to devote their time to raise money among the Hebrew trades" and had appointed the Socialist Party leader, Abraham Shiplacoff, treasurer of the fund to keep the bankrupt International alive.[13]

On February 17, 1927, in response to a request from William Green, the New York City Central Trades and Labor Council expelled the Fur Workers' Union Locals 1, 5, 10, and 15, and the International Ladies' Garment Workers' Union Locals 2, 9, 22, and 35.[14] Ironically, the left wing in the ILGWU was denounced for having lost its 1926 strike led by the Joint Board, while the fur workers' left wing was expelled after having won the great 1926 strike in its industry.

There was another irony. In late 1926 the AFL began a campaign for the five-day, 40-hour week.* This was just at the time the AFL pursued investigations which were designed to rid the Furriers' Union, the best example of how mass labor action could bring about such a working week, "of its communistic leadership and destructive influence."

On March 2, 1927, the General Executive Board of the International Fur Workers Union expelled thirty-seven officials of the New York Joint Board and of Locals 1, 5, 10, and 15 from membership in the union. Those expelled included Ben Gold, Jack Schneider, Joseph Winogradsky, Samuel Liebowitz, Lena Greenberg, Fanny Warshafsky, Esther Polansky, Mary Cohen, Esther Gumberg, and Lena Rabinowitz. The GEB ordered the immediate dissolution of the Joint Board and the local unions and demanded the immediate delivery of all funds and properties of the board and locals to the AFL's special committee. The members of the expelled locals were ordered to stop paying dues to the "illegal" bodies and pay them instead to a new union, called the Joint Council, which was launched by the AFL's special committee.[15]

In all, thirty charges were listed in the expulsion order, although not all of the thirty-seven expelled were included in each one of the charges. Most of them were based upon the report of the AFL's investigation committee, and one, the seventh charge, directed only against Gold, charged a conspiracy "to permit the Communist Party to shape the policies and the conduct of the strike." Several charges referred to the fostering of dissension among the fur workers, attending protest meetings against the union, and joining an organiza-

---

*The original resolution, submitted to the 1926 AFL convention by members of the Cloth, Hat, Cap and Millinery Workers' Union, asked that the convention "go on record" as favoring "the shortening of working hours in all industries to 40 hours a week," and that the Executive Council be "instructed to inaugurate a vigorous campaign in every industry throughout the country for the introduction of the five-day and forty-hour week." The substitute resolution, ultimately unanimously passed, made no reference to 40 hours except in its title, and merely placed the convention "on record as favoring a progressive shortening of the hours of labor and the days per week" while requesting that the Executive Council "inaugurate a campaign of education and organization" on the issue. (Proceedings, AFL Convention, 1926, pp. 197, 201-03.) President William Green, moreover, made it clear that the resolution meant that the AFL was only agitating for change in the "mining industry, the building industry, and the automobile industry." (Labor, Dec. 18, 1926.)

tion (the name of which was not mentioned) said to be "hostile to the union."[16]

RESPONSE OF THE JOINT BOARD

In his reply to the GEB in the name of the Joint Board, Gold branded the charges as "a tissue of falsehoods and flagrant inventions, evidently not made in the expectation that they would be believed, but in an attempt to find some excuse for ...actions, which are not only utterly illegal, but, if successful, would result in utter ruin of the union itself." He challenged the accusers to present the charges to a convention "of duly and honestly elected representatives of the rank and file of our International membership, as we stand ready to answer all charges before our own membership...."[17]

The Joint Board refused to recognize its expulsion, pointing out the unconstitutional nature of the proceedings, and it rapidly mobilized the workers around a defense committee organized to prevent the forcible takeover of the union. The fighting that went on in the fur district during the next few months was intense. The manufacturers and the police lined up with the Joint Council and its goons in an attempt to force the fur workers to register with the new union. The workers and their defense committee fought back with strikes and fists; the opposition with fists, blackjacks, and knives.[18]

ANOTHER ATTACK

On March 17, 1927, eleven active workers and leaders of the Joint Board, including Gold, were arrested and charged with felonious assault in connection with the picketing of a small scab shop in Rockville Center, Long Island, near Mineola, during the 1926 strike. A week later Mayor James J. Walker announced an investigation of the AFL charge of police bribery during the 1926 strike. He was "convinced that the allegations were sufficient to warrant a thorough inquiry." (He did not mention the fact that he had become convinced during a conference with William Green and Matthew Woll.) Magistrate Joseph Corrigan was named to conduct the official court investigation.[19]

The AFL "reorganizers" took steps to deprive the accused of adequate legal defense. Woll, Frayne and McGrady wrote to Green: "About April 1 your committee was informed that Clarence Darrow was coming to New York to confer with the communist leaders who desire to engage his services at a trial which was to be held at

Mineola, New York, where they were the defendants on a felonious assault charge and also to represent them at the investigation of the alleged police graft in New York City. Your committee met with Mr. Darrow and as a result he promised not to handle their case."[20]

George Z. Medalie, a member of the National Committee of the Republican Party and former State Attorney-General, agreed to serve as counsel for the union and headed the group of lawyers for the defense. The Joint Board also appealed to Frank P. Walsh, former chairman of the Federal Commission on Industrial Relations and Joint Chairman of the War Labor Conference Board, to undertake the defense of its leaders. Walsh refused to accept the cases until he had an opportunity to make an exhaustive investigation of the charges and counter-charges. For several weeks, Walsh and his entire staff of attorneys investigated the Mineola affair and the police bribery charges. They reached the conclusion that the charges against the leaders of the fur workers were "of the flimsiest nature," most of them being "based upon false accusations," and inspired by right-wing leaders of the International and the AFL "to eliminate the present Joint Board and their officers."[21]

Walsh not only agreed to take the cases; he helped organize a Committee of One Hundred to defend needle trades' workers who were either in prison or were facing imprisonment as a result of their activities in the furriers' and cloakmakers' strikes of 1926. The committee including leading writers, artists, playwrights, editors, ministers, and men and women prominent in humanitarian causes.* The formation of the Committee of One Hundred enraged the AFL leaders and their Socialist allies. McGrady charged that the liberals who were serving on the committee were being used as "window dressing" by the "Communist Joint Board of the Furriers Union." There was "no issue of civil or industrial rights" involved, he insisted, since they were all "Communists."[22]

Morris Sigman of the ILGWU wrote personally to the directors of the American Civil Liberties Union, advising "the individual Civil

---

* Among them were Forrest Bailey, director of the American Civil Liberties Union and President of the Civic Club of New York; Susan Brandeis, lawyer and daughter of United States Supreme Court Justice Brandeis; Professor Henry W. Dana; W.E.B. Du Bois, outstanding Black leader and editor of *Crisis*; James Weldon Johnson, leader of the National Association for the Advancement of Colored People; Arthur Garfield Hays, prominent lawyer and active in the American Civil Liberties Union; Rev. John Haynes Holmes; Upton Sinclair, famous novelist, and Rev. Harry F. Ward of the Union Theological Seminary.

Liberties members participating in this so-called 'defense committee' to keep their hands off." In reply Arthur Garfield Hayes accused Sigman of allowing "your emotion," to "have destroyed your sense of honor as well as your sense of fairness.... You even state that we who serve on the Committee must be 'inextricably bound up with gangsterism, fraud and corruption employed by those former leaders.' You must know that this sort of thing is preposterous and that statements of that kind merely reflect on your judgment and good faith."[23]

ROLE OF THE EMPLOYERS

Originally it had been planned that the employers should remain in the background while the leaders of the International and the AFL carried the ball in smashing the Joint Board. In this way, it was hoped, the fur workers would not see how deeply their employers were involved in the scheme to destroy their union. But the continued resistance of the workers forced the conspirators to drop the mask. The employers came openly into the campaign to force the fur workers to register in the new union. "As a result of these conferences," Woll, Frayne and McGrady wrote to William Green, "the Associated Fur Manufacturers agreed to recognize the contract of the International organization and the American Federation of Labor. It further agreed that it would instruct all members of the Association to employ none but workers in good standing in the International organization affiliated with the American Federation of Labor."

On April 2, fur workers entering the shops were informed by signs posted on the walls that anyone who did not bring a book from the Joint Council at the opening of the following week would not be allowed to work. "The period of slavery in the United States is past," the Joint Board warned the manufacturers. Should they continue their attempts to dictate to the fur workers what union they should belong to, the Joint Board would take steps to defend the workers' rights.[24]

Rarely had a union faced attacks on so many fronts at one time. Every day more and more workers reported to the Joint Board that they had not been allowed to go to work because they had refused to register with the Joint Council. Meanwhile, with the aid of the police and gangsters, the Council was trying desperately to fill the shops with scabs to replace workers who had refused to register. Woll, Frayne and McGrady informed Police Commissioner McLaughlin that it was absolutely essential that the Council receive the "full cooperation of the police department." McLaughlin instructed Deputy Inspector McGrath and Captain Hanley of the 30th Street Precinct to devote their full time to assisting the Council. Woll, Frayne and McGrady reported to Green that "it was agreed to ... let the police handle the situation. This procedure has ever since been followed."[25]

Under the threat of police intimidation and starvation, some workers did capitulate. The vast majority, however, held fast even though they were thrown out of their shops and deprived of their livelihood. Under pressure from the manufacturers whose fur garments were not being produced, the leaders of the Association demanded action from the AFL. "The Associated Fur Manufacturers called in your committee," Woll, Frayne and McGrady wrote to Green, "and said they were willing to go through with this fight provided your committee would pledge that the American Federation of Labor would stay until conditions were stabilized. This we promised to do."[26]

In the Mineola trial, the defendants were supposedly on trial for having broken into a scab shop and attacking the owner. But a good deal of the trial was conducted as if the defendants were guilty of political crimes. They were asked if they read the *Freiheit* and endorsed its principles. Did they know Charles E. Ruthenberg, general secretary of the American Communist Party? Did they oppose the capitalist form of government? Frank P. Walsh protested that these questions had nothing to do with the charge against the defendants and were asked only to prejudice the jury. Judge Smith overruled his objections. Two defendants—Gold and Shapiro—were acquitted. Nine others were found guilty. They were sentenced to two-and-one-half to five years in prison.[27]

Later, Supreme Court Justice Mitchel May in Brooklyn granted a certificate of reasonable doubt in the Mineola case on the grounds that even "a superficial examination of the records of this trial" revealed "an atmosphere...which would influence the jury against the accused." Justice May accused the presiding judge and the district attorney of going far out of their way in order to assure an "unfavorable verdict against the accused." "It is seriously questionable whether the defendants were able to secure the fair and impartial trial which the law insures," he concluded.[28] After two years of legal appeals in the courts and continuous mass pressure, seven of the nine who were found guilty in the Mineola trial were acquitted. The other two were imprisoned for two and one-half years.

Meanwhile, hearings were held on the police bribery charges before Magistrate Corrigan. But the record of police brutality during the 1926 strike demolished the charge that the furriers' leaders had bribed the police to keep them from arresting pickets. Police records put into evidence showed 874 arrests in three precincts alone and 477 convictions. In all, about fifteen hundred strikers had been arrested, hundreds had been brutally beaten by the police, and throughout the strike, protests had been lodged by the Joint Board against the police.

The investigation lasted for two weeks. Judge Corrigan finally ruled that there was "no evidence obtainable to sustain the charges" of the AFL officials. "Nothing has been brought out during this examination," he declared, "which in any way reflects upon the honesty of the Police Department or any members of the force." He dismissed the entire charge. The press conceded that this action was inevitable, since the police had rendered valuable service to the employers during the strike, and any charge that they had been bribed to be partial towards the strikers was simply too preposterous to hold water.[29]

For three months, the fur district was in a turmoil as the workers resisted efforts to force them into the Joint Council. The unionization of the whole New York fur industry was in danger, and the Joint Board called a tactical retreat. At the beginning of May, 1927, the left wing instructed its followers to register with the Joint Council and await further instructions. By May 10 about 6,500 workers, carefully screened to keep out the known militants, had registered with the AFL Joint Council. Actually, the vast majority of these fur workers did not go to register and obtain their union books in person.* Their employers registered for them, paid their initiation fees, obtained their books, and paid their dues to the Joint Council. But the workers still continued to pay dues to the Joint Board and to attend shop meetings in the Joint Board office. Thousand who refused to register with the Joint Council wandered from shop to shop, working a day or two in each place, until the boss would order them to either register or get out.[30]

In the Association shops, the employers lost no time in reaping the benefits of the chaos created by the expulsion of the Joint Board and the AFL "reorganization." Working hours were increased to forty-four and forty-six a week, and many furriers were forced to work

---

* In order to work in the shops, a worker was required to show his or her union book revealing that he or she was a paid-up member of the union.

fifty, sixty, and even seventy hours a week without overtime pay. Wages were cut sharply, in many shops as much as 50 percent. As in the case of the ILGWU, the sweatshop system now returned in full force. Contracting and sub-contracting again infested the indus try.[31]

THE 1927 STRIKE

While the new union was now in control of the fur market, it was either unwilling or unable to enforce the agreement won by the Joint Board in 1926. The Joint Board, on the other hand, mobilized the workers to resist the breakdown of working conditions in the shops, and on June 3, 1927, it took the offensive by calling the fur workers out on strike. The demands of the union were: reinstatement of the 1926 agreement, enforcement of the agreement in the shops, and recognition of the Joint Board.[32]

This was the real showdown, and the strike was the bloodiest ever seen in the fur district, already notorious for its violence. After a hurried consultation, Woll, Frayne, and McGrady decided to prevent the strike from developing. They turned for assistance to Joseph A. Warren, New York City Commissioner of Police, "The strike must not take place," they wrote. "To this end we venture to suggest, if it is within the propriety of your Department, that you call to your office the communistic leaders of the Joint Board."

But this maneuver failed. Then in a letter to Police Commissioner Warren, Edward McGrady, the AFL's general organizer, who was managing the crusade against the Joint Board, predicted that a mass demonstration called by the Joint Board for June would be completely successful "unless these groups are awed by the presence and activity of the police assigned to this district .... We are confident that your Department will adequately handle the situation." The police leaped to do his bidding. From the first day of the strike, numerous squads of police and Industrial Squad detectives patrolled the fur market and assaulted the pickets. Arrests of strikers increased daily.[33]

On the morning of the first great mass demonstration, the entire fur district was flooded with policemen and detectives. No sooner had the thousands of strikers started their march than the fur district was turned into a "war zone" as police and detectives, swinging clubs and blackjacks, tried desperately to break up the demonstration. "At times the press of strikers was halted only when detectives drew revolvers," wrote one reporter. But it was only a temporary halt, for the strikers moved along relentlessly and swept all scabs out of the market. Unable to break up the mass demonstration, the Industrial Squad took bloody revenge on individual strikers, particularly singling out women pickets for beating.[34]

Under the protection of the police, gangsters overran the fur market, spreading terror on every block. They rode through the district in big cars filled with weapons. At intervals, they would leap out, slash the pickets with knives and beat them with iron bars and other weapons. Here, again, women pickets were singled out for attack. "In a free-for-all fight yesterday afternoon on Sixth Avenue and Twenty-Seventh Street," the New York *Sun* reported on June 25, 1927, "four left-wing pickets, three of them women, were beaten with iron bars and stabbed within sight of police on strike duty."

When arrested, the strong-arm men said they were getting $50 a week from the International Fur Workers' Union. Aaron Gross was beaten, stabbed, and nearly killed by two men; the ten were arrested but promptly bailed out of jail by the IFWU.[35]

A cursory examination of newspaper headlines gives a clear picture of the violence against the strikers: "Police Arrest 11 Fur Strikers for Parading": "Arrest 350 Fur Strikers": "224 Fur Strikers Arrested"; "Forty Fur Pickets Sent to Prison"; "131 More Pickets Sent to Prison"; "The Big Parade—to Court."

The Jefferson Market Police Court was packed with sympathizers and fellow strikers, and cheers rang through the courtroom when 110 of the strikers announced that because of the excessive bail asked by the judge, they preferred to sit in jail rather than put their union to a great expense. "I have been to war," wrote one New York reporter the following day, "but I have yet to see anything which will compare with the indomitable courage and guts displayed yesterday by the striking furriers—men and women—on the picket line."

In one day alone, one fur worker was sentenced to eight months in prison; four workers to six months in prison; sixty-two to fifteen days in prison; thirty-four to ten days; and eight to five days in prison. Among those to whom this "justice" was meted out were fifty-four women. Two women, Ethel Shusterman and Ida Ishman, were among the famous five who were sentenced to eight and six months in prison for having "disturbed" the court when, outraged at the vicious sentences given their fellow pickets, they expressed indignation and horror.[36]

In vain the Joint Board pointed out that the penalizing of the workers for picketing peacefully violated a recent decision of the New York Court of Appeals upholding "peaceful picketing." The police continued their mass arrests and the magistrates continued to sentence the pickets to jail. But Edward McGrady complained that the authorities were still not dealing "severely enough" with the fur strikers. And when Magistrate Rosenbluth, who had sentenced scores of pickets to jail, ventured to suggest that the AFL leaders reach some agreement with the Joint Board "on the number of pickets to be used," McGrady immediately released a statement criticizing the judge. "There is no strike. There is no legitimate need or right to picket," he declared.[37]

After studying the situation as an observer for the American Civil Liberties Union, Norman Thomas, leader of the Socialist Party, who could hardly be accused of being biased in favor of the left-wing leadership of the Joint Board, wrote to Forrest Bailey; "As far as I could judge, the present attitude of the police would make proper picketing of the most peaceful sort a practical impossibility."[38] That "attitude" was given full meaning by A.C. Sedgwick, a *New York Times* reporter, when he described the treatment of arrested strikers at the hands of the police and the Industrial Squad:

> One detective takes a piece of rubber hose, which is part of the equipment of the detectives' bureau and is favored because it leaves no marks. Another takes out his blackjack. Others grab for anything—blackjacks and night-sticks. The prisoners fall to the floor. The blood pours from their faces. They spit and cough blood. The detectives still in a rage, look at them. The door opens. A young policeman in a uniform pokes his head in. "You fellers is easy with 'em," he says. "Is that so?" roars a detective and kicks a prisoner in the face, pulls him to his feet, props him against the desk, then with the butt end of his revolver makes a gash in his head...
>
> If it were asked of any official source what happened to the men it would be said that they received their injuries "resisting arrest," or perhaps that the "sidewalk came up and hit 'em."[39]

The extraordinary heroism of the strikers is shown by the attitude of forty women pickets who were arrested and sentenced to five, ten, and in some cases, thirty days and even six months imprisonment on Welfare Island. Those given five or ten days could have been freed if they were willing to pay their fines. But when a representative of the Joint Board came with the money for their release, they refused to allow the union's funds to be exhausted by the payment of fines. "We will serve our sentences," they declared, and not even the pleas of anxious relatives could sway them.[40]

By the time the strike was ended, after six weeks of battle, it was clear that it was the Joint Board that held the loyalty of the fur workers. While the strike ended in only a partial victory, union control and union conditions were reestablished in shops employing the majority of the workers. The Joint Board, moreover, was recognized by both independent and trimming association employers,* and although it was unable to win formal recognition by the major manufacturers' association, the Joint Board did compel many association members to agree not to oblige their workers to register with the Joint Council. Other association employers went through the motions of asking their workers to register but took no reprisals against those who refused.[41]

THE 1927 INTERNATIONAL CONVENTION

While thousands of fur workers were battling police clubs, arrests and imprisonment on the picket line in New York, the Eighth Biennial Convention of the International Fur Workers Union opened on June 13, 1927, in the AFL Building in Washington, D.C. According to the union's constitution, the convention was to have taken place in May, but Woll, Frayne and McGrady instructed the International officers on April 21 "that no call be sent out at this time for the holding of a convention." "As you well know," they pointed out, "your International Union is today being financed to a great part by the reorganizing activities going on here in New York City and that without this income your organization would be practically bankrupt." In a private letter to AFL President William Green, the AFL trio gave their reason for postponing the convention:

> There is an agitation being worked up around the country for the convening of the convention of the International Fur Workers' Union. This should have taken place in the month of May. Your committee delayed calling this convention until we had assurances that the International Organization would be able to control the situation....[42]

Only after they had received assurances from Shachtman that if a convention was called outside of New York City, the International would have thirty-one "favorable delegates and six unfavorable delegates," did the AFL "reorganizers" agree to call the convention to be held on June 20. The choice of the small council chamber in the AFL Building in Washington came after Shachtman pointed out that

---

* Three years before, the Fur Trimming Association had broken its agreement with the left-wing union. It represented employers who manufactured fur trimmings.

it would "prevent any possible demonstrations on the part of the vast majority of the Communists and their followers."[43]

The right-wing International leadership made sure they would control the convention. They refused to recognize the delegates from the New York Joint Board even though they represented more than 85 percent of the total International membership. The General Executive Board had chartered a number of locals in New York and elsewhere in order to pack the convention. When the convention opened, thirty-five delegates, headed by Ben Gold, elected by the fur workers to represent the New York Joint Board, were present. Although they knew they would be barred from the convention, these delegates were determined to put up a fight for recognition.[44]

But the Credentials Committee, composed entirely of right-wingers, presented a report recommending seating the delegates from the New York Joint Council. Together with the out-of-town paper delegates, they made up the convention majority. The legitimate New York delegates were not seated, nor were any anti-administration delegates from Newark, Montreal, Boston, Chicago, Winnipeg and Toronto. After a fruitless attack on the report of the Credentials Committee, the Joint Board delegates were barred from the convention.[45]

Meanwhile, a split was developing among the AFL leaders with respect to the situation in the New York fur workers' union. William Green and Edward McGrady were fed up with the constant conflict, had lost respect for the right-wing Socialist leaders of the International, and felt that purges among fur workers was a waste of effort. Matthew Woll, however, refused to go along, insisting that the AFL must continue its support for the right-wingers.[46]

Although it was Woll and not Green and McGrady who prevailed in the end, the AFL president did persuade the right-wing International leaders to permit the Joint Board delegates to present their case against expulsion to the convention before the delegates voted on the issue. In an impassioned speech, Gold branded as false the "charges" against the Joint Board. While accusing the right-wing leaders of having "annihilated the working conditions for which the furriers have fought so long and so hard," he emphasized that neither the issue of officers nor of communism should concern the convention. The problem was to achieve unity and a more effective union to serve the interests of the workers. He was prepared to resign as manager of the Joint Board if that would advance the cause of "peace and unity." "The real issue," Gold concluded, "is whether we shall be sold out to the bosses or whether our union shall fight to win better conditions for the workers. The real issue is majority rule versus gangster and boss control. It is democracy in the union; effective strikes and mass picketing versus surrender to the bosses .... Finally, the real issue is the creation of a strong, honest, democratic union in the industry."[47]

But the appeal fell on deaf ears. Matthew Woll urged the convention not to be taken in by "Communist oratory" and appealed for action completing the "reorganization" of the union. The next morning, the convention voted to approve the expulsions and lifted the charters of the Joint Board locals.[48]

FAILURE OF THE CONSPIRACY

Although the movement for peace and unity had failed in Washington, it did not end. On May 14, 1928, Local 30 of Boston adopted a resolution calling the GEB's attention to the spread of open shops in the fur manufacturing and fur dressing industries which was "breaking down the power of our local unions, cutting our wages to the bone and generally bringing in worse conditions in the union shops." The resolution went on to point out that because of the internal struggle in the union, the International was "spending all the money and energy on the war against the left wing instead of using them for organization purposes and for strengthening the locals." In view of these tragic developments, Local 30 appealed to the GEB to immediately call together a conference of local representatives for the purpose of putting an end to the internal struggle in the union. The resolution was forwarded to every local.

Within two weeks, three locals—Local 53 of Philadelphia, Local 40 of Toronto, and Local 58 of Brooklyn—had endorsed Local 30's demand. In addition, several locals were seriously debating the resolution. The answer from the right-wing GEB came swiftly. Local 30 was accused of "acting for the Communists who have instigated the officers of your local to this in order to get some publicity." It concluded: "The International Fur Workers Union as well as the American Federation of Labor have once for all taken the stand that there can be no unity, peace or compromise with the Communists."[49]

But the AFL leaders were growing weary of the battle, especially as an open split among the right-wing leaders flared in the New York Joint Council over which group should get the best positions. This convinced even the AFL leaders that their entire campaign against the fur workers had disintegrated to the point where it was no longer retrievable. On top of this, the Committee for Preservation of Trade

Unions informed the AFL leaders that their treasury was bankrupt and they could no longer carry the burden of financing the Joint Council. The AFL had already indicated that it could not keep pouring money into the Joint Council.

On July 6, 1928, Edward McGrady notified Shiplacoff that the AFL had decided to throw in the sponge and withdraw from the fur situation in New York:

> The committee representing the American Federation of Labor feels very much discouraged over this situation and as a result of the action of your Committee I have conferred with President Green on this situation, and we feel that inasmuch as the Preservation of Trade Unions Committee is not in a position to render any further assistance, the American Federation of Labor will surrender its control of the situation as soon as we can close the various matters up.
>
> If there is anything further that you think might be done in the immediate future I will be very glad to hear from you. Otherwise the American Federation of Labor will get out of the situation within the next few weeks.[50]

Five days after he had received McGrady's letter, Shiplacoff sent a hurried call for help to the right-wing leaders of the needle trades unions, inviting them to an emergency meeting in the Council Room of the ILGWU. Calling their attention to McGrady's letter, Shiplacoff reminded the right-wing leaders "that we cannot very well afford to have the Communists re-entrench themselves in the Furriers Union." "Just what can be done I don't know," he fairly wept, "but I do know that it would weigh heavily on your conscience and on mine if we did not make a serious attempt to prevent the recapture of the Furriers Union by the Communists."

In a telegram to the *Jewish Daily Forward*, William Green announced that not only would the AFL not "withdraw from the furriers' situation," but it would continue "to give its service" in the "fight against Communism and Communist influence" in the International Fur Workers Union. The Executive Council again assigned Woll, Frayne and McGrady "to the fur workers for an indefinite period." At the same time, Shiplacoff disclosed that the organizations represented at the emergency conference had promised to provide the additional financial resources to enable the AFL "to control the situation" in the Furriers Union.[51]

But statements could not breathe new life into the "corpse," as the workers called the Joint Council. All the money poured into the "corpse" would only pay the salaries of the right-wing clique and their strong-arm squads, and preserve it as a useful instrument of the employers to destroy the furriers' working conditions. On the other hand, the Joint Board was very much alive. It had just completed a highly successful drive for July raises. It had called and won several shop strikes despite the fact that the employers had new "agreements" with the Joint Council, and did not recognize the Joint Board. These successful strikes enabled thousands of workers in other shops to obtain July raises from their bosses.[52]

As the Joint Board re-established control, over the New York market and established ties with the out-of-town locals, and as the Joint Council faded away, it found that despite itself, it was operating as a dual union. In the summer of 1928, the fur workers proceeded with a conference with eight out-of-town locals and the "Progressive Block" which had split from the Joint Council. This conference issued a call for the formation of a new International Union for the fur industry of the United States and Canada.[53]* Unlike the left wing of the ILGWU, the left wing of the Fur Workers Union was able to take most of the members with them into the new union.[54]

---

* In 1927 the Trade Union Educational League's National Central Committee already envisaged such development, observing in an "Outline of Policy for Furriers Convention": "We must recognize that we are working in a split situation... and that strengthening of our forces and of the union necessitates another step in the direction of forming a Union independent of the Furriers International or of the forces claiming to be the International Union." (Daniel Bell Papers, Tamiment Institute Library, New York University.) As in the case of the Ladies' Garment Workers' Union, this decision to move towards an independent union was under consideration before the Communist International endorsed dual unionism in the spring of 1928.

CHAPTER 8

THE MEN'S CLOTHING AND MILLINERY WORKERS

During the 1920s all the needle trades unions underwent a prolonged period of internal struggle between right and left. In most instances, the union leadership was closely identified with the Socialist Party, and its hegemony was challenged by the new-born Communist Party and its ally, the Trade Union Educational League. However, in the case of the Amalgamated Clothing Workers of America, the situation was for several years quite different. As we have seen in our last volume, from 1920 through mid-1924, the Hillman leadership in the Amalgamated was allied with members of the Trade Union Educational League, most of whose members, if not all, were Communists, while the Socialists in the union fought against the union leadership for a variety of reasons, of which the most important was the enthusiastic support of the Bolshevik Revolution and the young Soviet Union by the Hillman leadership.*

The Trade Union Educational League did organize branches in the Amalgamated in the years 1920-1924, but they were in general support of the administration. But not uncritical support. Thus on March 7, 1924, the minutes of the National Committee, TUEL report:

> Amalgamated Clothing Workers
>
> Foster made the following recommendations regarding the ACWA: criticize freely the policies of the Hillman administration but in careful manner in order to prevent an open break. If a break comes, it should be left

---

* *See* Philip S. Foner, *History of the Labor Movement in the United States*, 9 (New York, 1990): 302-07.

clearly on the shoulders of the Hillman administration. An effort must be put forth to elect left-wing delegates to this [Amalgamated] convention, but not on the basis of an open struggle with the Hillman group, if this can be avoided.[1*]

It was not long, however, before the "open break" which Foster sought to avoid came to pass. Despite the Amalgamated's continued support of the Soviet Union, Foster's advice became more difficult to carry out. Hillman and his supporters believed that the only way the union could secure itself in the chaotic clothing industry was to promote order and organization in the trade, encourage the development of the larger manufacturers, and cooperate with these employers in applying the principles of scientific management.

As part of this strategy the Amalgamated in the 1924 strike refused to deal with individual employers and forced them to form an employers' association. They argued that such agreements were easier to enforce. The left wing vehemently disagreed. Its position was that the weaker the employers were, relative to the union, the more the workers could win from them in wages, hours, and working conditions. For the union to foster an employers' association was to engage in one of the worst forms of class collaboration.[2]

While this conflict over trade union policy played a part in the break between the Hillman leadership and the TUEL, it was a political question that proved to be the occasion for the parting of ways. When the Amalgamated leadership chose to support the LaFollette campaign in 1924, and not the efforts of the Communists, supported by the TUEL, to establish an "independent" labor party, the die was cast.[**] After this, the TUEL emerged as the center of the left opposition while the Socialists abruptly made peace with the union leadership, sensing a chance for a major assault on the Communists. In conducting a purge against the left, the Hillman group called on their former opponents in the Socialist Party for assistance.

---

* The report also included: "The National Committee should censor comrades in the Amalgamated Clothing Workers who are responsible for alienating the masses in the organization through their opposition to the 5% assessment for unemployment relief. The National Committee of the Needle Trades Section should draft a statement stating its position with reference to the 5% unemployment assessment as a local program for unemployment relief." (Daniel Bell Papers, Tamiment Institute Library, New York University.) The left-wing members of the Amalgamated had opposed the assessment for unemployment relief on the ground that this should have been imposed on the employers, rather than on the workers.

** See Philip S. Foner, *History of the Labor Movement in the United States* 9 (New York, 1990): 306, 346-47.

During the next few months, the breach widened as the left wing charged that Hillman's radical phrases were merely a blind used to keep a militant rank and file in line while he pursued a reactionary course of class collaboration.[3] While Socialists and liberals praised Hillman for his willingness to lend hard-pressed employers money from the union treasury, TUEL members in the Amalgamated condemned the action as opening the door to widespread wage-cutting. When B. Charney Vladeck of the *Jewish Daily Forward* called the Amalgamated's Bank "more valuable than all the writings of Marx and Lenin," the TUEL pointed out that the bank had fired its employees who were union activists. All needle trades workers were urged to attend a protest meeting called by the Office Workers' League "to voice objection to this discrimination against union members by a labor bank."[4]

In 1924, Hart, Schaffner and Marx of Chicago appealed to the Amalgamated to help it reduce the costs of operation in its factories. In response, the union took over numerous functions of the management and planned a reorganization of production to achieve a reduction in costs. Other large establishments in Chicago were similarly reorganized. The policy resulted in fewer workers in the shops, while those who remained had to do more work than ever before at lower piece rates. The TUEL criticized the union leadership for participating in an industry-sponsored speedup. Leaflets quoted an admiring journalist who wrote: "The Amalgamated statisticians, research men, and industrial engineers have supplanted the strike committeemen and picket line leaders to a great extent."[5] In 1983, after a very detailed study of how the Amalgamated's cooperation with employers in the production process operated, Steven Fraser concluded that "scientific management was either anti-union or prepared to work with trade union leadership willing to sacrifice the fundamental interests of their workers."[6] As the TUEL intensified its criticism of the Hillman leadership, a sharp battle emerged between that leadership and Local 5 of New York where the left-wing had its leaders as local officers. In August, 1924, the local held an open meeting to discuss a plan for the amalgamation of all the New York locals. The members of many of the other locals were there when Sam Lipzin, a member of the local executive board and leading member of the TUEL, attacked the GEB's request for a dues increase and accused the administration of employing many more people on its staff than were necessary.[7]

By the end of November, the administration decided to move against the TUEL. At the GEB meeting on November 29, 1924, Hillman gave a two-hour speech attacking factionalism. The GEB set a closed meeting for December 6 to deal with the issue. In the meantime the December 5, 1924 issue of *Advance* ran a large banner headline—"Hillman Attacks Factionalism in Union"—and some quotes from Hillman's lengthy speech, such as:

> We refuse to be a party to any single group or combinations of groups. We will no longer deal with a "good" league or a "fine" council...Our experience has been that neither faction has the interests of the Amalgamated at heart. We recognize the impossibility of carrying on any constructive organizational work if factionalism continues....[8]

Acting in response to the GEB, the New York Joint Board voted to reorganize as of December 20. When the reorganized board met, leading members of the TUEL were present, and the administration made a statement that this was acceptable as long as they ceased acting as representatives of outside forces. There was also some talk of revoking the charters of some unnamed locals (presumably Local 5), but this was opposed by Hillman as an action to be resorted to only when there seemed to be no other choice.[9]

The leadership of Local 5 was not cowed by these developments and pressed its attack on the administration. Then, when two members were discharged for allegedly either opposing production standards or fighting at work,[10] Local 5's Executive Board called the workers out on strike. The manager of the Joint Board stepped in and ordered them back while he negotiated with the employer. However, the local Executive Board refused to send the workers back, and the Joint Board manager sent in other workers. At this, the local Executive Board members marched at the head of the picket line, and Local 2 called its members out in a sympathy walkout. The GEB ruled that since under the constitution only the Joint Board could call a strike, the manager was right in sending in other workers, and it ordered the local to send its workers back to the shop. The local ignored the GEB order until the manager of the Joint Board had negotiated the return of the two dismissed workers.[11]

With this victory, the left wingers pressed on with their attack. On January 8, 1925, they called a mass meeting at which they denounced the officers of the Joint Board and the GEB and called on the workers to support them in their fight with the Joint Board. After this meeting and the circulation of leaflets publicizing the action, the Joint Board suspended Local 5's representatives. The GEB then stepped in to investigate. When the leaders of Local 5 openly assumed responsibility for the meeting and the leaflets and said they would continue, the GEB placed the local in receivership, suspended its Executive Board, barred left-wing leader Sam Lipzin and two others from all union activities, and began systematically to expel TUEL members.[12]

In August, 1925, Professor Earl R. Beckner of the University of Chicago observed in a study of the Trade Union Educational League: "The League has members in the Amalgamated Clothing Workers, but a severe struggle has not developed in that union .... The League considers the ACWA to be the 'leading labor union of America,' and does not condemn its officials as it does the officials of other unions generally."[13]

However, this was no longer an accurate picture of the relationship. In March, 1925, negotiations began between the Chicago manufacturers and the officials of the Amalgamated for a new agreement. In a leaflet distributed by the National Committee of the Needle Trades Section of the Trade Union Educational League, the policies of the Amalgamated leadership came under sharp attack. The leaflet accused the Amalgamated officials of abandoning "a militant policy of fighting the bosses," and of "adopting the method of aiding the employers at the expense of the workers." It noted that in its early days, the Amalgamated did not tolerate collaboration with the bosses. However, in recent years, there had "grown swiftly an unwillingness on the part of our officials, nationally and locally, to struggle. They look for a peaceful path, instead of class struggle and workers' solidarity." In short, "the union officialdom is cooperating with the bosses to enforce wage cuts and to speed up production." As a result, conditions in the shop "are becoming intolerable," and it was now "impossible to earn a decent living." The leaflet went on:

> Brothers and sisters!
> Let us not allow the Amalgamated Clothing Workers to disintegrate into a second United Garment Workers. You can prevent that!...
> Don't wait until it is too late. Let your voice be heard at the next meeting of your local union against the policy of collusion with the bosses.

The League's proposals for the new agreement urged open wage negotiations instead of "the present method of secret diplomacy with the bosses," "the forty-hour week, with pay for forty-four," to help solve the crisis created by the "development of machinery, which while bringing bigger profits to the bosses, is throwing hundreds and thousands into the unemployed ranks;" week work, "with a maximum standard of production and minimum scale of wages," instead of piece work; a genuine system of unemployment payments and shop committee control of the union with the employers recognizing "the shop committees as the union representatives, empowered to conduct all negotiations for the workers." But to gain these "needed demands," the expulsion policy must end!

> The expulsion of the militants, the supporters of the Trade Union Educational League, by the administration serves the interest of the manufacturers and evidences an unhealthy cooperation of the union officials with the bosses. The membership must prevent the attempts of the officials of our union to get rid of the vital elements, the militants and left wingers in the Amalgamated.
> Fight against the expulsions of the militants.
> Fight for the reinstatement of the expelled.[14]

It was the Trade Union Educational League which made the 40-hour week an important issue in the Amalgamated. To be sure, Hillman declared that the whole nation was ready for the 40-hour week, but in his own industry, the 44-hour standard remained intact after the negotiations, with only a promise "to consider the feasibility of introducing the forty-hour week" being granted by the employers. As in other needle trades' unions, it was the left-wing, mostly the communists, who made the 40-hour week an issue in the Amalgamated.[15]

The League also made sex discrimination in the union a central issue. Noting the small number of women in the leadership of a union where membership was 60 to 70 percent female, TUEL leaflets called for an instant change in this situation.

It was not a new problem. In Chicago's Local 39, a group of women led by Sarah Rozner had run as delegates to the 1920 Amalgamated convention on this very issue, but they were all defeated. The women were infuriated, especially since Chicago was the center of Hillman's strength, and he had not lifted a finger to help them. As Sarah Rozner recalled: "Up to that time I was mainly class conscious, but when I saw that they [the union leaders] were so ruthless, so indifferent to the biggest part of the organization, the women, I thought, how can we stand by and ignore it?" As a result, Local 275, the women's local in Chicago, was formed.

Through their own local, the women were able to occupy a place of leadership, for within the structure of the ACWA, every local had a representative on the Joint Board and every local nominated a business agent. Not only did the Amalgamated leadership grant local 275 its charter, but by the middle of the decade, there were women's locals in several cities. In October 1924, moreover, a Women's Bureau was launched within the ACWA, with Dorothy Jacobs Bellanca in charge.[16]

Unfortunately, the Women's Bureau was short-lived, and the Amalgamated leadership reversed its attitude with respect to meeting the special needs of women members. The TUEL seized upon this change, and issued leaflets which noted that:

> The constitution of the union stands for full equality in the rights, privileges, and duties of its membership, regardless of sex, creed, or nationality. The women members pay the same dues and assessments as the men. A special Women's Bureau was established a few years ago to encourage and stimulate activity on the part of women members.

But all that appeared to be simply for the sake of appearance:

> The membership of the union is approximately 50 percent female with an ever-increasing proportion of women in some of the large markets. Yet there is but one woman member on the General Executive Board. The number of business agents, local secretaries, or union officers of any sort is negligible. The special Women's Bureau lasted about a year. The rate of wages of women workers in the union shops is less than that of men.

And yet in strike after strike, the number of women pickets arrested and beaten up exceeded that of men. In the St. Louis strike of the workers of the Curles Manufacturing Company during the summer of 1925, "the great activity of the women workers" had aroused widespread comment in the local press, but it had had no effect in altering the second-place status of women members in the Amalgamated Clothing Workers of America.[17]

The attack on discrimination in the union brought support for the left wing from women members; One woman member wrote to *Advance* praising the TUEL for at least recognizing this problem, unlike the union leadership. "Discrimination against women in the union is no joke or invention," she continued. "It is a real live issue, insofar as the women are concerned .... It is going on constantly .... We feel that, if we take our places on the picket line, we are entitled to 'our' place in the shops."[18]

Women made up more than half of the left-wing group that organized the Amalgamated Joint Action Committee of New York, modeled on that of the ILGWU. Esther Baroff and Celia Levine, two militant TUEL members, were elected to the Committee's governing board.[19]

Prodded by the Joint Action Committee, the Amalgamated took on the International Tailoring Company, an open-shop company with plants in New York and Chicago, which represented a threat to the biggest markets in the country. The strike began in June and ran until November, 1925. Although it had previously scoffed at criticism by the left wing, the Amalgamated leadership now set out to demonstrate that it was no less militant than the left wing. It conducted an extremely militant strike, with mass picketing, violation of injunctions, and other vigorous strike tactics. The left, for its part, fully supported the strike, and members of the Joint Action Committee were among the many pickets who were arrested and beaten during the long strike.[20]

The Amalgamated leadership, however, viewed the left wing's support of the strike as merely a tactic. Indeed, it now saw an opportunity to eliminate the left completely. By July, 1925, the strength of the Amalgamated had declined from the 1920 level of 177,000 members to 103,000,[21] and the standing of the leadership had gone down commensurately. But the prestige acquired in the victory over the International Tailoring Company made it possible for the leadership to take on the left wing. The December GEB meeting appointed a committee of three, headed by Hyman Blumberg, to take over and reorganize the New York organization. The committee merged the men's and boys' clothing joint boards and brought in the notorious Abraham Beckerman to manage the consolidated Joint Board. The GEB also declared the Amalgamated Joint Action Committee to be a dual union, called for the expulsion of all associated with it and assigned Beckerman to declare war on the left-wing organization using gangsters and union strong-arm men for this purpose.[22]

On December 15, 1925, the *Daily Worker* carried a poem entitled, "The Ghost of Rickert.* Dedicated to Sidney Hillman by a Tailor Shop Worker," it read:

> The ghost of Rickert now draws near,
> With blackjack hand
> And ready gun.
> These highest symbols of his rule—
> Are here.
>
> Though newly clad,
> Though different name,
> We know him yet
> To be the same.

---

* Thomas Rickert was the corrupt and brutal leader of the United Garment Workers of America from which the clothing workers who formed the Amalgamated Clothing Workers of America had seceded.

And as his tyranny of yore
We fought until we won;
So now, O brothers! Let us fight
All those who rob at us of our right,
With blackjack and gun.

At this point an angry B. Marcus, a member of Amalgamated's Local 39, criticized the TUEL in a letter to the editor of the *Daily Worker*. He charged that the League's methods in combatting the Hillman leadership, which he charged was "more brutal and more corrupt" than even the bureaucracy of the United Garment Workers Union from which the Amalgamated had split, were totally inadequate. He urged the TUEL to combat the use of "a gang of thugs led by the scum of our union" who regularly raided meetings "with guns and blackjacks and slugged the men and women present," especially those who were identified as members of the TUEL. To meet this "dreadful situation," he recommended that the TUEL "start a movement" to have the membership refuse to pay dues as long as the brutal practice continued. In addition, he called upon the League's leaders to demand police protection against the hired thugs and gangsters of the Hillman administration:

> These thugs are known to the police because of the many crimes charged against them. When they attack us they know that no matter what they do, you of the TUEL will protect them against the police and in this way give them a free hand to terrorize the membership. [23]

Replying for the TUEL, Earl R. Browder informed Marcus that he had "made a mistake in tactics which has been committed often— much too often in America."

> That mistake is the idea that the progressive and left wing members can defeat the reactionaries by refusing to pay dues. But the reactionary officials cannot be defeated that way. The blow falls against the union as a whole, divides the membership into two camps fighting one another, and thus gives a new lease of life to the old officials, who come before the members in the role of angels of peace pleading for unity.
>
> The left wing will rally the membership for the support of class struggle policies as against the class-collaboration of Hillman & Co., and any attempt to rally the membership only on the destructive platform of non-payment of dues would wreck the left wing and the union. So the proposal of Brother Marcus cannot be accepted.

As for "the struggle against thuggery, which is now a burning question in the ACW," Browder made it clear that the left wing was not "pacifist," and did not "subscribe to the doctrine of Jesus to 'turn the other cheek.'"

Resistance must be organized to meet and defeat gangsterism. But this must be done by the members themselves. The police will not do it for us. And while we have no interest in protecting the gangsters from the police, neither have we the slightest idea that we can expect any police protection, nor does the left wing solicit it. The left wing depends upon the organized power of the membership.[24]

WAR AGAINST THE LEFT WING

Beckerman certainly had "a free hand to attack the membership," and he hit at the Joint Action Committee with a special flair. Strong-arm men were hired to beat up left-wingers and break up their meetings. Nor did it matter if the victims were women. One woman worker wrote:

> The news of my being beaten up on Sunday of last week by officials of the Amalgamated Clothing Workers and sluggers, and of the previous Friday's sluggings at the membership meeting, reached the shop where I worked before I did .... As I walked into the shop all eyes were turned towards me, and as I went past the other workers I was showered with questions from all sides.
> "How many sluggers were there?"
> "Do you know who hit you?"
> "Did they beat up other girls, too?"
> "How many 'gats' did they have?"
> While we continued work, pictures of the bandaged workers were passed around and newspapers containing the story. At the noon hour, the workers gathered around me while I answered their questions.
> One brother remarked: "Is this the result of our many years of struggle and sacrifice to build up the Amalgamated, to have our own brothers and sisters beaten up?"
> I was told how some of the brothers and sisters had been beaten up the previous Friday evening at a general meeting because they had dared to discuss the proposed $25.00 assessment....
> "But what can we do?" asked a girl member. "They have the sluggers and they have the money. And if you say anything, you lose your job."[25]

The combination of the strong-arm men and economic threats, such as loss of jobs, destroyed the Amalgamated Joint Action Committee in New York. B. Charney Vladeck gave thanks for this victory in an article in the *Forward* exclaiming, "Blessed be Beckerman's knuckles."[26]

In most of the other markets, less drastic measures were used to keep the left wing under the administration's control. In Rochester the left gathered strength in 1926, and the GEB sent Blumberg to investigate the situation. He reported back that the left's influence was based on very real grievances, and that their leader, Abe Chatman, was a very able young man. The GEB then took steps to alleviate the causes of unrest in Rochester and to isolate the left wing. Chatman was invited to have a talk with Hillman, and not long thereafter he was made manager of the Rochester Joint Board as a loyal Hillman supporter.[27]

Despite the expulsions and reorganizations of the mid-1920s, the progressive element in the Amalgamated Clothing Workers was not completely eliminated. From a Chicago woman member came the following letter to the *Advance* in 1927:

> Is it true that our membership consists of more than 50 per cent women? Is it true that the women in our organization helped to build the Amalgamated Clothing Workers of America and do they pay dues and assessments or are they exempt from the same? Does the constitution of our organization uphold discrimination against women workers in the industry or within the organization?... Is it a fact that the women have become permanent workers in the industry? What means do our leaders employ to combat the idea that women are not temporarily in industry? What methods do our officials use to promote greater activities amongst women workers since they have become a permanent factor in industry? What has become of the Women's Bureau for which the women have so long struggled?[28]

The editor of the *Advance* answered: "Leadership in a union is a prize to those who know how to win it .... There is no room for gallantry toward sex in the struggle for leadership."[29]

Nor did the editor of the *Advance* feel that there was any need to answer those women members who indignantly inquired why the Women's Bureau, established in 1924, was so quickly abolished.[30] On behalf of Local 275, the women's local in Chicago, Sarah Rozner introduced a resolution at the union's 1928 convention calling for the reestablishment of a Women's Bureau in the ACWA.* The Committee on Resolutions recommended non-concurrence, and two prominent Amalgamated women, Bessie Abramowitz Hillman and Mamie Santora, both spoke against the resolution, charging that it

---

* Sarah Rozner, who came to the United States from Hungary in 1908, was the first business agent of Local 275. A business agent was a full-time union officer, elected or appointed, who handled the union's financial, administrative, and other activities, especially enforcing the union agreement.

For the text of a leaflet drawn up by Sarah Rozner sharply criticizing male officials of the Amalgamated for discouraging "highly intelligent women ... from being active in the organization," see Rosalyn Baxandall, Linda Gordon, and Susan Reverby, eds., *America's Working Women: A Documentary History 1600 to the Present,* New York, 1976, pp. 260-63.

was a "Communist plot" to discredit the union. So, too, did President Hillman. The resolution was defeated.[31]

On December 9, 1926, the headline in the *Daily News Record*, journal of the garment trades, read: "Left Wing Is Beaten Says Sidney Hillman. Assures Manufacturers of Rochester Future Peace." Proposals by the left wing that an amnesty be granted to those who had been suspended or expelled for political reasons were rejected, and Hillman had let it be known that if those who sympathized with the TUEL wanted to stay in the Amalgamated, they had "to keep their mouths shut."[32]

In reviewing the defeat of the left wing in the Amalgamated, the *Jewish Morning Freiheit*, the Yiddish-language organ of the Workers' Party, pointed out that Hillman was much shrewder in dealing with his opposition than were the leaders of the ILGWU. Under his leadership, the Amalgamated often took positions on general issues which the left wing could and did support. Hillman was not part of the *Jewish Daily Forward* group which was in the forefront of the attacks on the left wing in the ILGWU. Nor was this independent union subject to AFL pressure to eliminate left wing entirely from the labor movement. Hence although there were occasional expulsions and suspensions of officers, Hillman rejected the tactic of expulsions. In its place he and his allies used violence. The *Freiheit* therefore attributed the defeat of the left wing to the fact that "right-wing officials of the ACWA freely resorted to the use of professional thugs and gangsters. Through alliances with gang leaders, these officials succeeded in establishing themselves as dictators in their local, terrorizing the membership and eliminating the opposition by violence or intimidation."[33]

However, William Z. Foster refused to accept the idea that the TUEL had been decisively defeated in the Amalgamated. On the contrary, he reported to the Central Executive Committee of the TUEL in 1926 that "in the Amalgamated the situation was now ripe for action." He called for "mapping out the program of struggle against the Hillman machine."[34] But there were no members of the TUEL left in the union to carry on such a "struggle." As William F. Dunne observed in that same year, "in the powerful Amalgamated Clothing Workers Union, the left wing is almost non-existent."[35]

Two years later, the Amalgamated's General Executive Board declared to the assembled delegates at the 1928 convention that "Factionalism in the Amalgamated has burned itself out." The Trade Union Educational League in the union was a thing of the past.[36]

In his study of Sidney Hillman and unionism in the Amalgamated, Steven Fraser notes that with this announcement, policies in any way resembling "the class struggle were being interred as well."[37] Although still kept out of the AFL, the Amalgamated Clothing Workers of America now functioned precisely as did the vast majority of the Federation's affiliates.

BATTLE OF THE MILLINERY WORKERS

In 1924 the United Cloth, Hat and Cap Makers' International Union was received back into the AFL after a six-year suspension and was given permission by the federation to include the millinery workers in its membership.[38] Although its influence in the International General Executive Board was not strong, the left wing in the United Cloth Hat, Cap and Millinery Workers International Union was important in many locals, and it had a substantial following. After the merger, the left wing raised the demand for the organization of the unorganized women millinery workers. A leaflet signed by "TUEL members of the United Cloth Hat, Cap and Millinery Workers International Union" pointed out the need for the campaign:

> There are 1,400 people in Chicago engaged in the millinery industry. Of that number the overwhelming majority is composed of women. The women are unorganized while the men have a union.
> The man milliner's working conditions are protected by his union agreement. His wages are $40 a week and thereabouts and he is paid time-and-a-half for overtime. This is very important, as during the rush season he often works twelve hours a day and seven days a week and there is a large semi-idle season. The work is mostly piece work.
> For not being organized, the women milliner pays in the following way. Her wages are $25 a week and thereabouts. There is no limit to her working hours a week and no extra pay for overtime. During the rush season the woman milliner toils from eight in the morning till eight at night. Sunday is included in the week's work with only one dollar extra.
> The boss hires and fires women milliners whenever and whomever he pleases. He fixes the prices for the workers to bring him the largest profits without interference from the girls. He is not responsible to anyone. He knows that the only thing a dissatisfied girl can do is to leave the factory. She has no union to protect her. Now that our union has merged with the hatters, it is time to begin to provide the woman milliner with a union to protect her.[39]

The International did nothing in response to this appeal, but locals with large left-wing memberships did launch organizing drives to unionize women millinery workers. Results In Chicago, Boston and a few other cities were significant, but the outstanding success was in New York, where Millinery Hand Workers' Union Local 43, composed entirely of women millinery workers, was organized. The members elected a left-wing leadership, with Gladys Schechter, an eighteen-year-old worker, as president.

Schechter, a member of the TUEL, earned the reputation of "the 'Joan of Arc' of the Millinery Workers' Union."[40]

Established with four hundred members in November 1924, by November, 1926, Local 43 had grown tenfold. It was made up mostly of young women under twenty-five years of age. It had become the second largest local in the international and, it claimed, "the largest local of women workers in the United States."[*] With four young women as business agents and organizers, the union had established control in many shops, where working hours had been reduced from fifty to forty-four, wages increased, and general working conditions improved. The local prided itself on the fact that it had "established an educational institution consisting of lectures, courses, and shop educational conferences dealing with the specific problems of women workers in the industry and the problems of the working class generally."[41]

But all this had been accomplished under left-wing leadership by members of the Trade Union Educational League. The right-wing international leadership was anything but pleased by this development, and it did not relish the organization of women millinery workers outside of New York under left-wing leadership. International President Max Zaritsky and Samuel Hershkowitz, the right-wing manager of the New York capmakers' local, determined to follow the pattern set by the right wing in the other needle trades unions by eliminating the left wing. Controlling the General Executive Board through paper locals outside New York created precisely for the purpose of giving such control to the right wing, they began their campaign at the 1927 international convention.[42]

The GEB report to that convention denounced the TUEL members in the organization and declared that although "we have practiced tolerance toward them and even employed them as organiz-

---

[*] On February 16, 1929, *Labor* referred to Local 105 of the National Federation of Federal Employees, with over fifteen hundred members in the Bureau of Engraving and Printing in Washington, D.C., as "the largest single organization of women workers in the United States and the largest local affiliated with the National Federation of Federal Employees." It had been first organized in 1909 and chartered by the AFL as Federal Labor Union No. 12,775. It affiliated with the National Federation of Federal Employees in 1918.

ers... we would recommend that the convention should express its condemnation in the strongest possible terms of those elements in our ranks who interfere with and obstruct the constructive work that the general organization is engaged in." The left-wing delegates fought back, led by the delegation representing the Millinery Hand Workers' Union, Local 43. Gladys Schechter declared:

> We contend that the developments in our union during the past two years since our last convention are in complete contradiction to the analysis and conclusion drawn by the General Executive Board's official report with reference to the activities of the left wing in our union. Not only have these elements not been a hindrance to the work in our organization, but on the contrary, they are the very ones who are responsible for and are to be credited with the gains made by our union during the past two years. The best example of this is Local 43, which, under a progressive administration, has carried through a successful organization campaign, increasing the membership from 400 to 4,000. Similar results have occurred in Boston, Chicago and Los Angeles. In all these locals, it was the left wing that constituted the backbone of the organization campaigns and made possible the achievements in which we all take pride.
>
> We believe the recommendations of the General Executive Board to express condemnation of the left wing in our organization is in complete contradiction to the policy of tolerance and not conducive towards the preservation of unity in our ranks.

Delegate Schechter then concluded:

> I am a member of the Trade Union Educational League. You claim the TUEL brings in dissension. As long as there are differences of opinion, there will be dissension. I would not belong to that organization one-half hour if I were under the impression that it is there to disrupt our union.[43]

Having led the defense of the left wing, Local 43 became the first target of the right-wing attack. Following the convention, the GEB established Millinery Local 24 in New York under Socialist leadership, then ordered Local 43 to dissolve and its members to join the newly created Local 24. The justification? That Local 43 was created and was functioning as a "dual union." When Local 43 rejected the charge as unfounded and refused to dissolve, it was subjected to a veritable reign of terror, climaxed by gangster attacks on Local 43 women strikers outside the shops they were picketing. In one instance Frieda Fraiclass, a Local 43 organizer, was attacked and severely beaten in her own office. In a plea for public support, Local 43 stated:

> Hundreds of women milliners, loyal to the union which they had built, were thrown off their jobs by the bosses at the demand of the International officials. Many of our members were brutally assaulted by the gang-

sters hired by the right-wing officials. Many members were clubbed by the police and imprisoned upon the instigation of the right wing.

Moreover, when our local carries on strikes for the enforcement and protection of the workers' economic conditions, the right-wing officials provide scabs for these firms and grant concessions at the expense of the workers.[44]

The attack on Local 43 was only the beginning. The charters of the locals of women milliners under left-wing leadership in Boston, Chicago and other cities were revoked. Demoralization swept through the ranks of the union's membership. Nevertheless, the right-wing offensive continued and by 1928, the situation was summed up as follows:

Zaritsky is determined to smash all the militant locals which stand for the maintenance of union conditions. He is trying to eliminate from the union all progressive and militant workers who distinguish themselves in organizing thousands of unorganized workers. Instead of combatting the open-shop danger, instead of utilizing the unified strength of the union for organizing the thousands of unorganized workers, instead of protecting the interests of the workers, Zaritsky is pursuing a policy of splitting and smashing locals, thus helping the employers to defeat the workers and destroy the union.[45]

The process was completed at the 1929 international convention. Left-wing leaders, including those of Local 43, were expelled, and the constitution was amended to ban membership in a dual organization and to authorize the suspension of any local that refused to obey the decisions of the GEB.[46]

In opposing this action, delegate Irving Smoliak of St. Paul [Minn.] declared: "Despite the policy of terrorism and intimidation practiced by the official leadership, we will continue to fight within the International for improving the conditions of the workers. But if we are expelled, we will not remain unorganized, but will join the industrial union that represents the interests of all the needle workers."[47] The "industrial union" was the Needle Trades Workers' Industrial Union, whose formation as an independent left-wing union we will examine below.

SITUATION IN THE NEEDLE TRADES

In describing the left wing in the United Cloth Hat, Cap and Millinery Workers International Union, William Z. Foster noted that while it had "developed a strong movement which was influential in the life of the union," it was "not able to win control of the organization," and wrest power "from the class collaboration leadership."[48]

With one exception, this was the situation in all of the needle trades' unions. By the middle of the decade, the left wing, headed by the Communists and united in the Trade Union Educational League, was leading opposition movements in each of the major needle trades' unions. In the ILGWU, the Communists and other insurgents, organized in the TUEL, built a small opposition into a mass movement. During the mid-1920s, they commanded a majority of the national membership's loyalty. By the end of 1925, they had gained control of the joint boards in the most important centers of the industry, winning the support of more than two-thirds of the entire membership. However, the right-wing Socialist bloc in the union continued to rule the International, under the leadership of Morris Sigman and David Dubinsky, a control which rested on a "rotten borough system." Nevertheless, throughout the 1924-26 period, the Sigman-Dubinsky administration lost key local union offices in Boston, Chicago and Philadelphia. In New York City, Locals 2, 9, 22 and 35, representing nearly half the ILGWU's national membership, were solidly left-wing.

The end of the long and bitter strike of 40,000 cloakmakers in 1926, with little to show for the months of struggle, gave the right wing its long-awaited opportunity. Sigman removed the officers of the New York Joint Board conducting the strike, settled the strike over the heads of the locals and the Joint Board, liquidated the existing locals—and then invited the members individually to re-register with the International or else lose their jobs in union shops. Great numbers of Communists were expelled from the union, after which the same right wingers denounced those expelled as "dual unionists" for organizing to protect their very livelihoods.

The internecine conflict of the next two years left the ILGWU in ruins. As Melech Epstein, an anti-communist labor writer, later summed it up, "the right had won the battle, but the union lay wrecked."[49]

The left wing, led by Communists, made many errors of judgment and policy, but this should not divert attention from the fact that the right-wing Socialist and AFL leadership both ignored and suppressed the will of the membership. It was not the bureaucrats, however, but the workers, including those not expelled, who suffered.

The left wing in the Amalgamated Clothing Workers of America was never able to achieve a degree of success comparable to that accomplished in the other needle trades unions. They were opposed by an administration with a progressive reputation and a pro-Soviet orientation—an administration that was quite flexible in its tactics, combining strong-arm methods, expulsions, and other undemocratic practices with the adoption of some of the key demands raised by the left wing. Faced with such a complex situation, it seems remarkable that the left wing did as well as it did.*

Only in the smallest of the needle trades unions—that of the fur workers—was the left wing able to win and keep control. The astute tactics and general ability of the leaders in the fur workers' union, headed by Ben Gold, stood in sharp contrast to the too often hesitating and vacillating left-wing leaderships in the ILGWU and the Amalgamated. Militant, brilliant, and resourceful himself, Gold was surrounded by men and women who shared many of these characteristics. It was the combination of this homogeneous leadership, the success of the 1926 strike (in contrast to the outcome of the strike that same year in the ILGWU), the thorough organization of the industry, and the solidarity of the membership that made possible the left-wing victory in fur. Mass expulsions by Socialist and AFL officials were ineffective because the left-led Joint Board and locals had organized the trade so thoroughly that employers could hire workers only through left-led locals.

The left leadership in fur defeated the coalition of the Socialist and AFL bureaucracy by uniting the workers and dividing the coalition. In vain the employers, the AFL and Socialist leaders resorted to gangsters and the aid of the police against the left. They were met and defeated by a united rank-and-file. "The Communists in the fur union," acknowledges Bert Cochran, "displayed a dazzling mastery of tactics to solve complex and varied problems, and ability of a high order to mobilize outside support for their cause."[50] Above all, they gained and continued to maintain the unwavering support of a united, militant membership.

---

* In a comment appended to one of Foster's reports on the Amalgamated Clothing Workers to the National Executive Committee of the TUEL, Daniel Bell cites one reason which he believed helps to explain "the relative weakness of the CP in the Amalgamated as compared to the other two unions... that the main strength of the Amalgamated was not concentrated in New York as was that of the ILG and the Furriers, particularly the Furriers, and that the Amalgamated did have strength in other cities, particularly Rochester and Chicago, giving them a more widespread basis of control." He conceded, however, that this was a "fairly simple explanation." (Daniel Bell Papers, Tamiment Institute Library, New York University.)

CHAPTER 9

THE AUTO WORKERS

By 1923 the automobile industry was the largest industry in the nation. Mass production, with its large scale production of identical items, interchangeable parts, and sequentially ordered moving assembly lines, was symbolized the world over by Henry Ford's Model T.[1]

By this time, the auto workers were divided into three main groups: white native-born workers, Black native-born workers, and foreign-born workers.[2] Unlike many industrialists, the auto employers did not seek to have a work force divided by language. "Perhaps," observes Joyce Shaw Peterson, "the threat of united worker organization seemed so slight that employers saw no need for special advantages...."[3]

Historians generally agree that the greatest obstacle to union organization of the automobile industry lay in its reputation as a high wage industry. From the initial lure of Henry Ford's 1914 five dollar a day wage through the high wage period of the 1920's—by 1925 the auto industry ranked first in yearly wages received by workers—labor in all parts of the United States was drawn to the auto industry in Detroit.[4]

However, as shop floor tensions emerged with increasing use of "efficiency engineers," followed by line speed-up and other assaults by employers on established working methods, unionization of the auto plants became a real possibility. Despite the reputation for high wages, actual conditions in the industry were abominable. After just two decades, the industry had come under domination of a few giant corporations who wielded absolute power over the workers. They paid piece rates which were cut every time the workers started earning more than the companies wanted to pay. Long lay-offs that reduced workers to near starvation alternated with working seven days a week, ten and twelve hours a day.

Job security was unknown. Lead poisoning and other job-related ailments were common. The speed of the production line reduced workers to physical wrecks. Talking was forbidden in auto plants, and talking union could get a worker beaten up and fired. Spies infested the plants—Ford's factories were patrolled by the notorious Service Department, made up of convicted gangsters and murderers paroled in the company's custody. The most insistent and persistent grievances of the 1920s "were workers' complaints about the tension of their work, the pace of the line, the inability to exert any control over the pace, the impossibility of making a mistake without having that affect everybody else. All of these features of mass production came to be concentrated around the concept of speed-up and, when organization finally came to the automobile workers, speed-up was one of the chief organizing issues." So writes Joyce Shaw Peterson in her study of the auto workers.[5] She quotes a Ford worker who observed:

> The weight of a tack in the hands of an upholsterer is insignificant, but if you have to drive eight tacks in every Ford cushion that goes by your station within a certain time, and know that if you fail to do so, you are going to tie up the entire platform, and you continue to do this for four years, you are going to break under the strain.[6]

Auto workers struck back by absenteeism, turnovers, restricting output, and sporadic walkouts that often lasted less than a day. But these outbursts were usually unsuccessful in having any effect on workers' conditions of employment, especially inhuman work rules, speed-up, and fluctuating and insecure employment.[7]

A machine-shop worker voiced his feeling about restricting output in a poem he posted on the shop bulletin board. It read in part:

Harmony:
I am working with the feeling
That the company is stealing
Fifty pennies from my pocket every day;
But for every single pennie

They will lose ten times as many
By the speed that I'm producing I dare say
For it makes me so disgusted

That my speed shall be adjusted
So that nevermore my brow will drip with sweat,
When they're in an awful hurry
Someone else can rush and worry
Till an increase in my wages do I get.[6]

In short, the industry cried out for unionization.

The auto industry was never entirely without unions. Craft unions like the carpenters or the upholsters had members in auto plants, but the unions themselves had little power within the industry. The Carriage and Wagon Workers Union, an industrial union chartered by the AFL in 1891, added "Automobile" to its name in 1913, and moved into the auto industry. But except for a few years around World War I, its membership rarely numbered even 3,000, and that membership was almost entirely among the skilled workers.[8]

The Industrial Workers of the World (IWW) maintained a local in Detroit from 1905, but it was not until 1910 that it showed serious interest in attracting auto workers. In 1910 the IWW established a Metal and Machinery Workers' Local No. 16. By 1911, the IWW in Detroit claimed more than 400 members, an increase from only fifty in 1910. By May 1913, 200 auto workers were counted among Detroit's IWW membership.

As we have seen in a previous volume, the IWW led a 1913 strike in three Studebaker plants in Detroit, 6,000 workers in all, that lasted one week. It was marked by several clashes between strikers and police, and was the first important industrial organized strike in the auto industry.* (The strike did not involve skilled workers.) While the strike did not bring any immediate results, it "aroused considerable apprehension among auto manufacturers and may have contributed to the introduction of the $5 day."[9]

The Carriage, Wagon and Automobile Workers Union saw the opportunity created by the IWW's presence and the Studebaker strike, and requested an organizer from the AFL. The union argued both the need to defeat the radicalism of the IWW, which it conceded was particularly appealing to foreign workers, and the need to take advantage of the enthusiasm for worker unity created in the Studebaker strike to move workers into the Carriage, Wagon and Automobile Workers. The AFL, however, rejected the appeal, arguing that it could not afford to send an organizer at the time.[10]

As an industrial union inside the largely craft union organization of the AFL, the Carriage, Wagon and Automobile Workers Union became increasingly involved in jurisdictional disputes within the Federation's affiliates in the automobile industry. The union was ordered by the AFL national convention to stop all efforts to organ-

---

* *See* Philip S. Foner, *History of the Labor Movement in the United States* 4 (New York, 1965): 383-90.

ize workers who came under craft jurisdiction in the auto industry, and to release to the nine craft unions those members who belonged to their respective trades. In 1914 the AFL ordered the union to drop "Automobile" from its name. For insisting on retaining "Automobile" in its title and persisting in organizing automobile workers without regard to the craft jurisdiction of other AFL unions, the Carriage, Wagon and Automobile Workers Union was suspended from the AFL in 1917 and expelled a year later.[11]

Reporting to his union's members, President William Logan of the Carriage, Wagon and Automobile Workers explained the cause of the expulsion:

> All the trouble between our organization and the A.F. of L. has been because of the fact that we stood uncompromisingly for industrial unionism. It was hardly possible for us, as an organization, to claim jurisdiction over all the workers in our industry, without stepping upon the toes and coming into conflict with other trade organizations also claiming jurisdiction over workers employed in different branches of the industry.[12]

In April 1918, under the same Socialist leadership it had before its expulsion from the AFL, the Carriage, Wagon and Automobile Workers Union (also known as the Automobile, Aircraft and Vehicle Workers of America, and more commonly, as the Auto Workers Union [AWU]), became an independent organization, claiming 23,000 members.[13] In 1919 it had grown to over 45,000 members and thirty-five locals in Detroit, Toledo, Cincinnati, Flint, Pontiac, Buffalo, Chicago and New York City. Its strongest and largest unit was Local 127 in Detroit, with sections in 15 auto companies and additional scattered members for a total in 1919 of between 30-35,000, and was adding 1,000 members a month. Its weekly paper, the *Auto Worker*, boasted a circulation of 50,000.[14]

In 1920 the union suffered a severe setback. Many politically advanced auto workers were deported during the Palmer Raids as foreign radicals.* On top of this, the open-shop campaign of the 1920s and the economic recession of 1920-21 took their toll on the union. By 1922, it was down to two or three hundred members in Detroit and only three thousand members nationally. In short, the union was "virtually finished."[15]

---

* See Philip S. Foner, *History of the Labor Movement in the United States* 8 (New York, 1988):21-22.

In 1922, the Workers' (Communist) Party assigned Edgar Owens to take charge of Communist organization in Detroit. Owens met with William Logan, the Socialist head of the Auto Workers Union, and explained to him that the Workers' (Communist) Party had endorsed the program of the Trade Union Educational League opposing dual unionism, and supported its program for amalgamation and industrial unionism, organization of the unorganized, support for the Soviet nion, and the formation of a labor party. If Logan would permit Owens to work for the AWU, he promised to bring twenty-five to thirty Communists into the union as organizers. They would be chiefly concerned with organizing the unorganized auto workers and recruiting them into the AWU, leaving the leadership of the organization in the hands of the Socialists. Fully aware that the AWU was by then merely "a shell of the old organization," Logan readily agreed.[16]

Communist auto workers who were still under the influence of dual unionism were told that the party's Industrial Commission expected all party members to join Local 127 of the Auto Workers Union. In the next few years, the Detroit Communists established small organizations, or shop nuclei, in nearly a score of auto plants, including Chrysler, Murray Body, Briggs, Buick, Packard and Durant Hayes. A typical auto nucleus consisted of only a dozen or so Communists scattered throughout various departments in a shop containing thousands of workers. In spite of their limited numbers, the shop nuclei were able to exercise a remarkable influence among the auto workers.[17]

COMMUNIST SHOP PAPERS

The Communists quickly made the Auto Workers Union an active agitational organization whose lunch hour plant gate rallies were a familiar sight to many workers.* The climate of fear in the plants made shop-floor organizing nearly impossible. Instead, the Communists relied on the shop papers that they distributed at the plant gates. The papers put out the party's view on issues of the day and

---

* Roger Keeran in his widely acclaimed study, *The Communist Party and the Auto Workers Unions* declares that the Auto Workers' Union until 1933 "was the only active union in the automobile industry." (Bloomington, Indiana, 1980, p. 96.) *In Auto Slavery: The Labor Process in the American Automobile Industry, 1897-1950* (New Brunswick and London, 1986), David Gartman devotes almost 100 pages to unions in the Auto industry from 1897 to 1933. But he does not even mention the Auto Workers' Union.

education about socialism. But their biggest feature was the anonymous workers' contributions exposing conditions in the shop—the only real outlet workers had to express their grievances.

The shop papers were small, crudely printed four-page sheets, selling for a penny, that appeared weekly, monthly or, as was most often the case, irregularly. Communist workers and their sympathizers provided the news about shop conditions that went into the papers, and they also surreptitiously distributed the shop papers within the auto plants. Communists not employed in the shops did the actual writing, editing, layout, and printing, as well as the distribution at the plant gates. Soon a large part of each issue was made up of descriptions sent in by auto workers of unbearable working conditions in the plants.[18]

In April 1926, the Ford shop nucleus published the first auto shop paper, entitled the *Ford Worker*. Above the title were the words: "Workers of the World, Unite," and underneath, "Issued by Exploited Ford Workers." In "Introducing ourselves," the *Ford Worker* announced:

> *Greetings* to all those who toil, irrespective of their race, color or creed. May this little missive, the first issue of a publication devoted to the interests of the Ford workers, reach all toilers, and be the means of drawing us all closer together in a common bond of working class interests.
>
> *May* it create the determination and unity needed in the effort to put our class in its rightful position, that of a ruling class instead of ruled. We aim to bring about a condition where the exploitation of man by man shall cease to be.[19]

Other shop papers issued by the nuclei were the *Dodge Worker, Fisher Body Worker, Briggs Worker,* and *Chrysler Worker*. The first issue of the *Dodge Worker* appeared in August 1926, and announced that it was "Issued by the Dodge Shop Nucleus of the Workers' (Communist) Party." Its introduction declared:

> This little paper is edited and printed by the Communists working in the Dodge Bros. plants. We who write these articles work side by side with you on the machine, the bench and the floor, in every department of the plant.
>
> It is our Aim to speak in behalf of the exploited worker in this shop, to point out some ways through which we can improve our conditions and put an end to the system of exploitation.
>
> We are Communists, and at some future time we will tell you about ourselves and the Great world-wide workers' Movement to which we belong....[20]

The *Fisher Body Worker* introduced itself with the information that "this little sheet is edited by a group of workers in this plant Each of

us is a member of the Workers' (Communist) Party. Our organization has a branch (Shop Nucleus) in almost every shop in the city."

> You wonder why we are doing this: Well, it's like this. We know that wages
> and conditions here are rotten and we have worked in other shops and
> there they are about the same. We want to interest you in this matter and
> create enough sentiment to *organize* and improve our conditions.[21]

The shop papers contained sermonettes on unionism, such as the
one in the *Ford Worker* called "Hornets Are Wise," which told how a
Negro farmer decided not to mess with hornets because the "rascals
are organized." It ended: "Moral: organize! In union there is
strength!"[22]

Workers were invited to send in accounts of their deplorable conditions, and there was no lack of response. A study of the shop
papers notes: "The descriptions covered wage cuts, speed-ups, lay-
offs, unhealthy and dangerous working conditions, confusing and
inequitable piece rates, tyrannical work rules and arbitrary and
prejudicial foremen."[23] One Ford worker wrote:

> The dirt and filth is awful! In some places it is an inch thick an the
> floor.... [There is no ventilation system worthy of the name. The men are
> compelled to work in these filthy, dusty rooms that are a menace to their
> health. During the hot weather we go home covered with cotton dust,
> grease and sweat .... On this second floor there is nothing to carry the
> dust away so it settles over everything. We breathe it into our lungs and
> eat it during the lunch period. We are not allowed to sit on the stock to
> eat so like pigs and dogs we eat on the floor.[24]

"Here's Just One Reason Why We Need A Union," was the title of
an editorial in the *Dodge Worker*. The answer read:

> For some time we were working short hours, and only two or three days a
> week. Now in many departments we work from ten to thirteen hours a
> day and six and seven days a week.
>   Trade unions tell the employers, "We're men and not machines."
>   Trade unions fight for shorter hours, and short hours mean steady
> work.
>   You can help build a union in the automobile industry in Detroit.
>   Join the Auto Workers Union, or the Machinists Union.[25]

A Dodge worker, writing of the colds and rheumatism that the
men in his department had contracted from having to work while
standing in water, concluded: "This is the price we pay for working in
an open shop." That message was driven home repeatedly by the
shop papers. But they also pointed to the way in which other workers
were uniting to solve similar problems. They were forming units of
the Trade Union Educational League. When the TUEL held a mass

meeting in Detroit on the eve of the 1926 AFL convention held in that city, a meeting to be addressed by William Z. Foster, Ben Gold and William F. Dunne, the *Worker* recommended that "all its readers be present at the TUEL meeting."[27]

Commenting on the AFL convention, the *Ford Worker* noted that "many workers find fault with the unions represented in the AFL and so does the *Ford Worker*. But let us call your attention to this. No matter what differences we have among ourselves we must have a united front against the bosses." The article continued:

> We can do this only by joining a union and becoming a part of the American labor movement. From the inside of the movement we can correct its shortcomings and mistakes, To criticize from the outside is equivalent to fighting the labor movement in the interests of the bosses. Let us watch the AFL convention. If we are for the unions we will join them, if we are against the unions we will fight them. That's what the boss does. *Where do you Stand?*[28]

As we have seen, the shop papers openly proclaimed their Communist origins and they consistently raised political issues beyond the immediate grievances of the workers. The shop papers supported the idea of a labor party, rallied support for Sacco and Vanzetti and appealed to the auto workers to vote for the candidates of the Workers' (Communist) Party.

> The *Ford Worker* calls upon its 20,000 readers to vote the straight Workers Party ticket on Tuesday, November 2 (1926). Because the Workers Party is the Party of Labor.
> The Workers Party is the only force today fighting for the interests of the Worker Politically and Economically.
> The Workers Party is your Political Party. Members of the Workers Party are publishing the *Ford Worker* and our members in other shops are publishing hundreds of such Shop Papers....
> By voting the straight Workers Party ticket you are registering your opposition to the Ford system of Slavery....[29]

The shop papers did not confine themselves to domestic issues. They also dealt with American foreign policy, emphasizing the necessity to oppose every aspect of U.S. imperialism. The *Fisher Body Worker* of May-June, 1927 carried an editorial entitled, "Hands Off China" which opened: "The Chinese workers and peasants are completing their revolution and will soon establish a Workers and Farmers Government in China. The Imperialist Powers are still scheming to overthrow the Chinese Revolution. Just a few days ago the American government has sent more Marines to China to defend the property of the American capitalists in China." The editorial concluded: "Our 100% patriots who have millions of dollars invested in China are now being told by the Chinese Workers and Peasants to get out if they don't like the Chinese Revolution, which is being fought in the interest of the Chinese toiling masses. The slogan of every worker in America must be: 'Hands Off China!'"

The May 1927 issue of the *Dodge Worker* featured an editorial entitled "The U.S. and Nicaragua." "Nicaragua is a small country in Central America," began the editorial. "Unfortunately it is rich in minerals, mahogany and other natural resources. We say unfortunately because this natural wealth attracted the attention of American financiers, and they did not rest until they got control of a good portion of this wealth. In order to get control they had to find native agents. With millions of dollars at their command they found native rascals who were willing to sell their country to Wall Street." But the Nicaraguan people objected, and they joined together to fight the "forces which served the American financiers." So aroused were the people that they "fought bitterly and were on the point of decisively defeating the conservatives, when American marines came to the rescue of the latter." Moreover, Henry Stimson, "the representative of President Coolidge," is threatening to use more "force if the Nicaraguans continue their resistance." The *Dodge Worker*'s analysis concluded:

> This "Dollar Diplomacy" of the American government may secure riches for our millionaires. But for us, the workers and farmers, it gets nothing. Nay, what is even worse, it gets for us the hatred of the Nicaraguan and other Central and South American peoples equally with hatred for Wall Street. Ultimately this policy must lead to war. We must say to our government: We reject Dollar Diplomacy; we demand Human Diplomacy.

The papers consistently advocated the goals of socialism and praised the accomplishments of the Soviet Union. They asked auto workers to support U.S. recognition of the first socialist state, and to oppose the anti-Soviet policies of the capitalist countries. The *Ford Worker* looked forward to the day when they, like the Russian workers, would be able "to create a government without room for capitalist domination and in which the chief claim to honor will be the work one performs and the services he renders for the benefit of the great mass of workers from whose labor all wealth comes."[30]

The *Ford Worker* achieved the widest circulation of any of the Communist shop papers. It claimed 20,000 readers, but the figure of six thousand may be closer to the reality. At any rate, that was the figure mentioned by Jack Stachel, a leader of Party trade union work. Each of the other shop papers had a circulation of between one hundred and three thousand.[31] But the employers did not underestimate the impact of the shop papers and made them their chief target of attack. In and near the shops, foremen and plant guards seized copies and harassed distributors. Workers suspected of writing for the papers were fired. The mobsters, pugilists, and ex-convicts of Ford's Service Department beat up distributors, and the Dearborn police arrested them. One distributor, Sarah Victor, was arrested three times in one afternoon.[32]

Despite the efforts to suppress them, the shop papers circulated "like wildfire" among the auto workers. Frank Marquart, who worked in the Detroit auto shops in the late 1920s, and who later became educational director of UAW locals 600 and 212, explained the reason for the wide circulation of the shop papers. "These papers," he recalled, "had the smell of machine oil about them. They fairly bristled with live, on-the-spot shop reports, exposing flagrant health hazards in the paint shop, describing brutal acts of this or that foreman toward the men under him, citing facts and figures about speed-up on specific job operations, revealing how workers got short-changed by a bonus system no one could ever figure out." Marquart recalled, too, how the auto workers told him they loved the shop papers.

"The papers gave them a visceral reaction; it spoke to them about the experience that impinged on their nerves, muscles and brains. The papers said what they felt." Marquart noted, too, that the papers publicized the employers' discriminatory practices, "the way Negroes were confined to the dirtiest and meanest jobs, particularly in the foundries and toilets." "I can credit these papers," he wrote, "for making men conscious of the fact that Negroes have special problems as a minority group, apart from the general conditions of wage workers." As for the impact of the papers on workers in general, Marquart declared: "I do know that those papers played a significant role in preparing auto workers' minds for the union thrust that was to come in the days ahead."[33]

COMMUNISTS GAIN LEADERSHIP OF AUTO WORKERS UNION

Over the years, relations between the Communists and Socialists in the Auto Workers Union deteriorated. In the presidential election of 1924, the Socialist leaders of the union endorsed Robert M. La Follette while the Communists, following the position taken by the Workers' Party and the TUEL, condemned the candidate of the Progressives as "a reactionary" and the "candidate of political gangsters."* It was a position that enraged the Socialist leaders. Nor did it gain much support among the auto workers. More serious was the split over the question of strikes. The Socialist leaders opposed strikes, especially spontaneous unauthorized walkouts, while the Communists insisted that they were necessary. When a series of departmental walkouts occurred during the summer of 1926, the Communists proudly claimed that they were "among the first to start the war and down the tools." On this issue the auto workers stood firmly behind the Communists.[34]

Before 1926, however, despite their differences, the Communists did not challenge the Socialists for leadership of the Auto Workers Union. They were satisfied to concentrate on organizing the unorganized and educating the auto workers on political, economic and social issues through their shop papers and meetings, many of them held before the shop gates.[35] In 1926, however, the Communist Trade Union Committee recommended that "all members of the party who are eligible to join the unions in the auto industry should be distributed proportionately with a view to capture the machinery of both the Auto Workers and Machinists locals in the various automobile centers." That same year Phil Raymond, a young, militant Communist, challenged Lester Johnson for the post of secretary of the Auto Workers Union. The Socialist leadership had tried to keep Raymond from running for office by changing the union's constitution to restrict eligibility to office to those who had been members of the union for at least a year. But by 1926, Raymond had been a member of the union for a year and he defeated Johnson by one vote. Phil Raymond became the first Communist officer of the Auto Workers Union.[36]

Within a year, the Communists had three or four members on the AWU Executive Board. In 1927, the Socialists gave up the struggle for union control. Lester Johnson left the union and entered law school. William Logan, head of the union, resigned, as did the secretary, Charles Dickenson. The union combined the offices of president and secretary into the post of executive-secretary to which it elected Arthur Rohan, the only Socialist in a leadership that had become increasingly Communist.[37]

The Communist leaders of the AWU decided to revive the union paper, which had gone out of existence in 1924. Renamed the *Auto*

** *See* Philip S. Foner, *History of the Labor Movement in the United States*, 9 (New York, 1990):339.

Workers News, it sold for one penny instead of, as previously, for fifteen cents. The price, however, was not the only similarity to the Communist shop papers. Like them, the *Auto Workers News* dealt with shop conditions and featured accounts of the workers' complaints against speed-up, industrial accidents, layoffs, short work weeks and the tyranny and favoritism practiced by foremen. In its very first issue, the *Auto Workers News* reported on a disastrous fire that took the lives of twenty-one workers at the Briggs Manufacturing Company, a body plant notorious for its hazardous working conditions. The Michigan Department of Labor and Industry blamed the fire on "an act of Providence," but the *Auto Workers News* placed sole responsibility for the blaze on the company's failure to provide an adequate ventilation system to dispose of the flammable fumes arising from the lacquering process. The paper also published the following verse entitled "Bodies by Briggs":

> Bodies by Briggs, this cinder heap
>   of things that once were men,
> Bone of our bone, our brothers, they
>   slain in the flaming den;
> Such is the tally of wealth and greed thru
>   all of mortal ken,
> Death marks the score in the worker's
>   blood using a golden pen.[38]

Headlines about industrial accidents were characteristic of future issues, "Another Victim of the Speed-Up System," "Six Workers Killed in Ford Rouge Plant," "Ford Speed-Up Maims Workers." Another headline read: "Human Scrap Pile Grows, Old Employees are Thrown Out of Work."[39]

AFL DECIDES TO ORGANIZE AUTO WORKERS

For some time, the Auto Workers Union was the only union under Communist leadership which operated as an independent organization. But that was not because of choice. Rather it grew out of the fact that the union had been ousted from the AFL and had to operate independently. Nevertheless, the Communists were convinced that they did not have the resources to organize the auto industry. They concluded that while they would continue to "stimulate the drive for organization among auto workers," they would prod the AFL into launching a massive drive to organize the industry.[40] They were under no illusions that this would be easy to achieve. The AFL leadership had indicated on several occasions that they favored a policy of labor-management cooperation and frowned upon aggressive organizing. As we have seen, William Green was a leading exponent of this doctrine, insisting that the "best interests [of workers] are promoted through concord rather than by conflict."[41] Nevertheless, a number of AFL leaders feared the growing Communist influence in the auto industry that was symbolized by the circulation and popularity of the shop papers. This fear led James O'Connell, head of the AFL Metal Trades Department, to introduce a resolution at the Federation's 1926 convention in Detroit, calling on the AFL to initiate an organizing drive among the automobile workers. Sharing O'Connell's fears, the delegates unanimously passed the resolution.[42]

Although they understood that the resolution was adopted because of their own developing influence in the automobile industry, and that they were certain to come under renewed attack as a result of it, the Communists declared that they were "pleased to hear" of the Federation's intention to organize the auto workers. Phil Raymond wrote to William Green that the Auto Workers Union was prepared to "render all assistance possible" to the effort and asked him "under what terms and conditions" the AFL would lift its suspension of the AWU.[43] Green immediately informed Raymond that the AFL was not interested in assistance from Communists and that the AWU could only return as a federal labor union. This meant that the union would have to relinquish control of its funds and strike decisions to the Federation and turn over its members to any international union that claimed jurisdiction over them. It was clear that the AFL had no intention of welcoming the AWU back into its ranks or of making use of the experience gained by the union's officials or by Communist auto workers since 1922.[44]

In furtherance of the AFL campaign to organize the auto industry, Green published challenges to Henry Ford in the *American Federationist* to meet with him and other Federation leaders so as to convince himself that they had no intention "to make war on industry," and to give them "a chance to mobilize the creative ability of workers and cooperate with management." In one challenge, Green argued that Ford needed organization among his workers "in order that they may tell him things he does not know about his production force."[45]

Similar challenges went to General Motors, but neither Ford nor GM even bothered to respond. It would also appear that the AFL craft unions were as little interested in organizing the auto workers as the employers. Of the original seventeen craft unions involved in the campaign, eight quickly dropped out. Even the nine who remained were anything but enthusiastic about the campaign, despite the fact that the AFL planned to organize the auto workers into federal labor unions which would be split up among the various craft unions. As Joyce Shaw Peterson notes:

> The craft unions were afraid that their jurisdictional claims might be overruled, and in addition, had no desire to incorporate into their unions unskilled and semi-skilled workers—many of them the despised "new immigrants." Unskilled workers, they suggested, did not have staying power when it came to unions and would not be committed members. That they might also be foreigners, blacks, or tinged with radicalism was no doubt also not in their favor.[46]

FAILURE OF THE AFL CAMPAIGN

The AFL's organizing campaign hardly got beyond the passing of the convention resolution. In June 1927, Green appointed AFL staff member Paul J. Smith to head the drive. Although Smith and a few organizers established a headquarters in Detroit, the organizing drive consisted of little more than an attempt to sell Henry Ford and General Motors the idea of union-management cooperation. In July 1927 and again in February 1928, Smith reported to Green that efforts to organize the auto industry had been totally unproductive.[47] On November 12, 1928, Green replied to an inquiry from Robert L. Cruden, chairman of the Student Industrial Commission in Detroit, requesting information as to what the AFL was doing to organize auto workers:

> Conforming to your request I am sending to you, under separate cover, a copy of the printed proceedings of the Detroit 1926 Convention of the American Federation of Labor. The American Federation of Labor is not yet prepared to make a formal report of its endeavors to organize the automobile industry. We are still actively engaged in this work in different sections of the country but as you can appreciate our activities are greatly restricted for financial reasons.[48]

The truth was that "greatly restricted" was simply a euphemism for no organizing activity whatsoever. "Thus ended," writes James O. Morris, "the AFL's first attempt in the 1920s to organize a specific industry by primary reliance upon selling employers on the virtues of union-management cooperation rather than upon selling workers on the merits of unionism."[49]

As we shall see below, the attempt to organize the southern textile industry on the same principle was "to meet the same ignominious fate."[50]

"Who Will Organize the Auto Workers?" asked a writer in the *Daily Worker* of August 25, 1928. He answered: "The Party must be the driving force in the whole movement.... There is no other group that can go through with an aggressive organizing campaign."[51]

To spread the message of unionism in the auto industry, the Communists used the *Auto Workers News*, shop gate meetings, gatherings in the homes of sympathetic workers, in the halls of nationality groups and the workers' social and fraternal clubs. In addition there was the support of strikes, most of them spontaneous as auto workers walked off the job to protest wages and conditions. In the period 1926-30, the Auto Workers Union reported the occurrence of over fifty spontaneous strikes. "Though the Communists initiated few if any of these," writes Roger R. Keeran, "they became involved in nearly half of them."[52] The Auto Workers Union helped considerably in the strikes at Briggs Meldrum in 1927, Fisher Body Plant No. 18 in 1928, and Graham-Paige and Murray Body in 1929. In the case of the Graham-Paige and Murray Body strikes, the strikers initially turned to the Detroit Federation of Labor for aid. Rejected, they then asked the Auto Workers Union to help them. The AWU instructed the strikers in the procedures of electing a strike committee and running strike meetings. In the end, the strikers voted to accept a compromise proposal and returned to work.[53]

The Auto Workers Union also benefited from the activities of the Communists in the Canadian automobile industry. Actually, it was a two-way street with many Canadian auto workers, including the 15,000 or so residents of Windsor, regularly coming into contact with one or other of the Communist "shop groups" in the Detroit plants, and bringing their message of organizing the unorganized and industrial unionism back to Canada with them.[54]

Communists began holding regular shopgate meetings in Canada at Ford in 1925, but these passed off uneventfully until 1927. In July of that year, Communist Party of Canada (CPC) industrial director Tim Buck mounted his soapbox outside Ford, only to be hauled down and arrested. But this did not halt the Communist organizing drive. Between March 1928 and March 1929, eight strikes occurred in the Canadian auto industry, all under Communist leadership. The General Motors Oshawa strike of March 1928 was the leading one, involving a majority of the work force—4,000 of 5,000 workers—and the victory for the strikers in forcing General Motors to rescind a cut in piece rates was seen at the time "as a potential breakthrough for the auto workers in both Canada and the United States." As Maurice Spector, leader of the CPC, put it: "Oshawa is a demonstration that the spell of industrial slavery can be broken even in the automobile industry."[55]

In the United States the Communists tried to do their part in breaking the "industrial slavery" in the auto industry. "In entering a strike," Roger Keeran points out, "the Communists helped the strikers to organize mass meetings," formulate demands, select strike committees, establish picket lines, write leaflets and obtain legal aid. The Communists impressed upon the workers that a successful walkout "demanded racial solidarity and such aggressive tactics as mass picketing."[56]

RESULTS OF COMMUNIST ORGANIZING IN AUTO

The Communists also used the *Auto Workers News* to drive home the importance of racial solidarity. The paper condemned the employer practice of paying Black workers less than whites, of giving them "the hardest and dirtiest work" and of trying to keep the workers divided by arousing "suspicions and prejudices." For a while, too, the *Auto Workers News* ran a special women's column and condemned the practice of hiring women at "substandard rates." "Girls must have a chance to earn a decent living," it argued, and it insisted that "one of the demands of the Auto Workers Union must be: 'Equal pay for equal work.'"[57]

Although the Auto Workers Union never divulged its exact membership figures, there is evidence that it had several thousand members in 1929. At the AWU Conference held on August 14, 1929, the union reported activity in Detroit, Pontiac, Flint, Grand Rapids and other auto centers, and that its membership was "being steadily increased."[58] William Chalmers, who attended many AWU meetings in order to gather information for a University of Wisconsin thesis, wrote: "The Communists ... have made a profound impression on the workers of the industry through their continuous and strenuous activity. It is they who have constantly urged the workers to organize, who have addressed impromptu meetings ... who have led spontaneous walkouts and strikes ... and who have aroused the opposition of the employers." Chalmers predicted: "[If] the industry is going to be organized 'from the outside' in the immediate future, it will be the Communists who will be responsible."[59] A recent study of Black auto workers in Detroit during the period from 1910 to 1930 concluded: "For all auto workers, Black and white, the 1920s were times of quiescence and passivity if measured by attempts to form unions and to contend aggressively with the auto industry."[60] This is hardly the whole truth. To be sure, the amount of activity during the 1920s seems small compared to the developments during the next decade. Nevertheless, by the end of the 1920s, the Communists had established their presence in the automobile industry and had spread the idea of industrial unionism to large numbers of unskilled auto workers. Communist shop papers played an important role in clarifying issues and mobilizing auto workers in struggles for higher wages, against the killing work loads and for industrial unionism. These same papers were effective in uniting the auto workers in the fight against racism and sexism and for the unity of Black and white and men and women workers. The left-led Auto Workers Union which, until 1933, was the only union active in the automobile industry, helped lay the groundwork for the founding of the United Automobile Workers (UAW).

In spite of four years of intensive activity, the TUEL and the Communist Party were unable to organize the mass of the auto workers. There were good reasons for this. The relative prosperity and easy credit of the 1920s; the powerful anti-unionism of the employers and the government; the prevalence and effectiveness of company espionage systems; the inexperience, diversity and migratory nature of the workers themselves, and the limited resources of the left wing were all important factors causing this lack of success. The Auto Workers Union signed up hundreds of members during the course of strikes, but most of them left the union after the immediate crisis was over. Phil Raymond explained that the auto workers regarded the AWU "like a fire department" that they could ignore except for those occasions "when they needed to call on it for help."[61]

One might say that Communist activity in the auto industry in the 1920s failed either to build a stable union or to stimulate a real AFL organizing drive. However, this would be a one-dimensional view. Although unsuccessful, the effort of the Communist-led Auto Workers Union did pave the way for an industrial union. As one auto worker said of the Auto Workers Union's educational work:

> They used to hold classes in public speaking. They were developing people in the sense of giving them confidence to get up on their feet and speak; they were getting some training in public speaking, they were getting some ideas, some background of the labor movement. All of this meant that when the upsurge came, you had people in factories and around Detroit who were able to get up and present an intelligent case for unionism and the ideas in the union movement as they saw them.[62]

Roger Keeran sums up the effect of the work of the Communist Party and the Auto Workers Union:

Both the Party and the union recruited and gave practical organizational experience to workers who later became active in the drive to form the UAW. Also, through the shop papers, shop gate meetings, and fraternal societies, countless auto workers who never joined the CP or AWU became acquainted with radical ideas. These workers became conscious of shared grievances. They learned of socialism, and they encountered the idea of an industrial union that would unite all auto workers in a struggle for a better life. In these ways, the Communists did more than anyone in the pre-union days to lay the foundation for a successful auto union.[63]

CHAPTER 10

THE TEXTILE WORKERS

In an evaluation of unionism in the textile industry published in 1923, the Trade Union Educational League observed: "Of the 1,000,000 workers in the industry, not over 100,000 are organized. These are split up into fully a score of unions, squabbling among themselves, and constructed according to every known type. The employers, on the other hand, are well organized and trustified. In no industry in America are the trade unions so variegated and the workers so helpless and underpaid as in the textile industry."

"There is no outlook for the textile workers better than that of slavery unless their great number of unions are brought together and united," the League declared. It announced that to end this state of affairs, the General Amalgamation Committee of the Textile Industry held its first national conference in New York on May 5, 1923. The Committee issued a statement entitled "The Textile Program" which asserted:

The vast army of textile workers must be organized .... But before complete organization can be brought about, the many unions in the field must be united .... A solid front of all the existing unions is the first essential to the organization of the textile industry.

This indispensable unity can be achieved only by thoroughgoing amalgamation.[1]

Strangely, "The Textile Program" of the General Amalgamation Committee of the Textile Industry did not mention a pressing problem confronting the textile workers in Fall River, Lawrence, New Bedford, Passaic, Paterson, Philadelphia, Manchester, etc. As a result of the southward movement of the textile mills to take advantage of cheap labor, by 1925 there were more spindles in the Southern textile mills than in New England.[2] Using southern competition as an excuse, northern manufacturers reduced wages and thereby triggered a series of bitter conflicts.

STRIKE IN WILLIMANTIC

The scene of one of the first of these strikes was Willimantic, Connecticut. The American Thread Company, the largest thread mill in the world, was practically the only industry in that city of 12,000 inhabitants, of whom about 2,600—80 percent of them women—were on the mill's payrolls. About 35 percent of the workers were organized in a local of the United Textile Workers, and most of its officers were women.

The American Thread Company was a British concern, owned by the English Cotton Sewing Company of Manchester. In 1924, even while it was running only part-time, the company paid its stockholders a dividend of 10 percent. However, the average wage of its workers was only $15 per week. Nevertheless, on January 9, 1925, the company announced a 10 percent wage cut and turned a deaf ear to conciliation efforts by the local Chamber of Commerce, citizens' committees and the U.S. Department of Labor. After trying in vain to negotiate some concessions from the company, all 2,600 workers responded to the UTW strike call on March 12. So complete was the walkout that it was not even possible to keep the steam under the boilers.

As indicated above, 80 percent of the strikers were women, and the strike was in the charge of a women's committee headed by Mary Kelleher, organizer for the United Textile Workers, and Amy Hooks, president of the Willimantic Textile Workers' Council. Each morning at seven, about a thousand pickets, mostly women, began their march before the mill gates, and for weeks they kept the mill closed. However, French-Canadian strikebreakers were recruited, and with the aid of the state police, the plant was reopened.[3]

On July 16, deputy sheriffs entered the company houses and began throwing out the furniture and other personal property of the tenant strikers. The evicted strikers were forced to move to a tent colony on land donated by a sympathetic citizen.[4] Relief funds were scarce, for despite some contributions from the Women's Trade Union League, the United Textile Workers, viewing the strike as impossible to win, was unwilling to give adequate assistance to the strikers, who, nevertheless, remained steadfast.[5]

After a year on strike and facing the threat of starvation, many of the strikers drifted to other cities in search of work, and a handful

even returned to the thread mill. At the end of thirteen months, the
only evidence of the long strike was an occasional demonstration at
the plant gates. The United Textile Workers conceded defeat and
called off the strike on April 22, 1926.[6]

The wage reduction at American Thread was only one of the
many "10 percent cuts" in the New England textile industry in early
1925.[7] The UTW did nothing to mobilize the textile workers against
these cuts. Since many of the workers were women, and since the
UTW had a defeatist attitude toward the organization of women
workers, it confined itself to complaining about the difficulty in mobilizing textile women to resist wage cuts.[8]* On the other hand, the
Trade Union Educational League distributed an appeal addressed
"To All Textile Workers—Organized and Unorganized," urging them
to "Organize and Fight!" The appeal said in part:

> The textile workers are either without any union or divided into small
> craft unions. There is no unity among the textile workers like there is
> among the bosses and this is the reason that wage cuts can be put over.
> The textile workers need a powerful industrial union—all the textile
> workers in one union.
>
> This is the immediate program of the Trade Union Educational
> League for the workers in the textile industry. An industrial union of the
> workers against the industrial union of the bosses: Resistance to all wage
> cuts and increases in hours![9]

"The Communists in the textile districts must see that this message
gets to the workers and that it is translated into concrete forms of
organization," the *Daily Worker* editorialized. Shortly thereafter, it reported that the Workers' (Communist) Party and the Trade Union
Educational League were bringing their message to the Willimantic
strikers, urging a "united front of all the unions and workers against
the textile barons and amalgamation of the unions into one huge
industrial union." Moreover, United Front Committees of rank-and-
file workers were being formed in mill towns throughout New England, and members of the Workers' Party were "taking a leading part
in the formation of the United Front committees and in the organization of mass meetings." They were seeking to organize resistance to
wage cuts and speed-ups in the mills.[10] In the summer of 1925, a

---

* After a detailed exposition of the shortcomings and failures of the United Textile
Workers, Robert R. Brooks concludes: "From 1922 to 1933, the union appeared to
consist almost entirely of a suite of offices, a complement of officers, and a splendid
array of filing cabinets." (Robert R. Brooks, "The United Textile Workers of America,"
Ph.D. dissertation, Yale University, 1938, p. 349.)

large group of textile workers, including those organized by militants of the TUEL, attended the United Front Committees' conference in Lawrence, Massachusetts. One of the decisions reached by the conference was to spread the principles of the TUEL and the United Front Committees among the silk and wool workers of New Jersey.[11]

THE PATERSON STRIKE

In the summer of 1924, Paterson had been the scene of a bitter strike over wages and loom assignments, the same issues that had caused the 1912 and 1913 strikes.* The Associated Silk Workers, the only union still active in Paterson, declared a strike on August 12, 1924, demanding the abolition of the four-loom system and a return to the two-loom system, an eight-hour day, a 15 percent increase in wages and recognition of the union. The strike was bitterly fought and there were so many arrests of strikers and such an effective curtailment of the right to picket that the union had to call in the American Civil Liberties Union to try to halt the "police terrorism." The ACLU did win the right of the union and strikers to hold meetings, but the strike still ended in defeat.[12]

The Workers' Party publicly called attention to the fact that its members were "taking an active part in the Paterson strike," and the TUEL made it clear that while it was not leading the strike, it was cooperating fully with its leadership.[13] Nevertheless, the TUEL was critical of the approach of the Associated Silk Workers toward women workers. TUEL members in the union urged the organization of the women winders and quillers. The answer they invariably received was that the weavers were the key to the union's strength and had to receive most of its attention. During the 1924 strike, no wage list was worked out for the winders, quillers or pickers,** nor was any special attention paid to them, other than to see that they did not go back to work. There was only one woman member of the strike committee. Left-wingers in the Associated Silk Workers tried to get the union leadership to organize a women's auxiliary, to mobilize the wives of the men and to educate them to the importance of standing by their

---

* For a discussion of the 1912 and 1913 strikes in Paterson, *see* Philip S. Foner, *History of the Labor Movement in the United States* 4 (New York, 1965): 351-72.

** Winders, quillers and pickers were the less skilled crafts in the manufacture of silk and were nearly all young women.

husbands. But the answer they received was: "We tried it once and nothing came of it."

In the strike itself, the women silk workers were conspicuous by their faithfulness and militancy on the picket line. But the union's failure to either highlight the women's grievances and demands in order to involve them more fully, or to organize the wives of the strikers into auxiliaries was, in the TUEL's view, one of the reasons for the strike's failure to gain its key demands.[14]

BACKGROUND OF THE 1926 PASSAIC STRIKE

The left wing soon had the opportunity to show what it could do in this important respect when it was leading a textile strike. The first big strike initiated and conducted by the TUEL was the Passaic strike of 1926. In fact, the 1926 walkout of over 15,000 wool and silk workers in and around Passaic, New Jersey was the largest strike in the 1920s under total left-wing leadership.

In 1926, more than 16,000 men and women worked in the mills within the Passaic city limits. Thousands more worked in the neighboring towns of Clifton, Garfield and Lodi. The Botany Worsted Mills, the largest, employed 6,400 workers; the Forstmann & Huffman mills employed 4,000, and Passaic Worsted and Spinning, Gero Mills, New Jersey Worsted and Spinning and Dundee Textile together employed another 3,300. They produced fine woolens that were used mainly for women's dresses, coats, hats and suits. Most of the workers were foreign-born, unskilled laborers, among whom were recorded thirty-nine nationalities, with Poles, Italians, Russians, Hungarians and Slavs the major groups. Women made up 50 percent of the work force. "They are of the recent immigration," one study noted, "from eastern and southern Europe—working in the mills is a matter of course to the foreign women in Passaic."[15] Eighty-four percent of these women surveyed by the Department of Labor's Women's Bureau at the end of 1922 were earning under $15 a week. An American Civil Liberties Union survey in 1926 disclosed that the men in the Passaic mills averaged $1,000 to $1,200 a year, while women averaged $800 to $1,000.[16] The women worked at least ten hours a day to earn these wages. Those employed on a piecework basis had to maintain a grueling pace. During the Passaic strike of 1926, one of the pieceworkers was asked why she had joined the walkout. She replied:

> The boss he laugh all the time, we say we can no make a living. He say, why you no work harder? I work piece work, so hard, my back and feet

ache all the time. When I stop a few minutes to eat, the boss he say, "What the hell for you eat? Why no work?" I say: "I work piece work, I eat a few minutes my own time, I no eat can no work."[17]

The hardships endured by the women who worked on the day shift paled by comparison with the lot of the women who worked at night. Their husbands had been employed on the day shift on the condition that they got their wives to work at night.

In 1925, the Women's Bureau of the U.S. Department of Labor issued a bulletin reporting on the "Family Status of Breadwinning Women in Four Selected Cities." The report revealed that there were nearly ten thousand women breadwinners in Passaic, the vast majority of them in the woolen mills, and went on to note: "The strikingly significant fact is that all of these breadwinning mothers had small children at home, requiring care." Again, it pointed out: "Over four-fifths of the breadwinning women, who were or had been married, were maintaining homes and hence were carrying the double burden of household duties and factory employment." Mill mothers left their children with their husbands or with other adults who were at home, or with neighbors, boarders, or landladies.

However, many "had to leave the children virtually without care except as such as would be given when there were other children."[18]

A report of the National Consumers League on women workers in the Passaic mills emphasized that "all the work is exceedingly heavy, involving standing, lifting and constant walking. Complaints are general that the number of machine tenders has been reduced, thus increasing the strain.... The noise and shriek of machinery, the oil-soaked floors, the close, humid air, and the strain of night work seem past belief." The hours of sleep snatched by the night workers ranged from none to four or five, or possibly six. "Most women shrugged their shoulders at the question and answered, 'one, two hours, maybe.'" Nor was this the worst of it. "One evil universally recognized was the prevalence of pregnant women on the night shift." In order to make ends meet, these women worked up to the last possible moment, "as is shown by the fact that births frequently occur in the mills."[19]

A New Jersey law prohibiting night work for women was scheduled to go into effect at the end of 1924, but since there was no provision for either enforcement or punishment of violators, the law was totally useless. Moreover, the Passaic Wool Council, the voice of the manufacturers, took court action to block any possible enforcement of the law. Night work was necessary, the employers insisted, because as far as the carding operation was concerned, should the machines be stopped, the fiber would have to be removed from each machine each day, thus reducing the employers' profits.

Testifying before the Senate Committee on Education and Labor on May 26, 1926, W Jett Lauck, an economist and economic consultant, noted:

> Our own original investigations have shown that the usual custom in Passaic is for the husband to work in the daytime, while the wife works during the night. Although this night work of women is forbidden by State law, the law is not enforced because of a legal tangle deliberately produced by the mill owners in an action against the State. Although the people of New Jersey have forbidden it, the Passaic industrial autocracy has by manipulation thwarted their will, and women are forced to work at night.[20]

The mother would leave for her shift at eight or nine in the evening, after putting her children to bed. She would return from work between 6 and 7 a.m. in time to prepare breakfast, see her husband off to work, and send the older children on their way to school. A certain amount of housework had to be done, lunch had to be prepared, and dinner still had to be managed. There was now the question of marketing. And somehow, during the hours between seven in the morning and six in the evening, she had to arrange for eight hours of sleep. At 8 p.m. or thereabouts, another twenty-four-hour cycle started.[21]

The Passaic mills were notorious not only for their deplorable working conditions but also for a network of industrial spying. Established and underwritten by the Industrial Council of Passaic Woolen Manufacturers, set up by the managements of several of the mills in 1916, it operated through an elaborate card system to ensure that no worker who was even suspected of "agitation" could get a job in any of the mills. Part of this system of blacklisting workers who advocated unionism surfaced in 1920, when Alice Barrows of the U.S. Bureau of Education was making a survey of adult education in Passaic. She called at the then existing local of the Amalgamated Textile Workers of America and inquired into the educational classes being conducted by the union. Labor spies reported her activities to the Woolen Manufacturers Council, which tried unsuccessfully to get Barrows ousted from her federal post. She, in turn, exposed the undercover system of the Council in the Passaic papers, but the employers' association still refused to change its practices. When the reformer Justine Waterman Wise, daughter of Rabbi Stephen S. Wise, took a job in one of the Passaic mills in 1924 she, too, was spied upon regularly.

In 1926, with the aid of Alice B. Hamilton, the Workers' Health Bureau of America conducted a health survey of 404 Passaic textile workers. The survey, funded by the American Fund for Public Service, demonstrated "an unusually high percentage of tubercular workers and an extremely high accident rate."[22]*

In its study "Breadwinning Women," the Women's Bureau concluded: "It is obvious that many of the problems connected with the breadwinning wives and mothers would be dissipated if the husbands and fathers were to receive a wage adequate for the family needs."[23] But such a description could hardly be applied to the wages in effect at the end of 1925. They stood around $24 per week for men and between $16 and $20 for women. Thirteen percent of the workers made less than $800 a year, 69 percent made from $800 to $1,300, and only 18 percent made from $1,300 to $1,600 a year. Compared with the figures of the National Industrial Conference Board, which found that the minimum wage at which an "American standard of living" could be maintained in Hoboken, about a dozen miles away, was $1,400, the wage level in the Passaic mills was painfully low. The mills themselves, however, were highly profitable enterprises, largely German-owned but controlled by resident officials. During the war, the mills had made mammoth profits, and while the woolen and worsted industry had suffered economic setbacks in the 1920s, they continued to generate profits. Botany Worsted Mills, with assets of $28 million net, made profits of over $6 million a year.[24]

As we have seen, the New England textile companies had cut wages 10 percent early in 1925, and in October of the same year the Industrial Council of Woolen Manufacturers of Passaic met to consider following the pattern set in New England. Colonel F.H.

* The Workers' Health Bureau of America was founded in New York City on July 29, 1921 by Grace Burnham and Harriet Silverman, who were joined later by another radical woman, Charlotte Todes. They regarded industrial disease as a function of capitalism, "only another example of production for profits with workers paying the price," and understood health as "a question which can never be settled satisfactory for Labor by anybody, except by labor itself." The Workers' Health Bureau has been called the "sole Marxist medical institution devoted to labor in the early twentieth century." (Angela Nugent, "Organizing Trade Unions to Combat Disease: The Workers' Health Bureau, 1921-1928," *Labor History* 26 [Summer, 1985]:430.) "Over a period of eight years," David Rosner and Gerald Markowitz point out, "the Bureau did a series of investigations, reports and organizing drives for a wide variety of labor organizations and was instrumental in bringing safety and health issues to the consciousness of hundreds of thousands of American workers." ("Safety and Health on the Job as a Class Issue: The Workers' Health Bureau of America in the 1920's," *Science & Society* 48 [Winter, 1984-85]: 473-74.)

Johnson, vice-president and manager of the Botany Consolidated Mills, favored the wage cut but most of the other mill representatives refused to go along, fearing a repetition of the textile strike of 1919 which, at its peak, involved more than 10,000 workers in and around Passaic. However, when Botany, the city's largest employer, proceeded to reduce wages by 10 percent on its own, all the other mills except Forstmann & Huffman followed suit.[25]

UNITED FRONT COMMITTEE

Although wages were already low, Colonel Johnson had been able to persuade the Botany workers to accept the wage cut with the argument that the alternative was to lay off a part of the labor force. But the Trade Union Educational League, under the name of the United Front Committee of the Textile Workers of Passaic and Vicinity (UFC), and led by Albert Weisbord, was already active in the wool city. Weisbord was the son of a Brooklyn garment manufacturer who had severed connections with his father after attempting to organize the employees of his factory. He was a Phi Beta Kappa graduate of the College of the City of New York and Harvard Law School. He had moved from the IWW to the Socialist Party, where he was elected national secretary of the Young People's Socialist League, and then to the Workers' (Communist) Party. After giving up his legal career, Weisbord spent a year working in the textile mills of New England, helping to spread the message of the United Front Committee of Textile Workers. In 1926 he brought this message to Passaic.[26]

The United Textile Workers protested the wage cut but did nothing to mobilize the workers to resist it. The AFL union explained that it had attempted over the previous fifteen years "to organize the textile workers of Passaic and vicinity, but we have been met by the opposition of city officials and the indifference of the workers."[27] Actually, Passaic had a long history of efforts to unionize the mill workers, but the AFL had abandoned that effort after an unsuccessful campaign in 1902. The IWW in 1912 and the Amalgamated Textile Workers of America in 1919 attempted to revive the campaign for unionism abandoned in 1902 by the AFL. Neither, however, was successful. The United Front Committee, however, was confident that even though the city officials would be opposed, the workers could be aroused to conduct a fight-back campaign. The committee distributed leaflets among the Botany workers, pointing out that they had been duped into accepting the wage cut. Within two months, the UFC had enrolled about a thousand workers and organized them to resist the wage cut. With the United Textile Workers and other textile unions virtually nonexistent in Passaic, the United Front Committee became the voice of the textile workers there.[28]

On January 21, 1926, a worker was discharged from the Botany Worsted Mills for "agitating" on behalf of the United Front Committee. A committee of three, elected by UFC members, met with Colonel Johnson to protest the firing. They were told that any people known to belong to the UFC would be similarly discharged. The members of the UFC met again on January 25 and voted to elect a committee of forty-five to meet again with the mill management, this time not to ask for reinstatement, but to present the following demands: (1) abolition of the 10 percent wage cut that had been in effect since October; (2) time-and-a-half for overtime and (3) no discrimination against union members. Colonel Johnson replied by promptly discharging the entire committee. The committee members ran back into the mill and called upon all the workers to walk out. The workers left their machines, and the strike was on.[29]

About four thousand workers participated in the first walkout, all of them from the Botany mill. Within an hour, a picket line was organized and was marching in front of the mill gates. Other mills were picketed, one by one, by the workers on strike. By the end of the first week, the workers of the Garfield Worsted Mill, the Passaic Worsted Spinning Mill, the Gera Mill, and the New Jersey Spinning Company had joined the strike. About eight thousand workers were out. and it was evident that a major battle was shaping up.

The formal demands of the strikers served to strengthen this feeling. They were: (1) abolition of the wage cut and a 10 percent increase in wages over the old scale; (2) reimbursement of the money taken from the workers by the wage cuts since the time the cuts were imposed; (3) time-and-a-half for overtime; (4) a forty-four-hour week; (5) decent sanitary working conditions; (6) no discrimination against union members and (7) recognition of the union. These demands were presented to the management of each mill after the strike had reached all the mills that had instituted the wage cut.[30]

PASSAIC STRIKE BEGINS

Within two weeks, most of the workers of the six mills that had cut wages were out. The next major objective was the Forstmann & Huffman Company, which owned three mills, the largest of which employed four thousand workers. If these workers joined the strikers' ranks, a serious blow would be delivered to the industry in Passaic.

But this mill had not imposed a wage cut and operated with a company union.

On February 9, the mass picket line of strikers started across a bridge from Passaic to Clifton to close down the Forstmann & Huffman mill in that city. When the unarmed picket line reached the bridge, the police assaulted the strikers, trampling and clubbing men, women and children. The next day the pickets, more determined than ever, were able to get to the plant, and workers inside who had already joined the United Front Committee poured out to strengthen the mass picket line. After several days of picketing, the Forstmann & Huffman mill force joined the strikers en masse. On February 23, the company closed its mills, declaring that it had ceased operations because the remaining workers were "in fear of their lives."

On March 9, the large United Piece Dye Works of Lodi, three miles from Passaic, were closed down. Italians and Blacks (the only Black workers in the area), along with Mexican workers, joined the picket lines. Within two months, the original four thousand strikers had grown to over fifteen thousand of the seventeen thousand textile workers in the community.[31]

On February 20, 1926, Elizabeth Gurley Flynn, acting for the American Fund for Public Service, hired Mary Heaton Vorse to serve as publicity director for the fifteen thousand Passaic strikers. Vorse directed the publication of the *Textile Strike Bulletin*, a newspaper distributed to strikers and outside sympathizers. Vorse's biographer describes the *Bulletin*:

> A women's column, with stories of the women strikers and workers' wives was one of the *Bulletin*'s most popular features. Poems of the strikers' children were frequently printed. Pictures were prominent. Humor, too, was prevalent, as in the pictures of the workers' ragged children over the caption "Outside Agitators." The newspaper was written in a simple style easily read by those new to the English language. It printed announcements of classes, meetings, and stirring reports of picket lines, police assaults, and outside support for the strike.[32]

To this Morton Siegel, in his detailed study of the Passaic strike, adds: "None of the issues of the Bulletin ever called on the strikers to join the (Communist) Workers' Party; none of the issues contained even indirect praise for Soviet Russia; none of the issues suggested that the dictatorship of the proletariat was an inevitable necessity, and none of the issues quoted any Marxist classic or source."[33]

On February 25, the first issue of the *Textile Strike Bulletin* quickly raised the spirits of the strikers. Another lift to their morale was provided by the appearance on the strike scene of Elizabeth Gurley Flynn—famous, among other reasons—for her role in the IWW strikes in Paterson and Passaic in 1913. Another of the many radical and liberal women who came to help the strikers, as we have seen, was Mary Heaton Vorse, who described the scene at strike headquarters: "An office that boiled, picket captains, strike sympathizers, magazine writers, authors like Fanny Hurst and Rebecca West. Sympathizers, such as Katherine Wiley .... Miss Jeannette Rankin, Mrs. Stephen Wise, Miss Justine Wise, streamed through the office on Main Avenue...."[34]

CONDUCT OF STRIKE

Mass meetings were held daily, and there was also a daily picket line. The long, singing line became a regular feature of the strike, creating an atmosphere and a feeling of unity and power. The strikers' families were drawn into all of the activities. Many of the women, of course, worked in the mills, but even those who did not joined their husbands on the picket lines. Women served on all committees, and a number of them were picket captains. They had to get up at four on the cold mornings to see that the picket lines around the various mills were organized.

The strike committee, which met every morning at nine, was organized so as to give representation to all the mills on strike, and to all important crafts in those mills, as well as to the principal ethnic groups and to both women and youth. The chairperson of the committee was twenty-one-year-old Gustave Deak, of Hungarian descent, who worked in the finishing department of the Botany mill. Another Botany worker active on the strike committee was Ellen Dawson, a twenty-six-year-old Scottish weaver known as "the Little Orphan of the Strikers." From the Gera mill came Ma Brezniak, who was called "a tiger on the picket line." Lena Cherneko, a founding member of the Communist Party and a militant garment worker from New York, came to Passaic to assist as an organizer, as did a number of other Communist leaders, men and women.[35]

Albert Weisbord described the women as "the greatest strike enthusiasts of all," and Jack Stachel, the Communist Party trade union strategist, added: "Particularly worthy of mention is the militancy of the women strikers. They are in the forefront of the picket line." As one account noted:

Many of the women on the picket line carry babies in their arms. In some cases one sees a woman with one child in her arms, and one or more children holding on to her ragged skirt.

We asked one such woman what she was doing there. She looked at us with distrust. But upon being assured by an official guide from the strike headquarters that we were "all right," she answered in her broken English:

"What do you mean, what I do here? I picket!" "But what about the children?"

"They are mine."

In the conversation which ensued, this woman worker told a story which sheds light on the condition of the textile workers. Her husband was employed in the Botany Mills, earning the full man's wage—$19.70 per week. This being insufficient ... for the entire family, this woman, a mother of six children, worked in the mill nights, thus adding $8 a week to the family income. During the day she took care of the home and the children. She never slept more than four-and-a-half hours a day, and yet, now that the strike gave her an opportunity to rest up, she spends her time on the picket line—with her children.[36]

A complete page in the *Textile Strike Bulletin* was devoted to the young strikers. Baseball teams and other athletic groups were formed to keep them occupied when they were not on picket duty.[37] The children of the strikers received special attention under the care of Miriam Silverfarb, Sophie Melvin and Martha Stone. They were urged to write poems and compositions for the strikers' newspaper, and a regular column was set aside for these contributions.

The children participated in the strike in more concrete ways as well. Groups of two to three hundred children paraded the streets of Passaic, publicizing the demands of the strikers and calling for public support for their parents' struggle. "In many ways," Weisbord later recalled, "the children were invaluable. They would ferret out where scabs lived and picket their homes. And many a scab quit because his child came home with a black eye after a fight in school." The strike was carried into the schools in another way as well. "The children demanded to know why the schools did not open free lunch rooms for the strikers' children."[38]

But no lunches were provided, and in order to "relieve the economic pressure on the parents and the relief organization, as well as give the children the benefit of a new environment and wholesome meals," the United Front Committee borrowed a leaf from the IWW's book in the Lawrence strike of 1912 by sending the strikers' children away to the homes of workers' families sympathetic to the strike.[39]

One of the most interesting organizations to emerge during the strike was the Council of Working Class Housewives, originally formed by a group of Jewish housewives in Passaic, most of them members of the Workers' (Communist) Party. Its members canvassed stores for donations of food and ran a soup kitchen for the strikers' children. Soon other housewives organized councils and affiliated themselves to the United Council of Working Class Housewives in New York City.*

Eleven Working Women's Councils, including both striking women and housewives, were also organized. They were English-speaking, Hungarian, Russian-Ukrainian and Polish. The Working Women's Councils raised money for strike relief, helped in the children's kitchens and mobilized for picket duty.[40] They also held educational meetings in Polish, Ukrainian, and other foreign languages, prepared the strikers' wall newspapers and posted them in the stores in Passaic, Garfield, Lodi and Clifton.[41]

The varied techniques employed for raising relief funds included tag days, solicitations by letter, bazaars, concerts, street corner meetings and appeals at union meetings and labor conventions. Help for the strikers also came from groups of local citizens. "Storekeepers in the industrial district," notes Michael H. Ebner, "took out advertisements in the *Textile Strike Bulletin*, extended credit, and in some cases made outright cash donations to the relief committees aiding the protesters and their dependents."[42]

A seven-reel motion picture—*The Passaic Textile Strike*—was produced and shown throughout the country to raise funds for strike relief. "Stirring—Thrilling—Educational." was the heading of an advertisement for the labor film, and it went on: "The millions of unorganized steel, rubber, auto, oil, coal, textile and transportation workers will receive inspiration from this film, [and] will be encouraged to cross swords with their exploiters for better living conditions." The motion picture began with a prologue enacted by the strikers them-

---

* The United Council of Working Class Housewives described itself as "an organization of trade unionists' wives and other workers' wives." It was organized early in 1926 by Communist women, with Kate Gitlow as secretary. (Gitlow now was also secretary of the United Council of Working Class Women, another organization founded by Communist women to help in strikes called by left-wing unions.) The United Council of Working Class Housewives did considerable relief work in Passaic and also helped in the organization of women into workingwomen's councils affiliated with the United Council. "The Council's relief work in Passaic," the organization reported, "amounted to $200,000, not to mention the invaluable work done in the kitchens and along organizational lines." (*Daily Worker*, May 23, June 12, 1927).

selves, dramatizing the life of a striker. The film then showed the strikers braving police clubs and shotguns, fire hoses in zero weather and tear gas bombs. The huge mass meetings, with ten thousand workers participating, were shown with the strike leaders and other speakers addressing the strikers. Relief activities were also depicted, as were the picket-line lunch counters, the Victory Playground for the strikers' children,* and the specific organization of women strikers and sympathizers. Audiences were deeply moved by the film, especially by the scenes showing the "atrocious police brutality against the strikers, including girl pickets and even the children of the strikers."[43]

ANTI-STRIKE VIOLENCE

On February 25, the Passaic City Council invoked a Riot Act dating back to Civil War days in order to prohibit meetings and picketing. Three days later, strike headquarters announced that picketing was legal and clearly intimated that the order would be defied. On March 1, two thousand pickets assembled in line, and although they were met by police, they were allowed to pass. The next day, the line formed again and was met by Chief of Police Richard L. Zober and a number of policemen lined up across the street down which the pickets were approaching. The front of the line halted but those in the rear, unaware of what was happening, pressed forward to see. Soon the police began clubbing the massed strikers, and when the clubs proved ineffectual, Zober tossed several tear gas bombs in front of the crowd. When even these failed to disperse them, he called upon the fire department to direct a stream of freezing water upon the crowd.[44]

The next day the scene was repeated, with the police clubs directed at spectators, newspaper reporters and photographers and their equipment, as well as the strikers. Two days later, the picket line reassembled, this time with steel helmets, and marched triumphantly past the onlooking police, while photographers in armored cars and even in an airplane recorded the event. This time, the lines were not

---

* Years later, Sophie Melvin recalled that on some days during the strike there were as many as a thousand children in the Victory Playground. "We fed them when they came in the morning and they stayed till the evening" ("Women in Textile Organizing: An Interview with Sophie Melvin Gerson by Anne Fishel," *Radical History Review* 4 [Summer, 1977]: 113)

molested, and to the tune of "The Battle Hymn of the Republic," the pickets sang a new version of "Solidarity Forever," which went in part:

The men all stick together
And the boys are fighting fine.
The women and the girls are all right
On the picket line.
No scabs, no threats can stop us
As we all march out on time
In One Big Solid Union.

Solidarity forever,
Solidarity forever,
Solidarity forever,
For the Union makes us strong.[45]

There were other attacks on strikers' gatherings on March 8, 18, and 25, and the police in both Passaic and Garfield arrested pickets and other strikers. Those arrested usually drew heavy jail terms for their alleged offenses.[46] "It seems to be no wrench on the patriotism of the Passaic police that they beat the heads of American workers to defend German stockholders," commented Elizabeth Gurley Flynn.[47]

In April, Norman Thomas, the Socialist leader and a member of the National Committee of the ACLU, along with Freda Kirchwey of *The Nation* and other distinguished individuals, went to Garfield to speak in a vacant lot in defiance of the Bergen County sheriff's virtual imposition of martial law. Thomas was arrested on charges of violating the state's "riot act," held on $10,000 bail, and later released but not before he had characterized New Jersey as a "slave state." Immediately, the ACLU started proceedings to obtain an injunction preventing the sheriff from again violating civil liberties. When the Reverend John Haynes Holmes and Arthur Garfield Hays went to Belmont Park to speak under ACLU auspices, dozens of armed police prepared to arrest them. At this point, the ACLU injunction was served on the sheriff, restraining him and his deputies from interfering with the meeting. The result was a victory—freedom for the strikers to hold their mass meetings in Belmont Park.[48]

Through the American Civil Liberties Union, Robert W. Dunn became deeply involved in the Passaic strike, The ACLU began a campaign to win freedom of speech and assembly for the strikers. On April 12, as Dunn ended a speech to five thousand workers, club-wielding police routed the strikers and arrested Dunn, along with six others. The Sheriff felt that "the backbone" of the strike had been broken by the arrest of "nearly all the leaders and particularly that of

'Dunn,' the jailed Weisbord's successor." "An idea," writes Gloria Garrett Samson, "that must have amused everyone. Dunn was merely
acting as an ACLU representative and had no official connection
with the strike or its membership." Oswald Garrison Villard offered
"to go" Dunn's $10,000 bail. Dunn's arrest prompted Socialist leader
Norman Thomas to go to Passaic, where he spoke out in protest and
was also arrested.

On June 25th, 250 organizations representing a quarter of a million workers sent delegates to support the Passaic Strike Conference,
where they were addressed by Elizabeth Gurley Flynn for the Garland
Fund* and Robert Dunn, out on bail, for the ACLU.

Because many strikers faced lengthy prison terms, the ACLU and
the International Labor Defense established the Joint Committee for
Passaic Defense to raise defense funds apart from strike relief. But
the police brutality never let up. Horses were ridden into the strikers'
lines by the police. Fire hoses, clubbings, and tear gas failed to break
their spirit. After one vicious attack on their lines, the renewed picketing was led by Elizabeth Kovacs, pushing a baby carriage. Nor were
the children spared. The presence of fifty school children at the
head of a mass of 2,500 strikers meant nothing to the police, who
attacked the demonstration, clubbing children as well as adults.[49] On
April 10, five thousand schoolchildren paraded alone, led by "a
dozen boys and girls bearing a large American flag." Barely had the
parade started when a detachment of police ordered the children
back. When they resisted, the police attacked. "Considerable disor-
der followed," reported the *New York Times*. "Excited mothers rushed
hither and thither among the scattering mass of children in search of
their own boys and girls." The next day's headline read: "Passaic
Police Rout Children's Parade. 5000 Youngsters Scatter in Disor-
der."[50]

On July 26, the Passaic police charged and clubbed a delegation
of 350 members of the Furriers' Union of New York who were parading in support of the textile strikers. The fur workers arrived in
busses and found the police awaiting them. Chief of Police Zober
objected to placards carried by the furriers reading: "Down with the

_____

* The Garland Fund, another name for the American Fund for Public Service, was
organized by Charles Garland in the summer of 1922 after he had turned down an
inheritance for his own personal use. (See Gloria Garrett Samson, "Toward a New
Social Order: The American Fund For Public Service: Clearing House for Radicalism
in the 1920s," unpublished Ph.D. dissertation, University of Rochester, 1987, pp. 33-
50.)

bosses." "All workers must stick with the textile strikers." When the delegation refused to discard the placards, the police charged. Six fur workers were arrested, four of them women, and a number were severely beaten.[51]

The strike strategy called for extending the strike to include the silk mill workers of Paterson and vicinity. Strikers in Lodi, where the dye houses were located, were active in this struggle. The police were particularly brutal in their treatment of these strikers, especially the women. Maggie Pittocco, a seventeen-year-old striker, was "repeatedly dragged from the picket line," and Reta Verlie "was so hurt when knocked down by a police officer that she had to be taken for an operation." When Sam Elam, a Black picket, went to her assistance, he was arrested and jailed.[52]

On July 23, Frances Riburdo, one of the striking textile workers from the United Piece Dye Works in Lodi, addressed a mass meeting of Paterson dye workers. She herself had already been on strike for twenty-five weeks, and her speech was hailed by Elizabeth Gurley Flynn as the "best speech to textile workers I have heard in fifteen years' association with the labor movement."[53]

"I've been working in the mills at Lodi since I was a bit of a girl," Riburdo began, "I've been there seven years now. Maybe I'll be there the rest of my life. That's why I want a union." Her wages were 18 cents an hour for working in the dye house, "breathing poison, getting poison on your hands." Then, when she and others went on strike, the boss came and said to her:

> "Those leaders of yours are against religion. They're Socialists." I asked the boss: "When you hired us you didn't care what religion we are, you only wanted us to work, work, work. Now, why you suddenly interested in our religion?" So I told the boss: "I don't care who our leaders are. I'm glad they woke us up. We should have been wise to our conditions long ago. These leaders helped us to get wise. That's more than you ever did. So lay off that religion stuff."
>
> Nobody, no, not even the boss, can tell us anything now. For we have the union in back of us. The union makes us men and women instead of slaves. It keeps the boss from squeezing the life out of us, and then throwing us away. Before the strike, the bosses would not rush us so much if we brought them a bottle of wine now and then or give 'em a kiss. No, I never gave the boss a kiss, or brought him a bottle of wine. That's why they call me a Bolshevik now. Because I tell the truth about the bosses."[54]

All accounts of the Passaic strike emphasized the important role played by the women strikers and their allies. Vera Buch (later Vera Buch Weisbord), a member of the Workers' Party and one of the strike organizers, considered this the most important aspect of the entire strike. She wrote in October, 1926:

> Labor leaders may well study the marvel of a strike that is still strong after ten months. The organized participation of the women had much to do with the remarkable vitality of the strike .... They had their own mass meetings where the issues of the strike and the problems of their own lives were explained to them. Then the Working Women's Councils were organized, which drew in not only the striking women but the wives of strikers and sympathizers. The United Council of Working Housewives opened kitchens for the children which the women themselves conducted. The Women's Councils went in for strike work with scabs and on the picket line. They raised money for relief. The housewives took charge of the strikers' children at the Victory Playground. An organization of women has been built up which has not only been a powerful support of the strike, but which the women will maintain after the strike is settled.[55]

INVITATION TO UNITED TEXTILE WORKERS

Various attempts were made to settle the strike. The Associated Societies and Churches of Passaic, composed of Poles, Slovaks, Russians, and Hungarians, in conjunction with a blue-ribbon panel of Protestant laymen, attempted and failed to achieve conciliation between employers and workers. Originally neutral, the organization later condemned the "Kaiser-like" attitude of management, sent a delegation of priests, ministers and laymen to Washington to urge a federal investigation, It also sponsored a mammoth Sunday afternoon parade to publicize the workers' conditions, and advocated the recall of Commissioner Abram Preiskel and John McGure, the city's mayor.[56]

The recall movement failed. So did all attempts to end the strike by mediation led by a citizens' committee, the Passaic Chamber of Commerce and another citizens' committee organized by the American Civil Liberties Union. In mid-March, 1926, Secretary of Labor Davis, after conferring with the mill owners, proposed that the strikers go back to work with their demands to be arbitrated afterward, but the workers turned down this proposal.[57]

On March 28, Albert Weisbord appealed to the AFL Executive Council for support. This was quickly rejected: President William Green made it clear that the Federation would deal only with the United Textile Workers and would have nothing to do with the "Communist-dominated United Front Committee."[58] However, the workers' determination to fight on was not daunted by the rebuff, by the wholesale arrests of leaders of the United Front Committee, by the most drastic temporary injunction in New Jersey history, (secured on April 16 by the Forstmann & Huffman Company, it forbid picketing, advising, encouraging, or consulting with employees of the company), or by any of the other attempts to intimidate the strikers. They continued to take their places on the picket lines even when they knew they would be attacked, and they refused to be driven back into the mills.[59]

In the wake of the fur workers' 40-hour settlement on June 11, the United Front Committee hoped that precedents had been set in that employers had bargained with Ben Gold, a Communist, and that the AFL had, however grudgingly, accepted Gold's leadership. The *Textile Strike Bulletin* rejoiced: "Victory of Fur Workers Will Carry Passaic Over the Top."[60] However, such a breakthrough did not occur. Despite widespread publicity unfavorable to the employers and the local authorities, no serious negotiations occurred. Spokespersons for the AFL indicated that the federation would probably enter the strike if the strikers invited the United Textile Workers to take it over but they also made it clear that Weisbord and his associates had to be eliminated from any connection with the strike.[61]

After a series of discussions, the Workers' Party and the TUEL reached the decision that "it would be incorrect to let the issue of communism stand in the way of a settlement," even though it meant that Weisbord and other communists in the UFC leadership would have to step aside. Weisbord opposed the decision, but finally agreed to step down as strike leader. He insisted, however, that the United Front Committee must remain and be taken in as a body by the AFL.

On August 12, a committee selected by the strikers conferred with officials of the United Textile Workers. An agreement was reached that the UTW should take over the strike, that Weisbord and his associates would withdraw, and that only actual workers in the Passaic mills would be taken into the AFL. Weisbord wrote to the committee and gave his specific promise to withdraw from the affairs of the union immediately upon the issuance of a charter to the strikers' organization. The United Textile Workers thereupon issued the charter for Local 1603 to the United Front Committee, Weisbord sent a public letter of resignation, and the United Textile Workers took over the leadership of the Passaic strike.[62]

The strikers chose as president of their new local Gustave Deak, a young striker who had worked closely with the Communists during the strike. Moreover, Rebecca Gratz, a Communist who had been active in relief work for the strikers before the UTW takeover now worked as field organizer of the Relief Committee of the Passaic Textile Strike, representing the new local. She traveled all over the country appealing for financial help for the strikers.[63]

Both UTW Vice-President James Starr, who was now in charge of the strike, and UTW President Thomas McMahon were convinced that they could achieve a quick settlement by just changing the tone of the strike—by employing fewer outside speakers and fewer posters to attract attention to the injustices from which the strikers suffered. But they were no more successful than their predecessors.

Before the AFL took over the strike, the mill representatives had indicated that they would probably be willing to deal with such an organization, but now that the United Front Committee, which the mill owners had claimed was plotting a "revolution" hatched in Moscow, was replaced by the United Textile Workers, the owners decided that they could not even deal with the conservative AFL and refused to consider a settlement under any circumstances.[64]

The strike dragged on but by November 1926, the strikers' resources showed signs of becoming exhausted. Alfred Wagenknecht, who had remained at his post as relief administrator and was one of the leading Communists in the organization of the strike, reported to a group of New York sympathizers that the landlords who had up to that point allowed the strikers to avoid rent payments to help them conserve their funds, were beginning to evict strikers who failed to meet payments. More serious was the fact that the surplus of $100,000 that the strikers had had in their relief treasury at the end of June was completely used up.[65]

END OF THE PASSAIC STRIKE

However, the strikers' determination, together with the demand from newspapers, citizens' committees, and ministers for a settlement, and the adverse publicity resulting from the violations of civil liberties, produced results. A "Committee of Five" made up of local residents and including three clergymen, succeeded where others had failed. On November 12, 1926, the first break came in the Passaic strike when the Passaic Worsted Company signed an agreement based on the following terms: (1) recognition of the union; (2) the right of the workers to bargain collectively; (3) no discrimination in rehiring; (4) arbitration of further disputes) and (5) no outside help to be engaged until all the strikers were reemployed. Since the wage cut had been rescinded before the settlement, it was not part of the agreement. Six hundred workers on strike at the mill met and voted to accept the agreement. "This is the first time in the history of Passaic," reported the *New York Times*, "that one of the larger concerns has formally recognized the American Federation of Labor and has conceded to its workers the right to organize."[66]

The Botany Mills came to terms with their striking workers on December 13 and, with minor exceptions, the agreement was similar to that of the Passaic Worsted Company. The Garfield Worsted Mill and the Dundee Textile Company then settled, restoring the wage cut and accepting the same terms as the other companies. These terms were also ratified by the strikers.[67]

But the Forstmann & Huffman plant still refused to come to terms. On February 14, 1927, the workers still on strike voted to bring their walkout to an end They did so without winning any agreement other than the company's assurance that it would "endeavor to reemploy as many of our former workers as we possibly can, without discrimination."

The Gera and New Jersey Worsted strikers voted to resume work on February 16 on the basis of their right to affiliate with the AFL and to be reemployed without discrimination. The United Piece Dye Works' strikers were the last to return. The only concession granted them was an oral promise by management not to discriminate in rehiring. On March 1, 1927, the great Passaic Textile Strike came to an end.[68]

The Communist Party and the TUEL viewed the outcome as a victory. Albert Weisbord, terming it "a great victory for the left wing," argued that as a result of its policies and tactics, the "wage-cutting campaign has been definitely stopped [and] a smashing blow has been given to the company union!" "This is the greatest labor victory of the year," exulted the *Daily Worker.* Furthermore, Passaic had clearly

> ... demonstrated woman's ability as a fighter in the cause of labor. It was the simple, unpolished women, mothers of families, who gave battle to the textile barons of Passaic ... who aroused the attention of the entire country to the shameful conditions prevailing in Passaic mills. With their babes in arms, they braved the Cossacks with their gas bombs on the picket line. Misery and starvation had brought these women together and taught them the lesson of solidarity.

"Can the Woman Worker be organized?" asked a workingwoman in the *Daily Worker*, and the paper answered:

> That women workers are highly organizable was demonstrated by the splendid, militant part they played in the Passaic strike, where they dis-

played much of the fiery spirit, the courage and the determination that characterized the strike.

Theresa Wolfson, a keen student of women and the labor movement, described the Passaic strike as "an epoch-making example of the ability of women workers to fight for what they consider to be their economic rights," and went on to note:

> At the beginning of the strike, the thousands of women of different nationalities could not understand one another and had nothing but their jobs in the same factory in common. After tramping on the picket lines, working in the food kitchens, attending mass meetings, and classes in English, for an entire year, these women were forged into union material, despite their language differences, their maturity, and their social problems

This "union material" ultimately produced "a union organization in a community where hitherto there had been none."[69]

For the time being, however, the situation was anything but optimistic. At a meeting of the National Committee of the TUEL, the following report was received:

> Union in Passaic has less than 200 members, 8,000 unemployed in Passaic. Agreements are broken down completely. Mills fire employees and then rehire them at cut wages as new workers. Members of the union have been eliminated entirely from the mills. Workers asked why they should pay $1 a month to the union. There are no answers. The(y) question, they drop out.[70]

EVALUATION OF STRIKE

The outcome of the Passaic strike left many dissatisfied, and this feeling increased over the next few years. While the result had been a victory for the strikers in the short run, few of the terms of the agreement were actually enforced and most were simply disregarded by the companies. Since it was the United Textile Workers and not the United Front Committee which emerged as the union representing the Passaic strikers, this could have been predicted. The UTW was not interested in mobilizing the membership for struggle to uphold the terms of the agreement. In fact, the membership became so disillusioned with the policies of the UTW that they abandoned the organization in droves. In less than two years, the union of twelve thousand was down to less than one hundred, and soon it disappeared altogether.[71]

It was not long after the strike that a feeling emerged in left-wing circles that the Communist leaders had made a mistake in agreeing to the terms for the takeover of the strike leadership by the United Textile Workers. Both Weisbord and his wife expressed bitter disagreement with the decision,* and Bert Cochran has charged recently that Weisbord was "forced to step out at Moscow's order, and that it was simply the result of a 'zig-zag' in Communist policy internationally—that it was an improvised and ill-conceived application of the Communist International's Sixth Plenum's campaign against the "ultra-left."[72]

However, the Comintern pronouncement against "formation of parallel unions" was not issued until the summer of 1926, and Weisbord had been trying to bring the AFL into the strike since March. Moreover, the *Daily Worker* did not view the Weisbord removal as an application of a new principle, but as bowing to expediency. The Communist paper criticized Weisbord's "forced withdrawal" as "merely another phase of the expulsion policy invoked by the Labor officialdom to insure the continued rule of reaction."[73] Later William Z. Foster described the "mistake ... of affiliating the Passaic textile strikers to the AFL, even at the expense of eliminating the Communist leadership" as a "wrong policy" and a "serious error." Foster acknowledged that the TUEL was "severely criticized" by the Red International of Labor Unions, based in Moscow, for its "whole course of action" in the Passaic strike.[74]**

This controversy cannot erase the fact that the Passaic strikers, under Communist leadership, exhibited labor solidarity at its highest level, which remained as an important symbol in American labor history, that gave substance to that symbolism, that was the concrete achievement of turning back wage reductions in an industry that was already paying at levels insufficient to maintain "an American standard of living!"[75]

Before leaving the Passaic strike, it is worth including the following report. On June 25, 1926, Robert Dunn of the ACLU chaired the "Support the Passaic Strike Conspiracy," held in New York City. The conference pledged itself to raise $30,000 to aid the Passaic strikers

---

* Weisbord insisted that while he "gave his word to comply," he resented the decision and did not vote in favor of it. He and his wife, Vera Buch Weisbord, charged further that the Communist Party leaders were "only too glad" to get rid of him. (Albert Weisbord, "Critical Moments in Textile Strikes," *Class Struggle* 1 [1930]:5; Vera Buch Weisbord, *A Radical Life* [Bloomington and London,1977] pp. 130-31.)

** Cochran fails to mention this criticism by the Red International of Labor Unions. (Bert Cochran, *Labor and Communism: The Conflict That Shaped American Unions*, [Princeton, N.J., 1977), p. 32.]

To raise the funds, Alfred Wagenknecht, a Workers' (Communist) Party leader, and Relief Chairman, General Relief Committee, proposed "Methods of Raising Money." It declared:

1. All unions, fraternal organizations and sympathetic organizations must again open their treasuries for the strikers. Money in the treasuries must be made to work for the labor movement in order that it may grow.
2. Make another shop collection.
3. Assess your membership.
4. Collect contributions of food.
5. Distribute your contribution lists among your members so that their friends may have the opportunity to help win the strike.
6. Help the Children's Campaign: Meals for the strikers' children. Buy a seal and you buy a meal for a textile striker's child. Milk Fund—Milk Tickets. Take strikers' children into your homes and camps. Make it possible for every striker's child to get its much needed outing!
7. Sell HELL IN NEW JERSEY, the Textile Strikers Pictorial. Every time a Pictorial is sold a meal is bought for a striker's child.
8. MOTION PICTURE of the textile strikers' struggle will be ready soon. Prepare to have it shown in your neighborhood! Prepare to see it.[76]*

---

*Steven J. Ross notes that the Passaic strike produced "the only labor movie that has remained virtually intact." It was produced by Alfred Wagenknecht; it was distributed by International Workers Art (IWA), created by the Workers' (Communist) Party in the 1920s for making films and newsreels and distributing Russian movies in the USA. (Steven J. Ross, "Struggles on the Screen: Workers, Radicals, and the Political Uses of Silent Film," *American Historical Review* 96 [April, 1991]:355.)

CHAPTER 11

THE TEXTILE WORKERS: II

"The mill owners of New England are determined to force their workers to accept the same conditions that prevail in the cotton industry in the South, where child labor, the sixty-hour week, unrestrained exploitation and wages averaging ten and twelve dollars a week is the rule." So declared John J. Ballam, secretary of the National Textile Workers Progressive Committee and a leader of the Trade Union Educational League, in announcing the New England Textile Conference to be held in Boston on February 20, 1927.[1] The Conference voted "to form local textile progressive committees in every textile town in New England to organize resistance to the wage-slashing campaign of the bosses."[2]

One of the most important of the committees was organized in New Bedford, Massachusetts.

CONDITIONS IN THE NEW BEDFORD MILLS

Although the mills of New Bedford were run by an "inefficient and antiquated management structure" in which "nepotistic control" dominated,[3] they were more modern and sanitary than those in Passaic. There was no night work for women. Living conditions were also far superior to those in Passaic. New Bedford is a seaside city, and the mills were built on the water. The mill workers' homes were clean and tidy, but the wages of these workers, who produced the finest cotton goods in the United States, were incredibly low even compared with those of the Passaic textile workers. Average weekly earnings in New Bedford, according to the reports of the Massachusetts Department of Labor for 1927, were $19.95, and for the first three months of 1928, they were down to $19.00. Yet in 1927, a New

Bedford family of five needed $2,204.04 per year to maintain standards of health and decency. Since the average New Bedford earnings were $1,037.40, the mill workers were receiving less than half of what was needed to provide a living wage for a family.

Nor did these average earnings tell the entire story. Women employed in the mills for as long as five years were making $8 and $10 a week. Not surprisingly, mothers as well as fathers had to go into the mills and children were sent to work as soon as the law allowed. Lodgers were a common feature of life in the families of mill workers.

Then at the beginning of April, 1928, the New Bedford Cotton Manufacturers' Association cut wages by 10 percent. The owners justified the reduction by referring to Southern competition. However, according to the *Springfield Republican*, it was actually management's response to the state legislature's refusal to modify the laws governing night work. In any event, on April 16, five to six thousand of the skilled workers, members of the American Federation of Textile Operatives (AFTO), walked out. They were led by the New Bedford Textile Council.

The Textile Council was made up of seven craft unions representing 8,000 of New Bedford's 30,000 textile operatives. The locals, consisting of Loom Fixers, Mule Spinners, Weavers, Ring Twisters, Slasher Tenders, Carders and Ring Spinners, and Warp Twisters, were affiliated with the American Federation of Textile Operatives, a national organization of textile workers independent of the American Federation of Labor. But in April and May, 1928, the locals joined the United Textile Workers, affiliated with the AFL.

Whether independent or affiliated with the AFL, the unions that made up the Textile Council represented only the skilled workers, most of whom were native-born and English-speaking. The Portuguese, predominantly unskilled, were discriminated against by the companies and the craft unions. They received the dirtiest and hardest jobs when they entered the mills, and were kept from advancing by the exclusivity of the craft unions. They were also excluded by the Textile Council when it called on the skilled workers to strike against the 10 percent wage cut.[4]

TUEL CALLS FOR STRIKE

The same day, April 16, that most of the skilled workers walked out, handbills were distributed among the unskilled and unorganized mill workers in New Bedford, urging them to strike; they were signed "Textile Mill Committee of New England." William L. Murdoch, secretary of the Committee, Fred E. Beal, Gus Deak, and Evan Stone had come to New Bedford to offer their aid to the Textile Council in bringing the unskilled workers into the strike. But the council leadership rejected their offer, and denounced the Textile Mill Committee as "communistic and a danger both to the unions and the manufacturer."[5]

Not in the least disturbed by this reaction, the Textile Mill Committee established a New Bedford branch in the city and announced its aim:

> Only 8,000 operatives are organized. About 27,000 remain free. It is our purpose to organize our committee from this free element, and members of the existing locals can join our group without hindrance and without relinquishing the membership they already have. We still stand ready to join with the New Bedford Textile Council even though they have refused our moral and financial support.[6]

The response of the unskilled mill workers to the strike leaflets was tremendous. On April 23, the press reported that "30,000 cotton workers, 60 percent of whom are female, struck 58 mills of the 27 companies affiliated to the New Bedford Textile Manufacturers' Association. Not a loom wove and not a spindle spun in even one of the mills as the workers went out in defiance of a 10 percent wage cut."[7]

Not only was the strike conducted separately by the New Bedford Textile Council and the New Bedford Textile Mill Committee, but the two organizations presented different demands. The Council demanded only the revocation of the 10 percent wage cut, while the Committee called for "a 20 percent increase in wages, the 8-hour day and 5-day week (40 hours), equal pay for men and women for equal work, and elimination of the speed-up system." In addition, the New Bedford Textile Mill Committee declared that in the event a mill closed down and moved South to operate with even lower wages and longer hours under non-union conditions,* the workers who were made unemployed thereby should set up an Unemployment Council of Textile Workers and seek to achieve the program adopted by the Trade Union Educational League to deal with such a situation. This included the demand for (a) work to be provided by the city and the state at prevailing union rates of wages; (b) maintenance of unem-

---

*There were many reports that the Manomet Mills of New Bedford, the largest cotton yarn manufacturing plant in the country, operating 318,000 spindles and employing between 4,500 and 5,000 workers, was preparing to close down indefinitely in the city and move to the South. (New Bedford *Evening Standard*, April 10, 19, 1928.)

ployed workers by means of a special unemployment fund to be created out of increased taxation on property; (c) the opening of food stations for the unemployed and provision of free fuel and clothing; (d) provision for free food for children in public schools; and (e) a moratorium on rents during the period of unemployment.[8]

CONDUCT OF NEW BEDFORD STRIKE

Not only were their demands different, but the New Bedford Textile Council and the New Bedford Textile Mill Committee handled their own relief measures separately. The Boston and New York branches of the Women's Trade Union League sent assistance to the Textile Council, and a New Bedford branch of the WTUL was established for the administration of relief programs.[9] Relief was a special problem for the unskilled, who were the lowest-paid workers, and the Textile Mill Committee, as leader of the strikers, worked energetically to meet the urgent need. Ann Washington Craton,[*] a veteran of the Passaic strike, was in charge of relief. As a result of her activity, Portuguese and Polish bakers contributed more than a hundred loaves of bread daily, while the South End grocery stores, sympathetic to the strikers, donated food supplies. Nearby, friendly farmers furnished potatoes and milk. In the main, however, the TMC had to look outside the community for aid. The Workers' International Relief, the organization set up by the Communists and their sympathizers, took over the work of raising funds and furnishing relief for the strikers organized by the Textile Mill Committee.[10]

Although officially in charge of relief, Ann Craton participated in every phase of the strike. She regularly addressed meetings of strikers. A reporter for the New Bedford *Evening Standard* wrote:

---

[*] Ann Washington Craton was born to wealth in North Carolina. As a college student in Washington, D.C., she had marched in cap and gown with fifteen thousand women in the suffrage parade that was brutally attacked by a jeering mob of men. After graduation from George Washington University in 1915, Craton worked briefly in a settlement house, and later as one of three hundred women field agents hired to gather statistics for the U.S. Bureau of Labor. After other labor activities, she joined the left wing of the Socialist Party. She received trade union experience as an assistant to Mary Heaton Vorse in the successful campaign by the Amalgamated Clothing Workers of America. (Alice Kessler-Harris, "The Autobiography of Ann Washington Craton," edited and with introduction, *Signs*, [Summer, 1976], pp. 1019-1037.)

The fact that only about 50 percent of the crowds she addresses understand English did not give Miss Craton any pause. She stands at the front of the platform, gestures little, speaks slowly and clearly, in simple language, repeats the expression, "Fellow Workers" constantly. Her face and manner draw the crowd. She gets applause .... A canvass of a typical audience reveals only one here and there who understands any question put to him in English. But these auditors stand quietly and listen to Ann Craton as she talks. The women sit, many of them with babes in their arms. The men stand behind the benches and against the wall.[11]

From the outset, Craton emphasized the importance of involving women in every aspect of strike activity. This was not a simple problem in New Bedford, where the Portuguese men looked with disfavor on activities by their wives and daughters that went beyond taking care of the family. Sophie Melvin, who came to New Bedford from Passaic, recalled later:

I actually saw the husbands become vicious against their wives who took a meaningful position in the union. I stayed with one family where one night, the wife, the two daughters and myself in the midst of winter had to get dressed and run out of the house because the husband came back drunk and he lashed out at his wife, primarily because she was at a meeting that night and spoke. It was horrible.[12]

But Sophie Melvin, Ann Craton and other militants insisted that women had to be active in the strike if the workers, male and female alike, were to have any chance of winning. Craton put it bluntly:

Women are better at this sort of thing than the men. They are more courageous than men. They will do more and suffer more. One of the distinctive sights in the Passaic strike was that of women with baby carriages leading the picket lines. Organize the women along with the men. Teach them to maintain the picket lines, and to organize collections, and let them learn to speak.[13]

And so, from the beginning, women constituted a major element of the pickets. Indeed, headlines in the New Bedford *Evening Standard* read: "Most of the Pickets Are Women," and "Four Out of Five Pickets Women." From the picket line, these women came to strike meetings and, some for the first time in their lives, spoke in public to audiences. A typical description of a strike meeting in the local press went:

A girl striker, Teresa Yolante, was the first speaker, introduced by another young girl, with alert features and bright black eyes, who cried: "I declare this meeting opened in the name of the Textile Mill Committee." Miss Volante, an attractive picture in light gray suit and scarlet hat, made an appeal for workers to collect money and to picket Monday morning. She was followed by Mr. Murdoch who spoke briefly and Miss Craton who spoke at more length. In fact, the meeting was dominated by women speakers, a number of whom spoke in Portuguese and Polish, and most of them were addressing audiences in public for the first time.[14]

When Murdoch and Beal were arrested and jailed for disturbing the peace, Ann Craton took over from the strike leaders. "I will lead you now," she told the strikers. "They have taken your leaders. But don't let them scare you! Other leaders will spring up to take their places. I am here to direct relief, but as long as it becomes necessary, I will lead you myself." She remained at the head of the strike committee for days until Murdoch and Beal were bailed out.[15]

"Children are rapidly becoming an important element in the strike here," the New Bedford *Evening Standard* observed on May 2, 1928. Under Elizabeth Donneley's leadership, clubs composed of boys and girls from five or six years old to ten and twelve were formed at the headquarters of the Textile Mill Committee. There they gathered after school each afternoon to hear talks by Donneley, to discuss the strike in their own words, to elect their own officers, to learn to sing the strike songs, and to shout the strike slogan:

Solidification, education, solidarity;
S–t–r–i–k–e;
Are we on strike? Yes, we are.
Strikers, strikers, rah! rah! rah!

Afterward, the children were fed "a substantial meal of bread and potato hash."

On April 30, children marched for the first time with their elders on the picket lines. "Keep the children out of it," cried the New Bedford *Evening Standard* indignantly. The New Bedford Textile Council called it a "crime" and "uncalled for"; the mayor of New Bedford termed it "contemptible," and the local Girl Scout Commissioner protested against "the child picket line."[16]

"It's the families' strike," replied Ann Craton. "For this work you need the women and their children." And she appealed directly to the women strikers:

You women who cannot leave your children at home, bring them with you. Let them understand what the strike means, so that when they have to go hungry, and when they have to go to school in ragged shoes, they will know why. Educate them to be good union men and women, for they are the workers of the future.

Nothing has a greater effect upon scabs than children. The presence of the little ones on the picket lines about the mills, singing strike songs and shouting, "Hey, you scab, don't take my dad's job!" has a tremendous influence.[17]

The children continued to picket the struck mills. "Marching thru the streets in strike demonstrations," one reporter wrote from New Bedford, "the children ... have done much to keep up the firm spirit of their parents."[18]

ARREST OF STRIKERS

On May 9, the first arrests occurred. For insisting on their right to continue picketing, two women strikers, Angelina Tsoupreas and Christina Simores, were arrested and charged with loitering and disturbing the peace. In court later, they were both placed on bail of $1,100 each, which was furnished by the Textile Mill Committee. Neither could speak English, and both pleaded not guilty through an interpreter. Both were back on the picket line at the Pennaquid mill the next morning.[19]

Three other strikers, two of them women, were arrested the next day. On May 23, all five of the arrested pickets were found guilty in the Third District Court, and three of them received harsh jail terms. Angelina Tsoupreas and Christina Simores, the first to be arrested, were sentenced to serve six months each in prison. Tsoupreas had an additional fine of $45 imposed on her, while Simores was fined $20. Frank Cunha, the only man arrested, was sentenced to thirty days in jail, while Mary Valente was fined $60, and Maria Silvia, $40. The International Labor Defense announced that the sentences would be appealed to higher courts.[20]

On June 10 Maria Katrikaros, called the "Ringleader of Strikers' Pickets," was arrested. Three days later, Elizabeth Donneley was arrested while she was leading children in singing on a picket line. The headline in the New Bedford *Evening Standard* the next day read: "Miss Donneley Arrested Leading Singing Children. Held in $300." Donneley stood in the women's dock and pleaded not guilty to the charge of disturbing the peace. "I've got a perfect right to sing," she told the judge. "I am an American and know my rights." But, as the *Standard* reported, she was held on $300 bail for trial later.[21]

At the same court session, a jail sentence of thirty days was imposed on Bessie Katrikaros, an eighteen-year-old weaver and sister of Maria, for shouting: "Tell the scabs to go to hell!" As she was pushed into the police wagon, she cried out: "God gave me my voice, and God is the only one who will keep me quiet!"[22]

Eula Figueredo was another of the Portuguese women strikers in and out of jail during the strike. By August 2, A.C. Gonzales Pinto, picket leader of the strike, had been jailed twelve times.[23]

Despite the arrests and jail sentences, the strikers stood firm. In July, when the owners attempted to reopen the plants under police and National Guard protection only about twenty workers returned.[24] One of the most dramatic events in the New Bedford strike took place when a rumor spread that eight scabs had started the looms in the Kilburn mill. It brought out eighteen thousand strikers, who continued to picket throughout the night. Pickets in fishermen's boats kept guard at the waterfront in what the New Bedford *Evening Standard* acknowledged was a "tremendous demonstration of workers' solidarity."[25]

At this point, the authorities stepped up their repression. Mass picketing was ruled illegal, and the militia continued to guard the mills. Arrests of strikers began to mount. Sadie Reisch, the Women's Trade Union League organizer, was among the hundreds of women arrested for picketing, and she was ordered to move out of her YWCA room. On July 13, the court imposed six months' jail sentences and $20 fine on each of 37 strikers tried on that day. They had been arrested for picketing on July 6. The International Labor Defense announced that all cases would be appealed immediately. Release of the strikers during the appeal required raising $20,000 in bail bonds.[26]

Day after day the New Bedford *Evening Standard* reported the number of pickets arrested. A typical report read:

> Four strikers arrested this morning. Three of them are women. Maria Valente, Laura Nunes, Joseph Gomez, and 16-year-old Blanche Almeda, after twice being driven away from the factory gates by a squad of police, came back to reform the picket line for the third time, which resulted in the arrest on charges of peace disturbance and loitering. Gemina Medieros, strike committee member, on her way to a meeting at union headquarters, was also arrested on a warrant issued against her on charges of "disturbing the peace."[27]

But neither arrests nor imprisonment could stem the strikers' militancy. On July 22, John Sullivan, president of the New Bedford Cotton Manufacturers' Association, declared that the Mill Committee's influence was growing: "Not only are they getting members from among the unorganized workers, but they are taking many members away from the established union, because some workers like aggressive tactics."[28]

STRIKE SPREADS TO FALL RIVER

In nearby Fall River, where 28,000 cotton workers were employed, representatives of fifteen textile mills met on April 22 to organize the Textile Mill Committee. The action followed reports that a ten percent wage cut was being prepared by the mill owners. Late in June, the announcement came of the wage cut. The Mill Committee immediately distributed the following leaflet at all Fall River mills:

FIGHT THE WAGE CUT
Join the Textile Mill Committee.

TEXTILE WORKERS:

The old wage scale must come back! No compromise. Every worker must organize and be prepared to fight to wipe out these wage cuts. Only T.M.C. comes with a fighting plan to the workers. The A.F.T.O. officials...do everything in their power to prevent a strike. The U.T.W. officials... jump around and do nothing....

Over in New Bedford the Textile Mill Committee has organized the workers and is leading them in a great fight against the bosses there. We must do the same here. The Fall River workers can fight just as the New Bedford workers can. Now is the time to fight!...

Fellow Workers:

Now is the time to join the T.M.C. The quicker we grow the quicker the bosses will take back the wage cut. The stronger we get the better we can fight. The sooner we begin to fight the better for ourselves and for our Textile brothers in New Bedford.

Don't delay. Now is the time. Come to our office at 161 So. Main Street, Room 6. Open every day: 9-11 A.M., 3-9 P.M.

And Join Up!

TEXTILE MILL COMMITTEE
Fall River Unit
Watch for our Big Mass Meeting Soon![29]

When the police of Fall River stopped a meeting called by the Textile Mill Committee, the Committee promptly issued a leaflet proclaiming:

POLICE STOP MEETING OF TEXTILE WORKERS
WHY?
BECAUSE THE MILL OWNERS OF FALL RIVER AND NEW
BEDFORD ARE AFRAID THAT A
REAL UNION WILL BE ORGANIZED
AND
A FIGHT FOR THE RESTORATION OF THE 10% WAGE CUT

WILL FOLLOW
THEY ARE RIGHT
     The Workers will organize and the Workers will Fight Even as the New
Bedford Workers Are Doing.30

On August 6, in response to a call from the Textile Mill Committee, 3,000 workers walked out of the American Printing Company in Fall River. Immediately the city was placed under martial law. Solid police cordons were thrown across the viaducts leading to the American Printing Company, and patrol wagons were drawn up at the curb, ready for mass arrests. When the strikers attempted to break through the police wall to picket the mill, men and women were clubbed and arrested. A pregnant woman striker was crushed against the iron railing of the viaduct and beaten by the police. She was taken, bleeding to the hospital. But the strike continued and spread to other mills in Fall River.31

As the strike progressed, the American Federation of Textile Operatives merged with the Textile Mill Committee, and its name was changed to the New Bedford Textile Workers' Union. Claiming six thousand members, many of them Portuguese and a large number women, the Communist textile union in New Bedford was prepared to carry on the struggle to victory. Mass picketing continued as did police clubbings and arrests.32 Meanwhile, a citizens' Mediation Committee, in collaboration with the Massachusetts State Board of Conciliation and Arbitration, proposed a compromise offer from the mill owners of a 5 percent wage cut. Although the New Bedford Textile Workers' Union insisted that the strikers hold out for their original demands, the United Textile Workers' officials, having raised only the single demand of revocation of the 10 percent wage cut, accepted the settlement offer, subject to a vote by the strikers.33

   Two ballots had to be taken before the compromise was accepted. The first vote rejected the offer, and the authenticity of the count on the second vote was questioned by a number of observers. Left-wing leaders were arrested to keep them in jail while the second vote was being taken, and Robert W. Dunn, who was at the scene, charged that the results were announced by the New Bedford *Evening Standard* a half hour before the voting ended. Actually, only two thousand workers voted on the final ballot, and the compromise was accepted by only a small margin.34

The New Bedford Textile Workers' Union tried to prolong the strike until several of the original demands were won. A drive was launched to provide "adequate clothing and shoes for the strikers and their children," and a store was set up in New York City to be used as a central receiving station for articles to be shipped to New Bedford and Fall River.[35]

"Three kids in our class saved up and we are sending the New Bedford strikers $2.90. It took us a month to save this money so we have to give up candy and movies." This letter to the Workers' International Relief was from Martha Rose, 12, of Chicago. "When we heard the strikers' children didn't have enough to eat," Martha continued, "I got two other girls in my class to give up candy and movies because we thought it wasn't right for us to have a good time while strikers' children were hungry. So here is our money order."[36]

But with the workers facing winter without any resources, the strike could not be maintained. On October 7, 1928, the Fall River Cotton Manufacturers' Association granted thirty thousand textile workers a wage increase of 5-1/2 percent. (Although the American Printing Company was not an association member, the three thousand workers received the same increase.) Since wages had been cut 10 percent in Fall River, the wages in both Fall River and New Bedford were now about the same.[37]

END OF STRIKE

On October 12, 1928, the longest strike in the history of the New England textile industry came to an end when the New Bedford Textile Workers' Union released its members from further "strike obligations." During the 26 weeks of the strike, a total of 2,000 arrests occurred, and 662 strikers had been indicted on 882 counts. Every defendant was convicted in the lower courts on practically all counts. Sentences were meted out to individual strikers from six months to three years, amounting to a grand total for all the strikers of 112 years of jail sentences and over $6,000 in fines.[38]

The New Bedford Textile Workers' Union insisted that these sacrifices by the strikers had not been in vain, for they had "succeeded in halting the terrific wave of wage cuts that was sweeping the country at that time."[39] The left-wing union also took satisfaction from the fact that it had enrolled about 6,000 members in the city.* Some of these members proved instrumental, during the

---

* "There wasn't a single Communist in New Beford before the strike," wrote A. B. Magil, who covered the strike for the *Daily Worker*. "Now there is a Party branch with over a hundred members, nearly all of them mill workers, a Young Workers League with about 90 members, and a branch of the Young Pioneers, embracing several hundred strikers' children."(*Daily Worker*, Sept. 27, 1928.)

latter stages of the strike, in organizing the Communist-led National Textile Workers Union. (NTWU). Others from nearby Fall River also joined the NTWU to make the New Bedford area the strongest center of the new organization.[39]*

As we shall see below, the National Textile Workers Union reflected a changed Communist trade union policy. Instead of concentrating almost entirely on "boring-from-within" (trying to transform existing unions) through the Trade Union Educational League, the new policy advocated placing more emphasis on the formation of independent unions to oppose the conservative AFL affiliates—with the aim of achieving what William Z. Foster called "the greatest and most pressing task now confronting the working class—the organization of the unorganized."[40]

---

* Even after the strike ended, 25 Communist leaders were indicted by a New Bedford grand jury on charges of "conspiracy to violate the city ordinance forbidding parades without a permit and conspiracy to disturb the peace."

CHAPTER 12

LABOR AND FASCISM

In March, 1919 Benito Mussolini, the former ardent Socialist,* organized the reactionary *fasci* in Italy. By the summer of 1920, there were one hundred organized groups of the fascist movement. By February 1921, the fasci had grown to more than a thousand groups. "Every day armed bands selected from the dregs and scum of the Italian gutters and recruited from the jails, the most savage, bloodthirsty gangsters go about ... setting fires to the Chambers of Labor, Leagues and Circles," the Italian-American anti-fascist paper *Il Martellos* (the Hammer) reported in April 1921. "There bands of assassins are known as the 'Fighting Fascist.' In fact they fight the poor at the order of the rich."[1]

Mussolini marched into Rome in 1922, and with the assistance of the Monarchy and the Roman Catholic Church, established the Fascist dictatorship in Italy. Coming to power on October 30, 1922, the *Duce* of Fascism consolidated his dictatorship in 1924-25, in the process almost totally restricting the liberty of the Italian people.[2]

Soon after Fascism appeared in Italy, it made its appearance in the United States. Black shirt squads were organized throughout the country, and began immediately popularizing the slogans that "Mussolini made the trains run on time," and that "Fascism is the antidote to Communism and Bolshevism."

Soon the Fascist League of North America, headed by Count Thaon DeRevel, was established, and every Italian in the United States who was in business with Italy had to become member.

---

* Before the war, Benito Mussolini was the editor of *Avanti*, central organ of the Socialist Party of Italy.

Through threats or the use of money, the Fascist League of North America turned the Italian-American press into a vehicle of propaganda for fascism in the United States. Organizations or individuals who refused to join the League were attacked and blacklisted. Their relatives in Italy were threatened or arrested.[3]

In April 1923, August Bellanca, a leader of the Amalgamated Clothing Workers of America (ACWA) returned from Italy. He was the first American labor representative to bring back an impression of the country since Mussolini had come to power as head of the Fascist government. Bellanca reported that Mussolini had "destroyed many of the labor unions and reorganized them into Fascisti unions on a program opposed to strikes, and stressing 'cooperation' between capital and labor" "Nearly every publication issued today," he continued, "is a government organ and partly subsidized by the government. The greatest part of the labor press has been destroyed by Black Shirt mobs. Every non-Fascist publication is subject to strict censorship. No wonder Fascism is encouraged in this country by the enemies of the labor movement."[4]

Bellanca was correct. Mussolini's regime was viewed favorably by the U.S. government, by industrialists and financiers, and as we shall see, even by Samuel Gompers, then AFL president. Almost the entire American press joined in the approval of Fascism.[5] But there was also from the beginning of the Fascist dictatorship voices of opposition in the United States, especially among Italian-Americans, even though many in the Italian community were mesmerized by *Il Duce*'s charisma. "America's first organized opposition to Fascism originated in the Italian-American labor movement," notes John P. Diggins.[6]

In April a cluster of labor organizations in New York created the Anti-Fascist Alliance of North America (AFANA),* which they hoped would become the focus of opposition to Mussolini's government. The AFANA was a socialist, syndicalist organization that revolved around the newspaper *Il Nueva Mondo* (New York), and was financed in part by funds from Local 89 of the ILGWU. Luigi Antonini, Local 89's general secretary, was one of a small group of syndicalists, anarchists, socialists, and labor organizers who initiated the anti-Fascist movement in the United States, and who continued to play a key role in these early years of Italian-American anti-Fascism.

* The organization was also known as the North American Anti-Fascist Alliance

Most of them had emigrated to the United States at the turn of the century with records of labor militancy in Italy.[7] Atonini worked closely with such men as Frank and August Bellanca of the Amalgamated Clothing Workers, the Socialists Girolamo Valenti, Giuseppe Lapis, and Vinni Montana, and the anarchist Carlo Tresca, all leaders of the Italian-American left and of the Italian-American anti-Fascist movement.[8]

Although predominantly made up of Italian-American labor activists, the AFANA was heartily endorsed by the Central Labor Union of New York, the ILGWU, ACW, TUEL, and hundreds of labor unions.[9] "In Italy the Fascisti have made it a crime to belong to a real labor union," an officer of the AFANA told the press. "Hundreds of Labor Temples are in ashes. Thousands of our best fighters in labor's battles have been murdered . Tens of thousands have been imprisoned and mistreated . Shall we wait until they are strong enough to do likewise in America, or shall we organize against them now.?"[10]

"Welcome the Anti-Fascist Alliance," declared the *Labor Herald*, organ of the TUEL. "It is of great importance that the Anti-Fascist Alliance should receive the complete cooperation and support of every militant unionist. Those desiring to assist in the work of preventing the Fascisti from getting a foothold in America and to help combat the blackshirts generally, should communicate with the Anti-Fascist Alliance, 231 East 14th Street, New York City."[11]

"Anti-Fascist United Front," was the headline in the *Industrial Worker*, organ of the IWW, in its issue of April 21, 1923. The article reported that "the attempt to organize the fascist groups in America had led to the formation of a vast anti-fascist UNITED FRONT."

Along with the formation of the Anti-Fascist Alliance of North America, the Italian Chamber of Labor, an independent body representing all the Italian local unions of New York City, and with a membership of 150,000, called a conference which was held on April 3, 1923, at the Italian Labor Center in New York. Over 100 delegates, representing local and central bodies of the Workers' (Communist) Party, Socialist Party, IWW, the ACW, ILGWU, the Mosaic and Terrace Workers, the Amalgamated Foodstuff Workers, the Journeymen Barbers, and other unions unanimously approved a plan of action for an anti-Fascist campaign proposed by the AFANA. The activities discussed and adopted included

a vast propaganda campaign by means of the printed as well as the spoken word in all the Italian centers of this country. Speakers will be routed across the country in order to present the fascist movement to the workers in its true light. A servile and corrupt daily press has consistently lied to the great mass of the Italian workers as to the character and aims of the Fascisti; this lying propaganda will be counteracted by the publicity planned. The movement will not limit itself to illuminating the Italian workers as to the danger of the fascist theories and activities to organized labor, but will present this problem to American labor also. The fascist groups in America will ... degenerate into subsidized agencies of GUN-MEN AND SCABS, maneuvered by American capitalists in order to destroy American labor organization. The Italian Chamber of Labor and the new anti-Fascist united front will bring this aspect of the situation before the highest councils of the American Federation of Labor in order to force official action in the matter.

Besides these purely defensive steps, the Anti-Fascist United Front, centered around the AFANA, planned to launch an offensive against the Fascist regime in Italy "because of its savage oppression and persecution of the Italian organized workers." The immigrants living in the United States would be told to boycott Italian products, withhold remittances and deposits from all Italian state institutions, and "to refuse to recognize the official representatives of the Fascist regime in America." The United Front would also launch a campaign for funds "to aid the victims of fascist banditry, the widows and orphans in Italy, the maimed and the refugees from the reign of terror of the Italian reactionaries." The statement closed: "The united front of Italian labor in America against Fascism will be an accomplished fact and Signor Mussolini will have something more to worry about."[12]

Following the meeting, the first move made by the AFANA was a petition to President Calvin Coolidge insisting on the recall of Italian Ambassador G. Caetani on the ground that he was "encouraging the spread of Fascism" in the United States.[13] The appeal was ignored, but the AFANA stepped up its efforts to achieve the recall of Caetani's successor, Giacomo de Martino, whom they charged with "having abused the privileges of his office by proselytizing and intimidating immigrants."[14] Again the petition was ignored, but the AFANA had made its presence known.

The AFANA distributed an editorial in the June 1923 issue of *The Railway Clerk*, official organ of the Brotherhood of Railway and Steamship Clerks, reporting a meeting between Elbert H. Gary, the open-shop president of U.S. Steel, who had broken the great steel strike of 1919, and Mussolini. The labor paper was convinced that "plans to Mussolinize the American workers had been laid out and are in process of execution." It asked:

Is it a coincidence that Mussolini begins to establish "state branches" of the Fascisti in this country so soon after Judge Gary's visit to him? Let the citizens of the United States beware of the menacing danger of Mussolini's agencies; we need no Fascisti in America.[15]

In the spring of 1923, the AFANA and the Italian Chamber of Labor jointly published a Manifesto "To the Workers of the United States and Canada," urging them "to come to the aid of their fellow workers of Italy." The appeal was directed "to all the Italian workers of the United States and through them to the entire labor movement." Charging Mussolini "with the crimes of high treason, perjury, murder, arson, burglary, rape, and continued violence upon the body and property of all the workers of Italy," the Manifesto charged the labor movement of the United States and Canada, "in the name of their own humanity to come to the aid of the working class of Italy before it becomes socially extinct." Warning that the "fascist octopus ... is attempting to extend its tentacles across the ocean and to bring to America the gospel of the torch, the bomb and the stiletto," the Manifesto summoned "all labor unions of the United States and all true and honest lovers of liberty to begin at once an energetic campaign so that this evil weed may not take root in the soil of the Republic." "But it is not enough for us," it continued

> to prevent the monster of Fascism from staining with blood and searing with fire our fair American land. We must also strive with tireless effort and unabated faith to wipe away from Italy the shame and abomination of her present inhuman government. We must revive the faith, still alive in the breasts of millions of Italian workers, with our support, our example, the tangible proofs of our solidarity, and by transfusing into them the certainty that we shall stand by them till the inevitable day of resurrection and triumph.
>
> Fascism, wherever it rears its bloody head, whatever weapon it uses, whatever livery it dons, must forever disappear from the earth with the lust of blood and dominion that gave it life.... Against it we proclaim now a war of extermination, declaring it outside of the moral law of mankind and beyond every mercy and forgiveness of the workers of the world.
>
> Down with international Fascism!
>
> Up with the banners of working-class solidarity![16]

Thus, under the leadership of its Secretary, the poet Arturo Giovannitti, the AFANA began its war against fascism.[17] Unfortunately, while some AFL unions did respond vigorously to the Manifesto, under the leadership of Samuel Gompers the AFL "offered neither moral nor material support to the Anti-Fascists."[18] At its 1923 convention, the AFL failed to pass an ILGWU motion denouncing all manifestations of Fascism, and adopted instead a mild and vague statement opposing the "imposition of tyranny" in America.[19]

On July 16, 1923, Egisto Rossi, an Italian trade unionist and Vice-Chairman of Emigration for the Italian Government, who had met Samuel Gompers when the latter had visited Italy shortly after World War I, wrote the AFL president assuring him that Fascism was of great benefit to the Italian workers. The labor organizations which had emerged under Fascism, Rossi claimed, "are much more in accordance with the spirit of American labor unions than were the old ones, most of which have become political organizations affiliated with Moscow, and the leaders of which were out-and-out Communists, caring not a snap of their fingers for the welfare and prosperity of the country to which they belong." The Fascist government's policy, he continued, "is anything but that of an oppressor of labor, as the maintenance of the eight hour day and of all existing social legislation, including insurance of the aged, the sick, the unemployed working man prove." Rossi was certain that Fascism would win "the hearty sympathies and support" of the AFL president. For Gompers had "constantly and consistently maintained that the true interests of the workingmen are not served by radicals who speculate on the ignorance of the masses to further their own selfish condition." Moreover his philosophy was committed, like that of the Fascists, to "the steady uplifting through better social legislation and more just working conditions of the mental and moral atmosphere surrounding labor, whose welfare can never be realized except by making it recurrent with that of the majority of the citizens of the United States."[20]

Gompers had returned from Europe after World War I more convinced than ever of the threat of radicalism, especially Communism. The importance Egisto Rossi placed on the role of Fascism in suppressing these influences in the Italian labor movement was intended to cater to Gompers' anti-radical prejudices, and they hit the mark. Indeed, he could not have been more satisfied with Gompers' response had he written it himself. Shortly after receiving the letter, Gompers wrote "An Analysis of Fascism" in the *American Federationist,* the AFL's official monthly, which he edited. Echoing Egisto Rossi and other defenders of Fascism, Gompers wrote: "It must be of course understood that at the time the Fascisti came into power in Italy and for sometime prior thereto there had been a rising and dangerous Bolshevik movement fostered under the direct guidance of the Moscow authorities. The information available is that had the Fascisti not seized the government just when they did the Bolsheviks would have done so not many days later."[21]

Most of Gompers' article was devoted to an analysis of Odon Por's book *Fascism*, issued by the Labour Publishing Company of London and shortly afterwards published in the United States. Pointing out that Odon Por was long associated with the Italian labor movement and was viewed as "a pronounced radical but an anti-Fascist," Gompers noted that in his book Por was convinced that "some good will come out of Fascism and he presents in great detail a constructive side of the movement of which little has been heard in America." Agreeing with Por's every comment favorable to Fascism,[*] Gompers welcomed Fascism as a movement "capable of decisive action on a national scale" and as a system that was "rapidly reconstructing a nation of collaborating units of usefulness." In place of the old industrial unions and the growing influence of Bolshevism among them, Gompers saw the new "vocational parliaments" instituted by Mussolini as a step in the right direction. In fact, Gompers was greatly impressed with Mussolini himself. "However repugnant may be the ideas of dictatorship and the man on horseback, American trade unionists will at least find it possible to have some sympathy with the policies of a man whose dominating purpose is to get something done; to do rather than theorize; to build a working, producing civilization instead of a disorganized theorizing aggregation of conflicting groups." After urging the American labor movement to make possible a "wide reading" of Por's book, Gompers concluded:

> Certainly the promise of industrial democracy in Italy, pledged in declarations and phrases which might easily enough have been taken from the mouths of American trade unionists, makes the book one of tremendous and exciting interest.[22]

Thus the president of the American Federation of Labor joined the Republican administration, the leading open shop industrialists and bankers, and almost the entire commercial press in hailing Fascism. In essence, "Gompers saw Fascism as a model of class reconciliation that vindicated his own trade union philosophy."[23] By the time Fascism emerged, Gompers had developed the view that organized labor should seek recognition as a partner of the large corporation. He now viewed society as a corporate entity in which workers and

---

[*] Gompers, however, criticized Por for speaking "with much sympathy of the Russian Soviets, a fact which is regrettable in view of the balanced judgment which he displays so generally in the remainder of book." (Samuel Gompers, "An Analysis of Fascism," *American Federationist* 30 [November 1923]: 928-29.)

management had equal stake in achieving industrial stability, order, and social peace, in which class reconciliation replaced class struggle.[24]

Gompers' support of Fascism proved to be embarrassing to the AFL. Timothy Healy, president of the Firemen and Boilers, challenged the AFL to be as forthright in opposition to Fascist Italy as it was to Communist Russia. "Why don't we say something about Italy and the Mussolini dictatorship?" he asked.[25]

With Gompers' death in 1924, the AFL had an opportunity to meet this criticism. While, as we have seen, William Green shared Gompers' view that labor and capital must be partners, unlike his predecessor, he was concerned by the Fascist attempt "to infiltrate the American labor movement."[26] When he was informed of the Fascist activities among immigrants, especially the Italian miners of Pennsylvania and the needle trades' workers of New York, Green addressed a letter to organized wage earners, warning then of the "'menacing' efforts of American Black Shirts, the violent methods of Mussolini, and the reactionary nature of Fascist unions in Italy." Making certain to assure employers that he had not gone over to the Left, Green coupled his attack on Fascism with a bitter onslaught against Communism.[27]

Green followed this up with an article, "Fascism and the Workers" in the *American Federationist* of February 1926. He charged that "the Fascists are resorting to all sorts of tricks and maneuvers to stir up trouble and bring about a state of affairs which they can use an excuse for recruiting their armed forces and proclaiming open war against the working class."[28]

The 1926 and 1927 AFL conventions reversed the stand taken at the 1923 convention and adopted resolutions condemning Fascism. The resolution introduced at the 1927 convention by A.I. Shiplacoff of Federal Labor Union No. 17873, New York City, had two parts. The first noted that the people of Italy had been ruled for the last few years by a dictatorship "which has deprived them of many of their civil, economic and political rights," a dictatorship which had particularly affected the workers of Italy, subjecting them to arbitrary laws in the making of which they had neither voice nor vote, and "practically reducing them to the position of vassals to the dictator and his Fascist supporters." It added that the "very basis of the Fascist idea was contrary to the idea of government by the people," and that it had been "authoritatively reported that the anti-democratic and anti-American Fascisti movement is attempting to exercise its influence in this country, particularly among our workers of Italian birth or descent." The resolution urged the delegates to roundly condemn "the Fascist movement and philosophy as a return to the days of autocracy and tyranny in government and opposed to the interests of human progress."[29]

The second part of the resolution declared that the American Federation of labor "can not and would not endorse any organization in the country or elsewhere engaged in fighting the Fascist movement." No explanation was advanced for this statement which contradicted the first part of the resolution.[30]

In its report to the convention, the Resolutions Committee concurred with the resolution "in so far as it denounces the Fascist form of government." It added: "In Fascism we find merely another form of dictatorship and autocracy, a principle of government which can never find anything but opposition in the minds of free people." As for the second portion of the resolution, the committee pointed to the record which showed that no organization had been endorsed. It went on, however, to add that it "approved" most cordially the declarations in behalf of human freedom contained in the resolution "opposing this form of dictatorship, just as we oppose the Communist dictatorship...." With this understanding, the resolution was unanimously adopted.[31]

Without endorsing the organization, William Green told the AFANA in 1926 that the AFL "will stand with you and work with you until we have succeeded in driving Fascism from the face of the earth."[32]

As John P. Diggins points out, both AFL and rival unions "gradually joined the campaign [against Fascism] as the typesetters, electrical workers and operators, locomotive engineers, barbers and bookbinders, moulders, machinists, and the American Federation of Teachers began attacking Mussolini in their respective publications."[33] One union which was not part of the AFL was not among those who "gradually joined the campaign." This, of course, was the Amalgamated Clothing Workers of America. *Advance*, its official organ, began early to publish articles and editorials of condemnation of Fascism and its method of terrorism.[34]

In June 1924, the Italian Socialist Deputy Giacomo Matteoti was murdered by Fascist "squadrists." Matteoti's slaying "raised one single cry of indignation and horror in Italy and abroad."[35] On June 26, an anti-Fascist demonstration was held at Carnegie Hall in New York by Italian and American anti-Fascist organizations. With 2,500 people in attendance, most of them workers and trade unionists, cries of "Down with Mussolini and Fascism" rang through the hall. Elizabeth

Gurley Flynn, the "rebel girl" of the IWW, told the audience that the murder of Matteoti had been approved by Mussolini because the Socialist Deputy was about to uncover scandals in Mussolini's government "which would have made the Teapot Dome scandals look sick."[36]

Gurley Flynn proposed a nationwide campaign of boycott against Mussolini's Fascism as a way of showing America's horror over the assassination of Matteoti. The proposal was picked up later on December 5, 1925 by *Il Martello* which in an appeal to all Italian-American Anti-Fascists urged them "to follow the following guidelines of boycott:"

> Workers, comrades: the best method to defeat our common enemy is to cut off monetary assistance and profit.
> If your doctor is Fascist; boycott him.
> If your lawyer is Fascist; boycott him.
> If your tailor is Fascist; boycott him.
> If your shoemaker is Fascist; boycott him.
> If your retailer is Fascist; boycott him.
> If your grocer is Fascist; boycott him.
> If your newspaper man is Fascist; boycott him.
> If your druggist is Fascist; boycott him.
> If your barber is Fascist; boycott him.
> If your landlord is Fascist; boycott him.
> If you know that Banks, Movie Theatres, Drug Stores, Insurance and Travel Agencies are owned by Fascists, boycott them. Do not buy products which bear the label "Made in Italy." You must boycott, wherever you are and always. In this way, we can weaken the Italian monster. It is like a horse; if it has no oats, it changes course.[37]

On August 26, 1926 *Il Nuevo Mundo* published the North American Anti-Fascist Alliance's "Manifesto to all Workers of the United States, Canada, and Mexico. To Those People Concerned About Italy's Constitutional and Civil Liberties." The "Manifesto" charged "fascism" with "crimes of high treason against the sovereignty and liberty of the Italian people." It accused "the fascist government of conducting a disruptive propaganda in this country among Americans and Italian-Americans to undermine the essence of the Declaration of Independence and destroy the ideals of equality and freedom," as well as "of organizing a center of espionage whose aims are to infiltrate among factory workers to foment strikes, unrest, disruption, and inefficiency."

The Manifesto conceded that when the North American Anti-Fascist Alliance was formed in 1923, "we thought that fascism would be a transient movement of collective madness. Today, instead, we have to affirm sadly that fascism is still operative and aggressive, in spite of national and international condemnation .... If this monster is not strangled soon ... it will undermine all liberties."

> To prevent these nefarious consequences, the North American Anti-Fascist Alliance is addressing this Manifesto to all workers, to the political parties, Liberal, Moderate, Radical, Communist, Socialist, Republican, to organize an opposition against fascism. Let fascism not triumph in the democratic countries of the world. Let America expel any fascist or pro-fascist element.[38]

The Manifesto had been drawn up by a group of trade union leaders of the Amalgamated Clothing Workers, the ILGWU, the Italian Trade Union Progressive Centre, and the editors and directors of several anti-Fascist Italian-American papers. Moreover, it was fully endorsed by the Italian Communist Party of America, the Italian Socialist Party of America, and by the Society G. B. Odiema, presided over by Giuseppe Lupis, an Italian Social Democrat. The Manifesto was thus a common attempt by anti-Fascist forces aimed at the condemnation of fascism, its ideology, and its tactics. Issued by a collaboration of Communists, Socialists, Social Democrats, and Republicans in exile, "it marked the high point of an organized United Front in the struggle against fascism."[39]

Unfortunately, the United Front was already on the verge of splitting apart. Led by Salvatore Ninfo of the ILGWU, Morris Feinstein of the United Hebrew Trades, and Girolamo Valenti of the Amalgamated Clothing Workers, a number of groups seceded from the North American Anti-Fascist Alliance. The seceding groups refused to continue a United Front which included Communists, no matter how much this approach weakened the anti-Fascist struggle. They reorganized under the auspices of the Socialists and adopted the new title, "The Anti-Fascist Federation for the Freedom of Italy." The new Secretary, John Vaccaro, welcomed "all labor, radicals, and liberal groups" who were opposed to both Communism and Fascism.[40]

Attacking the splitters, the *Daily Worker* praised the United Front which had enabled the Anti-Fascist Alliance to grow:

> The Anti-Fascist Alliance was organized in April 1923 and has done splendid work since its organization. It has conducted several campaigns

against fascism and has rallied the great majority of the Italian workers in America to its side.*

When Matteoti was murdered on the order of Mussolini, the Alliance organized great demonstrations in every large city in the United States—against the murderers. Mussolini sent emissaries to America to counteract this propaganda, but his speakers were never able to hold one successful mass meeting. Italian workers met his agents on the pier and the police had to protect them from the wrath of their antifascist fellow countrymen.

To weaken this splendid organization on the false issue of "Communist influence" is to strengthen the power of Fascism![41]

Equally troubled by the split, non-Communist anti-Fascists made attempts to persuade the Socialists to remain in the Alliance. But their pleas fell on deaf ears.[42]

The anti-Fascist labor forces were further weakened by the impact of the Great Depression on the key unions in the movement. The ILGWU and the ACWA, experienced a sharp decline in membership between 1929 and 1933. Not until the mid-1930's, and especially not until the outbreak of World War II, did the anti-Fascist movement in the United States reassert itself to oppose Fascism in Italy and to halt the spread of Fascism in the United States.[43]

Meanwhile, in the fall of 1927, the Italian anarchists in the United States became very active in the anti-Fascist cause. Prior to this, they had devoted much of their time and activity to the campaign to free Sacco and Vanzetti. "After the execution of Sacco and Vanzetti, the menace of fascism became the overriding concern of the Italian anarchists," notes Paul Avrich. "In little Italys throughout the country the anarchists emerged as the forefront of the anti-Fascist struggle, heckling pro-Mussolini speakers, disrupting rallies and engaging in fist fights and gunplays. On occasion they also employed dynamite, attacking fascist clubhouses and Italian consulates."[44]

However, the anarchists had little connection with organized labor in these anti-Fascist activities, and they declined as did the labor anti-Fascist forces. Anarchist anti-Fascism in the United States declined along with the disintegration of the anarchist movement as a whole, because of government repression and old age, so that "by

---

* For evidence that this is an exaggeration, see Vincent M. Lombardi, "Italian American Workers and the Response to Fascism," in George E. Pozzeti, ed., *Pane e Laboro: The Italian American Working Class*, Toronto, 1980, pp. 141-57.

the end of the 1930s the Italian anarchist movement in America was merely a shadow of what it had been two decades earlier."[45]

It was precisely during these years that the anti-fascist forces in the labor movement revived and made an even greater contribution to the struggle against fascism than they had during the 1920s.

CHAPTER 13

THE BLACK WORKERS

In our previous volumes, we have seen that despite official procla-
mations of racial equality by AFL officials and conventions, the Federation did little to organize Black workers other than adopt resolutions without creating effective machinery to put them in operation,
or establish any enforcement machinery to prevent its unions from
discriminating. Between 1910 and 1920 the number of AFL affiliates
denying admittance to Black workers by constitutional provision or
ritual had risen from eight to eleven. By the end of the 1920s twenty-
four international unions discriminated directly in their constitutions or rituals, while many others discriminated informally. Ten of
these unions were AFL affiliates. Expectations that the great north-
ward migration of African-American workers from the southern
states would open wide the doors of the AFL and the railroad brotherhoods proved illusory.[1]

TUEL AND BLACK WORKERS

William Z. Foster s experience in the packinghouse campaign of
1918 and the steel strike of 1919 had convinced him that no effective
organization of the mass production industries was possible unless
special attention was paid to the Black workers. Yet he also knew from
experience that there was strong opposition to white unions among
Black workers, growing out of frequent betrayals and their indifference to the Blacks' needs. Hence, both as a Communist influenced
by the Leninist approach to the special character of the Black question, and as a practical trade-union organizer, Foster called upon all
TUEL militants to join in a campaign "to open all unions to the
Negro workers." To this end, it was necessary to educate white unionists on the self-defeating effect of racism on organized labor and to

impress upon Black workers the need for joining with whites in a common struggle against the employers.[2]

The *Labor Herald*, official organ of the TUEL, helped in the educational work with articles on the Black worker and his problems. The April 1923 issue carried a story dealing with the Black worker who had migrated from the cotton fields to the steel mills only to find that his rent, food and clothing were costing more than he was making. He learned, too, that he was the last to be hired and the first to be fired. But, saddest of all,

> ...he learns to distrust the white workers, who will not take him into their unions, yet who call him scab because, as an unorganized worker, he must take whatever job is offered him. For years, various unions, while uttering official platitudes about no discrimination on the basis of nationality, color, creed, or politics, really followed the policy of Negro exclusion.

The article went on to point out that friction between Black and white workers was "being nourished and developed by the employers for the purpose of dividing the workers and forcing upon them a fratricidal struggle." Unless the workers confronted the employing class with their ranks united, regardless of race or color, they would never succeed: "All workers, Negro and white, foreign-born and native, skilled and unskilled, must organize industrially and politically, and thus present one front against the one enemy."[3]

Even more pointed was an editorial in the July 1924 *Labor Herald*, headed "Negroes and the Unions." It merits extensive quotation, for it was the most fully developed statement by the TUEL on the subject of Black workers:

> Trade unions that neglect or discriminate against the Negroes (and there are many such in this country) are following a narrow, short-sighted policy that will ultimately lead them to disaster unless it is changed.
>
> Leaving aside, for the moment, all questions of the interests of the Negroes themselves (which are an essential part of the interests of the working class), and looking at the matter only from the selfish interests of the unions as now constituted, it is becoming plainer every day that if the labor movement is to be saved from destruction at the hands of the "open shop" campaign...they must break down the prejudices instilled by capitalist institutions, they must accept the Negroes on a basis of equality and they must organize them into complete solidarity with the white workers, native and foreign-born.
>
> It is no accident that in the industries dominated by the most militant enemies of labor, the Negroes are being brought in, in constantly increasing numbers. Because the unions are so short-sighted that they neglect the organization and education of our black brothers, they are thereby inflicting deep injury upon themselves. They are forcing the Negroes into

the position of strike-breakers. They are delivering a terrible weapon into the hands of the employers.

For the preservation of the unions, to defeat the "open shoppers," in order to build up working-class power—the Negroes must be brought into the organized. labor movement on a mass scale. All discrimination must be abolished. Every worker must be united in the unions without regard to race, creed, or color. It is time to put our high-sounding principles into effect if we would preserve the trade union movement.[4]

Hence the section on the Negro in the TUEL program adopted in 1924 stated:

The problem of the politically and industrially disfranchised Negroes shall occupy the serious attention of the League. The League shall demand that the Negroes be given the same social, political and industrial rights as whites, including the right to work in all trades, equal wages, admission to all trade unions, abolition of Jim-Crow cars and restaurants.[5]

The leaders of the TUEL were not content to spout generalities about human brotherhood, which often were nothing but excuses for inactivity on the issue of Negro labor and a convenient mask for the prejudices of the trade unionists who uttered them. Instead, the TUEL leadership called upon the militants to work among the white sector of the trade union movement, saturated with prejudice against the Negro, and win the support of the white unionists for a policy of opening all unions to the "Black worker and assuring him an equal opportunity to work on the same terms as the white worker.[6]

James W. Ford, a Black delegate to the Chicago Federation of Labor, described how the TUEL militants worked in the early 1920s. At one meeting of the Federation, he charged the AFL leadership with discrimination and "immoral trade-union conduct" toward Negro workers. As he had anticipated, several white delegates accused him of defending a class of workers who were mainly strike-breakers. To his utter surprise other white delegates came to his defense, although he was the lone Black delegate. "They not only supported fully the charges I had lodged against the bureaucracy but succeeded in forcing it to permit me to continue my remarks." He later learned that these delegates were left-wingers and Communists, under the leadership of William Z. Foster, and that they were leading a fight as members of the TUEL for the rights of Negro workers. Ford immediately joined the League and later the Communist Party and became active in the battle against "race prejudice in the labor movement."[7]

The TUEL leaders were not generally successful in combatting racism in the unions or in recruiting Blacks. They grievously underestimated the resistance among white unionists to their program on

the Negro question and often found them so blinded by race prejudice as "to prefer exploitation to cooperation with the colored man."
The militants failed, too, to appreciate the resistance of the Black
workers to the white unions, caused mainly by their experience with
organized labor, but deepened by the influence of the conservative
Negro church and by the belief of many Blacks employed in industry
that their interests resided with the employing class rather than the
white unionists. "The experiences of the Negro seeking work," commented *Opportunity*, the organ of the National Urban League, in
October 1924, "has forced him to believe that there is as much sa-
credness about the principles involved in his right to earn a living as
were involved in the principles for which the white trade unionists
stood."[8]

While thousands of workers rallied to the TUEL and conducted a
series of strikes under its leadership, especially, as we have seen, in
the textile and needle-trades industries, few Black workers were involved in these activities. Few were touched by the great strikes in the
needle trades, "since few of them," *The Crisis* noted, "are in the cloth-
ing-making industry." The same was true of the textile industry. All
told, few Black workers were recruited into the unions by the militants.[9]

AMERICAN NEGRO LABOR CONGRESS

In an effort to accomplish what the TUEL had failed to achieve,
the Communists organized the American Negro Labor Congress in
1925. The Congress was sponsored by the Workers' (Communist)
Party, and two Black functionaries in the Party, H.W. Phillips and
Levett Fort-Whiteman, were instrumental in organizing the convention in October at which the organization was born.[10] Its central
objective was to generate a movement directed toward the organization of Black labor and to overcome their exclusion from the established unions.[11] The official call of the congress urged "the abolition
of all discrimination, persecution and exploitation of the Negro race
and working people generally; ... to remove all bars and discrimination against Negroes and other races in the trade unions ... and to
aid the general liberation of the darker races and the working people
throughout all countries.."[12]

Thirty-two Black delegates, men and women, and one Mexican-
American, predominantly working class and representing a scattering of trade unions and farmer organizations, responded to the call
and were present in Chicago. Greetings were sent to the congress by

the TUEL, and William Z. Foster was a featured speaker [13] The congress declared that

> .the failure of the American Federation of Labor officialdom, under the pressure of race prejudice benefiting only the capitalists of the North and South, to stamp out race-hatred in the unions, to organize Negro workers, and to build a solid front of the workers of both races against American Capitalism, is a crime against the whole working class. If the unions of the American Federation of Labor, through ignorance and prejudice, fail in this duty to the American workers in industry, we Negro workers must organize our own unions as a powerful weapon with which to fight our way into the existing labor movement on a basis of full equality.[14]

The formation of separate Black unions was to be supported where necessary, but this was not to be seen as a diversion from the main task of uniting white and Black workers in the same unions. The Congress favored the establishment of "local councils" in all Black population centers which would form a united front with existing unions and other organizations. It called for the creation of "interracial labor committees" to "meet jointly for the purpose of bringing the Negro workers into the trade unions, preventing discrimination, undercutting of wages, the use of one race against the other in strikes, etc., and for bringing about the action of all workers, Black and white, against lynching and race riots." The program approved at the Congress went beyond the labor question to cover all aspects of Black rights. To help push the program, the Congress launched a newspaper, *Negro Champion.*[15]

However, the Congress was able to attract few delegates outside of the Communists and their adherents. Still, the Communist *Daily Worker* hailed the Negro Labor Congress and predicted that it would enable Black workers to "become a power in the labor movement."[16] The Black press, however, was almost unanimously critical because of the Communist-inspired character of the Congress. The fact is, however, that the Congress aroused considerable interest in the country. The American Negro Labor Congress, Ira DeA. Reid points out, "succeeded in arousing more public interest and editorial comment on organizing Negro labor than has ever appeared in the public press."[17]

The sharp attack on the Congress by the AFL leadership deterred Black unionists from participating. AFL President William Green issued a public statement denouncing the Congress as a Moscow-hatched plot "to convert the American negro [*sic*] workingman to Bolshevism" and admonishing Black workers not to become "traitors to their Government." Green added that there was no need for the

Congress, since "The AFL stands ready to give you the protection of an organized movement."[18]

The American Negro Labor Congress had relatively little success in bringing Black workers into the white trade unions. It lasted five years, but it soon became clear that the Congress was isolated from the Black masses and therefore ineffective as a mass organization. It was superseded in 1930 by the League of Struggle for Negro Rights.[19]

Meanwhile, the AFL continued to warn Blacks not to be lured by "the Voice of Moscow," and to assure them that they had no need for the Communists since the Federation offered them the "protection and experience of the Trade Union Movement."[20]

UMW AND BLACK MINERS

When William Green succeeded Samuel Gompers as president of the AFL in 1924, the hope arose among some Blacks that he would lead a battle against the exclusionist practices of the Federation's craft unions and their policy of limiting Black workers, in the main, to segregated units. Green, after all, was a charter member of the United Mine Workers; he had served as a local union officer, subdistrict president, president of the Ohio district, and international secretary-treasurer. Even W. E. B. Du Bois, skeptical though he was about white trade unionism in general and the AFL in particular, entertained the hope that Green's background might cause him to combat the racial practices of organized labor.[21]

Du Bois praised the UMW for having "organized the black miners without discrimination...throughout the country."[22] He appears to have been unaware that, by the time Green became AFL president, the UMW's reputation for nondiscrimination was being seriously questioned.

During the 1920s, 20 percent of West Virginia's miners and 50 percent of Alabama's miners were Black. Yet there was not a single Black international officer in the UMW. In fact, not since the 1890s, when Richard L. Davis, a Black miner from Ohio, was elected to the International Executive Board, had a Black miner held any International office.[23]

Abram L. Harris found that Black members of the UMW in Pittsburgh "seem quite happy in being affiliated with the organization," but, after investigating the status of the Black miner for the West Virginia Bureau of Negro Welfare and Statistics, he reported that Black miners who had quit the UMW had done so because, while the union was good for keeping up wages, "in many instances Negroes could not get jobs by which to earn the union wages" owing to the "Ku Klux spirit" in the union. Harris concluded his survey by warning the UMW that the Klan's power within the organization "must be checked or it will disrupt the labor solidarity among white and Black workers at which the United Mine Workers aim." Harris's evidence revealed that the "labor solidarity" had already been seriously disrupted.[24]

In his study, "The Negro Miner in West Virginia," James T. Faing found that "the attitudes of union brothers who were also members of the Klan led some of the Negroes to withdraw from their locals."[25] This reaction was not confined to West Virginia. An important reason for it was the practice of UMW leaders and white members of indulging in racist attacks on Black miners, accusing them of being "natural strikebreakers." "We have some white scum also," a UMW organizer declared, "but the Negro is in the majority."[26] Certainly there was Black strikebreaking. But the fact that hundreds of Black miners stood firmly by the union, and that hundreds of Black strikebreakers joined it, were never pointed out by the International officers or the *UMW Journal*. It was easier for the Lewis administration to place the blame for UMW defeats on Black workers than to admit its errors.[27] Angered by the racism of the Lewis administration, Blacks quit the UMW in droves. Black membership dropped from 25,000 in 1920 to no more than 5,000 in 1927.[28]

"SAVE THE UNION" MOVEMENT AND BLACK MINERS

Late in 1927, the TUEL urged its members in the UMW to make the restoration of the confidence of Black miners in the union a key issue.[29] Hence the "Save the Union" conference in Pittsburgh on April 1, 1928, attended by progressive miners from all over the nation, went on record condemning the Lewis administration's racist policies and demanding equal jobs and equal pay for Black miners, A report on the conference in the *Pittsburgh Courier* stressed the fact that many Black delegates attended. The Black weekly also reported:

> William Boyce, a Negro miner from Indiana, made a telling recital of the wrongs inflicted by the administration upon the Negroes in the industry, who were allowed to pay dues but were discriminated against on every occasion.... Although Boyce was an active union man for the past 28 years, he declared that this was the first time he had an opportunity of addressing a miners' convention.[30]

Charles Fulp, a Black miner with fifteen years in the mines, told the delegates:

> The time to beg is past! We must assert ourselves and demand our rights! My father was a slave, but his son won't be one! Abolish all discrimination, or our fight is lost. If you discriminate against the colored miners and force them out of the union, what else is left for them to do but scab?[31]

Several Black miners, including Boyce and Fulp, were elected to the National Executive Board of the "Save the Union" Committee. "Such equal participation in leadership had never been practiced in the UMW," Linda Nyden points out.[32]

In the April 1,1928 issue of the *Coal Digger*, the journal of the "Save-the-Union" movement, Fulp described how the operators used racism and anti-Communism to divide Black and white miners. "You and I are white men, an operator tells the white miners! We own and rule this country and some day you may be the president of the USA! The black worker, on the other hand, is told that those dirty white bums are not half as good as the good Colored people and the bosses go on to say how they love the Colored people." He continued:

> Finally the oppression of the people is so severe that the white and black worker meets and talks this over and decides to unite for the interests of their class, and then we hear at once the Reds are getting in among the Negroes and making them radicals. But it is not the reds, it is simply that both the Negro and the white man realizes that they have one common enemy to fight—the bosses and not each other, since they belong to the same class—the working class.

The Lewis administration, as we have seen, used both racism and redbaiting to condemn the "Save the Union" movement. In May, 1928, the UMW began expelling the movement's leaders, charging them with dual unionism. In ordering the expulsion of Isaiah Hawkins, John L. Lewis declared:

> We white members cannot tolerate this sort of thing. This man Hawkins is getting too strong a hold. He already has attained the leadership of a large group of whites throughout Western Pennsylvania, West Virginia, and Ohio. He must be stopped before his following spreads throughout the country and creates an embarrassing situation .... It would not matter so much if his work attracted simply Negroes, but he has a large and growing following among whites.[33]

In November, 1928, William Boyce was suspended from the union "for a period of 99 years."[34]

THE AFL AND BLACK WORKERS

The fact that while he was an official of the UMW, Green never spoke against the Lewis administration's racism did not, to some Black spokespersons, bode well for the relationship between the Black worker and the AFL under his leadership. It was not long before the worst was known. An open letter from the National Association for the Advancement of Colored People (NAACP) to the 1924 AFL convention, also addressed to other groups of organized labor, read in part:

> For many years the American Negro has been demanding admittance to the ranks of organized labor.
>
> For many years your organizations have made public profession of your interest in Negro labor, of your desire to have it unionized, and of your hatred of the Black "scab."
>
> Notwithstanding this apparent surface agreement, Negro labor in the main is outside the ranks of organized labor, and the reason is first that white union labor does not want Black labor and secondly, Black labor has ceased to beg admittance to union ranks because of its increasing value and efficiency outside the unions.

Warning that the Black worker had already broken the great steel strike of 1919 and would soon be in a position to break any strike "where he can gain economic advantage for himself," even though this hurt both Black and white labor, the NAACP insisted that it was essential for Black and white labor to unite: "Is it not time for white unions to stop bluffing and for black laborers to stop cutting off their noses to spite their faces?" A proposal was advanced for formation of an Interracial Commission made up of the NAACP, the AFL, the railroad brotherhoods, and other bodies agreed upon, which would seek: (1) to determine the exact attitude and practice of national labor bodies and local unions toward Negroes and that of Black workers toward unions, and (2) to organize systematic propaganda against racial discrimination in local assemblies and unions. The NAACP stood ready to take part in such an effort and invited the cooperation of the entire labor movement. The appeal closed: "The Association hereby solemnly warns American laborers that unless some such step as this is taken soon, the position gained by organized labor in this country is threatened with irreparable loss."[35]

The NAACP plea for cooperation was acknowledged by the AFL and then forgotten. Green's only sign of awareness of the Black worker around that time was his warning to Blacks not to be enticed by the American Negro Labor Congress, and his assurance to them that the AFL stood ready to give them "the protection of the organized movement."[36]

At the 1925 AFL convention, a dispirited group of Black delegates who had been agitating since 1919 for wider recognition of their legitimate rights made their last effort. A delegate from a Black federal labor union introduced a lengthy resolution taking the AFL to task for its refusal to show an interest in the welfare of "Black workers. The resolution singled out the policy of separate organizations for Negroes, condemning it as hardly better than no organization at all and as seriously undermining the doctrine of labor solidarity—a principle the AFL was fond of proclaiming. The resolution urged the Federation to enter into negotiations with each affiliate for the purpose of eliminating all traces of racial discrimination. Finally, the Federation was asked to proceed with "the greatest possible dispatch and energy" in launching a drive to organize all Black workers in the same unions with white workers.[37]

The resolution fared no better than similar motions submitted in previous years. The 1925 convention, ignoring the criticism of the Federation's policy toward Negroes, boasted that all but a very few of its 110 member unions accepted Black members. The AFL practice of separate organizations was overwhelmingly approved. Then, rubbing salt in the wounds of the Black delegates, the convention rejected a petition from the Colored Coach Cleaners urging the Brotherhood of Railway Carmen either to issue them a charter or to give them direct representation in both the union and the AFL. (The petition noted that, by accepting limited membership in the carmen, the coach cleaners had relinquished their right to govern themselves and with it their right to send their own representatives to the AFL's annual convention.) All the convention offered the disenchanted Black workers was help in arranging another meeting between the coach cleaners and the carmen, in the slim hope that they could settle their differences.[38]

From 1925 through 1927, no resolution relating to Black labor was even seriously discussed at an annual convention. A. Philip Randolph, who attended the 1926 AFL convention, complained that as far as Black workers were concerned, "there was not a word on their problems, although the American labor movement cannot reach its goal without them." The *Pittsburgh Courier*, a leading Black weekly, made the same point even more strongly:

> The American Federation of Labor, with its steadily declining membership, cannot afford to allow discrimination to continue within its ranks .... Otherwise it will become a means for destroying the organizations they

have so laboriously built up. Some of the most loyal and militant workers in organized labor are Negroes. They have struck, walked the picket lines and starved in order that the right to bargain collectively with the employers might be established and maintained. The Negro worker demands the right to join every union, and having joined, he demands equal treatment with all other union workers regardless of race, creed, color or nationality. Otherwise organized labor cannot hope to retain his allegiance.[39]

But the AFL was simply not interested in retaining the Black worker's "allegiance." An attempt to have the Executive Council appoint a Black adviser and organizer failed. "None of the international trade unions, which refused membership to Negroes, at the beginning of the year changed its policy," the National Urban League reported in its survey of the industrial and labor scene at the opening of 1927.[40] Meanwhile, Blacks abandoned the separate federal and local unions in droves, so that by 1927 there were only twenty-one left in existence. As the resolution of the 1925 convention pointed out, Black members had learned from bitter experience that such unionism was hardly better than no unionism at all.

BROTHERHOOD OF SLEEPING CAR PORTERS

On a state and city level, Black labor was better represented, but how much better is difficult to measure. No one really knows just how many Black workers were in unions, since few organizations kept membership statistics based on race. A 1928 survey by Charles S. Johnson estimated Black membership in the trade unions at nearly 200,000 in occupations where Black labor was important—longshoremen, hod carriers, and miners—or in independent Black unions of railroad workers. But in 1930 the NAACP estimated the total at "no more than 50,000 colored members of national unions," and half of those were members of the Black Brotherhood of Sleeping Car Porters.

The Brotherhood of Sleeping Car Porters was launched on August 25, 1925, in New York's Harlem by A. Philip Randolph and a few score of Pullman porters. Its intention was to deal with the low wages, long hours, lack of adequate rest on trips, lack of bargaining power, and job insecurity in the porters' work. There were 15,000 Pullman porters traveling all over the country. Those assigned to regular runs began work at $67.00 a month; if they remained in service for fifteen years, they would thereafter receive $94.50. Tips increased their actual earnings, but the cost of uniforms, shoe polish, etc., was de-

ducted from their wages. The 11,000 miles of travel per month usually meant 400 hours, excluding preparatory time and time spent at
the terminals. To aggravate the situation, porters often "doubled out"
or ran "in charge" of a car, taking increased responsibility under
unfavorable physical conditions for added pay at a diminishing rate.
Porters were required to remain on call at sign-out offices for several
hours a day without pay; porters-in-charge often had to perform
conductors' work without adequate compensation for extra services,
and the Pullman Employee Representation Plan did nothing to correct injustices.* Many of the Pullman porters realized that only
through real collective bargaining could they hope for improvements.[41]

When federal control of the railroads ended in 1920, the Pullman
Company, eager to stifle the porters' efforts to organize, introduced
the Employee Representation Plan, which, in the words of E.F. Carey,
the company president, was "offered to our employees for the purpose of handling expeditiously and settling promptly and fairly all
questions which arise as to wages, working conditions, and such matters as may be important to the welfare of the employees."[42] Basically,
the plan was a company union. Like the antiunion schemes adopted
by many other American companies during the postwar years, it included a promise not to discriminate against workers for membership in any union or fraternal order but insisted that "the right to
hire and discharge shall be invested exclusively in the company." The
workers' representatives could appeal a discharge as a grievance to
the Bureau of Industrial Relations, whose decision was to be "final,"
but the bureau was simply the company's personnel department. Its
chairman, who supervised the entire Employee Representation Plan,
was appointed by the company, and the company controlled the

* Professor Robert Higgs challenges the prevailing view regarding the terrible working conditions of Pullman porters. He concedes that "A Pullman porter's job had
many unpleasant features including (before the 1937 collective bargaining contract)
being on call 24 hours a day and having to sleep if at all, on a couch in the men's
room." Then he adds: "But the job also had desirable attributes sufficient to attract
(voluntary, not coerced, certainly not enslaved) applicants chronically exceeding va-
cancies. Porters travelled the country and into Canada; they hobnobbed with rich and
famous passengers; and they received much higher pay than the average black worker
of comparable skill." (Review of Jack Santini, *Miles of Smiles, Years of Struggle: Stories of
Black Pullman Porters*, [Urbana and Chicago, 1989] in *Labor History* 32, Winter 1991:
152.) Professor Higgs' comment that Pullman porters "received much higher pay than
the average black workers of comparable skill" tells us nothing when one considers
that for many Black workers, the so-called era of prosperity in the 1920s was already a
depression era, and even Black college graduates might work as Pullman porters
because other work was not available.

operation of the plan by financing it and supervising the election of representatives.[43]

It was not long before some of the porters' representatives under the plan saw through it as merely a device to put a benevolent face on the Pullman Company and discourage union consciousness. Some of the porters were ready to organize a real union but were deterred by a fear of losing their jobs. A small group of New York porters, led by Roy Lancaster, Ashley L. Totten, and William H. Des Verney, continued to hold conversations on the need for a union. In 1925 Totten, who along with Lancaster and Des Verney, was a militant representative under the Employee Representation Plan, heard A. Philip Randolph speak and was impressed by the Socialist editor of *The Messenger*. He initiated a one-man campaign to "sell" the porters to Randolph and Randolph to the porters. Early in 1925, Totten invited Randolph to address the Pullman Porters' Athletic Association. Randolph accepted, and in a speech on trade unionism, he condemned the porters' participation in the Employee Representation Plan, and emphasized "the need for porters to have their own organization, free from company control." The speech "stirred and aroused the New York porters," and Des Verney urged Randolph to meet with a group of porters to launch the union effort.[44]

The meeting was held at Des Verney's home on the evening of June 25, 1925. At the meeting Randolph presided, read the motions he had drawn up in advance, and then voted for approval himself, so that those present could not be accused later by a company spy, certain to be there, of supporting a union. Totten, Lancaster, and Des Verney agreed that the solution of the porters' problems lay in a union. Randolph agreed to write about the porters in *The Messenger*, and a series of meetings followed, culminating on August 25, 1925 with a meeting at Elks Hall in Harlem. At this meeting, a "National Committee to Organize Pullman Porters into the Brotherhood of Sleeping Car Porters" was established, and Randolph was invited to become the union's leader under the title of general organizer. *The Messenger* would be the union's official organ. Des Verney, who had for thirty years been an operating porter, was chosen to assist Randolph, and Roy Lancaster, a former official of the Employee Representation Plan, became secretary-treasurer.[45]

Although most porters worked for the Pullman Company, the union did not choose the name Brotherhood of Pullman Porters. Rather, probably at Randolph's suggestion, the name chosen was "Brotherhood of Sleeping Car Porters." As William H. Harris points out: "From the beginning, its leaders decided to form an international union to represent all porters in the United States, Canada, and Mexico [46]

The rally publicly launching the Brotherhood was hailed by the *Amsterdam News* as "the greatest labor mass meeting ever held of, for and by Negro working men." It drafted a set of demands and announced that the porters would settle for nothing less than (1) recognition of the brotherhood (which, of course, meant abolition of the Employee Representation Plan); (2) an increase in wages to $150 a month, with the abolition of tipping; (3) a 40-hour week and relief from unreasonable doubling out; and (4) pay for preparation time.[47]

In August 1936, Frank Crosswaith, who in 1925 had been executive secretary of the Trade Union Committee for Organizing Workers and who soon became a special assistant for the Brotherhood of Sleeping Car Porters, eloquently declared:

> The soldiers of labor's cause must never be permitted to forget that fateful August night eleven years ago, when enveloped by the suffocating heat of a summer's night and the stifling smoke from a hundred cigars, cigarettes and a few pipes, several hundred Pullman Porters defiantly threw down the gauntlet of battle to the nation's mightiest industrial monarch.

He went on to praise the porters for demonstrating "a courage hitherto unsuspected among Negroes in industrial warfare" and for awakening "the labor movement to the serious menace of the company union."[48]

It was not easy, however, to win recruits for the Brotherhood. Although unemployment had decreased by the mid-'twenties, Black workers were still feeling its effects. A large number of unemployed Blacks were eager to become Pullman porters; indeed, it was often the only job a Black college graduate could land. Those who were already porters were reluctant to risk their jobs, and the company's welfare workers—ex-porters who paid visits to porters and their families and usually received twice the salary of the average porter—were quick to point out that Randolph, not being a Pullman porter and hence immune to the company's bitter hostility to unions, had nothing to lose. Welfare workers, anti-union porters and company inspectors rode the trains on which union men worked and invented charges of rule violations against them, which often led to their discharge. To overcome the fear this practice created, the Brotherhood had to assure the porters that its membership list was carefully guarded.[49]

Despite the stiff opposition of the Pullman Company, many porters were convinced that they needed a real union to end the outrageous conditions under which they labored. The Brotherhood's first organizing drive in Chicago, headed by Milton P. Webster, a former Pullman porter who exercised some influence in the city's Republican politics, met with a magnificent response, but the majority of local Black leaders were unenthusiastic. They argued that the porters could never successfully challenge the Pullman Company; that the company, because of its long record of hiring Black workers, was a benefactor to the race and should be supported and not attacked; and that Blacks should "not bite the hand that feeds you." The company made sure to distribute such statements by influential Negroes to rank-and-file porters, adding in its own releases that the Brotherhood's porter "nucleus" was made up of "derelicts who have been dismissed for incompetency," "traditional gripers," and "morons," and that Randolph was an "outsider," a "Communist agitator," and a "threat to our American way of life." Lancaster and Totten were fired, and Des Verney resigned before he could be dismissed.[50]

Spearheading the attack for the Pullman Company was Perry Howard, a Black Chicago attorney, a member of the Republican National Committee, and an agent for the Department of Justice. Howard, an orator in the style of Booker T. Washington and an advocate of the expansion of segregation in government employment, challenged Randolph to a public debate in Chicago with the avowed purpose of "blasting and demolishing the Brotherhood and its leadership once and for all." The hall was filled with Black workers. Howard charged that the Brotherhood was "the first of a series of Communist attacks against American capitalism," that "Moscow backed the BSCP and that the union intended to involve Black workingmen in the meshes of communism and socialism to the detriment of their happiness and prosperity." Howard was lustily booed while Randolph received an ovation.[51]

The debate received not a single line in the Chicago papers, but word spread among the porters and gave the infant Brotherhood much needed publicity. This marked the beginning of a nationwide offensive against the Employee Representation Plan. Totten drew on his wide experience and firsthand knowledge as a former official of the plan to condemn its inequities in *The Messenger*, in leaflets and in speeches delivered during an organizing tour across the country. Randolph and Totten swept victoriously through St. Paul and Minneapolis, Seattle and Spokane, Portland (Oregon), Oakland, San Francisco, Los Angeles, Salt Lake City, Denver, St. Louis and Kansas City, leaving in their wake an ever increasing army of converts to the

Brotherhood. At the risk of their jobs, porters began assuming active roles in the union.[52]

At first, the Pullman Company did not take the Brotherhood seriously, viewing it as just another of the many "fly-by-night" efforts of the porters to organize. But as the Brotherhood gained recruits, the company struck back viciously. Union stalwarts, several of them with decades of service as porters, were "dishonorably" discharged; thugs hired by the company struck down Brotherhood organizers in broad daylight, and part of the Black press was subsidized to launch an all-out offensive against the union. The Chicago *Whip* (which Randolph derisively termed the "Flip") and the *Defender* (which he called the "Surrender") not only advised porters to support the company union, but urged members of the Black community to "align themselves with the wealthier classes in America" as their only hope of salvation. (The *Whip* urged porters to stay aloof from organized labor, emphasizing that many members of the AFL belonged to the Ku Klux Klan and that the Railroad Brotherhoods were notorious for their racism and opposition to Black workers).[53] The *Argus* of St. Louis, up to that time a poorly financed publication, blossomed out in an increased size; its editorials flayed the Brotherhood "Reds" and charged that Randolph's purpose for working with the porters was to take their money and run to Russia." After all, Randolph was known "to like the Reds." The Pullman Company placed half-page advertisements in the *Argus* and distributed copies free to porters. Following an investigation for *Labor Age*, Robert W. Dunn wrote that "praise of the company has come from Negro papers all over the country in which advertising has been carefully purchased in return for a 'correct' editorial policy." There were a few exceptions, most notably, the New York *Amsterdam News*, the Chicago *Bee*, the Kansas City *Call*, and, for a time, the *Pittsburgh Courier*. Of these, the most important was the *Courier*. It criticized Perry Howard for his opposition to the union, advised readers not to believe reports that "Communists were behind efforts to organize the porters," and praised Randolph as "brilliant, honest, and able."[54]

In the face of opposition from "respectable" Black circles, the prompt firing of all who aided the organizing drive, and physical attacks on organizers, Brotherhood nuclei were established in several cities. Boston, Randolph acknowledged, was a "hard nut to crack" because porters there, like other New England workers, were steeped in conservatism and feared dire consequences for themselves from unionization, especially if it failed. But a nucleus appeared there as well.[55]

With the Ku Klux Klan operating in high gear in the South, the Brotherhood restricted its organizational drives below the Mason-Dixon Line to a porter "underground," which made contact with the personnel of southbound trains and distributed literature explaining the union's program. When an organizer was finally dispatched to Jacksonville, the Pullman Company used its influence to have him brought into court on a charge of preaching racial equality by distributing *The Messenger*. Given the choice of leaving Jacksonville within twenty-four hours, or serving a term at a convict camp, he left at the advice of the Brotherhood. Organization of the South would have to wait for some break in the hostile climate.[56]

To counter the anti-unionism of the Black papers, ministers and political leaders, the Brotherhood sponsored labor institutes and Negro labor conferences in the larger cities throughout the country. The discussions centered on the grievances of the porters and the need for Black workers in general to unionize. This work was facilitate by grants from the Garland Fund. The $11,200 the Fund gave the Brotherhood was not only for organizational work, but also to aid in the preparation of a survey of working conditions among the porters.[57]

While Milton P. Webster in Chicago first took charge of the actual organizing, Randolph devoted much of his time in a constant effort to win public support. He wrote to attorneys, congressmen, and other influential people to explain the importance of the Brotherhood. He spoke to colleges, professional and labor groups, ministers' alliances, and business associations, Black and white. He enlisted speakers, including Morris Ernst, liberal lawyer, and Mary McDowell, Chicago woman leader in the Meatpacking union, to speak to porters' groups "in a demonstration of white support " He organized a Citizens' Committee of 100, which included Louis Gannett, Norman Thomas, and Freda Kirchwey, editor of *The Nation*. The Brotherhood did win neutral or approving mention in the *New York Times*, *New York World*, and New York *Herald-Tribune*, and in Chicago, the *Daily News* and *Journal*.[58] *The Nation* carried an editorial, "The Pullman Porters," which urged wide support for the union:

> The porters are organizing for certain specified and immediate objects. Instead of allowing the public to underwrite the Pullman Company's payroll by giving in tips (sometimes) the difference between $72.50 a month the porters are paid by the company and what it costs them to support their families, the union wants, instead of the possible 400 hours a month the porters may be called upon to work, hours and "run" schedules more suited to the needs of a human being—even if there is a chemical deposit in the pigment of his skin. It wants a place provided in

sleeping-cars where this human being may occasionally secure a little sleep—when his interminable duties do not for the moment claim him. These are reasonable demands, and nobody with a spark of decency in his heart can do less than wish the porters godspeed in their fight.... The men who punch our pillows and shine our shoes and stow our bags under the seat bear in their black hands no little of the responsibility for the individual future of their race. Whatever greetings we may give them because we believe in their immediate objects must be increased tenfold when we realize the full import of their movement.[59]

On August 25, 1926, the Brotherhood celebrated its first anniversary. The *Daily Worker* hailed the event and reported: "The union has in its first year of existence won over half the 12,000 maids and porters employed by the Pullman Co. and challenged successfully the employee representation plan, or company union." *The Nation* went further and declared: "The union was organized last fall, and to gather in a majority of the employees of a nation-wide service in the space of seven months remains an achievement of no uncertain magnitude. As an American Federation of Labor speaker pointed out at a recent meeting of the porters, many a union has worked for seven years and for three times seven years without succeeding in securing any such percentage of union members among the total employed in its field."[60]*

Randolph, however, was more modest He mentioned no membership figures, but noted that the Brotherhood had "brought the porter's plight to the attention of university and college groups and to the conventions of many organizations," that "75,000 miles was covered by organizers," and that women's auxiliaries had been set up in New York, Chicago, Washington, Boston, St. Paul, Minneapolis, Oakland, Los Angeles, Denver, Omaha, and Salt Lake City. The Brotherhood, moreover, had advanced the cause of unionism among all Black workers, not just the porters:

> The brotherhood carried the message of labor unionism to over a million and a half black and white workers from Aug. 25, 1925, to Aug. 25, 1926. Over 500 meetings were held, with 100 or 2,500 or more at each. Thousands of Negro workers who had never heard about organized labor before were addressed. Over 60,000 heard the general organizer speak on the cause of black labor at the opening of the Sesqui-Centennial in Philadelphia.[61]

* Unfortunately, this praise did not impress the AFL leaders, and they spurned the Brotherhood's request for affiliation in 1926 (*Messenger*, April, 1926, p. 8; December, 1926, p. 375.)

By the end of 1926, more than half the porters had pledged allegiance to the Brotherhood. Pullman chose to ignore this fact and continued to deal with employees through its company union. However, it did step up its social welfare program of summer picnics, parades, and Christmas parties. In order to deprive the Brotherhood of one of its most effective organizing weapons—the porters' starvation wages—Pullman called a wage conference in 1926 and permitted the porters to elect delegates. At the conference, porters were granted an 8 percent wage raise. Company officials were quick to point out that the Employee Representation Plan was responsible for the porters' pay rise. They neglected to mention that, in the election of delegates to the wage conference, the company had noted the name of every porter who failed to vote, and that these porters, assumed to be Brotherhood members, were then threatened, suspended or dismissed.

The company's concessions did not deter the Brotherhood. In 1927, it pressed for the demands it had formulated two years earlier, but it was easier to formulate a series of demands than to win the porters' support for an all-out drive to realize them. Beset by company spies and detectives and subject to pro-company propaganda in much of the Black press and most of the churches, many porters and their families dropped away. Only underground cells of solid, tried members continued to function, and their number was diminished whenever a cell was penetrated by a company spy and the identified cell members dismissed. To let the Black porters know they were not indispensable, the Pullman Company began hiring a few Chinese, Mexican, and Filipino porters. The Brotherhood tried to assure the Black porters that U.S. immigration laws made this company threat meaningless, but the threat did have an effect.[62]

With shrinking membership and a corresponding decline in dues, the Brotherhood was forced to close many of its branch offices. It appeared that the efforts to unionize the Black porters would meet the same fate as previous attempts to organize the porters.

But the Brotherhood's long months of work and its courageous battles in the face of Pullman's vicious counteroffensive had won the admiration of many labor and liberal publications, which recalled Pullman's infamous record in the great strike of 1894. They urged support of the effort to curb the power of this long-time foe of unionism. Financial support came not only from the Garland Fund but from a number of needle-trades unions, such as the Amalgamated Clothing Workers, and the Chicago Federation of Labor, whose president, John Fitzpatrick, spoke at public meetings and over

the radio in behalf of the Brotherhood. Soon, other officials of the
AFL, including William Green, joined the supporting chorus. Worried about the influence of Communists among the Black workers,
they saw the Brotherhood, whose leadership was bitterly anti-Communist, as a bastion against the American Negro Labor Congress.[63]

Although most of the Black papers continued to be hostile—the
Pittsburgh Courier, formerly a champion of the Brotherhood, did an
about face and declared that the company had properly refused to
recognize the union because Randolph was a Socialist—*The Crisis,*
the New York *Age,* the *Amsterdam News* and other Black journals rallied to the Brotherhood's defense and sponsored benefits that raised
much-needed funds for the organization. The NAACP supported the
Brotherhood, and while the National Urban League did not follow
suit, its executive secretary, Eugene K. Jones, himself a former porter,
did endorse the union. Some Black churches even permitted it to
use their buildings for meetings. Most important of all, many, including Black workers, came to see the Brotherhood both as a symbol of
the Negroes' claim to dignity, respect, and a decent livelihood and as
a test of the ability of Black workers to build and maintain an effective union. As *The Nation* put it:

> It has been claimed that the black man is unorganizable. Again and again
> unscrupulous corporations have recruited from his ranks the "scab" labor
> which breaks or tries to break a strike of white workers.... If the porters
> can organize their industry, hold their ranks, prove their fighting ability
> in the interest of the working class, it will have a profound effect on the
> attitude of white organized labor. And it will have a profound effect upon
> the organizable capacity of Negro workers in other industries.
>
> These men who punch our pillows and shine our shoes and stow our
> bags under the seat bear in their hands no little of the responsibility for
> the industrial future of their race.[64]

"The fight of the Pullman porters is the all absorbing topic wher-
ever two or more Negroes gather in Harlem," one report said.[65]
Many Blacks knew the words of "The Marching Song of the Fighting
Brotherhood," set to the tune of "My Old Kentucky Home":

We will sing one song of the meek and humble slave
　　The horn-handed son of toil
He's toiling hard from the cradle to the grave
　　But his masters reap the profit of his toil
Then we'll sing one song of our one Big Brotherhood
　　The hope of the Porters and Maids
It's coming fast it is sweeping sea and wood
　　To the terror of the grafters and the slaves

(Chorus)
Organize! Oh Porters come organize your might,
   Then we'll sing one song of our one Big Brotherhood
Full of beauty, full of love and light.[66]

In its hour of distress, the Brotherhood also had the support of
the porters' wives and women relatives organized in the Colored
Women's Economic Council. The council formed women's auxiliaries in various cities, which staged rallies, bazaars, picnics, boat rides,
theater benefits, and other types of fund-raising socials. Of particular
importance was the help the auxiliaries gave to porters' families who
had suffered because of Pullman dismissals.[67]

Encouraged by this support, the Brotherhood moved against the
Pullman Company on a government level. On May 20, 1926, the
Watson-Parker (Railway Labor) Act had become law. It provided for
"the prompt disposition" of all disputes between railroad carriers and
their employees. In case of a dispute, the act called upon the two
sides to meet in joint conference to "make and maintain agreements" on rates of pay, rules, and working conditions. Employee and
employer representatives were to be designated without "interference, influence, or coercion," and any dispute that could not be
resolved in conference was to be submitted to a federal board of
mediation.[68]

After trying vainly to get E.F. Carey, the president of the Pullman
Company, to meet with the Brotherhood as the "designated and
authorized" bargaining agent of the porters, Randolph appealed on
October 15, 1927, to the Railroad Mediation Board to settle the
dispute between the company and the Brotherhood. Although the
Mediation Board ruled that the Brotherhood represented a majority
of the porters, it had no power to declare the Employee Representation Plan illegal and to force the company to deal with the
Brotherhood. In August 1927, the Mediation Board announced that
the parties had failed to reach agreement through mediation and
recommended arbitration. However, arbitration was voluntary, and
while the Brotherhood agreed, the Pullman Company rejected the
Board's recommendation. The Mediation Board had no power to
compel arbitration; in the event that one of the parties refused to
cooperate, it could only recommend that the president create an
emergency board to prevent a strike.

Faced with the failure of its appeal, the Brotherhood invoked the
quasi-judicial powers of the Interstate Commerce Commission
against the system of tipping as a substitute for adequate wages, urg-

ing the ICC to compel the Pullman Company "to cease and desist from directly or indirectly informing or instructing applicants for positions as porters that they may expect increment to their wages from passengers" on the ground that this was a violation of the Interstate Commerce Act.[69]

In March, 1928, the ICC ruled by a vote of four to three that it did not have jurisdiction in the dispute between the Pullman Company and the Brotherhood. Thus, the latter had met with failure in both appeals.

Faced with a dwindling membership, depleted funds and a government clearly unwilling to stand up for the Black workers, the Brotherhood announced that it would strike the Pullman Company as the only way to compel recognition of the workers' right to collective bargaining. As M. P. Webster, Chicago District Organizer, explained: "The porters will create an emergency by voting a strike and then it would be necessary for an arbitration board to take up their claims to abolish tipping in favor of a higher wages. The Pullman Company has refused to arbitrate and the strike threat will be used as a club to get legal arbitration."[70]

The strategy was to force President Calvin Coolidge to set up an emergency board under Section 10 of the Watson-Parker Act, to investigate the dispute and report its findings to him, and then, confident that the findings would support the Brotherhood, rally public opinion to induce the president to put them into effect.

The threatened strike made news in every paper throughout the country, and articles on Pullman's system of tipping as a substitute for proper wages filled many columns. Heywood Broun, writing in the New York *Herald-Tribune*, called the Pullman Company "a panhandler. Some federal police officers should take away the tin can from the corporation and confiscate its pencils ... I'm tired of tipping the Pullman Company."[71]

But the Brotherhood's strategy came to naught. The Railroad Mediation Board ruled that Section 10 of the Watson-Parker Act did not apply to the dispute between the union and the Pullman Company and that, "in the Board's judgment, an emergency as provided for in the said section does not exist in this case." Many porters, fed up with the company's stalling and the government's do-nothing policy, urged the Brotherhood to go ahead with the strike, indicating their willingness to risk the consequences. In a newspaper interview, Randolph announced that "this is the first time we have threatened a strike and we intend to go through with it if our men favor doing so." On April 24, 1928, Randolph informed the Railroad Mediation

Board that the Brotherhood had taken a strike vote, and that the strike had been approved by a vote of 6,053 to 17. He requested that the Board recommend that President Coolidge create an emergency board to prevent the disruption of rail service, but the Board refused.[72]

On June 6, 1928, the Brotherhood held a mass meeting in New York City at which Randolph and Webster notified the Pullman maids and porters that "a strike has been ordered for noon June 8th," "If there is no intervention by President Coolidge," the *New York Times* reported, "the strike will be effective tomorrow for more than 6,000 Pullman maids and porters affiliated with the union." The *Times* reported Randolph as saying:

> It is my earnest wish that a strike of porters and maids may be averted. The Brotherhood would like to settle the dispute according to modern, civilized, methods of negotiation, through discussion in conference as provided by the Railroad labor act.
>
> Since the Pullman Company recognizes its conductors' union, the porters feel that they are entitled to similar treatment. Our organization has resorted to every reasonable and honorable means to get the Pullman Company to meet the Brotherhood's representatives to talk over the cause of the dispute, but to no avail. For two and a half years the Pullman Company has employed an elaborate spy system of espionage, coercion and intimidation to prevent the porters and maids from joining the union.
>
> The union demands recognition, $150 a month and a 240-hour month or eight-hour day. The present wage is $72.50 a month and an hourage of nearly 400, with tips averaging $58 a month but out of which the porter pays $38 as occupational expense for shoe polish, food in transit and two uniforms a year.

The porters and maids were buoyed by William Green's statement to the press that the Pullman employees would receive "sympathetic support from the Federation, although the union is not affiliated with the AFL." Alexander Marks, AFL local organizer, also publicly pledged "the unlimited backing of our organization to the men." (He appears to have forgotten the women members.) "Your demands are reasonable and the American Federation of Labor will see to it that they are met," Randolph hailed the statements of Green and Marks, and proudly told the press: "The American Federation of Labor, the Big Four Brotherhood and labor organizations throughout the country have assured us of their united support." With such support, he assured the union members, "Filipinos, Japanese and Chinese strike-breakers will not be able to take the colored porters' place, satisfactorily. Apart from having to face bitter opposition from the strikers and their labor allies, these strike-breakers are too small in physique, are not numerous enough and will not be regarded as trustworthy by the traveling public."[73]

Frank R. Crosswaith, special organizer for the union, announced that "the wives and children of the porters will join the strikers on the picket lines when the strike begins." He continued:

> We expect a 100 percent tie-up of Pullman cars in New York, Chicago, Oakland and at many other points. As the strike progresses, we expect more porters to walk out. Of the 13,000 porters in the country, 7,000 will answer the first strike call and others will join us later.[74]

By the end of the day, June 7th, all of the branches of the union were notified to be ready to strike on the following day.[75] But on June 8 the front page headline in the *New York Times* read: "PULL-MAN STRIKE AVERTED BY GREEN." Although many Brotherhood leaders and the majority of the membership were ready and eager to walk out, Randolph had no intention of calling one. The strike vote had indicated that the porters were ready to strike and fight however long it was needed to secure their rights and win their demands, but "a strike vote doesn't mean that the porters will necessarily strike," Randolph declared. Three hours before they were scheduled to walk out Randolph received a telegram from William Green in which the AFL President declared:

> Even though the attitude of the Pullman Company is provocative to the extreme and the grievances of the porters and maids are great and exasperating, I am of the opinion that it would be unwise to engage in a strike now. Economic conditions are unfavorable to the success of such an undertaking. Because of a lack of understanding, public opinion has not been crystallized in support of your demands.[76]

So much for the tremendous barrage of reports hailing the era of prosperity in the United States. So much, too, for the intensive public relations campaign Randolph had waged for so many months.

Green counselled instead "a campaign of education and public enlightenment regarding the justice of your cause and seriousness of your grievances." On June 8, 1928, the same day the telegram was received, the Brotherhood's leadership called off the strike.[77]

Randolph's decision not go forward after being empowered to do so by the membership was a serious blow to the morale of the porters. But the Brotherhood's leaders argued that the mere threat of a strike had brought the union a great gain, since it had "reversed the conception of the American public stereotype of a shuffling, tip-taking porter to an upstanding American worker, demanding his right to organize a union of his own, as well as a living wage." But the *Pittsburgh Courier*, now strongly anti-Randolph, declared that the

Brotherhood had suffered a major defeat and insisted that the union had never intended to call a strike—that it had all been simply another "Randolph bluff."[78]

The Communists claimed a sell-out and charged that the whole episode smacked of "typical AFL and Railroad Brotherhood type of leadership." They charged that the Brotherhood leaders had sold out to the AFL in exchange for the promise of a charter in the Federation, and called upon the porters to replace the leaders with "a militant class-conscious leadership."[79] For years to come, Black Communists were to point to the calling off of the strike as a blow to all Black workers. "The chances of success were very bright. The rank and file of the porters were very militant. The Randolph leadership and the AFL called the strike off, betraying Negro workers in the interest of the labor fakers," *The Liberator*, a Black Communist weekly, declared on July 20, 1931.

The American Negro Labor Congress started a drive to reject the leadership that had sold out the porters and it made some headway, especially in the Oakland area.[80] Randolph, in turn, launched a campaign to kill the "reptile" of Communism, declaring that under no circumstances would the Brotherhood have anything to do with that "sinister and destructive crowd" and that any porter who cooperated with the American Negro Labor Congress would be expelled from the union.[81] Sperling Spero and Abram L. Harris argue that the Brotherhood leaders reached their decision because they knew the porters would not strike. However, all evidence indicates that the opposite was actually the case and even Randolph wrote that the strike "could have been effective."[82] He insisted that the strike had been merely "postponed," but by mid-July 1928, nothing more was heard of a walkout. The Brotherhood's membership had declined so seriously that the Pullman Company stepped up its practice of discharging porters who were known to be adherents of the union and circulated yellow-dog contracts among the rest, forcing porters to sign an oath of loyalty to the company as a condition of further employment.[83]

In the weeks following the aborted strike of 1928, Randolph concentrated on achieving the affiliation of the Brotherhood with the AFL. Originally critical of the AFL for its policy of craft unionism and its exclusion of Black workers, by 1925, Randolph had become conciliatory toward the Federation. Already in 1923, he had attempted to mend his bridges with Gompers, whom he had earlier condemned as the symbol of all that was evil in the AFL, by inviting him to contribute articles to *The Messenger*. At the time of Gompers' death,

Randolph announced his support of Gompers' position that the AFL could not insist that all affiliated unions grant Black workers entrance into their ranks or grant them equal rights, because southern whites would not accept Blacks as equals. From the beginning of Green's presidency in 1924, Randolph sought his advice, support, and practical knowhow in building the Brotherhood. Green, who was especially worried by Communist efforts to influence the Black workers, regarded the success of the fledgling Brotherhood and its affiliation with the AFL as a way of assuring that, if Blacks were to be organized, it would be under "wise leadership." The Brotherhood's leadership, sorely in need of Green's financial assistance and moral support, and sharing much of his aversion toward the Communists, found it beneficial to cultivate harmonious relations. Most of the AFL internationals did not share Green's enthusiasm for the Brotherhood, recalling Randolph's earlier attacks on their unions and remembering that, while anti-Communist, he was still a Socialist. But since the porters' union did not threaten the segregated job structure or their monopoly, they were prepared to support the union's entry within the "House of Labor." Even the railroad brotherhoods favored affiliation of the Brotherhood with the AFL, where it would be kept by jurisdictional rules from encroaching on railroad jobs set aside for whites only.[84]

To a number of Black papers and politicians, however, the proposed affiliation of the Brotherhood with the AFL was enough to kick up another storm of criticism of the union. The Chicago *Defender* denounced the Brotherhood for wanting to join the Federation, which it called "paradoxically plutocratic and communistic." Through the Louisville *News*, a Black politician urged the Brotherhood to have nothing to do with the AFL and, instead, "to seek to win the Pullman Company officials.[85]

As early as 1927, the Brotherhood had applied for an international charter from the AFL, but the application remained dormant because the International Bartenders and Beverage Dispensers of America, basing its claim on a 1920 decision of the AFL Executive Council, claimed jurisdiction over the porters.[86] Then in 1928, the Hotel and Restaurant Employees' International objected to a charter for the Brotherhood, claiming jurisdiction on the ground that the Pullman porters were really hotel workers on wheels. Green tried to persuade the Hotel and Restaurant Union to agree to the granting of an independent charter to the Brotherhood, but failed. The union insisted that the Brotherhood enter the AFL as part of its international, and the other internationals backed its claim. Randolph knew that if he consented to tie the Brotherhood to an organization like the Hotel and Restaurant Employees, which had a constitutional provision establishing the inferior status of Black workers, his leadership would be in serious jeopardy. He rejected the "feasible solution" offered by the AFL, and the porters gave him a resounding vote of confidence.[87]

In mid-1928, Randolph again applied for a charter for the Brotherhood. This time he found Green cool to the application. The latter had been told that Randolph "had close connections with Communists" and had mismanaged the finances of *The Messenger* magazine. He told Randolph that the AFL would "not tolerate communism in any form," and he advised the Brotherhood leader to make his position clear on this point. He was also to present a complete picture of his management of *The Messenger*.

Randolph's answer must have satisfied Green, since he again took up the question of the Brotherhood's application for a charter. At conferences with Green and Edward Flore of the Bartenders' League, Randolph made it clear that the Brotherhood would never consent to be just another dues-paying "Jim-Crow auxiliary." For his part, Flore refused to withdraw his claim to jurisdiction.

In the end, a compromise was reached under which Randolph, in order, as he put it, "to establish a beach-head," affiliated thirteen of the Brotherhood's largest divisions as federal unions directly affiliated with the AFL. When the Bartenders' League learned of this decision, it asked the AFL convention to overrule the agreement, but the delegates at the 1929 session upheld the Executive Council.[88]

Thus, the Brotherhood entered the AFL, not as an independent international union, but under the system which had long been used to deal with Black workers who could not gain membership in the regular unions of their crafts — in short, "a substitute for real unionism" and one which had long been resented by Black workers.[89] Some sections of the Black press, along with several Negro politicians and clergymen, denounced Randolph for having anything to do with the AFL, citing its general exclusion of most Black workers and its imposition of Jim Crow status on the rest. Most of all, Randolph was criticized for accepting "federal union" status when experience had proved that under it, Black workers had no control over their working conditions, since all authority rested with the parent white union. It was the type of unionism that had completely hamstrung the efforts of Black workers to improve their standards. The Communists termed Randolph's acquiescence another indication of the bankruptcy of the Brotherhood leadership.[90]

Randolph defended his decision as fundamentally sound, arguing that as the delegate of the New York division, he would gain entrance to AFL conventions. Once there, be could study at close hand this "American version of the labor movement" and wage a battle to remove the stumbling blocks it placed in the way of unionizing Black workers. Randolph saw the sleeping car porters as "the spearhead which will make possible the organization of Negro workers." He was convinced that the Brotherhood could best do so within the Federation.[91]

The NAACP supported Randolph's position, and speaking for the organization, Dr. Abram L. Harris declared that the Brotherhood had "taken a positive step by aligning with white organized labor." He predicted that it would eventually receive an international charter which would go a long way "toward bridging the gap between white and Negro workers.[92] The National Urban League dismissed this view. In an open letter to William Green, T. Arnold Hill, the league's director of industrial relations, condemned the issuance of federal charters, noting that it gave Black workers "the badge but not the protection of unionism." In fact, he maintained, federal unions weakened Black workers by placing them under the jurisdiction of an Executive Council made up of vice-presidents of the AFL, many of whose unions barred Blacks by means of specific clauses in their constitutions.[93]

In his reply, Green defended the federal union method, insisted that the AFL had done all it could in trying to organize Blacks, and, echoing Gompers, argued that if few Blacks belonged to international unions, the fault lay with themselves. Black workers had simply not yet gained a labor consciousness. "The Federation," Green wrote, "cannot effectively carry the gospel of unionism until workers [are] ready to hear and act."[94]

One result of the AFL's decision to charter individual Brotherhood locals rather than grant the union a national charter was to make it exceedingly difficult for the Brotherhood to maintain a national structure.[95] Yet it would be impossible for the Brotherhood to organize the porters for effective action against Pullman without a national structure. To meet this problem, Randolph decided to call the Brotherhood's first national convention in Chicago in 1929. He did so over the opposition of William Green, who called such action "premature." At the convention, the Brotherhood adopted a constitution and held its first election of officers. Randolph was elected president, Milton P. Webster first vice-president and Roy Lancaster secretary-treasurer.[96]

At this time, the Brotherhood was all but defunct. Its membership had declined to the vanishing point after the Pullman Company fired or suspended every porter found to have voted in favor of the strike. But Randolph was determined that the union of Black workers must not fail. "We are making history for our race," be emphasized in a letter to Webster. "We are sounding the tocsin for a new race freedom."[97]

CHAPTER 14

SACCO-VANZETTI

In 1921, the American people were confronted by two terrible miscarriages of justice. One was already several years old. Tom Mooney and Warren K. Billings, militant labor organizers, had been falsely accused of having planted a bomb during the San Francisco Preparedness Day parade of 1916, which exploded and killed ten people. Billings had been sentenced to life imprisonment and Mooney to death. International protests, including those in St. Petersburg, Russia, had forced President Woodrow Wilson to appeal to the governor of California to commute Mooney's sentence to life imprisonment, which the governor reluctantly agreed to do. Although evidence disclosed that Mooney had been several miles from the scene of the explosion when the bomb went off, and that the two men had been found guilty on perjured testimony, the state of California refused to either grant a new trial or release Mooney and Billings.*

In 1920, further evidence of perjured testimony came to light. Draper Hand, who had been the detective in charge of the witnesses during the trial, admitted to the California authorities that he had made up evidence against Mooney and had coached and rehearsed the witnesses to present such evidence to the jury. It was he who had coached and rehearsed the witness Oxman, whose testimony had convinced the jurors of Mooney's guilt. A year later, Earl Hutcher and his wife disclosed that Oxman had been visiting them in Woodland, California at the very time that he had testified to seeing

---

* For a discussion of the early history of the case, *see* Philip S. Foner, *History of the Labor Movement in the United States*, Vol. 7.

Mooney in San Francisco. That same year, the witness John MacDonald gave an affidavit to Frank P. Walsh, a member of the Mooney
defense team, in which he stated that "the essential points of his
testimony were dictated by the District Attorney of California." But a
special Grand Jury denied immunity to MacDonald, and the threats
made upon him were so great that he refused to testify before that
body. Walsh wrote that the same powerful capitalist interests that had
brought about the conviction of Mooney and Billings were still at
work in San Francisco.[1]

The result was that Mooney and Billings remained in prison for a
crime they had not committed.

Three thousand miles across the country, two other radicals—Nicola Sacco and Bartolomeo Vanzetti—were also in prison for a crime
they did not commit.

ARREST AND TRIAL OF
SACCO AND VANZETTI

In a previous volume, we dealt with the arrest of the two immigrant Italian anarchists.[*] The crime with which Sacco and Vanzetti
were charged took place on April 15, 1920. A shoe company in South
Braintree, Massachusetts was the scene of a robbery and murder. As a
paymaster and guard were carrying the $16,000 payroll to the fac-
tory, two men who had been waiting nearby shot and killed them,
seized the payroll and were then picked up by a car carrying three
other men. Sacco and Vanzetti were arrested three weeks later while
accompanying Mike Broda, an anarchist friend suspected of involvement in the crime, when he went to pick up his car from a repair
shop.

The trial of Sacco and Vanzetti for the South Braintree crime
began on May 31, 1921. Much was made by the prosecution of the
fact that the two men had been armed when they were arrested as
robbery and murder suspects, and that they had lied under the initial questioning, denying either knowing Broda or being anarchists.
This behavior, the prosecution charged, revealed a "consciousness of
guilt." But the truth is that they were armed because they feared for
their lives. Their arrests occurred during the period of the most
intense political repression in American history. The postwar Red

---

[*] Philip S. Foner, *History of the Labor Movement in the United States*, Vol. 8.

Scare culminated in the notorious Palmer raids of January, 1920, in which four thousand radicals were rounded up and several hundred eventually deported. Just before Sacco and Vanzetti were arrested, an anarchist comrade of theirs, Andrea Salsedo, either fell or was pushed to his death in New York City after weeks of illegal detention by federal authorities.[2]

The evidence against Vanzetti was incredibly thin. Only one man claimed to have seen him at the scene of the crime, and he identified the swarthy Vanzetti as the driver of the getaway car, contradicting all other witnesses who described the driver as of fair complexion. The prosecution also claimed, with little supporting evidence, that the .38 revolver Vanzetti was carrying at the time of his arrest belonged to the murdered guard. The defense, headed by Fred Moore, the radical lawyer in many IWW cases, produced thirteen witnesses, all Italian, to testify that Vanzetti had been selling fish on the day of the crime.

Some prosecution witnesses, in violation of standard police procedure, had viewed Sacco individually instead of in a lineup, whereupon their initial recollection of the murderer's physical appearance improved remarkably. Others incredibly claimed that Sacco had spoken to them in clear, unaccented, colloquial English.

The key testimony against Sacco was the assertion that the .32 bullet found in the body of the guard had been fired from the revolver Sacco had on him when arrested. Each side produced ballistic experts to affirm or deny the claim. The prosecution expert, Captain William Proctor of the State Police, testified that the bullet was "consistent with" having been fired from Sacco's gun. He later admitted that the prosecution had carefully coached him in that exact wording after he had said he could not make a positive identification. He added that he did not believe Sacco's gun had fired the shot.[3]

Sacco's alibi was that he had gone to Boston the day of the crime to obtain a passport to return to Italy. The defense produced witnesses from the Italian Consulate, others who had lunched with him in Boston, and a man who recognized Sacco as having sat across from him on the train. The prosecution did not destroy the alibi. Nor did the prosecution attempt to determine who had fired five of the six bullets found in the bodies of the dead men, to link the defendants with the stolen money, to establish a motive for the crime, or to present fingerprints as evidence, even though newspaper reports indicated fingerprints had been found in the getaway car.[4]

The prosecution was convinced that in the existing atmosphere of widespread hostility to aliens and radicals, no real evidence was nec-

essary. The entire trial was characterized by intense hostility toward
the defendants. The blatant prejudice shown by Judge Webster
Thayer and by prosecutor Frederick Katzmann shocked even sea-
soned newspaper reporters. During cross-examination, Katzmann
bullied the defendants as to their political beliefs. He asked Sacco
whether he loved America, why he had avoided the draft, what he
thought of Harvard University, and whether he sent his son to public
school. It turned out he did. Frank Sibley, the veteran reporter who
covered the trial for the *Boston Globe*, remarked of Judge Thayer's
conduct:

> What affected me more than anything else was his manner. It is nothing
> that you can read in the record. In my 35 years [as a newspaper man] I
> never saw anything like it .... His whole manner, attitude seemed to be
> that the jurors were there to convict these men.... The rulings against the
> defendants were done with the air of prejudice and scorn.

Judge Thayer later boasted to a friend: "Did you see what I did to
those anarchist bastards?"[5]

After a trial which more than justified later charges that the "legal
proceedings were permeated with unfairness," Sacco and Vanzetti
were convinced and sentenced to death in the electric chair. Their
"guilt" was that they were immigrants, and more important, anarchists active in the class struggles of their time. They symbolized the
alien threat to provincial Anglo-Saxon America. A prominent legal
scholar, Dean John Wymore of Northwestern University Law School,
linked Sacco and Vanzetti with, among other things, "the thugs of
India, the Camorra of Naples, the Black Hand of Sicily."[6]

About four years after the trial, a fellow prisoner of Sacco and
Vanzetti in the Dedham jail, Celestino Maderios, convicted of killing
a cashier during a bank robbery, confessed to involvement in the
South Braintree crime. He asserted that Sacco and Vanzetti were
innocent, and that he had participated in the robbery and murders
as a member of the Providence, Rhode Island-based Morelli gang.
But Judge Thayer dismissed the Madeiros confession, suggesting that
the convicted killer expected a payoff from the defense committee.[7]

Before Sacco and Vanzetti had been indicted for the crime, New
Bedford police were engaged in their own investigation based on the
supposition that the Morelli gang were the probable bandits. Joe
Morelli, the head of the gang, faced indictments involving the robbery of shoe factories in South Braintree, including one at the company where the crime occurred. After the indictment of Sacco and
Vanzetti, the probe by the New Bedford police was dropped. Not a

single effort was made by the authorities to determine whether there was any validity to Madeiros' confession.[8]

For six years, defense lawyers filed successive motions for a new trial, pleading new evidence, recantation of prosecution witnesses, the prejudice of the judge, and the confession implicating the Morelli gang in the robbery. But Judge Thayer rejected all motions, and in 1926, the Massachusetts Supreme Court upheld his decision. Finally, in the spring of 1927, Thayer reaffirmed the death sentence.[9]

During their long agony, Sacco and Vanzetti sat in prison awaiting their tragic fate. The case had become an international *cause célèbre*, attracting the support of thousands of workers here and abroad. Their steadfastness, dignity and transparent honesty also aroused the sympathy of many people who would not ordinarily have concerned themselves with the fate of two Italian anarchists accused of a brutal murder.

While in state prison at Charlestown, Massachusetts, Vanzetti wrote a series of autobiographical notes, translated from the Italian by Eugene Lyons. They were published in *Advance*, organ of the Amalgamated Clothing Workers of America in November and December, 1921 under the title, "The Story of a Proletarian Life." It was introduced with the editorial note: "The conviction of Vanzetti and his friend Nicola Sacco on a murder charge has roused the greatest international protest since the Mooney-Billings conviction."[10]

Advance also urged its readers to write Sacco and Vanzetti in prison, noting: "It is too easy to forget that Sacco and Vanzetti are not mere names but human beings shut away from the light, weighed down to the tedium of idle waiting, waiting, waiting, waiting ... for the hangman." It continued:

> Write to Sacco and Vanzetti. That is the request of the Defense Committee in Boston. By heeding it you will make life more bearable for the prisoners. If you are one of the thousands who believe in the innocence of Sacco and Vanzetti tell them so. If you are one of the thousands who, like the two Italians, are imbued with the spirit of the larger love which brooks no factions or frontier, tell them so.[11]

Editorially *Advance* noted that the government of the United States had demanded release of American prisoners in Russia. After pointing out that "no such demand is made upon other governments," it commented:

> There can be no grievance against the efforts of a government to secure freedom for its citizens, But why not begin at home where the government's authority is supreme? While Washington is threatening Moscow, American citizens are pleading with the American government for the

liberation of some of the best Americans at home. Why is Debs still in prison? Why is Mooney still in the penitentiary? When will the unceasing demand for their freedom be heeded? There is no sign of hope. There is every indication that Moscow will respect the demand from Washington sooner than Washington will respect the demand from its own people.

And while the old industrial and political prisoners are kept behind bars new ones are added to their number. The latest victims are the two Italians, Sacco and Vanzetti. They were charged with murder which could not be proven against them, but they were convicted of murder because radicalism, not denied by them, was proven against them. They paid for their loyalty to their class.

An appeal will be taken to a higher court. That will require funds which must be raised. Sacco and Vanzetti must not lose their lives because of lack of funds to save them. Labor organizations will be appealed to for assistance and there should be a liberal response.[12]

In June 1922, the Amalgamated Clothing Workers and the International Ladies' Garment Workers voted to raise money for the defense of Sacco and Vanzetti, and called upon their constituent locals to do likewise, urging them "to extend all moral and financial aid to the movements for securing the freedom of Sacco and Vanzetti." In a message telegraphed to the prisoners, the ILGWU expressed fervent faith in their innocence, and added: "Organized labor in America will not rest until the sinister conspiracy which resulted in your incarceration is exposed and your freedom won."[13]

Elizabeth Gurley Flynn of the Workers' Defense Union was introduced by Amalgamated President Sidney Hillman at union meetings in Cleveland and Chicago, as "among the first and most consistent champions of Sacco and Vanzetti. The former "Rebel Girl" of the IWW declared:

It is not only a question of these two young men, but it is a question even more vital than their lives and their liberties. The question is: Shall a workingman, especially a foreign-born workingman, put his neck in the noose, put his life in the shadow of death if he dares to speak the message of organization and the message of rebellion to the foreign-born workers in this country.[14]

COMMUNISTS AND THE DEFENSE MOVEMENT

From the earliest days of the case in 1920, when few outside the anarchist ranks had even heard of Sacco and Vanzetti, the Communists worked tirelessly to save the two men. In 1920 the Party had been decimated by the Palmer Raids, but Art Shields, arriving in

Boston to work with the defense committee, found the Communists distributing literature and holding meetings to rally support for Sacco and Vanzetti. The *Liberator*, the Communist cultural publication which replaced the *Masses* after that monthly had been forced to suspend publication as a result of persecution during World War I, published Art Shields' first defense article from Boston in December, 1920. Shortly after this, the Communist Party published Shields' pamphlet, *Are They Doomed?* with the cover illustrated by Robert Minor, the great radical artist and member of the Party's central committee. The first issue of the *Labor Herald*, published In March, 1922, referred to the case of Sacco and Vanzetti, The official organ of the Trade Union Educational League called out: "Labor! Act at Once to Rescue Sacco and Vanzetti!" When the TUEL held its first national conference in August of that same year, it adopted a special resolution pledging "entire and whole-hearted support" in the task of securing the release of Sacco and Vanzetti.[15]

On November 15, 1924, after the death sentence was imposed by Judge Thayer, the Communist International, the Red International of Labor Unions and the Communist Youth International issued an appeal from Moscow which the *Daily Worker* published, declaring that it "should stir the labor movement of America from one end of the country to the other." "The murder of Sacco and Vanzetti must be prevented," urged the appeal. "We must wrest these, our revolutionary brothers, from the claws of the American bourgeoisie! Organize mass demonstrations! Plaster this appeal upon every street corner! Demand the liberation of Sacco and Vanzetti!"[16]

The Workers' (Communist) Party followed with its own call to "save Sacco and Vanzetti from death." Signed by William Z. Foster, chairman, and Charles E. Ruthenberg, secretary of the Party's Central Executive Committee, the document read in part:

> The Workers' (Communist) Party of America declares that the cause of Sacco and Vanzetti is the cause of the whole working class. It declares that the attack on their lives and liberty is an attack on the lives and liberties of all workers everywhere. It believes that only the united action of the working class can free these worker victims of capitalism's courts and save them from death.
> The Workers' (Communist) Party of America declares that the persecution of Sacco and Vanzetti is part of the drive against the most militant of the workers in America—that the Communists and members of the I.W.W., trade unionists railroaded for activity in strikes, who are in jail or under indictment, are victims of the same class and the same government that tries to send Sacco and Vanzetti to their deaths.

The Workers' (Communist) Party of America calls upon all organizations of workers in America to join with it in a united front for Sacco and Vanzetti against their capitalist enemies and for their immediate release....[17]

March 17, 1925 was set by the Workers' (Communist) Party as "Sacco and Vanzetti Day," on which mass protest meetings were to be held in every industrial center. "Make Sacco and Vanzetti Day a Red Day for Freedom," the Central Executive Committee appealed. Demonstrations to free Sacco and Vanzetti took place that day in 200 cities and towns. The meetings were addressed by members of the Sacco-Vanzetti Defense Committee, a number of them Italian anarchist workers, and by leaders of the Workers' (Communist) Party.[18]

The first issue of the *Labor Defender*, (January 1926) the monthly magazine of the International Labor Defense (ILD), edited by Communists, carried an article on the case by Ralph Chaplin entitled "In the Shadow of the Electric Chair."[19] Thereafter, every issue carried articles on the case. ILD meetings for Sacco and Vanzetti were held all over the country. On April 25, 1926, Vanzetti wrote to the ILD from his prison cell:

> The echo of your campaign in our behalf has reached my heart. I repeat, I will repeat to the last, only the people, our comrades, the world revolutionary proletariat, can save us from the powers of the capitalist hyenas.[20]

And from Sacco's cell came this message eight days later:

> ...your unchanged solidarity towards your two comrades ... brought me a great relief, for your brotherly and upturned spirit that you are showing towards your brotherly comrades, victims of an unjust persecution.

When a liberal lawyer complained that "Communist propaganda" was endangering the campaign to save Sacco and Vanzetti, Frank P. Walsh of the defense, replied: "They were kept alive by propaganda, especially the Communist propaganda. Let's say nothing against Communist propaganda at this time. Let's have more propaganda."[21]

FELIX FRANKFURTER'S ANALYSIS

In 1927 Felix Frankfurter, then teaching at Harvard Law School, published *The Case of Sacco and Vanzetti*, which helped immensely to rally respectable opinion behind the two men. "By systematic exploitation of the defendants' alien blood, their imperfect knowledge of English, their unpopular social views, and their opposition to the war," Frankfurter wrote, "the District Attorney invoked against them a riot of political passion and patriotic sentiment, and the trial judge

connived at—one had almost written, cooperated in—the process."
Frankfurter wrote further that "Judge Thayer's opinion stands un-
matched for discrepancies between what the record discloses and
what the opinion conveys. His 25,000 word document cannot be
accurately described otherwise than a farrago of misquotations, mis-
representations, suppression and mutilation." Sacco and Vanzetti, he
insisted, never really made sense as the murderers. Neither had a
criminal record. As he wrote: "A good worker regularly employed at
his trade but away on a particular day which is clearly accounted for,
and a dreamy fish peddler openly engaged in political propaganda
neither do nor can suddenly commit an isolated job of highly professional banditry." As Frankfurter saw it, "the case against Sacco and
Vanzetti for murder was part of a collusive effort between the District
Attorney and the agents of the Department of Justice to rid the
country of these Italians because of their Red activities."[22]

THE LOWELL COMMISSION

Franfurter's presentation was a clarion call to all liberals, all aca-
demics, all concerned citizens and others who were impressed by the
future Supreme Court Justice's vindication of the innocence of the
two anarchists and the outrage of their trial. But it did not lead to a
new trial. However, along with the rising protest movement, it did
lead to the appointment by Governor Fuller of a three-man advisory
commission to consider the fairness of the verdict. Consisting of
Samuel Stratton, president of the Massachusetts Institute of Technol-
ogy, Robert Grant, a former probate judge, and at the head, A.
Lawrence Lowell, president of Harvard, the commission was thoroughly isolated from the experiences of Sacco and Vanzetti. As the
New Republic observed, "The life of an Italian anarchist was as foreign
to them as life on Mars."[23]

The Lowell Commission did not find anything wrong with the
evidence against the two men. They even offered a witness against
them, Lotti Tatillo, that the prosecution had been afraid to use because of her unreliability. The Commission, however, used her con-
tradictory testimony. "The woman is eccentric, not unimpeachable in
conduct," they wrote, "but the Committee believes that in this case
her testimony is well worth consideration." About Vanzetti, the Commission concluded: "On the whole, we are of opinion that Vanzetti
also was guilty beyond reasonable doubt."[24] By using the phrase "on
the whole," the Commission seemed to infer that a shadow of doubt
did exist. But Governor Fuller ignored this. The Commission's re-

port allayed any doubts that he might have had about the executions.[25]

The appeals process continued up to the Supreme Court of the United States. But the Court refused to interfere. The "great dissenter," Supreme Court Justice Oliver Wendell Holmes, not only refused to stay the execution, but would not even read the evidence in the case, "except on the limited points that came before me.[26]

DATE OF EXECUTION SET

On April 9, 1927 the sentence of death was again imposed on the two men by Judge Thayer, and the execution date set for July 10. It was later postponed to August 23, 1927.

Sacco stood up and told Judge Thayer:

I am not an orator. It is not very familiar with me the English language.... I know the sentence will be between two class, the oppressed class and the rich class, and there will be always collision between one and the other. We fraternize the people with the books, with the literature. You persecute the people, tyrannize over them and kill them. We try the education of people always. You try to put a path between us and some other nationality that hates each other. That is why I am here today on this bench, for having been the oppressed class. Well, you are the oppressor.... As I said before, Judge Thayer know all my life, and he know that I am never been guilty, never,—not yesterday nor today nor forever.[27]

And Vanzetti told Judge Thayer:

I would not wish to a dog or to a snake, to the most low and misfortunate creature of the earth—I would not wish to any of them what I have had to suffer for things that I am not guilty. But my conviction is that I have suffered for things that I am guilty of. I am suffering because I am a radical and indeed I am a radical; I have suffered because I was an Italian, and indeed I am an Italian; I have suffered more for my family and for my beloved than for myself; but I am so convinced to be right that if you could execute me two times, and if I could be reborn two other times, I would live again to do what I have done already.[28]

On May 27, 1927, Vanzetti wrote: "We are ready to ... die, but be men to the last."[29]

INTENSIFIED ACTIVITIES TO SAVE SACCO AND VANZETTI

As the day of execution drew near, various groups of protesters began to arrive in Boston to lend their services to the defense. The New York Sacco-Vanzetti Emergency Committee of the International

Labor Defense sent the "Sacco-Vanzetti Freedom Delegation" on buses to Boston. Led by Rose Baron and William L. Patterson of the Communist Party and the ILD, the group joined others protesting the impending executions. Later Patterson explained why he went to Boston:

> I viewed their murder as inseparably related to the attempted murder of Tom Mooney and Warren Billings, two labor organizers in San Francisco accused of bombing a First World War Preparedness Day Parade in 1916. I recognized in it a profound relationship to the savage persecution and the attempted terrorization of Blacks who, seeking to secure equality of political rights, opportunity and respect for their inalienable human right, found these social attributes to be summarily absent and ignored. They themselves were seized by state police or state police or state-inspired mobsters, charged with rape and lynched legally or otherwise....
>
> As a Communist, the fight for the lives of Nicola Sacco and Bartolomeo Vanzetti revealed to me the historic necessity to unify all exploited and oppressed in social struggle against a common foe....[30]

Among those who arrived in Boston to join the protests were an impressive array of writers. They included John Dos Passos, H.L. Mencken, Heywood Broun, Dorothy Parker and Katherine Anne Porter.* "Save them, for your honor, for the honor of your children, and

---

* In her memoir, *The Never-Ending Wrong*, published in 1977, Porter leaves the impression that the intellectuals were the only ones who took part in the campaign to save Sacco and Vanzetti from the electric chair. The memoir is permeated with vicious anti-Communism including the charge that the Communists used the case of Sacco and Vanzetti merely for propaganda, "hoping only for their deaths as a political argument." She reports that she expressed the wish to Rose Baron "that we might save the lives of Sacco and Vanzetti"—only to have Baron snap at her: "Alive—what for? They are no earthly good to us alive." (*The Never-Ending Wrong* [Boston, 1977], pp. 28, 32-34.) But all who worked with Rose Baron testified to her earnestness, sincerity, and the tireless efforts she put into the campaign to save the lives of Sacco and Vanzetti. (Art Shields, "The CPUSA Defends Its Class," *Daily World*, Sept. 24, 1977; Arthur Zipser, "Sacco and Vanzetti: Their Friends and Enemies," *Political Affairs* 57 [January, 1978]: 39-41).

In her biography of Josephine Herbst, the radical novelist and journalist, Elinor Langer reveals that Katherine Anne Porter, Herbst's close friend over many years, furnished the FBI with allegations about her past Communist associations and radical predilections. This information, based on material obtained by Langer under the Freedom of Information Act, throws additional light on Porter's anti-Communist bias. (Elinor Langer, *Josephine Herbst: The Story She Could Never Tell*, [Boston, 1984], 118-30.)

For an effective answer to the charge that the Communists used the case for their own purposes, and preferred to have the two men dead rather than alive, see Alfred J. Kutzik, "The Sacco-Vanzetti Case and the Communists," *Nature, Science & Thought* 2(1969): 164-83.

for the generations yet unborn," wrote French writer Anatole France in an "Appeal to the American People," one of the many important authors and thinkers who put their names to the call for justice. H.G. Wells, George Bernard Shaw, Albert Einstein, Madame Curie, and many others asked that the lives of the two men be spared.[31]

While intellectuals did help attract world attention to the case, it was the anarchists, Communists, and the labor movement who carried the burden. We have already noted the contributions of the Communists and the Workers' (Communist) Party. Italian anarchists organized the defense committees from the beginning of the case, and Italian-Americans provided the funds to keep the defense movement going. Most of the $300,000 that had been raised by the end of 1926 came in small donations from working people, a majority of them Italian, and from such organizations as the *Lega Antifascita* of Pittsburgh, and the Brooklyn Italian-Democratic Club. The International Labor Defense also played an important role in raising funds.[32]

Trade unions were involved in defense activities from the beginning of the case. But it was with the imposition of the death sentence after the trial, that the unions really became active. The 1924 AFL convention demanded a new trial for Sacco and Vanzetti, describing the defendants as "defenseless victims of race and national prejudice and class hatred." The 1926 convention unanimously passed a resolution calling for a Congressional investigation of the case and a new trial. Similar demands were voiced by AFL international unions, locals and city central labor councils across the country. By 1927 a dozen state labor federations had also demanded a new trial. Locals of the United Mine Workers, the International Fur Workers, and the International Ladies' Garment Workers were especially active in fund raising.[33]

On June 17, 1927, the Central Executive Committee, Trade Union Committee of the Communist Party adopted a statement that said: "In relation to Sacco and Vanzetti .. that the CP begin to agitate among the miners the idea of a short mass strike on behalf of Sacco and Vanzetti."[34] On July 4, 1927, 20,000 representatives of labor unions and Italian fraternal organizations marched in Philadelphia to protest the impending executions.

On July 7, twenty thousand workers gathered in New York's Union Square to voice their protest. By the second week in August, the protests took the form of strikes. On August 10, several hundred thousand workers downed tools to protest the impending execution. In New York City, over 200,000 workers were involved. Fifty thousand struck in Philadelphia, 20,000 in Detroit, 10,000 in Rochester and Newark. Coal miners in Pennsylvania and metal miners in northern Colorado stayed out of the pits. Five thousand demonstrated in Cleveland, while the cigar makers of Tampa, the building tradesmen of Mount Vernon, New York, granite cutters of Quincy, Massachusetts, and thousands of other workers demonstrated or stayed home. On August 22, when the news came that the Massachusetts Supreme Court had denied the final appeal, workers in shops, mines, factories, and offices all over the country walked out.[35]

On March 13, 1927, at Walsenburg, Colorado, twenty-seven delegates from twenty-two mines attended the first public meeting of the Industrial Union 210-220, organized by the IWW to challenge District No. 15 of the United Mine Workers of America, AFL. The meeting passed a series of resolutions urging support for Sacco and Vanzetti, Tom Mooney, and "others held in prisons and jails for their loyalty to the working class."[36]

At a second meeting of IWW's Industrial Union 210-220 on July 14, 1927, at Walsenburg, fifty-five delegates from thirty-two coal camps, voted a second expression of support for Sacco and Vanzetti.[37]*

During the summer of 1927, the international executive board of the IWW called upon the nation's workers to lay down their tools for three days to protest the impending execution of Sacco and Vanzetti.** On August 6, 400 miners attended a meeting at Walsenburg

---

*The meeting drew up preliminary demands, including a 6-hour day, the election of checkweightman and pit committees, and no coal loaded on idle days.

**The international executive board also announced that the IWW General Defense Committee had just won a stunning victory in the case of Fiske v. Kansas decided by the U.S. Supreme Court. Harold B. Fiske was a 26-year-old native of Clinton, Washington, and during the summer of 1923, he was working as an organizer for the IWW Agricultural Workers Industrial Union, No. 110. After admitting he was an IWW organizer, Fiske was arrested and charged with violating the Kansas Criminal Syndicalism Act which prohibited the advocacy of force or violence as a means of political or industrial change. After deliberating for two hours, the jury found Fiske guilty of violating the Criminal Syndicalism Act, and on September 20, 1923, he was sentenced to serve from one to 10 years in the Kansas state prison.

After losing the appeal in the Kansas Supreme Court, the General Defense Council appealed to the Supreme Court of the United States. On May 16, 1927, the Supreme Court unanimously reversed Fisher's conviction. As Richard C. Cortiner points out: "...the Wobblies had through their Legal Defense Committee made a significant contribution to a fundamental change in the protection of freedom of expression under the constitution." ("The Wobblies and Fiske v. Kansas: Victory and Disintegration," *Kansas History* 4 [Summer, 1980]: 30-37.)

to discuss this action. At this meeting they voted to accept the proposal, to stop work on August 8, and to picket all mines in the Walsenburg district, IWW or UMW led. Spokespersons for the UMWA predicted that "the walk-out would fail," but Sheriff Harry Capps of Huerfano county disagreed, pointing out that "fully two-thirds of the miners in the district were members of the IWW."[38]

Picketing began as scheduled at 5 a.m. on August 8. The sheriff told the local press that out of a workforce of 1,167 miners, 1,132 had stayed out of the pits. Although the United Mine Workers refused to have anything to do with this work stoppage, the local leaders declared that its members would not cross picket lines.[39]

The following day, August 9, the members of the State Industrial Commission met with A.S. Embree, Paul Seidler (IWW international executive committee representative in Colorado), A.K. Payne, and José Villa—the leaders of the walkout. Upon learning that the Attorney-General's office stood ready to issue an injunction at the Commission's request, these IWW officials agreed to ask the men to return to work.[40] Meetings of the striking miners were hurriedly called at Aguilar, Morley, Starkville, and Walsenburg. Embree addressed the Aguilar meeting:

> Friends and fellow workers: You have now been on strike twice as long as any strike that has been called for in any part of the country. ...We had originally planned the strike should last three days. I am sorry that we are still a day short, but circumstances and conditions must be taken into account. Your committee which you elected last night to confer with the state industrial commission considers the protest in the Sacco-Vanzetti case has accomplished its purpose. As far as this district is concerned, you have already done more than any other part of the country. The strike was called by your vote. It cannot be called off unless you vote to call it off.[41]

With only six dissenting votes, the miners at these four meetings decided to return to work.[42]

Although the IWW strike was an unexpected success, it was not the greatest strike action in support of Sacco and Vanzetti "than in any other part of the country." That honor belongs to the Italian community of Ybor City (Tampa) Florida, made up mostly of cigar workers. The entire community rose up in mass protest as the date for execution neared. On April 27, 1927, cigarworkers overwhelmingly approved a strike resolution and left the workbenches en masse for a one-day walkout. Three months later another one-day strike, involving 12,000 workers, occurred. When Massachusetts Governor Alvin T. Fuller announced on August 3 he would not intervene in the case, cigarworkers again struck; this time 15,000 workers went out On August 10 a walkout "again emptied the cigar factories." Ybor City's main thoroughfare, Second Avenue, was virtually deserted as every store fronting the street closed for the day after posting painted signs in their windows reading "Save Sacco and Vanzetti" and "Help the Innocents." The last and largest strike on August 28 ended with a memorial to "bid farewell" to our martyred comrades.[43]

The outpouring of workers around the globe was tremendous. In virtually every European city, in Tokyo, Buenos Aires, Montevideo, Mexico City, Rio de Janeiro, in Australia, the Philippines and Canada, workers took to the streets in strike and in protest to call for justice. Protest meetings were held in several cities in the Soviet Union. Even while under Fascist rule, the Italian working class managed to demonstrate its support.[44]

Sacco and Vanzetti were scheduled to be executed at midnight, August 10, 1927. At 11:30 p.m. on August 10, Governor Alvin T. Fuller granted the condemned men a twelve-day stay of execution so that final legal maneuvers could run their course.

During that day, August 10, 1927, Cardinal William O'Connell, Archbishop of Boston, received a telegram from the Right Reverend Paul Morella, Auditor of the Apostolic Delegation in Washington, D.C. It read: "Card. Gaspari requests if possible your charitable intercession of Sacco Vanzetti (stop). Please answer by telegram." Cardinal Pietero Gaspari was Secretary of State to Pope Pius XI.

Cardinal O'Connell replied by wire to Marelli: "We have already done so and will continue as long as there is hope." On the same day, Cardinal O'Connell sent an intercessory note to Governor Fuller in which he wrote: "I have been implored by people whose request I cannot ignore to do whatever is possible in this matter and I offer you my application for clemency trusting that it may be favorably received."[45]

It was all in vain. On August 23, 1927 two innocent workers were executed for a crime they had not committed.

VICTORY IN DEATH

On May 13, 1927, the New York *World* featured an interview in the Dedham jail with Sacco and Vanzetti. The headline over the account read: "VICTORY IN DEATH SEEN BY SACCO AND VANZETTI." The interview included a statement by Vanzetti which became world-famous:

"If it had not been for these things," said Vanzetti, "I might have lived out my life, talking at street corners to scorning men. I might have died, unmarked, unknown, a failure. Now we are not a failure. This is our career and our triumph. Never in our full life can we hope to do such work for tolerance, for justice, for man's understanding of man, as now we do by an accident.

"Our words—our lives—our pains—nothing! The taking of our lives—lives of a good shoemaker and a poor fish peddler—all! That last moment belongs to us—that agony is our triumph.[46]*

Only one day before the execution, Vanzetti wrote to Dante Sacco, the son of Nicola Sacco:

Remember, Dante, remember always these things: we are not criminals; they convicted us on a frame-up; they denied us a new trial; and if we will be executed after seven years, four months and 17 days of unspeakable tortures and wrongs, it is ... because we were for the poor and against the exploitation and oppression of the man by the man.

Sacco wrote to his daughter Ines how he wished he could "see you running, laughing, crying and singing through the verdant fields," But then he added, "the same I have wished for other poor girls ... the nightmare of the lower classes burdened very badly your father's soul."[47]

Both Sacco and Vanzetti were taught to read and write English in prison by wealthy New England women who had interested themselves in the case, and Vanzetti, in particular, became a highly articulate writer in English whose letters evoked a great emotional response. Sacco emerges from his prison letters as a man with a definite social outlook, a strong class consciousness, and a view of himself and Vanzetti as "the good soldiers of the revolution."[48]

* This eloquent statement became famous after it appeared in *The Letters of Sacco and Vanzetti*, edited by Marion Denman Frankfurter and Gardner Jackson, published in 1928. For a discussion of the history of Vanzetti's statement, see Fred Somkin, "How Vanzetti Said Goodbye," *Journal of American History* 68 (September, 1981): 298-312.

Vanzetti's statement is part of what Paul Avrich, the leading American scholar on Anarchism and Anarchists, calls the myth that Sacco and Vanzetti were "philosophical anarchists" and that in the words of Upton Sinclair, "there was no possibility of either being guilty of any crime." Avrich goes to great pains to show why Sinclair changed his mind and became convinced that both Sacco and Vanzetti were "dynamiters" who were ready to use the utmost violence to gain their ends. Most of Avrich's book is spent on this issue and concludes with his agreeing with Upton Sinclair. (Paul Avrich, *Sacco and Vanzetti: The Anarchist Background*, Princeton, New Jersey, 1991, *passim*, especially pp. 160-63.) It remains to be seen if scholars who are experts on "the case that refuses to die" will accept Professor Avrich's discussion and conclusions, and his one-dimensional treatment of this tragic episode in American history.

VINDICATION OF SACCO AND VANZETTI

The case of Sacco and Vanzetti has been called the "American Dreyfus Case." It has never been forgotten. Many books have been written about it, several of them novels. Scores of poems have been sung of their courage and pain; at least three plays have dealt with it; and in 1971 a film produced in Italy made the grim story come alive.

In 1948, G. Louis Joughin, the coauthor of *The Legacy of Sacco and Vanzetti* wrote that "the literary verdict is unanimously sympathetic to the executed men. Prosecution, judges, and the hostile Massachusetts public majority have not in twenty years found a single literary defender of their position."[49]

While most studies of the Sacco and Vanzetti case have upheld the view that the two men were innocent and were victims of a frameup, there were exceptions. In 1960, Robert Montgomery, a conservative Boston lawyer, published *Sacco-Vanzetti: The Murder and the Myth*, in which he challenged the view that the two men were innocent. In 1962, James Grossman, a New York lawyer, concluded in *Commentary*, the journal of neo-conservatism, that Sacco and Vanzetti were guilty. That same year, Francis Russell, in *Tragedy in Dedham*, upheld the same view. He based this largely on evidence he claimed proved that the bullets that killed the men in the robbery had been fired from Sacco's pistol and could not have been fired from any other. He concluded that Sacco was guilty, and that Vanzetti, at most, possessed guilty knowledge which would have made him an accessory to the fact.* In 1969, Herbert Ehrmann, the last surviving Sacco-Vanzetti counsel, published *The Case That Will Not Die*. He challenged Russell's thesis and upheld the innocence of Sacco and Vanzetti. So, too, does Roberta Strauss Feuerlicht, in *Justice Crucified: The Story of Sacco and*

---

* In an article in the conservative *National Review*, "Is This the Truth About Sacco and Vanzetti?" (11 [Oct. 21, 1961]: 261-64), Max Eastman wrote that he had asked Carlo Tresca, the anarchist leader involved in the defense of Sacco and Vanzetti, for the truth about the two condemned men. To Eastman's query, Tresca allegedly answered: "Sacco was guilty but Vanzetti was not." The conversation was interrupted, and never resumed. A few weeks later, Tresca was assassinated.

The alleged statement by Tresca was used by Francis Russell, as well as others, to charge that Sacco was guilty of the crime. But the validity of Tresca's statement is effectively challenged in "Carlo Tresca and the Sacco-Vanzetti Case," *Journal of American History* 66 (December 1979): 535-42.

Vanzetti, published in 1977, which is, in a number of respects, the best recent history of the case.

In 1986 Francis Russell published *Sacco and Vanzetti: The Case Resolved* in which he announced that he was now certain that Sacco was guilty and Vanzetti innocent. The justification for this conclusion is a letter he received in 1982 written by Ideale Gambera, who introduced himself as the son of Giovanni Gambera, lately deceased, who had been active in "the case from its beginnings." Gambera wrote that Russell was correct in inferring Sacco's guilt. But this and what Russell calls "corroborative" details add nothing to what is already known, and does no damage to the reputation of Sacco and Vanzetti.

Until 1977 the Commonwealth of Massachusetts never officially admitted the slightest error or acknowledged the two men in any way. When the Federal Writers Project guide book to Massachusetts was published in the mid-'30's, Governor Hurley discovered that it was favorably disposed to Sacco and Vanzetti. His protests forced the first edition to be recalled and a new edition to be written, revising the objectionable section.[50]

In 1947 the renowned sculptor Gutzon Borglum completed a bas-relief of Sacco and Vanzetti and the arm of a robed Justice holding a balance tipped in their direction. Over half of its space was devoted to a statement by Vanzetti: "What I wish more than all in this last hour of agony is that our case and our fate may be understood in their real being and serve as a tremendous lesson to the forces of freedom so that our suffering and death will not have been in vain."

The plaque was offered to the Commonwealth of Massachusetts for erection on the Boston Common by a group of U.S. citizens including Albert Einstein, Herbert H. Lehman, Eleanor Roosevelt, Provost Paul H. Backy of Harvard University, and Dean Wesley A. Sturges of Yale University law School. The offer was rejected by Governor Hurley on the grounds that public opinion was still divided on the matter."[51]

The long overdue official acknowledgement by the state of Massachusetts that injustice had been committed in the case came finally on the fiftieth anniversary of the execution. Governor Michael Dukakis asserted by proclamation that Sacco and Vanzetti had not been given a fair trial and that any stigma should be removed from their names. The proclamation was presented ceremoniously to Spencer Sacco, the grandson of Nicola Sacco, and to an Italian consul representing Vanzetti's surviving sister in Italy. As part of the official action, August 23, 1977, the 50th anniversary of the execution, was proclaimed "Sacco-Vanzetti Day" in Massachusetts.

236 The Trade Union Educational League, 1925-1929

However, Governor Dukakis refused to grant a posthumous pardon because it might connote guilt. His proclamation asserted neither the guilt nor the innocence of Sacco and Vanzetti.

But in 1985, in *Postmortem: New Evidence in the Case of Sacco and Vanzetti*, William Young and David E. Kaiser established beyond a reasonable doubt the innocence of the two Italian anarchists, in a first-rate investigation of evidence never before part of any previous evaluation. Based on an enormous file collection from the Massachusetts State Police, electronic recordings of Felix Frankfurter's conversations, informers' reports from the defense committee, and new records from the prosecution, the secret grand jury proceedings, and the federal surveillance of anarchists, *Postmortem* has settled a debate among scholars which has raged for sixty years over the innocence or guilt of Sacco and Vanzetti. The final verdict—innocence. Reviewing the book in the *Journal of American History*, William Preston, Jr. reaches the same conclusion: "Young and Kaiser conduct an objective and impartial investigation. The argument and the evidence ought to persuade others that Sacco and Vanzetti were framed and that sixty years of controversy may now come to an end."[53]

CHAPTER 15

MARITIME AND AGRICULTURAL WORKERS

Although the TUEL slogan "Organize the Unorganized" was put into effect in a large number of sections of the working class, there were areas where little or no activity took place. The former occurred among the maritime workers and the latter among agricultural workers.

MARITIME WORKERS

In spite of the longstanding reputation of maritime workers for militancy and radical consciousness—especially under the leadership of the IWW—the Communist Party and the TUEL paid little attention to the waterfront until 1926.[1] To be sure, there were occasional references to the need to organize maritime transport workers in the minutes of the TUEL Executive Committee before 1926, but nothing significant happened.[2]

Late in 1926 the Communist Party formed International Seamen's Clubs (ISC's) in several American ports in conjunction with the establishment of such clubs in port cities around the world. For the most part, the clubs played a social and educational role, providing facilities for reading, recreation, and dining. Although the clubs made it clear that they stood for industrial unionism, and opened their doors to all waterfront workers, the ISC's did no organizing on their own. Instead, in keeping with the concept of "boring-from-within," they encouraged seamen to agitate for a "class struggle program" within the International Seamen's Union (AFL) or the IWW.[3]

In October 1928, the first issue of the *Marine Workers Voice* appeared on the New York waterfront, announcing the formation of the Marine Workers' Progressive League (MWPL). The MWPL attacked the ISU and the IWW for their failure to organize the seamen, but did not, in accordance with the prevailing opposition to dual unionism, suggest the formation of a separate union of maritime workers.[4] Not until the new trade union policy was adopted by the Communist Party and the TUEL, and the Trade Union Unity League was organized, were real efforts made to organize the maritime workers.

AGRICULTURAL WORKERS

In the case of the agricultural workers, especially those in California, the Communist Party and the TUEL did nothing until 1930. The need for such organization, especially in the Imperial Valley, was enormous.

Imperial Valley had emerged as one of the nation's richest fruit and truck farm agricultural regions during the first decade of the 20th Century. Intensive agriculture, founded on irrigation and requiring large numbers of agricultural laborers during the harvest season, developed rapidly in the valley during the second decade. In the 1870s and the '80s the white growers who had dominated the state's agriculture since the mid-century began importing Chinese laborers to better insure a docile labor force. When protests by organized white workers curtailed Chinese immigration, growers turned instead to the supposedly equally docile Japanese, only to reject them when the Japanese formed successful ethnically based labor organizations and, ultimately, established themselves as the state's leading truck farmers. By the 1920s, growers recruited Filipino and then Mexican workers to insure a dependent, non-unionized, and more easily manipulated labor force. By 1920 Mexicans dominated the Imperial Valley's harvest work, and in 1928, persons of Mexican descent comprised ninety percent of Imperial Valley's field labor force [5]

Needing big work crews, growers did not bother to hire great numbers of workers directly. Instead, they utilized the services of labor contractors. Contractors were often men of Mexican descent who organized work crews, collected wages from employers and distributed the money to workers. In return for these services, contractors normally were allowed to deduct for themselves one-half cent per standard crate of melons from the pay of their workers. They distributed wages at the end of each work-week, withholding the first week's pay until the end of the harvest. Thus, after the last work-week, the contractor owed the workers two weeks pay. "When the workers tried to collect this last installment," Charles Wollenberg points out, "it was not uncommon for the contractor to disappear."[6]

In 1927 Dr. Paul S. Taylor of the University of California made a thorough study of the valley's Mexican population. He found that the average Mexican field worker earned only six to eight hundred dollars per year. Such a worker housed his family in a one or two-room shack, usually on the outskirts of one of the valley's towns. Most of the Mexican dwellings had no plumbing or sanitation facilities. Mexican children in most Imperial Valley communities attended segregated elementary schools.[7]

The agricultural employers who favored the use of Mexican labor over all other groups emphasized, among other factors, that the Mexican was especially tractable. However, dissatisfaction among the Mexican field workers of the Imperial Valley emerged sharply in 1927. The issue of wages, living conditions, and the contract system made them eager to organize. But no labor organization in the United States displayed interest in organizing these discontented Mexican workers.[8]

Until the mid-'30s, the American Federation of Labor, dominated by a racist approach to Chinese, Japanese, Filipino, and Mexican farm laborers, made no attempt to organize field laborers.

The Industrial Workers of the World had conducted important strikes of 1,500 hoppickers in Wheatland, California and of 2,000 grape pickers in Fresno in 1913.* But with the weakening, if not demise, of the IWW, nothing of importance occurred in regard to formal labor organization of farm laborers. The decade of the '20s was a period of quiescence in agricultural labor unionism.[9]

The need for organizational work among agricultural workers in the capitalist nations had been recognized by the leaders of the Communist International as early as 1920. As part of its agrarian "thesis," the Second Congress of the Communist International advised all Communist parties of the capitalist countries that it was the "fundamental task" of each nation's "town proletariat" to educate and organize the "agricultural proletariat" in order to win it over to the side of the "Soviet Power and the dictatorship of the proletariat."[10]

Despite the Comintern's directives, the Communist trade unionists in the United States "entirely ignored agricultural workers during

* *See* Philip S. Foner, *History of the Labor Movement in the United States* 4(New York, 1965): 232-38.

the 1920s."[11] The Trade Union Educational League made no effort to establish its influence among farm workers, probably because it was having its hands full fighting the expulsion policy of the trade union bureaucracy. The Workers' (Communist) Party did acknowledge in 1928 the disadvantaged status of agricultural workers, and argued both for their right to organize and for their protection under federal labor law. The party, however, did not show any strong interest in assuming the task of farm worker organization itself, or pressuring the TUEL to undertake this activity.[12]

Into this vacuum the Mexican farm laborers acted on their own to improve their conditions.* With the assistance of Carlos V. Ariza, the Mexican agricultural workers of the Imperial Valley organized La Unión de Trabajadores Del Valle Imperials in April 1928, soon after changing the name of the new union to the Mexican Mutual Aid Society of Imperial Valley in order to facilitate incorporation under the laws of the State of California. Claiming a membership of 1,200 workers, during the first week in May, when the melon growers were in the process of securing their field workers through the labor contractors, the union delivered a statement to the leading growers. Couched in the most conciliatory language, it read:

> To Whom It May Concern:
> Hereby we make to your acknowledgment, that on the 22nd day of April, of the year 1928, was formed the board of directors of the Union of United Workers of Imperial Valley, State of California.
> By the same means we opportunately believe on directing to you, soliciting your valuable help for a convenience agreement to the picking season of cantaloupes, tomatoes and watermelons.

---

* In 1927 in Los Angeles the Confederación de Uniones de Obreros Mexicanos (CUOM) was organized by Mexican workers. In March 1928, the CUOM stated: "That the exploited class, the greater part of which is made up of manual labor, is right in establishing a class struggle in order to effect an economic and moral betterment of its condition, and at last its complete freedom from capitalist tyranny.... That the corporations, possessors of the natural and social wealth, being integral parts of the international association of industry, commerce and banking, the disinherited class must also integrate by means of its federation into a single union all the labor of the world." The ideology of CUOM was influenced by the concepts of Ricardo Flores Magón, anarchist leader of the *Partido Liberal Mexicano* (PLM) which was a militant group opposing the dictatorship of Profirio Díaz, and which was especially strong in Los Angeles where many of its leaders and members settled to plan the overthrow of Díaz. There is no evidence that there were any ties between the CUOM and the union of Mexican farm laborers in the Imperial Valley. (Douglas Monroy, "Anarquismo y Comunismo: Mexican Radicalism and the Communist Party in Los Angeles during the 1930s," *Labor History* 24[Winter 1983]: 38-41; Philip S. Foner, *U.S. Labor Movement and Latin America*, vol. I, 1846-1919, South Hadley, Mass., 1988, pp. 98-99, 112, 118-19.)

In accordance with the bad occasions that we've had in the past years, it makes us necessary of a better understanding of our business among the Mexican people residing as strangers in the United States. We want to keep on cooperating with our hand of labor, but we claim a more liberal wages, enough to cover our most urgent necessities of the actual situations, and we hereby propose to you gentlemen the points of our wishes.

During the year we scarcely work 185 days, of which we acquire the sum of $555 in which we couldn't meet our expenses of alimentation, clothing, house rent, medicine, automobile, and other small exigents.

As you understand, with this amount above stated, we live in the most unhonorable and miserable way, in our concept. For instance, you know that the picking season of cantaloupes is at hand, and we make to your acknowledgment that the prices we are asking for are very reasonable according to justice of the companies and we union laborers.

We hereby note the prices in accordance with all the laborers and approved convenient, and we hereby wait for the approval of the honorable companies. The fact is that in the past years in cases like the present, they have demonstrated their willing attitude as we've said before in our sacrifices, in compliments of our labors, for such reason we wish that the prices we ask for will be approved.

Therefore, we ask of your valuable moral and material influence to our petition before the companies.

For the above anticipated, this union retires, giving you many thanks for the present.[13]

Appended to the statement were the union's demands: 15 cents per standard crate for picking cantaloupes; where the piece work rate did not prevail (frequently the growers employed additional pickers at the height of the harvest at an hourly rate); 75 cents per hour for picking and for sorting and handling crates; free picking sacks and free ice; free lumber and brush for the construction of workers' sheds; and the installation of "closets." In addition, the union demanded that in case of accidents during work, the employer would cover all expenses during the worker's sickness and "if further consequence appeared, caused by illness, the companies must pay indemnity as the law requires."[14]

Before they received the union's statement, the growers had already signed with labor contractors specifying 13-1/2 cents per standard crate for picking cantaloupes. Some growers furnished ice and picking sacks free of charge, others charged the workers for both. Their contracts specified that the contractor, not the grower, must comply with the provisions of the Workmen's Compensation Act of California. While the growers do not seem to have considered the union's demand for 15 cents per crate excessive, all of them considered 75 cents per hour exorbitant, having paid 50 and 60 cents per hour the previous year and in former years. In any event, the growers arbitrarily refused to recognize the union or to enter into negotiations with its leaders. The Brawley *News* reported that growers felt that granting the union's "reasonable requests" simply would open the door for "unreasonable demands." "With a union there is no limit."[15]

The union leaders did not plan a cantaloupe strike, desiring to come to an agreement with the growers through peaceful negotiations. But the members of the union were convinced that only by depriving the growers of labor and hitting their profits could the union prevail. As a result a spontaneous cantaloupe strike broke out on a majority of the ranches in the area of Brawley and Westmoreland. While not all of the workers were ready to walk out, some 2,746 out of approximately 4,500 Mexican workers needed to pick the cantaloupe crop, did strike.[16]

Regardless of the union's strength or weakness, or the conditions it had stipulated for an agreement, in the most respectful and conciliatory language, the very organization of a union by the supposedly "docile" farm laborers threw the growers into a state of alarm. Louis Bloch of the California Department of Industrial Relations, who observed developments at first hand, wrote:

> Heretofore they [the growers] had been accustomed to considering the Mexican workers as bovine and tractable individuals, best adapted to the climatic conditions in the Imperial Valley and therefore the most desirable workers in the valley. The organization of a union of Mexican laborers seems to have evoked in the growers an ardent wish for its earliest demise.[17]

The growers' wish was translated into action by the sheriff of Imperial County, Charles L. Gillett. He announced that he would permit no agitation, intimidation—or interference with the harvesting of cantaloupes by scabs—and immediately deputized forty men, many of whom were field inspectors, foremen, and superintendents of the growers, to enforce his personal injunction.[18]

On May 7, four days after the union had submitted its terms for an agreement, the first arrests occurred. This followed the complaint of a grower who charged that four union workers refused to leave the company's property after he had discharged them for refusing to work for less than the union's demands. Cooperating with the growers and the sheriff's office in an attempt to forestall an effective cantaloupe strike and break the union, the Justice of Peace of Brawley fixed the exorbitant bail of $1,000 each on the charge of disturbing the peace. Unable to raise the excessive bail, the workers remained in the county jail.[19]

On May 9, when groups of Mexican workers gathered in pool rooms and on street corners to discuss their difficulties with employers, the union's demands, and the first arrests, Sheriff Gillett and his deputies swooped down on them and arrested thirty-six Mexican laborers. They were charged with disturbing the peace and held in jail until May 17 in default of $250 bail for each. On May 10, the Sheriff, with his gun drawn, arrested four Mexican men and one woman for "resisting an officer." On May 11, one of the Mexican strike leaders (an American citizen born in Arizona) was arrested in El Centro and charged with disturbing the peace. His bail was set at $1,000. Elmer Heald, the District Attorney, persuaded him to accept a deal under which he would plead guilty, receive a six months' suspended jail sentence, with the understanding that he would leave the Valley.[20]

By personal edict, the sheriff ordered four pool halls in Westmoreland closed, and instructed his deputies immediately to arrest the proprietors if they dared violate his fiat. The sheriff justified his arbitrary action by charging that the pool halls were used by workers as meeting places where they were incited by "agitators." He then ordered the union's office in Brawley closed, warning that he would arrest the officers if they dared to reopen it. The pool halls remained closed during the duration of the strike. The *Imperial Valley Press* of May 9 reported:

> In warning the men at the jail yesterday afternoon, the sheriff made it clear that quick justice would be meted out to anyone caught seeking to bring about a riotous gathering and warned those that are not satisfied with conditions here that they might better return to Mexico. He intimated that at the first outbreak of any kind as a result of the movement now afoot, a general deportation movement of all Mexican laborers employed in the valley would begin. In closing his talk, the sheriff made it clear that those abiding by the laws and not taking part in the strike movement would not be molested in any way.[21]

For their part, the growers issued circulars throughout the valley warning the Mexican laborers that thousands of outside Mexican and other workers were ready and anxious to be imported into the valley to take their places. One circular argued that the Mexicans owed loyalty to the growers and shippers in return for their opposition to federal legislation to place Mexican immigration to the United States on a quota basis.[22]* But many circulars maintained that

---

* In the early months of 1928, legislation applying the 1924 immigration quota system to Mexico and the rest of the Western Hemisphere was introduced by Congressman John Box of Texas. Imperial County's Western Growers Protective Association joined with similar organizations in California, Arizona, and Texas to fight the Box bill. The bill was buried in committee. (Charles Wollenberg, "*Huelga*, 1928 Style: The Imperial Valley Cantaloupe Strike," *Pacific Historical Review* 38 [February 1969]:49.)

the strike was called by "reds" who incited dissatisfaction among the workers. The sheriff and his deputies joined the campaign to arouse public opinion against the union and its supporters, by spreading reports charging that radical agitators had entered the valley from Mexico, that union workers had conducted a parade under the "red" banner, and that union workers were planning to burn the valley's packing sheds to the ground.[23]

Growers' circulars claimed that the Mexican worker "never caused trouble except when he indulges in intoxicants," But "agitators or communists or whatever they are... have come with their comrade stuff and with threats have intimidated the workers." An *Imperial Valley Press* headline screamed: "Radicals to Blame." And from the Los Angeles *Times* came a report that "I.W.W. members are in back of the movement."[24] But a spokesperson for the workers replied, "We are not a bunch of Bolsheviks or I.W.W.'s."

He and his fellow laborers had organized a union to gain "better wages for the benefit of our families."[25]

After a detailed study of the strike, James Gray concluded that there was "not a shred of evidence" to indicate that the new union was started by Communists or that the workers who withheld their labor "were induced to do so by local or outside agitators."[26] By May there were still about fifty workers in custody on charge, of vagrancy and disturbing the peace. Bail had been set at between $250 and $1,000 and, of course, no prisoner was in the position, given their meager wages, to post bond. In an effort to get the prisoners back picking cantaloupes, District Attorney Heald offered them six-month suspended sentences if they would plead guilty and return to the fields. As Heald explained, "if the judge would hold them on bail, they would enter pleas of guilty next day and would go to work and behave themselves."[27]

Faced with long prison terms if they rejected Heald's offer and unable to raise the high bail, many workers had no choice but to accept. However, on May 15, Alfred Blaisdell, a Calexico attorney hired by the Mexican consulate, entered the case on behalf of the defendants. Blaisdell advised his clients to refuse the prosecutor's terms, and instituted *habeas corpus* proceedings in an attempt to free the prisoners. He argued that the trials had been delayed too long and bail set too high. Blaisdell was unable to obtain freedom for several prisoners held in Brawley, but on May 16 he did win the release of thirty-three prisoners in Westmoreland. "The decision," writes Charles Wollenberg, "was hardly a landmark for civil liberties.

Justice of the Peace F.T. Cook decided that the city of Westmoreland no longer could afford to feed thirty-three prisoners."[28]

But by this time the strike had been broken by the sheriff and the vicious campaign charging it with being "communist-inspired and directed." Although the growers refused to recognize the union or deal with it, the strike was not a complete failure. Most of the growers decided to raise the rate for picking cantaloupes from 13 1/2 to 15 cents per crate. Eventually, court cases against the arrested workers were dismissed.[29]

The strike had been broken primarily through the use of force by the valley's growers and law enforcement officers.[30] Nevertheless, the strike was the first attempt at a major workstoppage organized by Mexican farm workers. As we shall see in our next volume, the stage had been set for the entrance of the Trade Union Unity League and the Communist Party into the Imperial Valley to organize the field workers, to lead them in strikes for higher wages and better working conditions.

CHAPTER 16

A NEW TRADE UNION POLICY

DIFFICULTIES CONFRONTING THE TUEL

The period following the election of 1924 was a difficult one for the Trade Union Educational League. Its official organ acknowledged that "the League is experiencing a sharp period of isolation," that "within the past two years the influence of the League, in certain respects, seriously diminished in the unions" and that "the movement undoubtedly lacks the broad sweep that it once had. Especially has the League largely lost leadership over the so-called progressive elements, which played such an important part in its early activities. The masses in the unions are not responding to its slogans as they once did."[1]

Several critics blamed this state of affairs on the split between John Fitzpatrick, president of the Chicago Federation of Labor, and William Z. Foster; on the formation and rapid abandonment of the Federated Farmer-Labor Party, and on the isolation of the League from the La Follette movement.[2] Others pointed to the ever-increasing intimate relationship between the League and the Workers' (Communist) Party, noting particularly the statement of the League to the Third World Congress of the Red International of Labor Unions that the "chief aim of all its [the League's] efforts shall be the building up of a revolutionary mass political organization of the working class, the Workers' Party. To this end, all the struggles of the workers shall be directed into the political channels, and all the campaigns of the League on the Labor Party, amalgamation, etc., shall be utilized to strengthen the membership of the Workers' Party." In short, the League and the Communist political organization were so intimately connected that it was hardly surprising that the masses in the unions were "not responding to its slogans as they once did."[3]*

While conceding that there was merit to this argument, Foster placed the main blame on the labor bureaucrats and said that events had proved that they were "hopelessly reactionary." No matter how strong the pressure of the rank and file, he maintained, the high officials were ready to go to any lengths to crush it: "Under our leadership, fully half of the whole labor movement demanded amalgamation. Yet the bureaucrats ignored the demand completely. With the utmost indifference to the needs of their membership they beat it back. Hardly a single amalgamation have they permitted to take place."[4] Then there was the "expulsion policy." Unwilling to alter their class collaboration policies and to carry out "the TUEL's fighting program," they expelled all militants—Communists, non-Communist TUEL members, and any workers who endorsed the League's program. Small wonder, then, that it was becoming more and more difficult for the League to attract mass support.[5]

What should League members do under these circumstances? The answer, Foster insisted, was not to revert to dual unionism and split away from the "old reactionary unions." Rather, the militants had to intensify building "fires under the reactionary leaders":

> The revolutionaries in the Trade Union Educational League must renew and intensify the fight for the adoption of militant policies by the unions .... The fate of the labor movement depends upon the growth and development of the revolutionary forces in the unions. We must realize this fact and we must redouble our efforts for the extension and estab-

---

*J.B.S. Hardman, labor educator and journalist, reported in *Advance* of March 12, 1926 that Foster had published an article in the Russian daily *Pravda* in which he urged the Communist International to demand that the opposition in the U.S. labor movement, "be led by the Trade Union Educational League and not by the Workers Party." Commenting on this report, Hardman observed that "there was a time, several years ago, when Wm. Z. Foster had it within his power to make his efforts count in the upbuilding of the progressive forces of American labor. His TUEL was originally intended as a rallying center for the live and wide awake individuals and groups in the trade union movement." But, Hardman argued, "Foster allowed the W(orkers) P(arty) to abort his potential usefulness and rendered him impotent to the point of uselessness."

Hardman failed to add that if the TUEL had been rendered "impotent," the leaders of the trade unions would not have had to resort to the vicious expulsion policy to assure their continued rule.

lishment of the Trade Union Educational League in every phase and state of the trade union movement [6]

TUEL "PROGRAM FOR BUILDING THE TRADE UNIONS"

In keeping with this approach, the Trade Union Educational League presented a detailed "Program for Building the Trade Unions" to the 1926 AFL convention in Detroit. The document, consisting of twenty proposals, was not introduced by any delegate to the convention, since no delegate dared to acknowledge a relationship with the League for fear of immediate expulsion. Rather, it was distributed as a leaflet to the delegates as they arrived in Detroit. It was also published in the special "Labor Day" edition of the *Daily Worker*, which introduced it as "one of the most significant declarations of the labor movement."[7] It began:

> The American labor movement is in a crisis. Everywhere the employers are attacking the workers' conditions of labor and standards of living and trying to destroy the trade unions. In nearly every industry, wages have been cut, either directly by a straight-out reduction, or by speeding up of the workers to a vastly increased production ....
>
> While capital is thoroughly organized, there are only 3,500,000 organized out of 20,000,000 organizable workers. The unions have lost more than a million members in the open-shop war. Company unionism is gaining, with over a million workers bound up in these fake organizations.
>
> The trade unions, weakened by craft divisions and top-heavy with an official bureaucracy which refuses to fight the employers, have retreated almost everywhere under the employers' attacks. The bureaucrats have adopted a policy of surrender to and collaboration with the employers ....
> In politics, the bureaucracy trails behind the coat-tails of every capitalist politician of both capitalist parties, seeking "friends" by "non-partisan" politics and thus reducing labor's political power to zero, instead of building up a powerful party of labor alone.[8]

To remedy these conditions and to build the trade unions "into powerful organizations," twenty measures had to be adopted by the AFL convention. The first and most important was to "Organize the Unorganized." Much of the weakness of the labor movement, said the TUEL, resulted from the fact that only about ten percent of the workers were organized, and that these ten percent were mostly skilled workers in the light industries. It was therefore imperative that the AFL call upon the entire labor movement "to embark on a general campaign to organize the many millions of unorganized, giving special attention to the basic and key industries, including steel, railroads, marine transport, mining, electrical manufacturing, chemicals, rubber, automobile, lumber, textile, etc. Emphasis must be laid on the organization of the unskilled workers."

The convention was urged to create a general organizing committee to supervise the work of organization. Campaigns should be initiated nationally in the various crafts and industries, and locally on a general scale. A special organizing fund should be created. A system of shop committees should be established to mobilize the unorganized and induct them into the unions. A special campaign should be waged against company unions "designed to convert them into real trade unions or to destroy them and to build the trade unions in their place."

To facilitate organization of the unorganized, a general reduction of initiation fees should be recommended to those affiliated internationals with high fees. The AFL, moreover, should hold conventions in the future "in big industrial centers," discontinuing the practice of holding then in summer resorts, like Atlantic City. In industries where no organization existed, the unions to be established should be "based on the industrial form." In industries where a whole group of conflicting weak unions claimed jurisdiction over the mass of unorganized workers, the jurisdiction should be awarded to the basic unions of the industry—to the Amalgamated Association of Iron and Steel and Tin Workers in the steel industry, to the International Association of Machinists in the automobile and electrical industry to the Amalgamated Meat Cutters and Butcher Workmen in the meatpacking industry.

Nineteen additional proposals followed, including demands for "Improved Living Standards," "A Labor Party," "Nationalization of Industry," "Against Company Unions," "Fight Against Injunctions," "Political Prisoners," "Against Racial Discrimination," "Corrupt Labor Papers," "Centralization of the Trade Union Movement," "Amalgamation," and "Democratization of the A.F.L." Most of these are self-explanatory.

In "A Policy of Militant Action," the TUEL called upon the AFL to "decisively condemn trade union capitalism, as reflected in labor banks, labor investment corporations, trade union life insurance companies, etc., and to demand the transformation of these institutions into genuine co-operatives." This was followed by a demand which was hardly likely to appeal to the "labor bureaucrats" of the AFL: "The investment of the workers' savings should be in the socialized industries of the Soviet Union."

Three other proposals dealt with the Soviet Union. In a proposal on "International Affiliation," the TUEL called for the AFL to "endorse the Anglo-Russian Trade Union Unity Committee, and support its program of a world congress" for trade union unity to include the Amsterdam International, the Red International of Labor Unions, the American Federation of Labor, and the unions of South America, China, India, etc." It also asked the AFL to recommend to its affiliated internationals that they affiliate with the "respective industrial federations of the Amsterdam International on the basis of the admission of the Russian trade unions and the holding of a world trade union unity congress."

There was a specific demand that the AFL urge the United States government to "recognize the Soviet Union and establish full diplomatic and commercial relations with that country." Noting that the Soviet Union had been recognized by scores of nations, "among them the most important countries," the TUEL felt that it was tragic that "only the United States withholds such recognition."

Finally, with respect to the Soviet Union, the TUEL urged the AFL to "accept the invitation of the Russian unions and send an official delegation to visit the Soviet Union and submit a report to the American labor movement." The Federation was reminded that the trade unions of Europe "have practically all sent delegations to investigate the conditions of labor under the Soviet government" "The American trade unionists," the TUEL declared, "have a right to know at first hand why it is that the whole world capitalist class is so bitterly opposed to the Soviet government and what are the conditions that 8,000,000 trade unionists share under that government."

The proposal dealing with the British miners' strike of 1926 called upon the AFL to "pledge its complete and active support to the strike," to "call upon the marine transport and railroad unions to halt coal destined for Great Britain," and to "call upon all affiliated members each to donate immediately to the strike relief fund a sum of not less than two hours' pay." It also called upon the AFL "to organize a loan of not less than $3,000,000 from the labor banks to the Mineral Federation of Great Britain."*

---

* The miners' battle (a seven-month lockout) was part of the great General Strike of 1926 in England. The miners held out after the General Strike was ended, but they finally returned, defeated, in November 1926.

The AFL was also asked to help the United Mine Workers in the United States, which was facing "collapse" because of the "open shop attacks of the coal operators" and the "reactionary leadership of the Lewis machine.... The fight must be to save the Miners' Union, whose threatened destruction menaces the progress of the whole labor movement."

The TUEL demanded that the AFL "condemn the imperialist policy of the American capitalist class," and called for the immediate and unconditional freedom for the Philippines and Puerto Rico, and "a policy of hands off Mexico and other Latin American countries." It called, too, for the transformation of the Pan-American Federation of Labor "into an instrument of struggle against American imperialism, now beginning in the Latin-American countries under the leadership of the All-American Anti-Imperialist League."

Another proposal urged the AFL to emphasize "the special importance of organizing women and youth workers" and to call upon its affiliated unions "to remove all constitutional barriers existing against these workers and to intensify the work of organizing them." The AFL, the TUEL insisted, must demand "equal pay for equal work, prohibition of night work, child labor and excessive hours, and propose that their demands be brought forward in wage movements by trade unions in industries in which they are employed."

The proposal "Against Racial Discrimination" merits quotation in full. It read:

> The trade unions must include wage workers regardless of race, creed, sex, age or color. The AFL must declare for the removal of all bars against Negroes, Japanese, Mexicans and other races, and national groups, which are being discriminated against in entering the trade unions. It must demand the abolition of all Jim Crow laws, practices and discriminations and the elimination of lynching.
>
> The AFL shall initiate an active campaign to organize Negro workers and demand that they be given equal pay for equal work, and extend to them the utmost protection in the trade unions. Special campaigns should be launched to organize the Mexican and Japanese workers in this country.

The final two proposals dealt with "Amalgamation" and "Democratization of the AFL." The "Amalgamation" plank was brief; it stated that the AFL "shall indorse the principle of industrial unionism and call a series of conferences in the various industries for the purpose of amalgamating the many craft unions into industrial organizations." In carrying through this amalgamation, "the principle of organization on the basis of the shop, instead of the miscellaneous local union, shall be introduced." And finally: "Amalgamation is a powerful weapon against company unionism."

In the eyes of the TUEL, the task of democratizing the AFL was crucial to the future of the labor movement. The AFL was urged to launch a drive to include within its ranks the Railroad Brotherhoods, the Amalgamated Clothing Workers and other independent unions. After this was achieved, the Executive Council should be enlarged to 45 members, representing principally mining, railroad, metal, textile and other "key and basic industries":

> We must look forward to the time when, with a democratized AFL and an educated membership, all affiliated unions, before presenting demands to their employers shall first have them passed by the executive council, whereupon the executive council shall mobilize the support of the labor movement behind these demands to the extent and in the manner required by the situation.

To achieve the democratization of the AFL, an end had to come to "the present system of complete control of the AFL and its component unions, AFL convention, etc., within the hands of an autocratic bureaucracy to the exclusion of rank and file participation and control...." The TUEL demanded that at least 25 percent of the members of the Executive Council "shall be actual workers," and that the representation of the various international and local bodies in the AFL convention "shall consist of at least 60 percent of rank and file workers employed at the trades." All convention delegates should be selected by general referendum vote of their respective organizations. The convention representation of the State Federations and Central Labor Bodies should be increased from the present system of one delegate each to from two to ten, and two to five, respectively, according to the size of these organizations. Upon the demand of 25 percent of the members of the Executive Council, or of 25 percent of the delegates at the AFL convention, or of 1,000 local unions, "any question, including the election of officers, shall be submitted to a general referendum vote." The final proposals read:

> In order to make a start at correcting the glaring evil of an overpaid officialdom, the salaries and expense accounts of the general officers of the AFL shall be reduced 50 per cent, and the general organizers accordingly.
>
> The agenda system shall be introduced by a provision providing that two months before the holding of the annual convention, an agenda shall be made up touching upon the most vital issues confronting the labor movement, and such agenda shall be submitted to the various organizations for their consideration.

Full freedom of expression shall be guaranteed to minorities in the unions, The foregoing general proposals for democratization shall also be introduced into all the affiliated unions of the American Federation of Labor.[9]

FACTORS LEADING TO FORMATION OF INDEPENDENT TRADE UNIONS

Since Foster had already characterized the AFL convention that had preceded the 1926 gathering as "the worst ever in the history of the American Federation of Labor" and as furnishing incontrovertible proof that the "bureaucrats now at the head of the trade unions are unwilling and unable to adopt a labor policy suited to the needs of the American workers,"[10] it is obvious that the TUEL had no hope of seeing any of its twenty proposals adopted. Hence, it came as a surprise that the Detroit convention, as we have seen, unanimously adopted a resolution calling on the Federation to initiate an organizing drive among automobile workers. Even though the TUEL knew that the delegates supported the resolution out of fear that the Communist-led independent Auto Workers Union might succeed in organizing these workers if the AFL did not, the convention's action was hailed by the TUEL, which offered to cooperate in the organizing campaign.[11]

The AFL rejected the offer and soon demonstrated, as noted above, that its own organizing campaign in auto was little more than a paper resolution. Among other factors, the rivalry among the eighteen international unions that claimed jurisdiction in the automobile industry prevented concerted action.[12]

The AFL fiasco in auto intensified the criticism of the Federation by the TUEL. William F. Dunne accused the Federation of "surrender" and "conscious reaction."[13] Foster charged that the leadership had gone completely over to "class collaboration" and was concerned only with the protection of "their group interests as a bureaucracy."[14]

While most Communists continued to oppose dual unionism and to favor working inside the existing unions, others felt that the policy of building "fires under the reactionary leaders" had produced little in the way of organizing the unorganized. In the main, however, the formation of new unions was branded as "dual unionism" and as constituting a disruptive influence in the labor movement. In their work among the textile workers in Passaic, New Jersey in 1926, the Communists had at first operated independently, but had later agreed to abandon independent unionism and to enter the AFL United Textile Workers. Apart from the Auto Workers Union, little effort was made to organize the unorganized independently. Meanwhile, thousands of militants were expelled from the existing unions and left without any labor organization in which to operate.[15]

The issue of whether or not to begin work to establish new unions was debated at the third national conference of the Trade Union Educational League in New York on December 3-4, 1927, of 297 delegates, 107 of whom were from the needle trades. The majority of the delegates were long-time opponents of dual unionism, and they strongly resisted any demand for the establishment of new unions. Instead, the conference directed that all efforts be concentrated toward continuing work inside the AFL, and called upon the expelled workers to fight for reinstatement into their former unions. The conference put forth as a central slogan, "Save the Trade Unions."[16]

Fearful of dual unionism, the leaders of the TUEL hung back. It took the intervention of the Red International of Trade Unions (Profintern) and the Communist International to change that position. On March 17, 1928, the Fourth World Congress of the RILU opened in Moscow. The Congress adopted a program committing the left-wing of the trade union movement to the establishment of new unions in those industries where none existed or where current organizations barred effective alliances with other left-wing groups. The resolution referred specifically to the TUEL, stating:

> The vital and immediate task of the TUEL is to become the leading organization struggling to organize the unorganized, concentrating especially in mining, steel, oil, automobiles, rubber, textile, chemicals, marine, transport and lumber industries....
>
> The TUEL, when necessary, may fight for the affiliation of the organizations of the AFL, but only on conditions which guarantee class leadership and a militant programme.

While the resolution emphasized the need to build new unions in the United States and made the organization of the unorganized the central TUEL task, it also noted the necessity of developing work in the AFL: "At the same time it must use all the possibilities of working inside the existing unions and fighting for the leadership [of the workers organized] in them."

In the summer of 1928, the Sixth World Congress of the Communist International endorsed the RILU policy, especially the founding of new, revolutionary unions designed to meet the challenge of what Joseph Stalin called the "Third Period"—an era of extreme capitalist contradictions and crises, of intensified class struggle, and of a new revolutionary upsurge.*

The basic principles of the Profintern resolution were brought home clearly to American Communists in an article by Arnold Losovsky, President of the RILU, published in the *Communist International*. Losovsky criticized the British, German, and American Communist parties for their trade union work. The Americans came in for perhaps the strongest criticism. Losovsky argued that the TUEL leaders, by relying on the AFL leaders and by making a fetish of anti-dual unionism, were neglecting the organization of the unorganized. He pointed to the conduct of the Passaic strike of 1926 and condemned the TUEL and the Workers' (Communist) Party for having turned over the independent textile workers' organization to the "reactionary United Textile Workers." He insisted that the TUEL must develop more of an independent leadership, and that while the work in the AFL unions must be continued and developed, the TUEL should give more attention to the actual organization of the unorganized into new industrial unions where the old unions did not exist or could not function.

Losovsky noted that "boring from within" had succeeded in bringing Communists to power in only one union, the small fur workers union. In other unions it had merely led to expulsions:

> The situation in America is such that it is necessary to form unions in all those branches of industry where there is either no organization or where what exists is practically negligible. Unions must be organized in those branches of industry where the unions are breaking up because of the tactics of the trade union bureaucrats.

There were some disagreements, however, with some parts of Losovsky's criticism. Opponents in the Party, said the CEC, had seized upon Losovsky's statement "and misinterpreted it into a repudiation of the entire program of working in the old unions and the initiation of an entirely new policy of dual unions." "Such added emphasis as may now be laid upon the formation of new unions is not a repudiation or rejection of our previous policy, but a development of it in accordance with a changing objective situation." When the old unions had a much wider mass base, when they were "the

---

*The three periods delineated by Stalin were: Period I, 1917-1923, the revolutionary upsurge in Russia, Germany, Hungary, China, India, and Korea; Period II, 1924-1927, the "relative, partial stabilization" of capitalism; Period III, 1928— new class conflict during the period of capitalism's crisis.

chief organs of the struggle of the workers, it was correct that our party concentrate its main attention upon working within and through them, even though at that time also the question of organizing new unions in wholly unorganized industries was a burning one." But as the base narrowed, as these unions "became restricted to skilled workers," and on the other hand, the great mass of unorganized workers became more militant, "the necessity of our Party to concentrate its major attention upon building new unions among the masses of unorganized workers became manifest."

It would be a mistake to imply, as did Losovsky, that the Party totally concentrated attention on the AFL unions to the neglect of forming new unions: "The fact is, our policy is based on AFL unions only in those industries and crafts where they have real mass organizations. In industries where the unions are decrepit or dying,...our policy is based either entirely upon independent unions, or increasingly so." Nevertheless, the Party could "be justly criticized for not making greater progress in the actual building of new organizations." The May resolution noted a "decline of the traditional craft unionism and the beginning of a new unionism among the great masses of unorganized" and called upon the Party to take the lead in building new unions among the unorganized workers. At the same time, however, the work in the old unions was to be continued, although the major attention of the Party was to be directed to building new unions among the masses of unorganized, who, "under the pressure of wage-cuts, speed-up, unemployment, etc.," were beginning "to acquire new militant moods," The resolution warned against any tendency to neglect and desert the old unions, which was to be "counteracted by clearly stating the necessity of Communists working with the AFL unions and laying down programs for this work." Thanks were extended to Losovsky, for while his writings contained "several unjustified criticisms of our policy," they had "served to focus our attention more definitely upon the whole question of formation of new unions and our relations to the old organizations."[18]

In an article explaining the Central Executive Committee's position, Foster noted that the "old trade unions are manifestly unable to meet the situation and to serve as the organ of struggle for these discontented masses of semi-skilled and unskilled workers." The situation was far different during the years 1919-22: "Then the old unions were widely established in the basic industries, including railroads, coal, steel, meat-packing, marine transport, etc." But in 1928, the conditions were "radically changed." The old unions had been driven out of various of the basic industries completely, "or their power has been so badly shattered that they can no longer function effectively." They had become "more and more restricted to skilled workers," and indifferent to the unskilled. The leadership "not only will not organize the great mass of workers, but they are one of the principal obstacles in the way of such organization."

Because of these factors, because of the growing mood for struggle among the masses of unorganized workers, "and the inability of the trade unions to furnish them with the necessary organization and leadership, the formation of new unions among these workers becomes imperative." The new unions had to be "industrial in character. They must be led by militant fighters and be imbued with a revolutionary spirit. Craft unionism and all its practices are obsolete in trustified American industry."

Foster revealed that new unions would soon be built in the coal mining and needle trades industries, and that "the development of new union tendencies" in those two industries, "together with the building of separate unions among the totally unorganized workers, shifts all the more decisively our center of gravity to the formation of new unions as our basic trade-union policy."[19]*

* Later, Foster wrote that Losovsky's "main point was well taken," and that the TUEL "in its deep-seated and profoundly correct antagonism to dual unionism, had leaned somewhat backward in handling this question and had undoubtedly neglected unorganized fields where independent unions might have been built." (William Z. Foster, *From Bryan to Stalin* [New York, 1937], p. 214.) It was Foster who was especially fearful that any change in trade union policy would revive the tradition of dual unionism in the Left, which he had fought since he had left the IWW in 1912. (James Prickett, "Communists and the Communist Issue in the American Labor Movement, 1920-1950," unpublished Ph.D. dissertation, University of California at Los Angeles, 1975, pp. 104-05.)

In her memoirs, edited with the assistance of Maurice Isserman, Dorothy Healy reports that she remembers Foster telling her "when I first met him in 1946 that the biggest mistake he ever made was agreeing in the late 1920s to have the Trade Union Educational League, which tried to work with the AFL, transformed into the Trade Union Unity League...." (Dorothy Healy, Maurice Isserman, *Dorothy Healy Remembers: A Life in the Communist Party*, New York, 1990, pp. 58-59.)

In my own interviews with Foster at my home in Croton-on-Hudson, New York, a few miles from his summer home in Peekskill, he acknowledged that it was a shock for him to abandon his opposition to dual unionism and support the formation of the Trade Union Unity League. But he quickly added that the opportunity for militants to work inside the AFL and most AFL unions for progressive trade unionism had all but disappeared by 1928-1929, and that to cling entirely to the TUEL would have meant standing still. Some Communists, he also made it clear, did continue to function where they could inside the AFL, and did work with those who formed the new unions, but the opportunities were very limited.

Actually, it was in three, not two industries in which new unions were established before the end of 1928—mining, textile, and needle trades.

NATIONAL MINERS' UNION

During the 1927-28 United Mine Workers' strike, the operators had succeeded in rolling back wages and working conditions that had taken union miners thirty-seven years to win. From a high of over 500,000 members in 1921, UMW membership fell to a low of 80,000 by mid-1928, two-thirds of whom worked in Illinois. It was then that Communists and other progressive miners decided to form a new union. A "National Miners' Convention Arrangements Committee" was established in Pittsburgh, with John J. Watt as chairman and Pat H. Toohey as secretary. It issued a call for a conference to be held in that city on August 17, 1928 which then set September 9 as the date for a convention to establish the new miners' union. In its appeal to the miners to send delegates to the September convention, the Arrangements Committee declared:

> Coal miners in all fields, break completely with the Lewis machine, make no further dues payments to these corrupt officials. Henceforth affiliate your locals with and send your dues to the National Miners' Convention Arrangements Committee. Take control of your local unions.... Remove all officials who stand in the way and select now officers from your own ranks who are ready to help build the NEW NATIONAL MINERS' UNION ....
>
> Workers everywhere, come to the defense of the coal miners, their struggles are your struggles. The destruction of the UMWA threatens your own union. The building of a new, powerful miners' union will become a real aid in beating back open-shop attacks everywhere.
>
> The National Miners' Convention to be held in Pittsburgh, Pa. September 9 to 16, will be ruled by the rank and file. They will take matters into their own hands, select new leaders.
>
> Militant rank and file miners, you have shown in the past that you know how to build an organization. Unitedly we will build a new union.
>
> Stand together all soft coal and anthracite miners!
>
> Lewis and his whole corrupt machine must go!
>
> Come to the National Miners' Convention.

Shortly after this was issued, the Arrangements Committee announced that "reports from practically every organized and unorganized field are uniform in declaring that the sentiment for the new union is rising. Everywhere miners are saying, 'We are going to build an honest, militant union, and a thousand Lewises can't stop us!'"[20]

On September 9, 1928, more than 700 delegates representing thousands of miners in Pennsylvania, Ohio and Illinois met in Pittsburgh to found the National Miners' Union. Lewis was unable to stop the union from being founded but he forced it to be born in jail. The *Coal Digger* reported:

> About 200 plug uglies, captained by Lewis officials, appeared near the hall almost two hours before the time set for the opening of the Convention. Time and again they made a rush for the door, attempting to break through, but the attacks were repulsed by the squad of 300 delegates who got into the hall in the early morning, The gangsters then turned their attention to the delegates who were coming from their hotels, attacking them with blackjacks, razors and other weapons.

Only after the delegates had cleared their convention hall of thugs did the city police arrive. They then hauled the delegates away in patrol wagons, arresting 120 of them. The jailed delegates proceeded to hold their convention and establish the National Miners' Union in the jail.[21]*

The statement of policy adopted by the convention began by analyzing the starvation of the miners and the profits of the companies, rationalization, speed-up, and showed how the Lewis bureaucracy in the United Mine Workers had cooperated completely with the employers' policy, smashing locals, betraying strikers, signing one district at a time, separating anthracite from soft coal, and abandoning the Jacksonville scale. The statement of policy continued:

> John L. Lewis and his corrupt clique can no longer speak in the name of the coal miners.... Break completely with the Lewis machine and join the National Miners' Union.
>
> We solemnly declare to use every ounce of our energy to fight to the last to remove every obstacle to build an organization to comprise the whole of the rank and file coal miners. An industrial organization taking into its membership all men employed in and around the mines, except the bosses. Within our ranks we welcome the colored miner as well as the white, the foreign-born miner as well as the American. We pledge ourselves to fight for complete equality for all in every respect, regardless of race or nationality.[22]

---

* In 1892 Western copper miners involved in the bitter Coeur d'Alene strike were sentenced to prison for violating a court injunction. While quartered in the Ada County jail, a group of the strikers discussed labor strategy and tactics, During these discussions the idea emerged of establishing a federation of Western miners. This led to the formation of the Western Federation of Miners. (Philip S. Foner, *History of the Labor Movement in the United States* 2 [New York, 1955]: 233-35.)

The Preamble to the NMU Constitution proclaimed:

> Regardless of color or nationality every working miner must become an integral part of our union. We declare we will not only organize the Negro miners in every field but also draw them into full participation and leadership of our organization. To this end we propose to educate the miners against the practice of discrimination.

The Constitution also specified that a "special Negro representative" should sit on the National Executive Board, adding that this should "not prevent any Negro member of the union from aspiring to any other office." Ora Boyce, who represented the Indiana women's auxiliaries,* sat as a "special Negro representative" on the National Executive Board. Her husband, William Boyce, the veteran Black miner from Clinton, Indiana, was elected Vice-President of the new NMU. John Watt from Springfield, Illinois was elected president; Pat Toohey from the Pittsburgh district was elected secretary-treasurer.[23] Ora Boyce praised the union for its stand against racism: "The new union is not discriminating against any miner, regardless of race and color, and is not making the same mistake UMW officials made. As a result, we may expect the Negro miners to rally behind the new union. They know they will get a square deal." *Opportunity,* the organ of the National Urban League, felt that the Black worker now had a new alternative, "the radical wing of the labor movement."[24]

The very first local to join the NMU was the all-Black Lincoln Hill mine local, just outside of Washington, Pennsylvania.[25]

THE NATIONAL TEXTILE WORKERS' UNION

On July 16, 1928 the *Daily Worker* carried what it described as "the official call for a convention of textile workers organizations and mill committees for the formation of a national industrial union of all textile workers." Signed by Albert Weisbord, national secretary of the Textile Mills Committee, the call was addressed "To All Textile Workers' Organizations, Textile Workers, Mill Committees, Textile Workers Clubs and Associations, Textile Unions." It noted that the textile industry was increasingly becoming characterized by "intense speeding up, mass unemployment, longer hours and wage cuts," and that in New England over one hundred thousand cotton workers had

---

* Forty-two women representing women's auxiliaries were among the delegates at the founding convention of the National Miners' Union.

already received a ten percent wage cut. But just as the Passaic workers in 1926 "did not take a cut lying down," but under Communist leadership, "put up a great and memorable struggle," so "again under our leadership," the textile workers were "battling against this new ten percent wage cut." The "brave fight" of over 28,000 textile workers in New Bedford "shows that everywhere the textile workers are ready to move," Unfortunately, outside of a few "tiny independent groups," the only union in the field was the small union of the American Federation of Labor, the United Textile Workers.

Not only were the officials of the UTW "of the most reactionary character, with a long series of betrayals to their credit," but after many years of existence, it still represented only "a small handful of skilled workers, pitifully helpless to resist the attack of the bosses."

> This situation means that especially now, the textile workers must take things in their own hands and build a national textile union, that will be a real workers' union, organizing the over one million textile workers in this country and actually resisting the wage cuts and worsened conditions imposed by the employers. This is the immediate task at the present time, the building up of a national textile union that will mobilize the workers for effective struggle.

To accomplish this objective, all *bona fide* textile workers' organizations were invited to elect two or more delegates to attend a national convention to be held in New York City on September 22 and 23, 1928.[26]

"The call for a new union comes like a beacon of hope to all those who are suffering in the textile hells," declared the National Textile Mills Committee "With a militant leadership, the same leadership that conducted the splendid fight made by the woolen workers in Passaic two years ago and is now in charge of the spirited battle being put up in New Bedford and Fall River, with such a leadership the workers feel confident that their ranks will be organized and mobilized for struggle."[27]

On September 22, 1928, one hundred and fifty delegates, fifty of them women, from cities in seven New England and Middle Atlantic states, met in New York City and established the National Textile Workers' Union. Most of the delegates were unskilled workers from the New England cotton centers, the Paterson silk and dye plants, the Passaic and Lawrence woolen mills, the hosiery plants of Philadelphia, the carpet factories of Connecticut, and the knit goods factories in New York City and Brooklyn. But it was the New Bedford and Fall River delegates, the majority of them unskilled Portuguese workers who had been unorganized before the 1928 strikes, who aroused the greatest interest:

> From the moment the strikers marched into the convention hall here, singing strike songs, swinging down the aisles in picket formation, they became the heart of the great millworkers' gathering. Nearly every member of the delegation was under sentence for strike activities, with terms running from three months to three years. Cameiro Cameiras has been arrested twelve times and Marion Betelho eleven times.

Perhaps the most unusual delegate was Emma Rodrigues, a fourteen-year-old Fall River striker. Emma had become a "doffer" (picking up bobbins) in the American Printing Company when she reached her fourteenth birthday and was in the seventh grade at public school. She received $6.17 for a 44-hour week. When the strike began at the American Printing Company, she joined her father and sisters in walking out and became a militant leader of the strikers. Asked by reporters at the convention in New York what her plans were for the future, she told them that her "greatest aim and ambition was to be an organizer for the new Textile Union."[28]

Stella Correca, a New Bedford striker, was another delegate who aroused great interest at the convention. Along with her daughter, Mary, Stella had become a familiar figure on the picket line. She described how both she and her daughter had been repeatedly clubbed and jailed by the police, and she told why she felt the "new militant union" was an absolute necessity. In view of the failure of the United Textile Workers' leadership to concern itself with unskilled women workers, she said, "the road is clear for our new union to recruit many women."[29]

James Reid of Providence and Albert Weisbord were chosen president and national secretary, respectively, of the National Textile Workers Union. Ellen Dawson, who had played an active part in the Passaic strike and was a chief woman organizer in New Bedford, was chosen second vice-president—the first time a woman was elected to top leadership in a national textile union. Of the thirteen-member National Executive Committee, three were women.[30]

The new union called for organization of all textile workers, including those who were unemployed; for the establishment of a fund for the relief of the unemployed, "maintained by the employers and controlled by the union," the 44-hour, 5-day week, abolition of the speedup system and equal pay for equal work for women and young workers. A resolution called for the formation of a labor party "to represent the interest of the workers and which would not permit the use of government machinery to break strikes." Another resolution condemned "the capitalist murderers of Sacco and Vanzetti, executed on August 23, 1927 for a crime they did not commit." Special resolutions called for "the organization of the children into permanent bodies that are to be involved in all activities of the workers," and for "the greatest diligence in organizing women who constitute almost half the total number of workers." "Everywhere," declared the new union, "attention must be paid to attracting the working women into our union, and to developing them for actual leadership." The Passaic, New Bedford, and Fall River strikes had clearly demonstrated the importance of the textile woman worker and had given to many workers outside the industry "a most thorough appreciation of the role of the working woman."

The union advanced the following specific demands for textile women:

1. Equal pay for equal work.
2. Minimum wage for women.
3. No night work.
4. Prohibition of work in heavy and dangerous occupations.
5. Vacations with pay for two months before and two months after childbirth.
6. Permission for mothers with infants to leave their work every three hours to nurse their children.
7. Factory nurseries for workers under the administration of the union, free of charge to all mothers who work in the plant.
8. Rest rooms in the mill to be provided for the women.[31]

Although not a single delegate at the founding convention of the National Textile Workers' Union represented the South, and although the union was at the outset based totally in Northern textile factories, it was determined to carry its program to textile workers throughout the industry. With the experience gained from Passaic and New Bedford, the National Textile Workers' Union would soon turn its attention to organizing the South.

NEEDLE TRADES' WORKERS' INDUSTRIAL UNION

Before adjourning, the founding convention of the National Textile Workers' Union sent greetings to and endorsements of the "new Mine Workers Union recently formed in Pittsburgh, the new Furriers Union and the National Organization Committee of the International Ladies' Garment Workers Union, formed to organize a new union."[32] The National Organization Committee, as we have seen above, was organized early in May of 1928 during the ILGWU convention in Boston with the aim of rebuilding the union "over the heads of the Sigman-Schlesinger clique." The NOC planned to unionize the open shops, establish new shop chairman's bodies and mount an offensive against the evils of the industry.

It was not clear whether or not the NOC was to operate as an independent union or seek to gain control of the ILGWU. But at a meeting of the Political Committee of the Workers' (Communist) Party on May 16, 1928, a resolution was adopted recommending that the National Organization Committee "proceed to function as a regular union." The "Resolution on the Needle Trades" condemned the AFL policy of divide-and-rule and proposed that organizational steps be taken to form a new garment union. It suggested that the headquarters of the new union be in New York, that it operate on a shop delegate basis, endorse the TUEL, and adopt militant policies designed to regain economic control of the industry.

The National Organization Committee held a mass rally at Bronx Stadium on August 8, 1928, at which 15,000 workers adopted a resolution stating that "the time has come when the workers of the ladies' garment industry must begin building our new union controlled by the rank and file, which will lead us in struggle against the bosses and the company union." A few days later, the National Organization Committee called on the workers in the cloak and dress manufacturing industry to "tear up the books of the company union and join the cloakmakers' union of and for the workers":

> Strike while the iron is hot. Let all together begin the task of building a union. Every worker in the industry must become a member of the union. Every shop in the trade must immediately put itself under the leadership of the National Organization Committee. Let the employers feel the united strength of the cloakmakers who are fighting to abolish the chaotic condition in the industry brought about by the Sigman-Schlesinger clique.
>
> A cloakmakers' union as against the company union! This was the slogan launched by the 15,000 cloak and dressmakers gathered at the large mass meeting in the Bronx stadium.[33]

On August 12, 1928, delegates representing nearly every fur workers' local in the United States and Canada plus the New York Joint Board and the former so-called Progressive Bloc of the right-wing Joint Council, met in New York City. The conference formed an international united-front committee for the purpose of building a new International union in the fur manufacturing and fur dressing industries upon the scattered ruins of the right-wing organization. As a first step, the united conference called a mass mobilization meeting of the fur workers. The declaration announcing this decision read in part:

> We repudiate the policy of expulsion of members because of their political convictions and affiliations, and we declare for a union of all workers, recognizing the right of every worker to his race, color and religious and political beliefs.
>
> We are fully cognizant of the probable persecution of every worker signed to this declaration, but we also recognize that the urgent task of building one united international union of all fur workers, a union democratically controlled and managed by the workers only, and the task of restoring and bettering of the union conditions and union wages, stand above every consideration of self-interest and safety .... All of those who are honestly and sincerely desirous of helping the workers to build their union are welcome to join our ranks.
>
> International United-Front Committee.[34*]

On August 15, 1928, over four thousand fur workers at New York's Cooper Union unanimously resolved to organize a new International Union. It empowered the representatives of thirteen locals and the "Progressive Bloc" to form a provisional National Executive Committee "for the purpose of uniting and mobilizing all of the locals and all of the fur workers ... for the organization of a real union." It also empowered the Committee to call a convention of all local unions "for the purpose of forming a new International Union of fur workers of the United States and Canada." Another resolution opened a drive to raise the sum of $25,000 to organize the open shops.[35]

Thus, within a week of each other, the cloak and dressmakers and the fur workers moved to establish a new industrial union. While the furriers' provisional National Executive Committee was engaged in sponsoring a series of mass meetings throughout the country in support of the new union movement, it was invited by the National Organization Committee of the cloak and dressmakers to join in forming a single industrial union as the first step toward complete amalgamation in the needle trades unions. The letter pointed out

---

*The signers were headed by Ben Gold, representing the New York Joint Board, and included Jack Schneider of Local 1, Joseph Winogradsky of Local 15, Hyman Sorkin of the "Progressive Bloc," S. Soulounios of the Greek Branch of the Joint Board, Morris Langer of Local 25, and Sam Burt of Local 53.

that the workers in these industries "have had to contend with and meet the same enemies. On the picket line we a were faced with similar gangster squads. Our enemies are the same; our problems are the same."[36]

Hailing the amalgamation proposal, Irving Potash, secretary of the provisional National Executive Committee for a new Furriers International Union, replied to the National Organization Committee of the cloak and dressmakers: "We are convinced that the immediate amalgamation of the cloak and dressmakers and furriers unions, which have freed themselves of the grip of the bureaucrats, will place in the hands of our workers the most effective weapons in their struggle for better working and living standards and lay the basis for the all-embracing unification of all needle trade workers despite the sabotage of the labor bureaucrats."[37]

Two conventions, one of the cloak and dressmakers and the other of the furriers, opened in New York City on December 28 and 29, 1928.

Two days later, after the amalgamation proposal had been unanimously adopted by both conventions, the Needle Trades Workers Industrial Union was organized by delegates representing thousands of workers in all the important centers of the garment industry.

The joint convention laid the foundation of the new union. A constitution was drawn up, resolutions were adopted, and national officers and a General Executive Board were elected.

The principles and structure of the new union marked an important advance in democratic trade unionism. It recognized the principle of proportional representation and the election of general officers by referendum, with the right of recall. It established the shop delegate system, with the shop as its basic unit, as the foundation for the union, an important step toward drawing more and more of the rank and file into the union's activities.

The economic program adopted by the Convention included: a 40-hour, five-day week; minimum wage scales; wage increases; abolition of piece work and the establishment of week work; 40-week yearly guarantee of employment; limitation on contractors with the aim of their eventual elimination; the right to the job with no discharge or reorganization; elimination of sweatshops, home work, section contracting and sub-contracting; unemployment insurance to be paid by the employers and administered by the workers, and protection of youth and women in industry.

The Convention adopted a series of important resolutions. It voted to send delegates to all conferences called by militant unions in the country and to conferences called by the Trade Union Educational League. It demanded immediate release of Tom Mooney and Warren K. Billings and all other class-war prisoners languishing in jails. It recognized the special need of organizing Black workers and women workers. It sent fraternal delegates to the next congress of the new International of Labor Unions that had been organized to combat the Socialist-dominated Amsterdam trade union international.

It its last session, the Convention elected the new union's officers. Louis Hyman of the cloak and dressmakers was elected president and Ben Gold of the furriers as secretary. An executive board composed of thirty-nine other well-known militant needle trades workers was chosen to lead the new union. The members of the executive board included Negro workers, Russian-Polish and Greek workers, women and a representative from the youth.*

Hyman set the tone for the new organization in his inaugural address: "We believe in a union controlled by the workers, subject to the dictates of the rank-and-file, a militant, aggressive organization, a union which will express the will and aim of all needle workers." And Henry Rosemond, the fur worker who was one of two Black members of the General Executive Board, added; "The new union is far from being the old union that used to discriminate against Negro workers. The new union will seek to secure the same advantages for all workers regardless of their creed, color and race." The *Negro Champion*, organ of the American Negro Labor Congress, published in Harlem, endorsed Rosemond's statement:

Negro workers have everything to gain and nothing to lose by organization. We are today the most exploited section of the American working class, principally because we lack organization: the prejudiced AFL bureaucrats refused to organize the Negro workers and even barred us from their unions when we applied on our own initiative for admission.

But the Needle Trades Workers Industrial Union, in line with the Left-wing policy of giving positions of leadership and responsibility to Negro members of the left-wing unions, elected two Negroes to its General Executive Board at its first convention. It has also placed Negro members on other committees of the Union, and takes every precaution

*The general executive board included Sam Burt, Irving Potash, Jack Schneider, Samuel Leibowitz, Joseph Winogradsky, Rose Wortis, J. Papas, Lena Rabinowitz, Charles S. Zimmerman, and A. Zierlin. The Black members of the Board were Virginia Allen, dressmaker, and Henry Rosemond, furrier. M. Jensky was the youth delegate.

with the American Negro Labor Congress, to safeguard the interests of its Negro members.

Negro needle trade workers! Support the new union![38]

The TUEL group in the Amalgamated Clothing Workers' Union called a rank-and-file shop delegate conference to support the new industrial union. It appealed:

Every shop must be represented. Every worker who is ready to fight for better conditions, every worker who realizes the necessity of a union to serve the interests of the workers, every worker who suffers from the inhuman speed-up system in the shops, every worker who realizes the danger of company unionism, must see to it that his shop sends representatives to the conference in order that with united ranks, like the dressmakers, the cloakmakers, and furriers, he will be able to organize for a struggle against the bosses and their agents in our union.

Fight for a union to serve the interests of the workers! For the unity of all needle trades workers! Support the Needle Trades Workers Industrial Union.[39]

Despite the setbacks it had suffered and the obstacles and struggles that lay ahead, the left-wing was confident that it had made the correct decision in the formation of an independent union in the garment industry. As one left-winger put it:

The struggle of needle trades workers is not a needle trades struggle. It is an integral part of the entire struggle of the left-wing and revolutionary workers against the corrupt trade union bureaucracy and [its] Socialist Party partner, their fake program, the strike-breaking government and class collaboration schemes.[40]

A NEW TRADE UNION POLICY

By the and of 1928, a definite shift had occurred in Communist trade union policy. While the Trade Union Educational League was still in existence and efforts to influence the existing unions by "boring from within" still continued, much greater emphasis was being placed on the formation of independent unions. Organization of new unions was always part of the Communist trade union tactics, but since the Party's endorsement of the TUEL, the main stress had been on work within the existing unions. But by 1928, the Communists found themselves expelled from the very unions they had helped to build and isolated from the large bodies of unorganized workers in American industry. The criticism and advice of Arnold Losovsky, speaking for the Communist International, brought home sharply to American Communists the realization that a reexamination of their trade union theories was urgently needed. When this reexamination showed that a change in the objective conditions required a corresponding change in the application of their theories, the Communists were ready to acknowledge it and to take the necessary action.

It has generally been argued that the shift in Communist trade union policy in 1928 had little or nothing to do with internal developments in the American labor movement and was determined solely by the dictates of Soviet leaders. Thus, Irving Howe and Lewis Closer write:

> In December, 1927 ... the TUEL reaffirmed its opposition to dual unionism .... But then with bewildering suddenness, a shift of trade union policy was announced in Moscow. Dual unionism was the order of the day.[41]

Jack Barbash, Harvey A. Lowenstein, and Bert Cochran also explain the shift by tying it to Soviet policy.[42] Theodore Draper mentions the expulsion of the militants from the AFL, but attempts to minimize their importance. The adoption of the new trade union policy, according to Draper, "had nothing to do with the expulsion of 'left-wing forces' from the AFL," since "the most notable case of the expulsion of a Communist—that of William F. Dunne—had occurred in 1923, and there were no significant expulsions in 1928 or 1929."[43] But, as we have seen, it was in 1927-28 that it became clear that the expelled militants would not be able to win reinstatement into the needle trades, miners and other unions. The 1927-28 conventions of the International Ladies' Garment Workers Union, International Fur Workers' Union, and United Mine Workers ratified the expulsion of a majority, in some cases as many as two-thirds, of the union's members. No new expulsions were necessary.

In each of these cases, the administration preferred a small shell without the Communists and the workers who supported them to a large union *with* such members. In each of these cases, the administration preferred disorganizing the organized to organizing the unorganized. Even some anti-Communist labor historians concede that the union office-holders, Socialist and non-Socialist alike, were callous, ruthless and dictatorial in their attacks on the majorities that followed the Left, and that the triumph of these leaders prostrated the unions, drove workers' conditions down and left great masses of workers unorganized.[44]

Evaluating the situation in 1928, the Communists concluded that concentrating on working inside the existing AFL unions meant isolating themselves from the masses of American workers. Since 1920, when union membership was a little over 5 million, the number of organized workers had declined by more than a million and a half. Unions in 1928 covered only fragments of the working population, primarily those in the traditional crafts, with only a few inroads made in the basic industries. There was little union membership in the majority of the industries in this category, such as steel, automobiles, textile, rubber, electrical equipment, oil and cement.[45] After the faint-hearted attempt by the AFL to organize the auto industry, all efforts by the Federation to unionize the basic industries ceased. "The aggressive morale needed for organization was absent," Irving Bernstein points out, "nor were funds available to contest the large corporations. Many labor leaders were more concerned with maintaining a hold on existing crafts, and spent their energies in jurisdictional disputes."[46]

While the left wing acknowledged that a number of other factors were also responsible for the decline of the union movement after 1920, especially the anti-union practices of employers protected by law, it attributed it mainly to the craft structure of most AFL unions, the failure of the Federation to adapt structurally to the new era of mechanization and large corporations and, along with all this, the nature of the AFL leadership. It was a leadership dedicated to class collaboration, unwilling and unable to meet the basic needs of the working class—a leadership determined to hold on to power regardless of the consequences to the labor movement.[47]

In his recent book, *The Communist Party of the United States: From the Depression to World War II*, Fraser M. Ottanelli takes issue with the view of Howe, Closer, Barbash, Lowenstein, Cochran, and Draper. He points out succinctly: "The Party's shift to dual unionism, while originating in Moscow, was not without justification in the United States .. Red baiting in the AFL and other unions had reached such a level that it was objectively difficult for Communists to continue to work within them."[48]

Moreover, there was no immediate prospect that this bleak situation would change. The objective conditions in 1920-1922 had required emphasis on "boring-from-within"; the objective conditions in 1927-1928 required organization of the unorganized into new industrial unions. The radicals hoped to accomplish through independent unionism what they bad been unable to do in the established unions: reverse the decay of working conditions and the decline in union membership and organize the unorganized by creating a dynamic, militant, aggressive labor organization.

CHAPTER 17

REVOLT OF THE SOUTHERN TEXTILE WORKERS

The year 1929 marked the puncturing of an illusion that had been carefully nurtured by the Chambers of Commerce of every city and town below the Mason-Dixon line—that Southern workers, most of them fresh from the farms and hills, were so docile and obedient that they would accept any wages or conditions offered them.

To give credence to this notion, letters were sent out to all the New England textile mill owners, accompanied by attractive folders describing the South's excellent climate, its cheap labor and its proximity to the raw material. They also stressed the alleged individualism of the Southern workers which made them unreceptive to union propaganda, certainly as compared with the Northern textile workers, many of them foreign-born, who were said to be far more susceptible to organization.[1]

CONDITIONS IN SOUTHERN TEXTILE MILLS

Partly as a result of this intensive campaign of the Southern business interests, mill after mill moved south from New England. The owners of those that remained frequently voiced the threat that if the Northern workers continued to press for higher wages, additional mills would move south. This proved to be more than just a threat. Between 1923 and 1929, over a million textile workers were added in the South.[2]

Nevertheless, when, in the fall of 1929, the *New York Evening World* featured an article emphasizing that Southern textile workers were "happy and contented," a "working mother" in a North Carolina textile mill replied:

It is a lie. We are not happy and by no means contented. who could be with wages so low as ours and food so high? There is nothing left after we pay our grocery bill. I have five children and my husband doesn't make $20 a week. We have to send our children to school when they haven't enough clothing to keep them warm in the winter I had pellagra about two years ago but discovered it in time to take a treatment. The doctors said it was due to my working too long and to overworking and breathing cotton lint and bad air.[3]

Beginning in late 1921, Southern mill owners had sought to over-come the effects of the postwar depression in the textile industry by lowering wages and extending the already long hours of work. They were confident that no effective protest could be mounted. After all, the power of the mill owners and managers extended far beyond the factories. The workers lived in isolated villages in which the compa-nies owned the shacks, provided whatever schools there were, paid the teachers, if any, ran the stores, extended credit, built the churches, subsidized the ministers, and administered "law and order" through mill guards, company spies, and deputy sheriffs. Moreover, every effort to establish trade unions in the Southern mill towns had ended in failure. The latest one had been that of the AFL's United Textile Workers of America in 1919-1920. Invariably, after a promis-ing start, each of the strikes led by the UTW had been broken, and the union was forced to retreat from the South, leaving the mill workers at the mercy of the managements. The owners took immedi-ate advantage of the situation. In 1926, while the average textile worker in New England was earning $21.49 for a 48-hour week, the average worker in the South earned $15.81 for a 55-hour week. And this was only the average. Neither a sixty-hour workweek nor wages as low as $1.81 a day for women were uncommon.[4]

In the mid-twenties, mill owners sought to reduce labor costs even further by introducing so-called efficiency experts. These individuals produced studies that resulted in the introduction of the "stretch-out" system—a revision of production schedules calling for increased productivity from the already overworked employees, with no accom-panying increase in wages, thereby making it possible to produce more with fewer workers. The "stretch-out" quickly became the focal point of a variety of labor's grievances. George Tindall tells a story about the Loray mill workers in Gastonia, North Carolina, who were demonstrating against the "stretch-out": "Loray workers paraded a coffin down Gastonia's main street. At intervals an effigy of the su-perintendent rose up to ask: 'How many men are carrying this thing?' The group shouted 'Eight.' 'Lay off two,' the effigy re-sponded, 'Six can do the work.'" As Tindall points out: "The comedy masked a growing tension."[5] Dissatisfaction had been growing steadily among the female textile workers in Southern mills. Newspapers and magazines told of girls and women, some as young as fourteen years of age, who worked from 5:40 in the morning until 6 at night, at temperatures near 85, with thirty minutes for lunch. Their wages were $5 a week. Many women workers were paid nothing during the period in which they learned their jobs.[6] There were also accounts of women who had worked in the mills for twenty years and were still earning only $12.90 a week.[7] One survey reported: "The girls who work in the Southern mills as winders on the Foster machines make $9 a week, and the work is so hard that few do not get sick at it They have to mind 36 to 42 ends and soon cannot work at all. Tuberculosis gets them after a few years of speed-up and bad working conditions."[8] To married (or divorced or widowed) women mill workers, the double oppression of household work and long mill labor was especially gruelling.

In the most detailed and biting criticism of conditions in the Southern textile industry, Tom Tippett indicted it for long hours, low wages, night work, employment of underage children, and the "stretch-out" system. He published pictures of female rayon workers in Elizabethton, Tennessee, displaying their paychecks of $8.75, $7.50, and $5.45 for a week's work. He used the powerful account of one of the workers, Lucy Sparks, to describe conditions in the Clinchfield mills of Marion, North Carolina. She told of constant spitting on the floor in an area where many of the workers were tubercular. The mills were swept while all were working, "filling our breath with lint and dust full...of germs." The toilets were "filthy and ill-smelling." Drinking water was obtained from a pail placed in the toilet room with a community dipper; "that is why many of the workers wait until after they go home at six o'clock to drink water." No time was allowed for a lunch break: "If a worker is caught up with work they cannot leave the mill. One worker worked hard and got one-half day ahead. She stayed home and was docked for losing the time." It told of a widow who had a little girl of ten and an invalid father to support, and whose sister and mother were too old to work in the mill: "The widow makes eleven dollars a week to support all of them. She is a spooler, and stands on her feet from six in the morning until six at night.* She underwent an operation six years ago—she isn't strong."[9]

* A spooler tended the machine which spooled the yarn

Lucy Sparks also told of conditions in the mill villages. The houses were "very open and cold in the winter time. .haven't been painted inside in ten years; are smoked and dirty;...roofs leak badly." Toilets in the villages were of the earthpit variety. New pits had to be dug by the mill workers when the old ones filled up and ran into the streets. "I hope," Sparks concluded, "there is some information here that you do not have. I am very sorry I haven't education enough to write as I wish."[10]

Educated or not, however, the textile workers knew enough to understand that until they organized and fought back, conditions would never change. In August, 1927, a textile strike took place in Henderson, North Carolina. Although the walkout was quickly crushed by the National Guard, it left a legacy of some five to six hundred new members of the United Textile Workers.[11] But the AFL union did nothing to further the organization of Southern textile workers unions until the formation of the National Textile Workers' Union in September, 1928. Then the alarmed United Textile Workers warned AFL President William Green that if a Southern organizing campaign was not started, the new textile union, "communistic in character," would fill the vacuum. And *Labor* prophesied: "Southern workers will be organized. If this is not done by responsible craft unions, it will be done by the Communists."[12]

While the AFL and the UTW dawdled, the Communists began to move. Early in 1929 the Trade Union Educational League announced:

> The new, fighting National Textile Workers Union, affiliated to the Trade Union Educational League, which led the New Bedford strike of 28,000 textile workers, has now launched an organizational drive in the South. Every militant must support the Trade Union Educational League and the textile union in its work of organizing the Southern workers, transforming their sporadic strikes into one organized, sustained movement against speed-up and for higher wages and shorter hours, and linking them up with the strike movement looming in New England, and other textile centers, into a great, unified, nationwide campaign of textile workers against the increasing pressure of rationalization.[13]

The "sporadic strikes" referred to by the TUEL were spontaneous uprisings against the long hours, low wages, the poor working conditions, and the "stretch-out." In 1929, over 350 mills in three Southern states—Tennessee, North Carolina, and South Carolina—were closed by such spontaneous strikes.

THE ELIZABETHTON STRIKE

The first began in Elizabethton, Tennessee. On March 12, 1929, a foreman in the inspection department of the German-owned Glanzstoff rayon plant demoted Margaret Bowen from her position as a section leader because she had demanded a pay raise. More than five hundred employees refused to work until Bowen was reinstated and their own wages raised.[14] Within a few days, five thousand workers, about 70 percent of them women, left the mills protesting a 56-hour week at wage scales ranging from $8.64 to $10.08 a week, or 16 to 18 cents an hour. They included two thousand employees of the Bemberg plant, who also refused to work. With the aid of local unionists and Matilda Lindsey, a Southern field representative of the Women's Trade Union League, a United Textile Workers local was formed with an initial membership of a thousand. Organized on March 15, when there was not even a UTW organizer in Elizabethton, the local's membership grew to over four thousand within a week. Margaret Bowen was chosen secretary-treasurer.[15]

The original strikers were very young girls. "An outstanding feature of this most unusual rebellion is that it was led by children, the little girls in the 'inspection rooms,'" wrote a labor reporter. "They were not only the first to come out, but among the most determined. Numbers of them addressed the mass meetings of strikers which were held every day, pleading, in their piping, childish voices, for the 'grown folks' not to weaken."[16] And they didn't. Despite the use of injunctions, the National Guard, and the arrest and jailings of pickets, the strikers held firm to their demand for wage increases. On March 22 the strike was settled, with increases of from 5 to 15 percent for men, 11 percent for women, and a commitment to rehire all workers. Matilda Lindsey had visions of this triumph as the first step in the unionization of the South.[17]

Her enthusiasm was soon shattered as the company reneged on the agreement, refusing to pay the wages the workers thought had been agreed to and discharging the active union members who had presented grievances.[18] Then, early on the morning of April 14, armed gangs separately seized Edward F. McGrady, who had been sent by the AFL as President Green's personal representative to save the sagging agreement, Alfred Hoffman of the UTW and a striker, transported them out of Tennessee and dumped them with a warning never to return. The abductors, probably businessmen, threatened the union officials with death if they returned to Elizabethton.[19]

These events, coupled with the company's reneging on the wage increase and its dismissal of active unionists, led to a second strike on April 15. In a determined effort to crush the new walkout, a company union, called "Loyal Workers," was launched, and over eight hundred National Guardsmen, two hundred special police, and a hundred deputies were sent to the town. Workers were evicted from their homes. More than 1,250 strikers, including girls from fifteen to seventeen years of age, were arrested and thrown into jail. Machine guns were used to protect the scabs.[20]

Nevertheless, the strikers' morale remained high. When the company attempted to open the plants early in May, not one of the five thousand strikers offered to return to work. At the hour set for the opening of the mills, a parade, six blocks long, marched along the highway to close the plant. Then the strikers marched back to their meeting place and voted unanimously not to return until they had obtained a satisfactory settlement.

Margaret Bowen had eight injunctions served on her. Several women were seriously injured when a bus carrying scabs charged into picket lines on the highway. "They're doin' everything they can to discourage us," Bowen told the delegates to the 1929 convention of the National Women's Trade Union League in Washington. "But we won't get discouraged. Two of the girls—neither of them is 15 years old—have been put to jail because they can't pay their bills."[21]

But neither could the UTW, whose relief funds were depleted. As for the AFL, it was "indifferent to the urgent financial requirements of Elizabethton."[22] On May 22 the UTW accepted a settlement negotiated by Anna Weinstock of the U.S. Department of Labor. The terms provided for the rehiring of most workers, with no discrimination against union members if their activities were "legitimate" and "not carried on at the plants," established a grievance committee and appointed a new plant manager, B.T. Wilson, a personnel man from a textile mill in Passaic, New Jersey, who was to act as an "impartial person" in disputes between the union and the company.[23]

The textile workers were assured that the new plant manager would be more sympathetic to their needs. However, National Textile Workers' Union organizers in the area exposed the fact that Wilson had represented employers in the 1926 Passaic strike and was notorious for his opposition to unionism. They urged rejection of the settlement and called on the workers to insist on higher wages and better conditions. But William F. Kelley, UTW vice-president in charge of the strike, told the strikers they had no choice. "If the plants will take our workers back and not discriminate, the strike is ended," he declared. Reluctantly, the strikers voted to end their walkout.[24]

In the days following the end of the strike, the workers began to register for reemployment. Immediately, the new manager showed his true colors, and hundreds of strikers were blacklisted. In the next few months, hundreds of other workers were discharged, and Wilson vigorously promoted a company union. On September 19, notices were posted announcing: "The management does not intend at any time to discuss any matters...with outside individuals or organizations." Employees who disapproved were advised "not...to remain in our employ."[25]

The textile owners eventually broke UTW Local 1630. Hundreds of blacklisted workers left the area, and since those who remained were threatened with dismissal if they were identified as union members, the membership of the union declined from a high of 4,500 during the strike to 200. In a vain effort to enlist Federation support, Matilda Lindsey told the 1929 AFL convention that either the union would survive in Elizabethton or the South was lost to organized labor.[26]

THE GASTONIA STRIKE

While the strike in Elizabethton was ending in a complete defeat for the union, less than a hundred miles away, on the other side of the Smoky Mountains, the next important strike was beginning in Gastonia, North Carolina. It soon became the most famous of the revolts of the Southern textile workers. Though by far the smallest of the major Communist-led strikes of the period, the 1929 Gastonia walkout is perhaps the most celebrated.[27] Set in the leading textile center of the aggressively open-shop state of North Carolina, the strike came to be viewed as a symbol of whether or not the entire Southern textile industry could be organized.

The largest mill in Gastonia was the Loray Mill, located a few miles from the town proper in Loray Village, a typical "company town." The mill had been built in 1900 and was originally controlled by local interests, but it had been sold in 1919 to the Manville-Jenckes Company of Rhode Island and had become the first Southern mill to be owned and operated by Northerners. It was also the first in the South to introduce the "stretch-out," which was put into operation in 1927. It was so effective in increasing the work load per operator that by the end of the year, F. L. Jenckes, president of the parent company, congratulated his resident agent in Gastonia, G. A. Johnstone, on reducing the Loray payroll by half a million dollars without decreasing production. Jenckes urged him to cut twice as much "and still keep your production up." As a result, during the next fifteen months, the mill reduced its working staff from 3,500 to 2,200 without any cut in production. At the same time, naturally, wages declined sharply.[28]

In March 1928, fifty Loray workers struck to protest the "stretch-out" and the deep wage cuts, but to no avail. As the year ended, Manville-Jenckes, under pressure from the local clergy, replaced its mill superintendent in charge of the "stretch-out." Although the move evoked joyous celebrations on the part of the millhands, it produced little in the way of reform at an enterprise which had already laid off more than a third of its 3,500 workers while still maintaining production. Since it took the wages of about three family members to earn enough on which the average family could live, such layoffs meant not only much harder work for those still employed, but also mounting debts at the company store. The speed-ups brought the issue of working hours into sharp relief. As one worker explained: "It used to be you could get five, ten minutes' rest now and then, so's you could bear the mill. But now you got to keep a-runnin' all the time. Never a minute to get your breath all the day long. I used to run six drawing frames and now I have to look after ten. You just kain't do it."[29] Publication of one month's pay envelopes of Mattie Hughes, a woman with three children and a mother to support, revealed these figures: "March 30, [1929], 60 hours, $7.47; April 6, 60 hours, $7.36; April 13, 60 hours, $7.13, less grocery bill of $3; April 20, 60 hours, $5.53; total, less grocery bill, $24.49, for 240 hours' work."[30]

Into this cauldron, in January 1929, came National Textile Workers' Union organizer Fred Beal. Beal, a former Wobbly and ex-Socialist, had helped to lead the New Bedford textile strike. He had been elected to the Executive Committee of the National Textile Workers' Union and was chosen organizer of its Southern District as well. After the New Bedford strike ended in October, 1928, he was directed by the NTWU, which had no locals in the South, to begin a Southern organizing campaign. He arrived in Charlotte, North Carolina on New Year's Day, 1929 together with another NTWU organizer, Mario Thumod. Beal had been told that the Loray Mill in Gastonia was the key to organizing the entire South, that the Gastonia workers were bitter toward the United Textile Workers because that union had signed up many workers in the district in 1920-1921 only to withdraw after losing a strike, and that they were ready to move into a new union. He made his way to Gastonia and, together with a single local mill worker, decided to set up a secret union local and begin taking in only a few members. After he left for New York to ask for help, close to sixty Loray workers signed up with the secret union local. However, the company learned about some of them and they were fired. When Beal returned to Gastonia, he found the workers ready for a strike. Although he hesitated, fearing that they were unprepared for the confrontation, a meeting of the secret union local reached agreement on the holding of an open meeting on the following Saturday afternoon, March 30.[31] On April 1, 1929, the *Daily Worker* carried the first of scores of articles datelined "Gastonia, N.C." It reported that an enthusiastic mass meeting of about one thousand workers of Manville-Jenckes' Loray plant had entrusted full authority to the organizers of the National Textile Workers' Union to proceed with strike preparations "in the event that the mill owners discriminate against any worker for joining the union."

Before April 1, when the mass meeting was to be held, the mill dismissed five union members. The night shift workers enthusiastically endorsed a strike at their meeting. Immediately, a large majority of Loray's 2,200 workers, possibly as many as 1,800 or 2,000, walked out.*

Most of the strikers were women, for, as in Passaic, men were frequently hired only on condition that their wives also worked. "Manville-Jenckes won't hire a man who has a wife without both of 'em working," one woman striker declared. "If the woman's about to have a baby and can't keep up with the work, or if she has a very young baby, they fires the husband too."[33]

On April 3, with the strike just two days old, the unionists drew up a list of demands which reflected both the general aspirations of the workers and the special concerns of the women. These included a 40-hour, five-day week (down from 60 hours weekly), an end to the "stretch-out," the abolition of piece work, removal of the bank clocks (which measured the yarn that was spun), equal pay for equal work

---

* The actual number of strikers is a matter of some dispute. Mary Heaton Vorse stated that 1,700 strikers walked out initially and cited the strikers' lawyer, Tom P. Johnson, as her source. (*Harper's Monthly* 159 [November, 1929]: 701). *The Outlook and Independent* (153[Oct. 16, 1929]: 253) put the figure at 2,000, but *The Nation* (138 [May 1, 1929]) thought that there were fewer than 1,500. The highest estimate is by William Z. Foster (*From Bryan to Stalin*, [New York, 1937], p. 234), whose figure is 5,000.

Irving Bernstein described the millhands as having walked out "almost to a man," He correctly captured the near-unanimity among the workers but erred with regard to their gender. (Irving Bernstein, *The Lean Years: A History of the American Worker, 1920-1933*, Boston, 1960, p. 22.)

for women and children, a $20 weekly minimum wage, a fifty percent reduction in rent and light charges, free baths and better toilets in the mill, screening in the company houses and union recognition. Loray Superintendent J. A. Baugh took only three minutes to reject the demands.[34]

Mass demonstrations, picketing and parades began immediately, but so, too, did the repression. As early as the fourth day of the strike, the National Guard was sent into Gastonia to protect strikebreakers brought in by the company and to prevent picketing on mill property. Court injunctions quickly forbade all strike activity, and anyone arrested for picketing was fined $50 and sentenced to a thirty-day work shift on the chain gang.[35] On April 4, a full-page advertisement in special edition of the Gastonia *Gazette*, signed by "A Group of Citizens of Gastonia," virtually appealed for violence against the strikers by calling upon a "all American citizens and church people" to prevent further organization by the National Textile Workers' Union. The strike, it said, was solely for "the purpose of overthrowing the Government and destroying property and to kill, kill, kill. The time is at hand for every American to do his duty."[36]

The injunctions kept strike activity away from the mills, but, despite the presence of a howitzer company of the National Guard, protests continued, aided by the increasing presence of Communist organizers, including Vera Buch, Albert Weisbord and Ellen Dawson. The strikers distributed leaflets to the troopers in an attempt to win them over to the cause, and Weisbord advised the women strikers "to go to the soldiers and ask them if they want to kill working women and children for the bosses."[37] The appeal had no effect. Nevertheless, the strikers fought on. Tom Tippet, who was in Gastonia, reported: "The strikers were clubbed and beaten in the streets and carted off to jail *en masse*." He marveled at their reaction to this "unwarranted brutality": "Their parades were broken up by force every day, and just as consistently the strikers would form again the following day to march, with full knowledge of what they were doing, into the clubs and rifles." He saw a woman striker knocked down and struck with a bayonet "until she bled profusely. She struggled to her feet and marched on in the parade." In his study of the Gastonia strike, Liston Pope notes that the women were acknowledged to be "the most outspoken and determined of the strikers; they ordinarily were placed in the forefront of the picket lines and parades, and on several occasions they used clubs on militiamen and deputies."[38]

On April 15, with relief slow in arriving and the AFL opposing the strike, the mills partially reopened. Two days late, a relief depot was opened by the Workers' International Relief in an attempt to remedy the situation. Strike leaders appeared unfazed by episodic returns to work. As Beal noted:

> ...the scab of today was the striker of tomorrow. This, and the fact that most of the strikers were related to each other, established a unique attitude on the part of the strikers to the scabs.... In Gastonia the scab was considered merely a potential striker. Those that worked all day attended union meetings in the evening. I began to organize the scabs to have periodic walkouts to support the regular strike.[39]

In the face of the steadfastedness of the strikers, local commercial leaders, politicians, newspaper owners and American Legionnaires joined in escalating attacks on the strike. During the night of April 18, undisturbed by nearby troops, a mob of armed and masked men attacked the union headquarters and completely demolished it. They then proceeded to destroy the Workers' International Relief Store, wrecked its furnishings, dumped the food into the street, doused it with kerosene, and set it afire. The troops slept through the incident, arriving on the scene directly after the damage was done, at which point they arrested Workers' International Relief representative Amy Shechter and some of the strikers.[40]

Despite the unprecedented terror, many workers refused to abandon the union. Ella Mae Wiggins, a mother of nine, did much to maintain morale by her frequent presence on the picket line and her union ballads. The life of this 29-year-old mill worker, militant unionist and balladeer, was riddled with tragedy. Before the birth of her second child, her husband was crippled for life when a heavy log fell on him. She bore nine children in ten years, and after her husband's death, she and her family moved from "back in the hills" to the cotton mill district, coming to Bessemer City to work in the American Mill. While she was working sixty hours a week as a spinner, the older children had to stay home to care for the babies. "They couldn't get no schoolin'," she explained. When four of her children became ill, the "super" refused to put her on the day shift so that she could care for them.

In desperation, she quit, only to find that she could not afford medicine for her ill youngsters: "So they just died. I never could do anything for my children, not even to keep 'em alive, it seems. That's why I'm for the union, so's I can do better for them."[41]

She not only joined the NTWU, picketed, and spoke at union meetings, but she also wrote what she called "song ballets" about the union and the strike, using mountain folk tunes. "Ella May was singing when I arrived," wrote a correspondent later, and he went on:

> She was a "slightly built" woman rather short and round, with lively brown eyes that had survived the early aging of the Southern working woman. She had a clear, true tone in her untaught voice, an unmodulated vibrancy that touched the emotion more nearly than the purer notes of trained singers. Hundreds of workers stood in the pine grove, their faces upturned to the singer, their lips following the words:
> "We're going to have a union all over the South.
> Where we can wear good clothing and live in a better house.
> Now we must stand together and to the boss reply,
> We'll never, no, we'll never let our union die."
> It was her own "Song Ballet" put to the ringing tune of "Floyd Collins."... It would travel through the textile towns, telling better than speeches or leaflets of the people's faith in the union to give them a better life.[42]

Ella Mae Wiggins, like many Communist organizers and local militants, worked hard to organize Black workers and recruit them into the union. Although Blacks made up about 15 percent of the population of Gaston County, only a few of them worked in the textile mills, which were reserved for "poor whites."* The few who did were engaged in heavy, unskilled labor outside the mill. The Loray Mill had possibly less than one percent Blacks. However, Weisbord insisted that "on the Negro question, there must be absolutely no compromise." But it proved difficult to convince the white workers to take Blacks into the Gastonia local, and at a union meeting in Bessemer City, Black and white workers were separated by a wire. However, when Otto Hall, the Negro organizer for the National Textile Workers' Union, was on his way from Bessemer City to Gastonia, white workers, fearing that Hall might be lynched by vigilantes, formed a bodyguard and took him in an automobile to Charlotte where they collected enough money among themselves to pay for his railroad fare back to New York. After Hall had left, a mob broke into the house where he had been hidden before his departure.[43]

---

* "There were only four hundred Negroes employed in the Gaston County cotton mills in any capacity whatever," notes one student of the strike. (John Garett Van Osdell, Jr., "Cotton Mills, Labor, and the Southern Mind, 1880-1930," unpublished Ph.D. dissertation, Tulane University, 1966, p. 152n.)

Even when white workers were persuaded to accept the Black workers, the Blacks were suspicious and responded slowly. Ella Mae Wiggins was convinced that once the Black workers saw that she was "poor and humble like themselves," they would listen to the union message. After a while, she had enough cards signed by the Black workers to call a meeting, which was held in Stumptown, where the Black workers lived, and they were welcomed into the union. News of the meeting immediately prompted the company to distribute hand-bills among the strikers, asking: "Would you belong to a union which opposes white supremacy?" At the same time, company supporters played on the fear that Blacks might enter the textile labor force in numbers for the first time as strikebreakers.[44]

In general the efforts to unite Black and white in Gastonia met with only mixed success (and any compromise with local race preju-dice met with bitter censure of some organizers in the Communist press). But the very attempt to apply equalitarian policies further enraged both local officials and vigilantes.[45]

Through May, mill production failed to return to normal. The company then undertook to break the remainder of the strike by forcibly evicting participants from company housing. The Workers' International Relief set up tents for the evicted strikers, and the union posted armed guards for protection. Although the National Guard was removed after a series of protests, a Committee of 100 organized by the mills insured, as one historian has put it, "the con-tinuance of the reign of terror on the strikers."[46]

On June 7, a carload of police armed with a warrant invaded the strikers' tent colony and were met by the union's armed guards. In the ensuing gun battle, Chief of Police O. F. Aderholt was fatally wounded. A union organizer was seriously wounded and three depu-ties were wounded slightly. A reign of terror followed. "The residents of the tent colony were hunted like wild beasts," wrote one observer. "They fled from their homes into the woods to escape the fury of the mob."[47] Seventy-five of the tent colonists were arrested and grand jurors later indicted sixteen for murder and seven for assault. Of the sixteen indicted for murder, three were women: Vera Buch, organizer for the NTUW, Sophie Melvin, organizer of the children's section in the strikers' tent colony, and Amy Schechter, Workers' International Relief director since the early days of the strike.[48]*

Throughout the summer, the NTWU was more occupied with conducting a defense campaign than a strike. In the campaign for funds the union received the support of the International Labor Defense and the *Daily Worker*. The ILD widely distributed copies of one of the most popular of Ella Mae Wiggins' "song ballets." It began:

> Come all of you good people and listen to what I tell;
> The story of Chief Aderholt, the man you all knew well.
> It was on one Friday evening, the seventh day of June.
> He went down to the union ground and met his fatal doom.

The song ended with the same refrain cited above:

> We're going to have a union all over the South,
> Where we can wear good clothin', and live in a better house,
> Now we must stand together and to the boss reply
> We'll never, no, we'll never let our leaders die....[49]

After several weeks in jail, the three women were informed that the state was not asking for the death penalty in their cases, and they were able to post bail. But with bail set at $5,000 each, the necessary funds could not be raised immediately, so the three women organizers remained in jail until August 3 when the Garland Fund contributed the necessary $15,000. Then they departed on a national tour to bring the story of Gastonia to workers in several cities and to raise funds for the ILD defense.[50] Black newspapers supported their appeals, and the *Chicago Defender* and the *Pittsburgh Courier* urged support for the defendants. The *Courier* observed:

> Colored people need to be concerned about this trial of white people in the South. If whites who are poor and disadvantaged have no rights of self-defense and no rights of legal procedure, the blacks will know where they stand .... These poor whites were striking; the policemen were in the influence of the employers. That is clear.[51]

---

* Vera Buch's first assignment as an organizer had been in the Passaic strike, where she organized the women's section and where she met and married Albert Weisbord. Following an assignment in the Pennsylvania coal fields in 1928, she was sent as an organizer to Gastonia. Sophie Melvin was only nineteen years old, but she had already had considerable labor experience and had been in jail several times for helping strikers. British-born Amy Schechter, the daughter of an Oxford professor and a graduate of Barnard College, had been arrested for picketing in the New Bedford strike and had been involved in relief work for strikers for several years. She had been in charge of the Workers' International Relief store in Gastonia since it was established. (*Daily Worker*, June 9, 10, 12, 1929; Anne Fishel, "Women in Textile Organizing: Interview with Sophie Melvin Gerson," *Radical History Review* 4 [Summer, 1977]: 111-13.)

The trial of the sixteen defendants began on August 26 in Charlotte, with the International Labor Defense and the American Civil Liberties Union serving for the defense. On September 7, after the selection of the jury, the prosecutors hauled in an effigy of the dead police chief dressed in his blood-spattered clothing. The sight of the effigy drove one juror insane, and the incident forced Judge Burnhill to declare a mistrial.[52]

Further mob violence greeted the news of the mistrial. On the night of September 9, five hundred vigilantes raided the strikers' headquarters in Gastonia and Bessemer City, kidnapped and beat strike leaders.[53] A union rally to protest the repression met with additional and more tragic violence on September 14. As they headed for the demonstration, a truckload of unionists encountered ten automobiles of vigilantes who blockaded the road and fired into the group of strikers in broad daylight. The volley of shots killed Ella Mae Wiggins, the union organizer, ILD secretary and union bard of Bessemer City.[54]

At her burial, her fellow workers gathered around her plain wooden coffin and Katie Barnet sang her best-loved song, "The Mill Mother's Lament":

> We leave our homes in the morning,
> We kiss our children goodbye,
> While we slave for the bosses,
> Our children scream and cry.
>
> And when we draw our money,
> Our grocery bills to pay,
> Not a cent to spend for clothing,
> Not a cent to lay away.
>
> And on that very evening
> Our little son will say,
> "I need some shoes, dear mother,
> And so does sister May."
>
> How it grieves the heart of the mother,
> You, everyone, must know,
> But we cannot buy for our children,
> Our wages are too low.
>
> Now listen to me, workers,
> Both you women and you men,
> Let us win for them the victory,
> I'm sure it will be no sin.

Then Dewey Martin, local NTWU organizer, spoke and repeated what Ella Mae Wiggins had told him not long before her death: "I want the children to live a decenter life than what I did. I'm fightin' for better conditions for my children. I want them to get some educating and have a better chance than I ever got and I want to learn them to be good union leaders and stick to their fellow workers." Mary Heaton Vorse recalled: "The last time I saw her, she said to me, 'I belong to the union because of my children. I haven't been able to do anything for them. I never sent a child to school. How could I buy shoes or books? Even if I could, I couldn't let the oldest go. She has to take care of the smaller ones while I am at work. But when they grow up they won't have to work twelve hours a day for nine dollars a week.' She looked at me with extraordinary earnestness and said, 'They would have to kill me to make me leave the union.'"55*

Five Loray employees were charged with the murder, but even though the crime had been committed in broad daylight and witnessed by more than fifty people, all of the accused were acquitted. No one was ever convicted for the murder of Ella Mae Wiggins.56

The mob violence in Gastonia did generate nationwide protests that were strong enough to cause the dropping of the charges against the three women and six of the thirteen men indicted for the murder of Chief of Police Aderholt. The second trial of the seven remaining defendants began on September 30, 1929. Although the defense established that Aderholt and two of his aides were drunk and that none of the raiders had any legitimate business at the tent colony, the prejudice of the jury with respect to Communism, racial equality and religion was so exploited by the prosecution, with the consent of the judge, that, as one contemporary conservative observer concluded: "The accused never had a chance .... The defendants were really tried for what they thought, not what they did."57 Seven of the defendants were convicted, the four Northerners sen-

---

* Mary Heaton Vorse published a novel in the fall of 1930 entitled *Strike* which was based entirely on the Gastonia strike. In the novel Mamie Lewis, the name given to Ella Mae Wiggins, is one of the fearless characters in the strike. The novel bore the imprint of Horace Liveright, a progressive New York publisher. Mike Gold praised the novel in the *New Masses* as a glorious example of "proletarian realism." Roger Baldwin called the novel "an enduring memorial to a great strike." (Dee Garrison, *Mary Heaton Vorse: The Life of an American Insurgent*, Philadelphia, 1989, pp. 237-38, 358.)

In *Strike*, Mamie Lewis is asked how she was able to get along. She replied: "I don't git along....I can't even afford to git a house in the mill hill! The rent ain't much but I cain't even afford that. I live out o' town over a mile and a half with some kin o' mine in a shack. They got one room and the kitchen hole and I got the other" (p. 12).

The Gastonia strike inspired Fielding Burke's novel, *Call Home the Heart* (1932), Myra Page's *Gathering Storm* (1938), and William Rollins' *The Shadow Before* (1934). Grace Lumpkin's *To Make My Bread* (1932) was a slightly fictionalized biography of Ella Mae Wiggins.

tenced to prison terms of from seventeen to twenty years, the three Southerners to lesser sentences.[58]*

After the late September retrial, the strike dwindled. It ended with none of its original demands gained although it did help to cause the adoption of a 50-hour week at Loray and other mills.[59]

It has generally been assumed that even though the Gastonia strike lasted from the beginning of April to the end of September, it was "lost almost as soon as it started," and that by April 15, "the strike as a strike was over," with the Loray mills virtually back to normal production. According to this view, the strike was prolonged for six months because the Communist Party and its organizations—the Trade Union Educational League, the Trade Union Unity League and the National Textile Workers' Union—viewed Gastonia as a windfall "for propaganda purposes."[60] The truth is, however, that many Gastonia workers, especially the women in the Loray mills, wanted the strike to continue and were ready to fight as long as necessary. "Some say the strike is over, that we have lost and that we know it," a young female mill worker wrote on June 14. "I for one know the strike is not over, for we intend to win if it takes ten years to do so." Others shared her determination, and they persisted until the very end, along with the Communist organizers, in the face of mass hysteria, mob violence and sheer hunger.[61]

Both the Trade Union Educational League and the Trade Union Unity League pointed up the importance of the Gastonia strike and issued appeals to "the whole left wing to rally to the defense of the victims of the bosses' rapacity in the Southern textile mills."[62] But the role of both organizations in the strike was limited. When the Gastonia strike began, the Trade Union Educational League was in the process of being transformed into the Trade Union Unity League as "a new militant labor union center," and the strike was practically over when the latter body was established.

There is no doubt, however, that the Communist Party directed its main forces in 1929 at the struggle in Gastonia. William Dunne exaggerated only slightly when he wrote in July, 1929: *The Gastonia case is the highest political issue in the South today.*[63] The *Daily Worker* made

---

* The seven convicted NTWU members jumped bail and went to the Soviet Union after their convictions. In 1933, Fred Beal returned to the United States and spent the next five years as a fugitive from justice. In 1937, he published *Proletarian Journey*, an autobiography, in which he attacked both the Communist Party of the United States and of the Soviet Union. Captured the following year, he served in a North Carolina prison until 1942, when he was paroled.

the same point: "It is because Gastonia is the symbol of the higher stage of the class struggle in this country and because the movement for revolutionary unionism is a challenge to the whole capitalist class, that the fire of the enemy is today concentrated upon Gastonia."[64] It is not surprising, then, that the Communist Party also "concentrated upon Gastonia." According to one study, about twenty-three Communist organizers took a direct part in the Gastonia strike.[65] Communist women militants were among the full-time organizers who stayed in Gastonia throughout the bitter months of the unequal struggle. They included, in addition to Buch, Melvin, and Schecter, Ellen Dawson for the NTWU, Caroline Drew for the Workers' International Relief, Edith Saunders Miller, who represented the Young Pioneers of America—the Communists' children's organization—and Ann Burlak, who was soon to be elected secretary of the National Textile Workers' Union.*

The presence of Communist organizers and the wide support for the cause of Gastonia in the Communist Party and among its sympathizers have led a variety of journalists and historians, most of them unsympathetic to Communism, to attribute the defeat to the ability of the Gastonia mill owners to make the Communist issue the prime consideration, and to what is referred to as the Communist practice of subordinating economic to political issues throughout the strike.[66] Yet it was clear to many contemporary observers that the Communist issue was mainly a smokescreen for the mill owners' anti-unionism. Ella Mae Wiggins was correct when she stressed, "But understand, all workers, our union do they fear." It is difficult to disagree with *Nation* correspondent Paul Blanshard who expressed doubt during the strike that a conservative AFL union would have been any better received in Gastonia.[67]**

---

* Born in Bethlehem, Pennsylvania in 1911, Ann Burlak went to work in a textile mill at the age of 14 to supplement her fathers earnings as a steel worker. Working 54 hours a week for $9 (while the men earned $12 for the same work), she went with a group of women to the United Textile Workers for help in organizing a union, but the UTW was not interested. Burlak joined the Young Communist League in 1927, and a year later, she went to New Bedford to help the strikers. She attended the founding convention of the National Textile Workers' Union, but when she attempted to form a branch in Bethlehem, she was fired and blacklisted throughout the region. As a full-time organizer for the NTWU, Burlak organized women mill workers in Scranton and Wilkes-Barres and then went to Gastonia to replace the women who had been jailed following the fatal shooting of Chief Aderholt. (Interview with Ann Burlak Timpson, Jamaica Plain, Massachusetts, December 22,1979.)

** AFL organizers might have been misled in this respect by the fact that when the Amalgamated Clothing Workers set out to organize the runaway shops that had moved

We have already seen that in the Elizabethton strike, Just a few weeks before the Gastonia upheaval, the police and militia brutally arrested and jailed women strikers who were members of the AFL United Textile Workers, that AFL officials were kidnapped, driven over the state line, and warned not to Ɪeturn to Elizabethton "under pain of death," and that in the end the United Textile Workers' local was destroyed almost as ruthlessly as the National Textile Workers' Union in Gastonia. Yet at no point were the Communists involved in the Elizabethton strike.

THE MARION STRIKE

While the Gastonia battle was still raging, the Southern mill owners had another opportunity to demonstrate that they made no real distinction between the Communist-led NTWU and the AFL's UTW. This time, the scene was Marion, North Carolina.

In April 1929, three Marion mill workers decided to form a union, and one of them journeyed to Elizabethton, where the strike was on in full force, to meet with Alfred Hoffman, the UTW organizer. Armed with Hoffman's promise to help, the Marion workers began laying the groundwork for unionization. Management responded in June by firing twenty-two employees who were union members. On July 10, Hoffman arrived in Marion to assist the fledgling labor organization. The following day, a local committee of the organized workers met with R.R. Baldwin, president of the Marion Manufacturing Company (popularly called the "Baldwin Mill"), to submit a list of grievances, Requests for a reinstatement of the twenty-two workers

from New York City to the little mining towns of Schuykill County in Pennsylvania, the runaway employers who feared an Amalgamated victory in their factories called on AFL affiliates—the United Textile Workers and the United Garment Workers—to battle the Amalgamated and organize their workers, guaranteeing them recognition. As Dee Garrison points out: "Employers preferred to deal with the conservative AFL unions, which had demonstrated less obvious concern for the welfare of women workers." (*Mary Heaton Vorse: The Life of an American Insurgent*, p. 165.) Many of the women workers, who made up the bulk of the workers in the runaway garment factories, were under 15 years old and worked for as little as $3.50 a week—a 6-day week and an 8-9 hour day. The older women—widows, or women with large families or sick husbands—did piece work at home. They were paid an average of ten cents an hour. With the aid of the unionized miners, the Amalgamated succeeded in organizing the runaway shops of Pennsylvania. Mary Heaton Vorse and Ann Craton played important roles in organizing the runaway sweatshops. (*Ibid.* pp. 165-67.) Southern textile employers felt that they had no need to follow the lead of the runaway employers in Pennsylvania. They were confident that with the aid of state officials, the state troopers and local police, and the courts, they could defeat both the AFL and the Communists. Moreover, there were no organized workers in their communities who, like the union miners, could help the textile workers in their struggle to unionize.

fired for supposed union activities and for an agreement to meet with an employee committee on further grievances were summarily rejected.

Acting against the advice of Hoffman, who knew that the national union's policy was not to support strikes unless the local unions had been in existence for at least six months, 650 desperate workers, a large number of them women, walked out on July 11. They were joined by thirteen hundred workers, many of them women, from the Clinchfield mills, who had been locked out by the management. One of the women strikers told the press:

> I work twelve hours and twenty minutes a day and I am completely worn out at stopping time. Men and women who work in the mill are weak and sallow-looking, some of them just dragging along half-dead and over-worked until they don't know what it is to take a rest and feel good. The average workingman or woman makes from $1.60 to $2.70 a day, and some have families of from three to seven and sometimes more depending on them for a living .... Do you blame us for striking?[68]

The lack of any effective support from the UTW, the issuance of a sweeping injunction, which the strikers ignored, the presence of two companies of militia, the evictions of strikers from company homes, and the arrest of scores of pickets on trumped-up charges (such as "insurrection against the State of North Carolina")—all combined to compel the strikers to return to work on September 11. The company agreed to lower the workweek from sixty to fifty-five hours, but at the same wage scale, which meant a reduction in pay, and to rehire the strikers with a few exceptions. No formal record of the settlement was made: it was treated as a "gentleman's agreement."[69]

The mills reduced hours as they had promised, but they also blacklisted a hundred workers for union activities, and families known to be friendly to the union were evicted from the mill villages. Because the company refused to discuss its violation of the agreement, the night shift went out in a spontaneous walkout on October 2 and congregated before the mill. Marion Sheriff Oscar Adkins and eleven deputies were called in by the mill owners, and the deputies fired tear gas at the demonstrating strikers. A 68-year-old lame man, half-blinded with tears, struggled with the sheriff. As he was being clubbed and handcuffed, deputies fired into the crowd, killing three strikers outright, mortally wounding three more and seriously injuring twenty-five others, one of them a woman. Although most of them had been shot in the back, the plant manager proudly proclaimed: "I think the officers are damn good marksmen. If I ever organize an army, they can have jobs with me." B. M. Hart, president of the Clinchfield mill, commented: "I cannot see that there is any difference between this so-called conservative union and the Communist union in Gastonia."[70]

Twenty-six strikers were arrested and four convicted for "insurrection and riot," but the sheriff's deputies were quickly acquitted of second-degree murder. With this, the Marion strike was effectively ended. "The mill owners," Herbert J. Lahne observes, "had accorded the orthodox UTW a no more peaceful welcome than they had extended to the Communist NTWU."[71]

Whether led by the NTWU or by the UTW, the Southern textile workers were met not only with a refusal by employers to bargain with unions but also with a disregard for the civil liberties of the strikers.

Although unionism appeared to have been crushed in the Piedmont region, the struggles of the Southern textile workers had not been in vain. The eyes of the nation had been centered on the degrading conditions in the Southern cotton mills,[72] and the uprisings of the textile workers in Tennessee and North Carolina "made the first significant breach in Southern anti-unionism."[73] There were others to come in the future.

In an appeal to left-wing militants, the Trade Union Educational League urged: "Special efforts must be made to bring Southern textile workers to the Trade Union Unity Convention. Bring the Trade Union Unity Convention call to the Southern textile workers."[74]*

---

* On March 1, 1987 the *New York Times* carried a dispatch from Gastonia in which Christopher L. Scott, president of the North Carolina branch of the AFL-CIO called for the "straightening out" of the history of the area which had been greatly influenced by the textile strike of 1929. "Unions are not violent and are not filled with a bunch of Communists," he insisted. However, Michael B. Black, Southeastern Coordinator of the AFL-CIO's Industrial Union Department told the *Times* that the events of the 1929 strike had been distorted. "I heard about the 1929 strike as a child," he declared. "Growing up in Gastonia, the strike was taught in the schools, never with a positive slant." To which he added: "It Is never easy to win, especially in a town like Gastonia."

This was the last official act of the Trade Union Educational League before it was transformed into the Trade Union Unity League, a Communist-led federation of unions and organizing committees to further "the organization of new revolutionary industrial unions in industries where there are no unions and in industries where the existing unions are corrupt and impotent."[75] Thus, the Southern textile strikes of 1929 marked the final stage in the history of the Trade Union Educational League.*

---

* For a vivid personal account of the Gastonia strike, see Carl Reeve, "The Great Gastonia Textile Strike," and "Gastonia: The Frameup, the Heritage," *Political Affairs*, March, 1984, pp. 37-41; April, 1984, pp. 23-32.

Carl Reeve was the representative of the International Labor Defense and its magazine, *Labor Defender*, at the Gastonia Textile Strike.

CHAPTER 18

THE AMERICAN TRADE UNION DELEGATION TO THE SOVIET UNION, 1927

As we have seen in the "Program for Building the Trade Unions" presented by the TUEL to the 1926 AFL convention, the TUEL urged the AFL to "accept the invitation of the Russian unions and send an official delegation to visit the Soviet Union and submit a report to the American labor movement." A labor delegation from the United States, although bitterly opposed by the AFL leadership, did actually visit the Soviet Union in 1927 and submit a report of its findings.

In 1925, for the second time British labor sent an investigating delegation to the Soviet Union. (The first went in 1920.) The delegation was elected from the General Council of the Trades Union Congress of Great Britain which also published the delegation's report. The delegation consisted of seven leaders of the British trade unions, four of whom had the reputation of being more critical than favorable to the Soviet Union. The seven were: Herbert Smith, President of the Miners Federation of Labor and delegate to the AFL convention in 1922; Ben Tillett of the Transport Workers, a labor leader for forty years; John Turner of the Distributive Workers; John Bromley of the Locomotive Engineers; Albert A. Purcell of the Furnishing Trades, who had been President of the Trade Union Congress in 1924, and was to be a delegate to the 1925 AFL convention, and who had also been a member of the British Trade Union delegation to the Soviet Union in 1920; A.A.H. Findley, of the Pattern Makers, and Fred Bramley, who was the conservative secretary of the Trades Union Congress.

The delegation's Report was unanimous. It went into an examination of the state of the Soviet political and economic system, coupling words of praise with those of criticism. Thus it reported:

> The delegation is of the opinion that the Soviet system and its scheme of constitutional and civil rights, so far from being undemocratic in the widest sense of this word, give in many respects to the individual a more real and reasonable opportunity of participation in public affairs than does Parliamentary or party government. In other respects, such participation is still severely restricted.

On the issue of the Russian trade unions and labor conditions, the Report said:

> A report on labor conditions in the Union of Socialist Soviet Republics must begin by pointing out that in Russia the workers are the ruling class. For unless the reader bears this in mind throughout, he will be misled by much in Russian labor conditions that at first sight seems very much the same as with us. Really everything is quite different; because in Russia we have a regulation of the workers' rights that they have put upon themselves for their own well being. Elsewhere we have a restriction of the workers' rights put upon them by the wealthy. Such regulations are in Russia the result of agreement between the workers and their own expert governors and managers, to whom they have entrusted their institutions and their industries, their factories and their farms. Elsewhere such regulations are the results of treaties and truces between the entrenched interests of a wealthy ruling class and the assaults of a working class that as yet never rules but only rebels....
>
> The right to strike, under an industrial system based on private capital, is a constant protection against the exploitation of the workers by the wealthy. The right to strike is maintained in Russia. But since all industry is either conducted or closely controlled by the community, the strike has changed its function. The worker enjoys all profit from the industry after proper provision for equipment, reserves, etc. He no longer strikes to protect himself or the community from exploitation by private interests, but only as a protest against mismanagement or malpractice, such as delay in wage payments, etc. There were during 1923 only 11 strikes involving 1,026 workers in government enterprises, and these were small ones.

The delegation laid special emphasis upon the remarkable state and vigorous activities of trade unions under the Soviet system, particularly the fact that "the trade unions have been able to engage in educating the workers as citizens and rulers."[2]

Albert A. Purcell, a member of the British trade union delegation to the Soviet Union, was the fraternal delegate from the British Trades Union Congress to the 1925 convention of the AFL. In his address to the delegates, Purcell suggested that one of the primary obstacles to the improvement of working conditions throughout the world was the imperialist policy of the major industrial powers. Their policy, Purcell argued, was to enable private industry to reduce labor costs by exploiting indigenous labor in the underdeveloped countries. The result, he contended, was to depress the wages of unionized workers in such highly industrialized nations as the United States and Great Britain.* In order to reduce the competition of underpaid workers and to narrow the disparity in working conditions throughout the world, Purcell urged the AFL to unite with other trade unions "in one powerful Trade Union International," which would be a potent weapon in the hands of international labor and would enhance the ability of the AFL to protect the interests of its constituency. To achieve international trade union solidarity, Purcell favored bringing the Russian trade unions into the international labor community. He therefore urged the delegates to establish fraternal relations with the Russian workers and to follow the example of the General Council of the Trade Union Congress of Britain by sending an official labor delegation to the Soviet Union.[3]

AFL President William Green rose to answer Purcell's proposals. He reported that "when the revolution developed in Russia (in February, 1917), the American labor movement sent congratulations to the working people of Russia, complimenting them upon their revolutionary action in overthrowing the power of Czarism and all it stood for. And we succeeded in having appointed upon a commission representing our Republic outstanding men of labor, so that on their trip to Russia...they could properly convey to the workers of Russia, the real, humane, brotherly sentiment of the working people of America."**

He did not mention the fact that the AFL leadership was enraged by the overthrow of the Provisional government and the rise to power of the Bolsheviks. Regarding the new regime as the most "monstrous or degrading government ever...set up anywhere in the world," the AFL allied itself with a succession of administrations in Washington in an effort to isolate the Soviet government and sever it from all contacts with the West. As a matter of policy, the AFL under Gompers and Green categorically prohibited all forms of intercourse

---

* V.I. Lenin took an opposite position in his famous work *Imperialism*, pointing out that the skilled aristocracy of labor in Great Britain and the United States profited from the exploitation by the imperialists of the indigenous populations of the underdeveloped countries.

** For a discussion of this Commission and the attitude of the AFL to the February Revolution, *see* Philip S. Foner, *History of the Labor Movement in the United States*, 8 (New York, 1987): pp. 44-45.

and fraternization between American labor and either the Bolshevik government or the Russian trade unions. It was therefore not unexpected that Green, in rejecting Purcell's proposals, denied any basis for fraternal relations between American and Russian trade unions, which unions, he observed, were instruments of a system seeking "not to cooperate with us but to capture and control us...and substitute for our philosophy the philosophy of communism." This they were seeking to achieve through agents in this country such as the Trade Union Educational League:

> The Trade Union Educational League here in America, which is the creature of the Communist Party, controlled and directed by a man who at one time was active in the trades union movement, frankly announces that its policy is to "bore within" the labor movement, to destroy it and substitute for our philosophy the philosophy of communism. We are not ready to accept that, and we wish that our friend (Mr. Purcell) who has so kindly advised us and has offered us such frank suggestions might take back to the Russian Red Internationale this message, that the American labor movement will not affiliate with an organization that preaches that doctrine or stands for that philosophy.

To the applause of the delegates, Green rejected the proposed labor mission to the Soviet Union.[4]

Green's rejection of Purcell's proposal was endorsed overwhelmingly by the delegates to the convention. Refusing to be discouraged, Purcell visited twelve cities, urging that American labor send a delegation to learn at first hand labor and economic conditions in Europe and the Soviet Union. Moved by his views, small labor groups in these and other cities, "united by a shared distaste for the [AFL] leadership's policy, began to act."[5] In New York City, representatives of forty-nine labor unions met to plan a reception in Purcell's honor. On November 17, 1925, at a meeting of thousands of trade unionists, Purcell's views were endorsed enthusiastically.[6]

Evidently Purcell's speaking tour in behalf of a trade union delegation to the Soviet Union produced results, for on December 24, 1925, "By Direction and Authority of the Executive Council," Green swiftly sent a letter "To All Organized Labor," declaring:

> Information has reached me that central labor bodies and local trade unions in various parts of the country have been asked to contribute to a

fund to be used to send a committee of alleged labor representatives to Russia for the same purpose that a committee of communists from Great Britain visited Russia and sought to make the world believe that the soviet government was representative of the people *

Green charged that the agitation for the creation of the committee to visit Russia was "being carried on by the members of the communist organizations and those who are in sympathy with communism." Such a plan, he wrote, "is not in the interest of the wage earners of the United States, or the people generally. It is in the interest of the few communists who are endeavoring to hold power in Russia, to strengthen that power and to extend its influence throughout the other nations of the world." Finally, Green warned that such a committee

> will not be representative of the labor movement and will not be recognized by the American Federation of Labor. It will be organized in the interest of the communists and against the interest of the American labor movement.
>
> No loyal trade unionist will give his aid or support to this nefarious scheme.
>
> Whenever applications are made to central bodies or local unions for contributions I hope I will be informed. Under no circumstances should contributions be made to this unworthy cause.

In the same message, Green wrote: "While the agitation is in progress, representatives from the Russian government have banqueted with American bankers and are now sowing the seed of their pernicious doctrines in the capital of our nation."[8] The technique of linking the interests of American bankers with those of the Soviet government had been used by Samuel Gompers ever since the triumph of the Bolshevik Revolution, and was continued by William Green who had succeeded Gompers as president of the AFL. "By creating the impression that the banking community, viewed as a traditional enemy of workers," writes Simeon Larson, "was willing to cooperate with the Bolsheviks for profits, the Federation hierarchy hoped to attract more support for its anti-Soviet policies from the rank and file."[9]

"The idea [of a labor mission to Russia]," Albert F. Coyle, acting editor of the *Locomotive Engineers' Journal*, informed Green on June 10, 1926, "started with Brother Tim Healy who put in the bank a

---

* It came as a distinct shock to British labor and even to the government that the members of the British Trades Union Congress' mission to the Soviet Union were all "communists." Such perversion of the truth revealed how paranoid Green had become on the subject.

fund of several thousand dollars consisting of money raised at the
meetings which Brother Purcell addressed when he was in this country."*10 Timothy Healy was president of the Brotherhood of Stationary Firemen and Oilers, an AFL affiliate. His union's 1925 convention had authorized him to make a trip in the summer of 1926 to
survey trade union conditions.

He discussed the matter with Frank P. Walsh, former co-chairman
with ex-President William Howard Taft of the War Labor Board, and
a frequent legal adviser to and defender of trade unions, and even
Communists. They decided to use the money to "send a group of the
ablest and most dependable labor leaders in the country to go to
Europe, observe trade union conditions there first hand, and to take
along several recognized economists to make an expert study of industrial conditions generally."11

The group appointed Coyle and Fred Hewitt, editor of the *Machinists' Monthly Journal*, to communicate with William Green and
invite him or his representative to join the delegation. The committee preferred to have Green himself, "for we covet both your com-
panionship and your knowledge of sound trade union principles as a
background for your observations." The committee was also dele-
gated to assure the AFL president that as a matter of policy

> no Communists, Socialists, or even of any of our Jewish brethren should
> be asked to make the trip with us, but only men of outstanding position
> and repute in the labor movement, who are in no way connected with
> any of the radical groups.12

Coyle must have been aware that like most anti-Semites of the period,
he automatically linked "our Jewish brethren" with radicalism.

To minimize Green's opposition, Coyle informed him that the
following had definitely decided to go on the mission: E.J. Manion,
president of the Order of Railroad Telegraphers; Timothy Shea, assistant president of the Brotherhood of Locomotive Firemen and Engi-
nemen; William H. Johnston, president of the International Association of Machinists ("if his doctor will permit him to go"); Phil E.
Ziegler, editor of the *Railway Clerk*; Fred Hewitt and Healy; W.B.

* The original idea was for "eight international trade union executives" to make a trip
to Europe in late summer of 1925, "to enable them to see and understand what
organized labor is doing, all the way from Britain, France and Belgium, through
Austria, Fascist Italy, and Russia, returning through the Scandinavian countries." (Albert F. Coyle to William Green, June 10, 1926, Box 2, William Mitch Papers, Pennsylvania Historical Collection and Labor Archives, Pennsylvania University, Library, University Park, Pennsylvania.) Hereafter cited as Box 2, Mitch Papers

Preenter, President of the Brotherhood of Locomotive Engineers, whose presence on the delegation depended on whether he had recovered sufficiently from illness to make a trip to Europe by the end of July. Two or three other international union executives had not yet made definite decisions but "have expressed a desire to join our group if it can be conveniently arranged."[13]

Coyle tried to persuade Green to recognize the potential the trip offered to strengthen the entire labor movement:

> It will afford a splendid opportunity for some of the best men in the Railroad Brotherhoods to become more intimately acquainted with some of the finest leaders of the A.F. of L. Brother Green, we ought all to be affiliated with one great labor organization. I have used my influence to that end even since I came here. But the best, and possibly the only way that goal can be realized is by intimate friendly contacts; that will build up the necessary confidence and real fraternal spirit, which alone can bring about a closer union between us. And the trip we have in view, which will last about two months, affords a wonderful opportunity for just such a growth in friendship and understanding.[14]

It was all in vain. Green immediately declined the invitation, informing Coyle of this decision first by telegram and then by follow-up letter. He reminded him that a similar suggestion by Purcell at the AFL convention was rejected by the delegates who "manifested strong disapproval of the suggestions which he offered." Such a labor commission, Green wrote, "would be of little value unless such commission were created by action of the American labor movement, and were authorized by the American labor movement." This meant that it had to be officially sanctioned "by action of the American Federation of Labor, or by the Executive Council of the American Federation of Labor." He was "confident" that the AFL Executive Council would "look with disfavor on the whole idea," but he was willing to submit the question to the members of the Executive Council at a meeting to be held in Cincinnati late in June.

To assuage Coyle's feelings somewhat, Green added: "I am in hearty accord with the sentiments expressed in your letter in favor of affiliation of all labor organizations" ...[15]

Speaking for the mission, Coyle assured Green "that there has been no thought of making this an official delegation to speak for the A.F. of L., or for any other section of the labor movement." It was possible, Coyle noted, that a majority of those making the trip would come from the Railroad Brotherhoods or other unions not affiliated with the AFL.* As a further gesture of friendship, he emphasized that the commission "carefully refrained from asking anyone to go who would be obnoxious to the A.F. of L."[16]

At its meeting in Cincinnati, the AFL Executive Council released a statement on June 28, 1926 to all newspapers and press associations in order "to correct any wrong impression which might prevail among the membership of organized labor and within the public mind" regarding the formation of a labor mission "for the express purpose of visiting the Soviet Union, and incidentally other nations in Europe, for the ostensible purpose of making an investigation of economic, industrial, social and political conditions." The Council repudiated the commission. "We do not feel that any good purpose could be served through such action. In fact, we seriously doubt the good faith of such a self-constituted commission." It described the venture as resulting from "the efforts of the soviet government of Russia to have a labor whitewashing commission sent forth from the United States to that country," and implied that the money used to pay expenses would come from groups allied with radical causes. It also charged that such a self-constituted commission, "despite all denials, would assume to represent labor and to create the impression that it speaks for labor." It vowed to oppose any visit to Russia by a group of labor executives "unless authorized to do so by the American Federation of Labor." Finally, the Executive Council expressed gratification "to learn that a number of officers and members of organized labor have declined invitations to serve on this proposed commission."[17] Coyle wrote to Green expressing his surprise and grief at "the bitterly hostile attitude of the Council," especially in view of the fact that he had made it "very plain" to the AFL president "that the party was in no way official, and did not seek an official status." He had also made it clear that the majority of those going "were executives of unions outside the A.F. of L., concerning whose personal plans the Executive Council, of course, could not with propriety speak." In a tone of exasperation and disbelief, Coyle asked how the Executive Council could possibly "question the honest motives of these men—long time members and officers of their unions." He pointed out that since most of the executives going "desired to pay

---

* This may have been written to remind Green that the AFL should not regard itself as being the entire labor movement in the United States, a frequent technique employed by the Federation's leadership. Another was also the frequent assertion that the AFL represented all workers and spoke for them.

part or all of their expenses the amount required is not large, yet the Executive Council openly insinuates that the funds for this trip will have to come from improper sources."[18]

In a telegram the next day, Coyle furiously attacked as "false and libelous" the allegations that the commission was being "sponsored by Russian Soviet Government and constituted a Labor Whitewashing Committee." He demanded that Green send a "complete retraction of this falsehood" to all papers and press associations. "Only thus can serious breach be avoided."[19]

Green disavowed the offensive sentence. He claimed that it was included and issued by a publicity representative in Washington while he was absent from headquarters. "I personally disclaim responsibility for this statement," he wrote to Coyle. However, he did not retract the statement publicly nor send such retraction to any newspaper in the country.[20]

Early in July, Coyle announced that the labor mission would leave at the end of August for a two-month trip to the industrial centers of Europe. The statement included a new advantage that might accrue from a successful trip, namely, that it would bring together the principal labor groups in both continents, "undermining, in effect, the AFL's policy of nonaffiliation with any European labor organizations."[21]

On August 28, 1926, the *New York Times* reported that the labor men would not leave for some time. It explained that the AFL's opposition had influenced conservative leaders among the Railroad Brotherhoods who advised officials of participating organizations to withdraw, if only temporarily. In their opinion, the time was not propitious for organized labor to appear to condone the practices of the Soviet government.[22] As a result, the departure date was indefinitely postponed.[23]

Coyle confirmed the postponement but not the reasons for it as reported in the *Times*. On August 18, 1926, William Mitch, Secretary for Indiana of the United Mine Workers, informed Coyle that he would "make every effort" to join the European trip. In reply Coyle welcomed the UMW official and indicated that the trip had been postponed until July 1927. He added:

> Several of the labor executives have recently advised me that, inasmuch as the United Mine Workers is the largest labor organization in America,[*]

---

[*] Coyle seems to have been unaware that the United Mine Workers had lost many members under John L. Lewis's disastrous leadership, and was no longer "the largest labor organization in America."

and the problem of the coal industry is not only a critical one in this country but in practically every other country of Europe as well, that we should invite another prominent officer in the United Mine Workers in addition to yourself to join the delegation. Would you be good enough to write me whom you think the second representative should be?

Coyle himself had both John Brophy and Frank Keeney in mind as the "second representative," but he believed Brophy "is so completely tied up in his election campaign that he probably would not consider the matter."[24]

Mitch indicated reluctance to recommend any one for the Commission from the United Mine Workers. He felt, however, that the UMW "could be induced to have representation on this Commission. I talked with [John L.] Lewis and he stated that he had an indirect invitation. He did not give me anything definite about the commission other than mentioned [sic] some of the personnel." Mitch made it clear that "I for one, whether I am a member of the commission or not, feel that the objective is a worthy one and labor especially should seek the truth." While he had "no desire to become entangled in a factional fight,"

I cannot understand the American Federation of Labor and other organizations would desire to go on blindly and evade learning the truth of the situation in Europe. I have written to Secretary William Green on this subject.[25*]

Coyle informed Mitch that Dr. W. Jett Lauck, "a very warm personal friend of President Lewis," felt that both President Lewis and Vice-President Murray "were so heavily encumbered with official duties that they could not possibly make the trip." The delegation did not pursue the matter further, convinced that Mitch, because of "the respect which all factions in the organization" held him, "would be the best possible officer of the U.M.W.A. to make the trip."

At the time he was writing, Coyle explained, the delegation would be composed of four executives from the Railroad Brotherhoods and five from AFL unions, including Mitch. It was quite possible that a sixth AFL executive would be able to join the delegation by the time it left in July, 1927. He then emphasized:

---

* Green had been Secretary of the United Mine Workers of America before he was elected to succeed Gompers as AFL president.

There is no question of a factional fight involved, since our delegation is not going in any official capacity and does not ask or need the official authorization of either the A.F. of L. or the railroad brotherhoods. The labor executives concerned are going on their own personal responsibility, as they have an absolute right to do as American citizens. As President Timothy Healy of the Brotherhood of Stationary Firemen and Oilers, an A.F. of L. union, recently wrote to President Green: "It would be a most unfortunate perversion of the rightful authority of the A.F. of L. if it should concern itself with the personal plans of the executives of affiliated unions."

I have mentioned this matter in some detail so that you will see how carefully the labor executives have observed all due propriety and courtesy to the A.F. of L.[26]

In late September of 1926, Coyle informed Mitch that L.E. Sheppard, president of the Order of Railway Conductors, who had become chairman of the delegation, had authorized Coyle, its secretary, to send a "formal announcement of our trip" to the press.[27] The press release announced that the delegation would leave the following summer, and that "executives from five of the most influential international unions in the A.F. of L." would join the prominent officers from the Railroad Brotherhoods already committed to the trip.[28]

Coyle further informed Mitch that at the suggestion of President Healey of the Stationary Firemen and Oilers, "the names of the A.F. of L. executives in the party have been omitted until after the A.F. of L. convention, since Brother Healy felt that it might possibly stir up unnecessary friction there by publishing them at this time." He himself did not see "what possible objection any intelligent A.F. of L. leader could have to this delegation, since it is in no wise purporting to be an official body." But Sheppard felt that the delegation should comply with Healy's request "as a matter of courtesy."[29]

The idea that not publishing the names of AFL union leaders on the mission would prevent stirring up "unnecessary friction" at the 1926 AFL convention was exceedingly naive, and pointed up a serious weakness in the delegation. Apart from Coyle, the trade union leaders on the mission were very reluctant to face the AFL leadership head-on and rally popular support, especially among workers, for their objective. Even Coyle had to give way to the cautious approach of the other members, both of the Brotherhoods and the AFL.

The debate on the mission to the Soviet Union took center stage at the AFL convention. The issue was introduced by the resolutions committee which, in opposing a resolution favoring recognition of Soviet Russia by the United States, supported the Executive Council's declaration that the AFL deemed any mission to investigate conditions in the Soviet Union as "wholly unnecessary."

A general debate followed. The leadership's position was upheld by John P. Frey of the Molders' Union, John H. Walker of the Illinois State Federation of Labor, James Wilson, president of the Pattern Makers' League and a Vice-President of the AFL, and John L. Lewis. It was opposed by Tim Healy, president of the Stationary Firemen, and Max Hayes, the Socialist delegate from the Typographical Union.

A summary of the opposition lists the following arguments raised against the mission:

(1) ample information concerning all aspects of Russian, life was available in this country;

(2) personal experiences with Communists precluded further investigation;

(3) the Red Internationale, the Communist party of the United States, and those organizing the mission to Russia, particularly Albert Coyle, were connected with each other.

(4) the Communist Party in Russia was the source of all propaganda intended to discredit the leadership of the AFL; and

(5) the internal struggles in many national unions could be traced directly to the Red Internationale, whose work in this country was being carried on by the Trade Union Educational League (TUEL), a firm supporter of the mission.[30]

Healy made a stirring speech against the recommendation of the resolutions committee. Although, largely to appease the AFL officialdom, he refrained from favoring the immediate recognition of Soviet Russia by the United States, he finished his speech declaring: "I know that our government will recognize Russia within a few years. That to my mind is as sure as that the sun will rise tomorrow morning."

At this point Green tried to pin Healy down. The questions and answers flew back and forth between them. The stenographic report reads:

President Green: I would like to ask Delegate Healy a question.
Delegate Healy: Certainly.
President Green: I understand from your remarks that you are not advocating the adoption of a resolution (for the recognition of the Soviet Union), but rather leading for the creation of a mission to visit the Soviet Union.
Delegate Healy: You are right, Mr. President.
President Green: I presume you mean a delegation to be created by this convention?
Delegate Healy: By the American Federation of Labor.
President Green: And that would be regarded as an American Federation of Labor commission?
Delegate Healy: Of course, it would.

President Green: Well, unless this convention creates a commission you, as a delegate in this convention, would not go on any other commission?

Delegate Healy: You are seeking information, Mr. President. I will answer that by saying that as a citizen, as a member of this Federation, I feel myself free to go where I like, not to represent this Federation. I want nobody to tell me where I shall go, what church I shall go to, where I shall go or stay. I think that is my prerogative and I claim that right.

President Green: That is granted, but there is a difference in going as an individual and going on a commission that would be classified as an alleged labor commission. I mean you wouldn't accept appointment on an alleged labor commission unless it was authorized by this convention.

Delegate Healy: So long as it would not go under the guise of representation of the American Federation of Labor.

President Green: Then a direct answer "yes" or "no" would satisfy the delegates best. It would me.

Delegate Healy: We will come to that later, Mr. President.[31]

Healy was immediately followed by Vice-President "Jimmie" Wilson, of the Pattern Makers' Union, who declared that "recognition of Russia is of minor importance to us." He forgot all about the resolution before the convention, and launched into an attack on the opposition to Lewis among the coal miners. He tried strenuously to show a conspiracy between the Trade Union Educational League,* the Federated Press, and Albert F. Coyle.

He capped it all by referring to a letter written by Coyle to Powers Hapgood, the close associate of John Brophy. Published in the press, the letter, dated September 3, 1926, mentioned the names of "Jay" and "John." It was disclosed that these referred to Jay Lovestone, a prominent member at that time of the Communist Party, and John Brophy. According to the letter, Coyle had arranged with "Jay," to found a new miners' newspaper that would support Brophy's candidacy against Lewis for president of the union. A friend of "Jay's" would be an assistant editor, though his name would not be listed lest it "give Lewis an opportunity to denounce the new paper and forbid his members to read it." Coyle suggested Hapgood for editor, as he

---

* Wilson referred to the TUEL repeatedly as Worker's Educational Bureau, a part of the educational activities of the AFL. Vice-President Matthew Woll had to insert a special correction on this point in the minutes, in order to keep the record straight.

could not be "branded by Lewis as a 'Bolshevik.'"* Acting as a sort of corroborating witness for "Jimmie" Wilson, Lewis used the letter to link Coyle, the mission to Russia, and the internal unrest in the UMW with the Communist party in the United States, and the Soviet government. He charged that the Communists were responsible for the troubles of the Nova Scotia miners, and had been behind their decision to adopt "reckless policies" which led to the expulsion of their district from the UMW.** Pointing to William Z. Foster, director of the TUEL, who was sitting in the visitors' gallery, Lewis charged that he was present to observe how faithfully Coyle had organized sentiment at the convention to reflect their mutual objectives.[33]

Before a vote was taken on the resolutions committee recommendation with regard to the labor mission, Healy urged adoption of a new resolution to appoint members of the AFL Executive Council to join the mission. Its purpose would be to investigate conditions and report its findings to the convention. He pleaded with the delegates to keep their minds open, noting that "the term 'Russia' aroused such prejudice in some as to prevent a rational judgment on the issue."[34] The proposal was not even considered. Instead, Green called for such a decisive vote in favor of the resolution committee's opposition to the labor mission "that there will be no doubt where the American Federation of labor stands." The mission, he said, was part of a worldwide effort "radiating from Moscow" to gain control of American labor and substitute the philosophy of communism, "for the philosophy of the trade union movement as we understood it since its foundation."[35]

The report of the resolutions committee declared that "The American Federation of Labor not only cannot join in any mission to investigate conditions in Russia, but deems any such mission as wholly unnecessary." It further declared "that no trade unionist should permit himself to participate in any such adventure." The report was adopted unanimously. When no delegate arose to oppose it, another delegate called the opposition "yellow." William Z. Foster

---

* For the text of the letter, *see New York Times*, Oct. 13, 1926, 3. Coyle did not deny the letter's authenticity, but the TUEL announced later that it was a decoy to trap the Lewis crowd and expose the methods he used against his opponents. The seizure of the letter, it charged, added rifling of the mails to his other crimes. (J. Louis Engdahl, "'After Gompers—What?' Answered," *Workers Monthly*, December 1926, p. 634.)

** For the full extent of Lewis's distortion of these events, see Philip S. Foner, *History of the Labor Movement in the United States*, 9 (New York, 1990): 230-244.

agreed. "The one thing," he told the press, "I concur with is that those who opposed the committee's report were 'yellow.'" [*sic*] [36]

Preparations for the mission to Russia resumed in the spring of 1927 and immediately the AFL campaign intensified, the leadership hoping that if knowledge of the mission became public, it should result in greater pressure on the delegation to discontinue the trip or, at least, cause some of the delegation's members to drop out. On May 28, 1927, Green's statement on the "so-called labor delegation which proposes to visit Russia and other countries in Europe," was widely published in the press. It reported that information had reached the officers of the AFL that "nine well-known trade union officials have already arranged with their organizations for leaves of absence and will be ready to start the early part of the summer; and that a staff of expert economists would accompany the delegation. "Thus far," Green continued somewhat ominously, "the names of the nine well-known trade union officials who are to constitute the delegation, or the staff of expert economists, have not been made public." He then threatened that the AFL would:

> notify the officially organized labor organizations in European countries in case Mr. Coyle and his associates consummate their plans to visit Russia that they cannot be regarded as a labor delegation in the true sense of the word, clothed with authority to speak for American labor and for the American Federation of Labor.[37]

Responding to Green's accusation and threat, the "American Trade Union Delegation to Russia," now the group's official name, issued a public statement reporting that "this Delegation will leave the United States shortly after July 15 to spend two months in Europe. Half of this time will be devoted to the countries of Western Europe and the other half to countries of Eastern Europe, including Russia." In order to make certain that the Delegation would have friendly access to all sources of information in Russia, it had already cabled the heads of the Russian Trade Unions "who have requested and secured from the Government of Russia absolute assurances on this point, permitting access to all persons and sources of information in Russia."*

In addition to those previously named, the labor members now included John Brophy, who was listed as a recent president, District No. 2,

---

* A similar request had been made to the Fascist Government of Italy, but assurances for an opportunity to investigate conditions were not forthcoming.

United Mine Workers, William Mitch, Indiana state secretary of the UMW, and James W. Fitzpatrick, president of the American Artists' and Actors' Federation.

The Delegation's statement observed:

> We know much less about what is happening in Russia today than about yesterday's developments in the interior of China. And yet Russia is the largest country of Europe, with vast territory in Asia, embracing about one-seventh of the inhabitable land and one-eleventh of the total population of the globe.
>
> From practically every country of Europe, delegations and commissions have visited Russia since the Revolution, but not one of them has made an expert economic research into actual social and industrial conditions in that country. The American Trade Union Delegation proposes to undertake this important task. It has already received the assurances of Senator William E. Borah of the Senate Committee on Foreign Relations that a special session of the Committee will be called to hear and consider this economic survey upon the return of the Delegation from Russia.
>
> The Delegation proposes to publish the report of its staff of economists without change or comment. It will also set down the personal observations of the members of the Delegation as to developments in Russia. These reports will be available for widespread public distribution and should prove invaluable to intelligent American citizens of every class and position who desire the impartial and uncolored facts, about the Russian experiment.

Because of "the large public service to be rendered," and unable to secure funds from the AFL, the delegation felt justified to appeal to "persons outside the ranks of organized labor" to help defray the cost of "employing its staff of economic experts, of paying their traveling expenses, and of covering the publication and distribution of the resulting report."*

The delegation made it clear that it wanted no publicity before its task was completed. Instead of going public, therefore, it was requesting "contributions of from five hundred to one thousand dollars from persons of means who appreciate the high value of the public service undertaken by the Delegation." A finance committee of Healy, Marion, and Shea had been appointed.[38]

***

* Simeon Larson states that the money was to be used "to help pay the costs of the trip." (Simeon Larson, "Opposition to AFL Foreign Policy: A Labor Mission to Russia, 1927," *The Historian 43* [May, 1981]: 355.) Actually, the labor members of the delegation paid their own expenses.

With the release of this statement, the AFL intensified its attacks. John Frey and Matthew Woll joined actively in the assault on the labor mission. Writing in the *Molders' Journal*, which he edited, Frey explained that the AFL's opposition derived not from its attitude toward the Russian government or internal conditions in that country, but from the nationwide campaign, sponsored by Moscow, "to destroy the A.F. of L. and to put communist-led labor unions in its place." "It requires no mission going to Russia," the editorial continued, "to discover the purpose of the Bolsheviks and the Red Internationale so far as the American trade-union movement is concerned." Not even a report favorable to the Bolshevik regime (which Frey anticipated) would have any effect on the attitude of the AFL to the Soviet Union.[39]

Woll threw caution to the wind in his attack, declaring in his union journal, *American Photo Engraver*, that everyone associated with the venture was "a loyal adherent of the Bolshevik cause; that the mission's sole purpose was "to strengthen the Communists' position at home and abroad"; that the entire affair was a "communistic scheme," in which Senator Borah, by promising to invite the delegation to testify before a Senate Committee "was playing a communistically inclined part."*

Woll was overjoyed when Timothy Healy lost the presidency of the Brotherhood of Stationary Firemen and Oilers, for he considered Healy to be "a leading figure in this latest of communistic moves."[40]**

At the last moment, Sheppard, Shea, Ziegler, Manion, Preenter, Mitch, and Johnston resigned from the Delegation and did not join the group which left for Europe. The leaders of the transportation unions cited coming wage negotiations or other pressing union business that would keep them home. Sheppard expressed his regret explaining that "I would very much like [to go] and it is a quite a disappointment as it is a chance of a lifetime." He hoped that the fact

* Borah refused to be intimidated. Upon the delegation's return, he again informed Arthur Fisher, a member of the delegation's technical and advisory staff, of his intention to grant the group a hearing before the Senate Committee on Foreign Affairs. However, a formal decision would be made when the Senate Committee reassembled with the opening of Congress. When it did, Borah's bid was rejected by a majority of the committee. (Robert F. Kelly to Secretary of State Kellogg, October 1, 1927, RG59,861.51/2152, National Archives; Fraser, *op. cit.*, p. 355n.)

** When Healy died in 1930, *Advance*, the organ of the Amalgamated Clothing Workers, stated that he had lost his post as president three years before because of his consistent advocacy of the recognition of the Soviet government (Aug. 15, 1930:2).

that some members could not make the trip "will not prevent others from doing so."[41] He remained as Honorary Chairman.

While Johnston's reason for his inability to leave was understandable since he had long been in poor health, that of Mitch's was more complicated, In a letter to Green, he gave two reasons:

> One is that I am tied up at home with official duties and the other that I have no desire or intention of doing anything that will be in opposition to the policies of the American Labor Movement. Our fight is tough enough when we fight together and I do not appreciate some of the opposition we get in our own district in a small way from those who work under cover and with ulterior motives and we realize that you have this in a big way.[42]

Naturally, Green was delighted that Mitch had yielded to AFL (and John L. Lewis's) pressure, and he assured Mitch that he would have no occasion to regret his decision.

> Because of the motives of some of the so-called economic experts associated with the Commission we are of the opinion that instead of the Commission going to Russia for the purpose of making an impartial investigation of economic and social conditions, it will be a propaganda committee. The names of the so-called experts lead many representative trade unionists to believe that it is a pro-Russian Commission.[43]

In the end, the opposition of the AFL leadership paid off insofar as the composition of the Delegation was concerned. Timothy Healy told the *New York Times* of July, 18, 1927, that the hostility of the AFL leaders disrupted the elaborate plans made by those interested in the mission. Not only had it been virtually impossible to get leaders of the AFL to make the trip, but sponsors of the idea were compelled to seek financing from sources outside the labor movement.

Still, despite renewed opposition from the AFL and the departure of a number of its most prominent trade unionists, the American Trade Union Delegation to the Soviet Union departed on July 27, 1927. James H. Maurer, former Socialist Party candidate for Vice-President of the United States and president of the Pennsylvania Federation of Labor, became chairman. He left with Brophy, Palmer, Fitzpatrick and Coyle. A technical and advisory staff accompanied the delegation. It included expert economists, sociologists, and educators.[*]

---

[*] Members of the technical and advisory staff were: Bartlet Brebner, assistant professor of history, Columbia University; Stuart Chase, director, Labor Bureau; George S. Counts, professor of education, Teachers College; Alzada Comstock, professor of economics, Mount Holyoke College; Jerome Davis, professor of practical philosophy, Yale University; Paul H. Douglas, professor of industrial relations, University of Chicago; Robert W. Dunn, research worker; Arthur Fisher, former professor of Law, University of Montana; J.A.H. Hopkins, chairman, Committee of 48; Carlos J. Israels, editorial

After stopovers in London and Paris, the delegation arrived in Russia on August 14, 1927. It broke up into five sections, each traveling in a different area, to learn as much as possible in the short time available, Each member covered the area of his own specialty.

Palmer, Maurer, and Brophy met William D. ("Big Bill") Haywood at the Lux Hotel in Moscow. The former IWW leader had fled to Russia to avoid returning to Leavenworth Prison for twenty years, after the Supreme Court upheld the frame-up trial, conviction, and long prison sentences and heavy fines handed out to over 100 Wobbly leaders who were found guilty of violating the wartime Espionage Act by simply being radical labor leaders. Brophy, who kept a diary of the trip, reported that Haywood "denied reports in American newspapers that he was critical of Soviet Russia and wanted to leave. He would not give one Gobernia for all the United States." "Haywood," Brophy noted, "reaffirmed his support of the Soviet system and emphasized his hostility to the capitalist world."[44]

The hostility of the AFL leadership and its paranoia on the subject of the labor mission followed the delegation to Russia. When the *New York Times*, in reporting interviews by the delegation with leading government officials, including Chikerin, Stalin, and Trotsky, referred to the group as an "unofficial delegation of the American Federation of Labor,"[45] the Federation's leadership hit the roof. Immediately the *AFL Weekly News Service* spread the leadership's view that such a designation gave "them a standing that they do not possess." The report was pictured as "an attempt if not a conspiracy participated in by the delegation, the *Times*, and others, to prepare the groundwork for the eventual recognition of Soviet Russia by this country."[46]

One interesting aspect of the interview with Stalin was the question he asked the delegation about the conservative policies of the American Federation of Labor. "How do you explain," he asked, "that on the question of recognizing the U.S.S.R. the leaders of the American Federation of Labor are more reactionary than many bourgeois?" Brophy answered first, arguing that the hostile attitude of the AFL was primarily due to two factors: (1) the difficulties Communists at home caused American labor leaders, and (2) the conservative attitude of a majority

board, *Columbia Law Review*, R.G. Tugwell, associate professor of economics, Columbia University; Carlton Washburne, superintendent of public schools, Winnetka, Illinois; and *Jurisconsult* Silas B. Axtell, member of the International Seamen's Union of North America.

of the American working class. The AFL leaders, therefore, simply reflected the thinking of their membership. The working class of America, Brophy insisted, was not interested in international affairs and as regards the USSR, was influenced in its thinking by the capitalist press.

Coyle, on the other hand, denied that a majority of the American working class opposed recognition of the Soviet Union, and stated that even the AFL membership had no real input into the Federation's policy on this issue. The conservative position of the AFL was mainly the result of a "leader caste...consisting of a few scores of individuals who receive enormous salaries...and into which it is extremely difficult to penetrate."[47]

On September 26, 1927, having spent a full month in Russia, the American Trade Union Delegation to the Soviet Union returned to the United States. Shortly thereafter, it issued a formal report of its findings, signed by Maurer, Brophy, Palmer, and Coyle.[48] Only Fitzpatrick dissented, stating in a letter to the *New York Times* that he was "in complete disagreement with the published interim report of the delegation."[49] However, neither in his letter nor elsewhere, did he give reasons for his dissent.

The technical and advisory staff, each advisor contributing material in the field he had investigated, issued its own report, which was published in book form early in 1928.[50*]

Topics discussed in the report of the trade union delegation included economic progress, structure and administration of Russia, trade unions, wages, labor laws and social insurance, housing, consumers' cooperatives, agriculture, education, structure of the government and Communist party, and civil liberties.

On the subject of the trade unions, the report said in part:

> The Soviet trade unions are revolutionary bodies, with constitutional preambles much like that of some of the militant socialist unions in America. They are not interested solely in a fair day's pay for a fair day's work. They stand on the basis "of the international class struggle of the proletariat," and aim "to foster the world-wide revolutionary class struggle for the overthrow of capitalism and the realization of socialism through the proletarian dictatorship."

---

* Stuart Chase, Robert Dunn, and Rexford Guy Tugwell, eds., *Soviet Russia in the Second Decade,* New York, 1928. The other authors were Melinda Alexander, John Bartlet Brebner, Alzada Comstock, George S. Counts, Paul H. Douglas, Arthur Fisher, J.A.H. Hopkins, Carlos L. Israels, and Carleton Washburne.

The Soviet unions are thus more than "socialist unions" in the continental sense of the term, for they have already passed through their period of revolutionary conflict and are now devoted to the to the business of consolidating the state power of the workers and peasants and the building up of a non-capitalistic society.

In addition to these general aims, the more immediate day-to-day objects of the unions at the present stage of their development are: To protect the economic and legal interests of their members and to improve their material conditions; to raise the general cultural level of the workers; to participate in the organization of production in their particular trade or industry.[51]

Since the delegation regarded the "Production Work of the Unions" as one of the most important aspects of their activities, it is worth quoting their views at some length:

"Union-management cooperation" is a fact in Soviet Russia. They condemn the B&O plan and other such experiments in America, but have introduced in their own plants the most friendly collaboration between the technical managers and the trade unions.

The report quoted the following from the resolution adopted by the congress of the Federal Council of Trade Unions in 1926: "The industrialization of the country, the need for capital and the raising of the material and cultural standards of the workers requires the further raising of the efficiency of work. It requires the constant attention of the trade unions...." The report continued:

To carry out the resolutions on production, passed at this as well as at previous All-Russian congresses, the unions, through the factory committees, have organized in all state factories and enterprises production committees. There are over 50,000 of these committees in the U.S.S.R. They have also called production conferences, the purposes of which are to "draw more workers into the building of our economy," to teach them more about production, improve their qualifications, to stimulate invention and to establish a stronger social control over the economic organs of the state.

Everywhere we went we found these production conferences at work, composed of all the workers in the factory who show a voluntary interest in increasing and improving production....

The production committee, composed both of workers and technical personnel, helps to arrange the program for the production conference and also sees to it that its resolutions are "put into life."

Noting that "the unions have trained thousands of their own members for technical posts," the report pointed out, "chain systems, technical operations, 'straight-line' production, specialization and standardization are a part of their dream of an industrialized Russia, just as they are the topic of constant discussion and planning among the union workers."

> Summarizing the work of the production committees and conferences during the past two years, President Tomsky [of the Central Committee on Trade Unions] told us that they have increased the output of the individual workers, facilitated inventions, and helped in the rationalization of industry and the organization of work by scientific methods. They serve to free the plants from many petty defects in the work and organization which have tended to decrease output.

"This production work," the report on this section concluded, "is one of the most stimulating and novel tasks of the unions in Russia. It is capable of unlimited development. And it brings out clearly the part that the trade unions are playing in the whole economy."[52]

"We asked Tomsky," the delegation reported, "what was the most important achievement during the last few years. His answer was:

> The most notable development in the Russian trade union movement is the tremendous progress of cultural activities. Through these activities great masses of the working class are aided in their cultural development. Tens of thousands are being prepared for participation in government as well as in the economic and trade union life. They are brought nearer to the realities of life, and that is the most important factor. Such a development exists nowhere else. No union abroad is doing a tenth of what we are doing in that direction.

"After examining the cultural-educational work of the trade unions," the report noted, "we are inclined to agree with Tomsky." And it concluded: "The cultural work of the unions is one of the most important achievements of the new Russia. There is no precedent or parallel for it anywhere in the world to-day."[53]

On the subject of Strikes and Disputes, the report said in part: "The first questions asked by labor men in arriving in Russia are: 'Do the workers have the right to strike? How are labor disputes settled?'" On the basis of their investigation, the delegation answered:

> We are satisfied that the workers have the legal right to strike. There is no anti-strike law, and nothing resembling American injunctions to curb strikes and the activities of the unions. The hiring of strikebreakers is prohibited by law. Anti-labor judges, courts and government officials are naturally unknown, since the officials are also workers.
>
> However, strikes are not frequent. This is because, as one of the workers told us, "We see no reason for striking against ourselves." From the general union point of view it is naturally desirable to avoid disputes when the costs are clearly borne by the workers themselves. The Soviet government is a workers' regime, and trade unions participate in the government. The leaders are able to look upon strikes not as a weapon of class conflict, as in other countries, but rather as a warning signal that the

unions are not responding to the desires of the workers. When a strike occurs, they quickly see to it that conditions out of which it grew are remedied and that where the local trade union officials are responsible for the situation they are either severely reprimanded or removed from office.

Of course, strikes in privately owned industries are quite another matter. The Russian unions are not slow to strike if they see their interests jeopardized by a private factory owner or concessionaire. There have been a number of such strikes in the last few years.[54]

Answering the question, "Are the Trade Unions controlled by the State?" the report declared:

The unions have a very definite relationship to the state, but the government does not control the unions. It would be more accurate to say that the trade unions control the government. Yet neither statement expressed the truth. Under war communism the trade unions were practically a branch of the state; membership was compulsory and dues were checked out of the pay envelope. But with the creation of at the state trusts and corporations under the New Economic Policy, the unions took on defensive functions similar to those of unions in other countries.

The unions have always been clear in their avowal of their determination to support the soviet government in industrializing the country and in "building up socialism." Believing in the philosophy and practice of socialism, they naturally support the government they have created and defended with gun in hand.

When the Russian workers whom we met in factory, shop and mine were questioned as to whether their unions were "controlled" by the government, their answer was usually an amused smile or a complete failure to understand the point of view of the questioner. "It is *our* government. They are *our* unions," was the reply in many cases. "This is a dictatorship of the proletariat, not a capitalist country" was another. "Our government never broke a strike," or "There are no injunctions and anti-trade union laws in Russia."[55]

On the subject of "Civil Liberties," the report began with a picture of enforced conformity: "No opposition is permitted in Russia, nor any paper which attacks the fundamental principles of communism. Active opponents of the existing regime are not allowed to address public meetings. All books, pamphlets, moving pictures and programs have to be passed on by the department of Censorship in the Commissariat of Education, and any material which attacks the fundamental principles of communism is not allowed to be presented." Yet, the report continued, this was not the entire picture:

But while organized opposition to the system is not permitted, a great deal of criticism by individuals is nevertheless allowed. Peasants and workers are free in the main to criticize the government for its policies. ... The peasants are subject to virtually no suppression; the urban workers are almost equally free. Every industrial or commercial establishment of any size has its wall newspaper, and this generally contains criticism of the administration of that enterprise. There are also workers' life columns in practically all of the newspapers, to which approximately 250,000 correspondents contribute criticisms. Representatives of the government and of the industrial enterprises frequently report to workers' factory meetings, where they are subject to criticism by the workers....

Western liberals and those opposed to the Soviet Government frequently confuse political freedom with real freedom. The former is a part of the latter, but without economic freedom it does not greatly benefit a man. The Russian workers possess this economic freedom to a degree enjoyed by the workers of no other country. Thus they cannot be discharged from employment without the consent of their representatives, and are therefore free from the fear of unjustified dismissal which constantly haunts the workers elsewhere. Their representatives are also members of the governing bodies of the nation's industry, and help to determine its policy. The managers of the factories and workshops must be satisfactory to them. They are also free to criticize the factory administration at any time or at any point. They fix by collective bargaining the pay and the conditions of their work. The managers are compelled to explain the major problems of the business to them. They are also free to criticize the factory administration at any time or at any point. Their help is actively solicited in improving production. The mills, mines and natural resources of Russia are theirs to make of them what they can. As production increases they and the peasants receive the full product, without any deduction for rent or profits. There is no parasitical leisure class to waste without earning and to stir up envy.

The great masses of the people have infinitely more political freedom than they had under the Czarist regime. They elect the members of the soviets, which are responsible to them. They can influence the decisions of the government to a degree which was formerly impossible....[56]

While mainly descriptive, the delegation's report did contain one substantive recommendation—that the United States recognize Soviet Russia. Among a variety of reasons advanced by the writers for this recommendation was that it would be advantageous not only to American capitalists but also to labor:

Such solicitude for the profits of American capitalists may seem somewhat incongruous on the part of a delegation of American workers. We are not concerned about the gains of American capitalists. They are quite able to take care of themselves, and many of them openly favor the recognition of Russia as a direct benefit to their own economic interests. Yet American labor has even a greater interest in this question than the capitalists, involving not profits for a few but employment for thousands. Every intelligent worker can see that a large loan to Russia to finance the purchase of American machinery would directly result in giving a bigger pay envelope to American labor and would stimulate the prosperity of the primary producers of the nation.[57]

The delegation hoped, finally, that an official delegation from the AFL and other labor organizations would eventually undertake a visit to Russia, and it foresaw the possibility that representatives of Russian labor might visit the United States to gain a better understanding of the objectives and structure of American trade unions.[58] The report concluded:

> After all, Russia is a workers' government. If it has made mistakes, or if mistakes are now being made, this ought not to cause complete outlawry from association with the workers in the United States. Only by creating the fiction of a situation which does not exist can the fact of this workers' government be ignored. We hope that this fiction will in time give way to the truth and that the official body of American workers will at least go to see and try to understand.[59]

The report of the technical and advisory staff declared in its Preface:

> When we crossed the Polish border, we were met by a delegation from the Russian trade unions—who are not to be confused with the Russian government. These men and women acted as our hosts during our stay. One condition they made in return for their hospitality, and only one; that on our return to America, we tell the truth about actual conditions as we found them. At no time were we ever embarrassed by any departure from that condition; by an attempts to place the good things too prominently in the foreground at the expense of the bad things. Indeed, as Americans, supposedly skilled in the arts of scientific management and technical efficiency, we were frequently consulted about various difficulties and troubles, in the hope that we would have some helpful advice to offer.[60]

In the chapter of the report of the technical and advisory staff entitled, "The Trade Union Movement," written by Paul H. Douglas* and Robert W. Dunn,** the authors pointed out that "anyone who has attended general meetings and delegate meetings of Russian workers could have little doubt as to the freedom of expression exist-

---

* Paul H. Douglas was the author of *Wages and the Family*, *American Apprenticeship and Industrial Education*, joint author with Dorothy Douglas of *What Can A Man Afford?*, a joint editor of *The Worker in Modern Economic Society*, and a contributor to various publications in the field of economics, statistics and political science.

** Robert W. Dunn had done research and organizing for American trade unions, and wrote regularly for the Federated Press and labor journals. He was at one time acting director of the American Civil Liberties Union, and was later connected with the Russian-American Industrial Corporation which is discussed in our previous volume. He was the author of *American Foreign Investments*, *Company Unions*, and *The Americanization of Labor*. He was also the co-author with Sidney Howard of *The Labor Spy*. Before departing on the research mission in the Soviet Union, he had published *Soviet Trade Unions*, a volume in the Vanguard Press series on Russia.

ing among the class that gained most by the Revolution. As Chairman Tomsky of the C.C.Y.U. told us, in answering a question as to the possibility of intimidation under a system of voting by show of hands. 'Our workers are not meek and cringing. They know how to vote, not only with one hand, but with two fists if necessary.'" Douglas and Dunn continue:

> Because they are economically freed from the intimidation of the employer and the club of a hostile employers' state the workers in these unions are expressing themselves creatively as no other group of workers in the world. With the power of the private employer removed they are growing into the full stature of articulate and self-reliant citizens. And what is more, the top leaders who are predominantly Communists are apparently doing their utmost to develop every form of expression and criticism among the workers. They seem to want them to talk, think and act like workers who have been emancipated and not like the virtual industrial serfs they were before 1917. Perhaps the leaders realize that without this unlimited opportunity for the "broad masses" to express themselves, the dangers of red tape and bureaucracy that beset a socialist state cannot be overcome. Indeed, whenever local union leaders have grown arbitrary and dictatorial, and have not responded to the will of the workers, strikes have resulted in the state industries, particularly in the textile trades in 1925. The workers have somehow learned to react rather quickly against such tendencies both among the governmental and trade union leaders. The half-peasant half-worker elements, fresh from the villages, have displayed a particularly sturdy independence in this respect.[61]

Pointing to the protection provided workers against "possible tendencies of administrators to discriminate against men whom they do not like," Douglas and Dunn noted: "This protection is of course thrown around non-communists as well as party members. This protection against bureaucracy is further intensified by the fact that the managers appointed by the state trusts to take charge of the factories must be acceptable to the unions and that if a manager later becomes obnoxious to the workers it is generally possible for the union to bring sufficient pressure upon the trust to have him removed." They continued:

> In practice, the workers' representatives are very reluctant to approve such discharges and limit the management very strictly. This unwillingness to drop men is but natural and it gives the workers much greater security than they enjoyed under capitalism. But it militates at the same time against industry attaining the highest possible efficiency since men are frequently retained who have been drinking heavily and who have a high percentage of absenteeism....
> Yet if we take Russia as a whole there does not seem to be much abuse of this privilege nor an abnormal percentage of absenteeism. Thus in the

third quarter of 1926, the average number of days of excused and unexcused absences of 2.1 million workers, excluding illnesses and vacations, was 2.4. This was only 3.2 per cent of the total possible working time which does not indicate any great abuse.[62]

"The life of the Russian worker," Douglas and Dunn noted, "centers around his factory. The factory is not looked upon simply as a dirty work place from which one escapes at the end of the day's grind. Instead, it has been remarked that one could spend practically a whole life in a Soviet factory and have one's social and general cultural and artistic demands reasonably well satisfied by the union."[63]

The conclusion of Douglas' and Dunn's chapter is lengthy but still worth quoting in full:

> The state power in the U.S.S.R. being in the hands of a workers' and peasants' government, the unions naturally do not attack the state as do revolutionary unions in other countries where the state is controlled by another class. But although the Russian unions usually cooperate with the Soviet state, real conflicts and disputes frequently arise between them and the overzealous administrators of the trusts and institutions. In such conflicts the unions act as the proper defense of the labor force against all those "bureaucratic tendencies" which they realize are so likely to develop even in a partly socialistically organized society. One of the main tasks of the union is to organize the workers' power against all such tendencies even though they may manifest themselves in a Communist or in the reddest factory director. The "defects in the state machinery" are frequently the subjects of spirited discussions in union meetings. The unions feel it is their social duty to correct and remedy them.
>
> But while attempting to perfect the "apparatus" of the Soviet Government and its economic organs the unions are not unmindful of the danger that their own inner government may become just as bureaucratic. Trade union leaders sometimes, as the Russians put it, get "detached from the masses." When this happens, as we have noted, steps are usually taken to elect officers more responsible to the wishes of the workers and more democratic in their methods.

The Russians, Douglas and Dunn noted in their conclusion, because of having wrestled with the problems of democracy and administration under a "proletarian government," had developed "what we in America would call a 'social conscience'... Regarding themselves as the virtual owners of industry, they have developed a cooperative and proprietarian attitude toward both the state and the industries that is inconceivable under a system of private ownership." They went on:

> Along with this social mindedness goes what might be roughly defined as international mindedness. We found the ordinary Russian worker to be

greatly interested in questions concerning labor progress beyond the Soviet borders. This international outlook is a thoroughly revolutionary concept of life and society. Being under the leadership of the Communists and affiliated to the Red International of Labor Unions (Profintern) the Russian unions are eager to see the downfall of imperialism and the establishment of workers' rule in other countries. They are permeated with the Marxian class struggle ideology. And they desire to see a similar point of view grip the unions in other countries, inducing them to become "class trade unions" and thus to take the lead in overthrowing capitalism in those countries. Because of this fixed idea of the Russians the conservative unions elsewhere contend that they find it difficult to work with them toward common objectives. On the other hand the Russians accuse many of the leaders of the foreign unions with being little more than the labor agents of their imperialistic governments.

In spite of these wide differences in outlook the Russians on their part are most eager to build closer inter-trade union relations with workers everywhere. They will not rest, they told us, until they have established the sort of international labor unity that will serve both as a wall of defense for the Soviet Republics and at the same time assist the unions abroad in their struggles with capital.[64]

The group that visited the Soviet union in 1927 was not as distinguished a body of trade union officials as it had been before the withdrawal of a number of its original members. But, as Simeon Larson points out, "fourteen labor leaders at one time or another had committed themselves to joining the mission. Five were presidents of unions, one was an ex-president, and another had recently been defeated for the office; four were editors of labor journals; one was an assistant president, another was a state director of a national union; and another was a president of a state federation of labor....

"In sum, while an overwhelming majority of trade union officials conformed to the wishes of the AFL leadership in the area of foreign policy, a small but significant minority did question that policy."[65]

They did so in the face of a vicious campaign by the AFL leadership to intimidate those who had agreed to become members of the delegation and any labor figure who contemplated such membership. They did so, too, at a time when the reverberations of the "Red Scare" of 1919-1920 were still evident, when "most trade union officials were therefore reluctant to engage in any activity that might, in any manner expose them or their organizations to charges of being pro-Bolshevik."[66] In his study of the period, Irving Bernstein notes that progressives within the AFL were "reluctant to propose reforms for fear of being branded communists themselves."[67]

It will be recalled that in closing his speech at the 1926 AFL Convention against the recommendation of the resolutions committee rejecting the idea of a labor mission to the Soviet Union, Timothy Healy made the prediction: "I know that our government will recognize Russia within a few years. That, to my mind, is as sure as that the sun will rise tomorrow morning." It took seven years before this prediction became a reality. While the union delegation had failed to convince the AFL leadership of the need for closer relations between the United States and the Soviet Union,* it had contributed to the growing feeling in the United States in favor of such an approach, a feeling that led to the recognition of the Soviet Union by this country. In March, 1933, over the bitter opposition and objections of the AFL leadership, President Franklin D. Roosevelt recognized the Soviet Union.

---

* Larson believes this failure was "due, in the main, to their reluctance to challenge the Federation openly and forcefully and to take precise administrative steps to effectuate their viewpoint," (*op cit.*, p. 364.) There is truth to this, but it was almost impossible under the way the AFL was structured and functioned for any dissent from the leadership policies to succeed. (*Ibid.*, p. 361)

Notes

CHAPTER 1: ENTER WILLIAM GREEN

1. *Proceedings.* AFL Convention, 1926, pp. 16-17.
2. Louis Engdahl, "After Gompers—What? Answered," *Workers Monthly,* 1926, p. 630-32.
3. Craig Phelan, "William Green and the Ideal of Christian Cooperation," in Melvin Dubofsky and Warren Van Tyne, editors, *Labor Leaders in America,* Urbana & Chicago, 1987, p. 136.
4. *Ibid.,* p. 145.
5. James O. Morris, "The AFL in the 1920's: A Strategy of Defense," *Industrial and Labor Relations Review* 11 (July, 1958): 579.
6. *Proceedings,* AFL Convention, 1926, pp. 52-56.
7. *Machinists' Monthly Journal,* November, 1925, p. 624.
8. *Proceedings,* AFL Convention, 1926, pp. 134-35.
9. *Ibid.,* pp. 186-87.
10. *Proceedings,* AFL Convention, 1925, pp. 210-16.
11. *Ibid.,* pp. 218-20.
12. *Proceedings,* AFL Convention, 1926, pp. 314-16.
13. *Ibid.,* pp. 334-36.
14. *Ibid.,* pp. 372-75.
15. *Ibid.,* pp. 384-91.
16. Morris, *op. cit.,* p. 581.
17. *Ibid.,* p. 387.
18. *Ibid.,* pp. 390-91.
19. *Ibid.,* p. 393.
20. *Ibid.,* p. 394.
21. *Ibid.,* p. 395-96.
22. Proceedings, AFL Convention, 1926, pp. 397-99.
23. *Ibid.,* pp. 402-03.
24. Joyce Shaw Peterson, *American Automobile Workers, 1900-1933,* Albany, New York, 1987, p. 122.

CHAPTER 2: THE MINERS

1. Daniel Mason, "John L. Lewis—Hero or Villain?" *Political Affairs,* August, 1980, p. 28.
2. Melvyn Dubofsky and Warren Van Tyne, *John L. Lewis,* New York, 1977, p. 98.
3. *Ibid.,* p. 150.
4. *Daily Worker,* March 24, 1924.
5. *New York Times,* Feb. 20, 1924.
6. George Voyzey, "What the Miners' Union Needs," *Workers Monthly,* April, 1925, p. 271; Dubofsky & Van Tyne, *op. cit.,* p. 135.
7. U.S. Congress, Senate, Committee on Interstate Commerce, *Hearings on Conditions in the Coal Fields of Pennsylvania, West Virginia, and Ohio,* Washington. D.C., 1928, pp. 166, 378-80.
8. George Voyzey, "What the Miners' Union Needs," *Workers Monthly,* April, 1925, pp. 271-72.
9. John L. Lewis, *The Miners' Fight for American Standards,* Indianapolis, 1925, pp. 22-23.
10. *Ibid.,* pp. 33-35.
11. *New York Times,* Sept. 2, 1925.
12. Dubofsky & Van Tyne, *op. cit.,* p 141.
13. *New York Times,* Nov, 23, 1925.
14. *Workers' Monthly,* November, 1925, p. 18.
15. *Ibid.;* *Scranton Times,* Nov. 11-12, 1925.
16. *Philadelphia Inquirer,* Feb.13, 14, 1926; *Daily Worker,* Feb. 15, 1926.
17. *American Federationist* 33 (March, 1926):276; Harold K. Kanarek, "Disaster for Hard Coal: The Anthracite Strike of 1925-1926," *Labor History* 15 (Winter, 1974): 58.
18. *New York Times,* Feb. 19, 1926; Dubofsky & Van Tyne, *op. cit.,* p. 143.
19. *Daily Worker,* July 12, 1926.

20. David M. Schneider, *The Workers' (Communist) Party and American Trade Unions*, Baltimore, 1928, p. 55.

21. Perlman and Taft, *op. cit.*, p. 564.

22. Schneider, *op. cit.*, pp. 55-56.

23. Perlman & Taft, *op. cit.*, p. 565.

24. Schneider, *op. cit.*, p. 56.

25. *New York Times*, Oct. 18, 1926.

26. Dubofsky & Van Tyne, *op. cit.*, p. 128.

27. *United Mine Workers Journal*, Dec. 1, 1926; Coleman, *op. cit.*, p. 109.

28. William Z. Foster, "A Dangerous Situation," *Workers Monthly*, September, 1926, pp. 493-95.

29. McAllister Coleman, *Men and Coal*, N.Y., 1943, p. 109.

30. Dubofsky & Van Tyne, op. cit., p. 128.

31. David J. McDonald and Edward A. Lynch, Coal and Unionism, Indianapolis, 1939, pp. 160-61; Dubofsky & Van Tyne, *op. cit.*, p. 126.

32. Quoted in Dubofsky & Van Tyne, *op. cit.*, p. 128.

33. Minutes of National Committee, TUEL, Meeting, Jan. 27, 1927, Earl Browder Papers, Series 21, Box 19, TUEL Folder, George Arents Library, Syracuse University.

34. *United Mine Workers Journal*, Feb. 13, 1927; Dubofsky & Tyne, *op. cit.*, p. 129.

35. Schneider, *op. cit.*, p. 58; Dubofsky & Van Tyne, *op. cit.*, p.128.

36. Schneider, *op. cit.*, p. 59.

37. James A. Wechsler, *Labor Baron*, N.Y., 1944, p. 32.

38. W.Z. Foster, "The Immediate Task of the Left Wing in the Coal Mining Industry," (2/25/27), Daniel Bell Papers, Tamiment Institute Library, New York University.

39. Anna Rochester, *Labor and Coal*, New York, 1931, pp. 204-06.

40. Minutes of Meeting of Trade Union Committee of Central Executive Committee, April 12, 1927, Earl Browder Papers, Series 2, Box 19, "Trade Union Committee of Central Executive Committee,"

George Arents Library, Syracuse University.

41. Minutes of C.E.C. Mining Sub-Committee, held May 25th, Earl Browder Papers, Series 2, Box 19, "Trade Union Committee of General Executive Committee," George Arents Library, Syracuse University.

42. Rochester, *op. cit.*, pp. 2-7-10; Irving Bernstein, *The Lean Years: A History of the American Worker 1920-1933*, Boston, 1960, p. 130.

43. Dubofsky & Van Tyne, *op. cit.*, p. 149.

44. *Daily Worker*, Oct. 15, 1927.

45. Peter Gottlieb, editor, "Black Miners and 1925-28 Bituminous Coal Strike: The Colored Committee of Non-Union Miners, Montour Mine No. 1, Pittsburgh Coal Company," *Labor History* 28 (Spring,1987):238-39.

46. *Ibid.*, p. 236.

47. *Ibid.*, p. 237.

48. *Daily Worker*, Sept. 7, Oct. 3, 1927.

49. *Daily Worker*, Oct. 3, 1927.

50. Perlman and Taft, *op. cit.*, p. 567.

51. Daniel Bell Papers, Tamiment Library, New York University.

52. Philip S. Foner, *Women and the American Labor Movement: From World War I to the Present*, New York, 1980, pp. 246-47.

53. *The Communist*, 7: (March, 1928): 175-80.

54. *Daily Worker*, April 1, May 1, 1927; Colston Warne, "The Coal War," *The Nation*, April 4, 1928, p. 370; National Save the Miners Union Conference, *Save the Miners Union from the Coal Operators and the Corrupt Lewis Machine*, Washington, D.C., 1928.

55. *Daily Worker*, April 18, 1928; *New York Times*, May 12, 1928; Coleman, *op. cit.*, p. 132; Dubofsky & Van Tyne, *op. cit.*, p. 145.

56. *New York Times*, July 19, 1928, *Daily Worker*, July 19, 1928.

57. "On the Miners Settlement—A Strictly Confidential Report Submitted by Foster," Daniel Bill Papers, Tamiment Institute Library, New York University.

58. Saul D. Alinsky, *John L. Lewis: An Unauthorized Biography*, New York, 1949, p. 61; United Mine Workers Journal, Nov. 15, 1928, p.17; Linda Nyden, "Black Coal Miners in Western Pennsylvania, 1925-1931: The NMU and the UMW," *Science & Society* 41 (Spring, 1977): 86-87.

59. Dubofsky & Van Tyne, *op. cit.*, p. 130.

60. *United Mine Workers Journal*, Nov. 15, 1928, p. 17.

61. *Daily Worker*, March 31, 1928.

CHAPTER 3: MACHINISTS AND CARPENTERS

1. Minutes National Committee, TUEL, Dec. 14, 1924, Daniel Bell Papers, Box 6, "Metal Workers History," pp. 10-11, Tamiment Institute Library, New York University; Edward P. Johanningsmeier, "William Z. Foster: Labor Organizer and Communist," Ph.D. dissertation, Univ. of Pennsylvania, 1988, pp. 618-19.

2. David Montgomery, *The Fall of the House of Labor: The Workplace, the State and American Labor Activism, 1865-1925*, New York, 1987, p.422.

3. William Z. Foster, *Misleaders of Labor*, Chicago, 1926, pp. 61, 71, 73-76.

4. *Labor Age*, August, 1923, p. 5; Johanningsmeier, *op. cit.*, pp. 619-20.

5. Schneider, *op. cit.*, p. 21.

6. *Machinists' Monthly Journal*, March, 1925; *Daily Worker*, March 19, 1925.

7. William Z. Foster, "The Situation in the Machinists Union and the Immediate Tasks for the Left Wing," Daniel Bell Papers, Metal Workers History, Box 6. Tamiment Institute Library, New York University.

8. *Machinists' Monthly Journal*, July, 1925, p. 538; Schneider, *op. cit.*, pp. 22-25.

9. Mark Perlman, *The Machinists*, New York, 1958, pp. 120-21.

10. F.S.T.E.C. Davison, "The Communist Plague in Our Union," *Machinists' Monthly Journal*, November, 1925, pp. 584-88, 637. *See also* "No Room for Communists in the I.A.M.," *Ibid.*, October, 1925, p. 612.

11. *Machinists' Monthly Journal*, May, 1925; Johanningsmeier, *op. cit.*, p. 490.

12. Minutes National Committee, TUEL, September 10, 1925, Daniel Bell Papers, Tamiment Institute Library, New York University.

13. "Resolution of Fight against the Expulsions in the Machinists Union," undated, Daniel Bell Papers, Tamiment Institute Library, New York University.

14. Minutes, National Committee, TUEL, September 10, 1925, Daniel Bell Papers, Tamiment Institute Library, New York University.

15. Perlman, *op. cit.*, pp. 322-23.

16. William Z. Foster, "The Situation in the Machinists Union and the Immediate Task of the Left Wing," Daniel Bell Papers, Tamiment Institute

17. John M. Laslett, *Labor and the Left*, New York, 1959, p. 25.

18. Schneider, *op. cit.*, p. 251.

19. *Ibid.*

20. Robert A. Christie, "Empire in Wood: A History of the United Brotherhood of Carpenters and Joiners of America," Ph.D. dissertation, Cornell University, 1954, P. 483.

21. *Ibid.*, p. 484.

22. *Ibid.*, p. 486.

23. *What's Wrong with the Carpenters' Union*, New York, 1928; Christie, *op. cit.*, p. 487.

24. Christie, *op. cit.*, p. 487.

25. *Ibid.*

26. *Ibid.*

27. Minutes of Meeting, National Committee, TUEL, Daniel Bell Papers, Tamiment Institute Library, New York University.

28. *Ibid.*

29. *Ibid.*

30. *Ibid.*

31. Christie, *op. cit.*, p. 48

32. Comment by Daniel Bell appended to Minutes of Meeting, Na-

tional Committee, T.U.E.L., Daniel Bell Papers, Tamiment Institute Library, New York University.

33. *What's Wrong with the Carpenters' Union.*, pp. 7-15.

34. Christie, *op. cit.*, pp. 488-89.

35. *Daily Worker,* June 2, 1925.

36. *Ibid.,* June 20, 1926.

37. *Ibid.,* June 28, 1926.

38. *Proceedings,* United Brotherhood of Carpenters and Joiners of America, 1928 Convention, pp. 240-45.

39. *Ibid.,* p. 255, ff.

CHAPTER 4: THE LADIES' GARMENT WORKERS

1. Stanley Nadel, "The Communists and the Needle Trades, 1920 to 1928," MA thesis, Columbia University, 1973, pp. 25-26; Stanley Nadel, "Reds Versus Pinks: A Civil War in the International Ladies Garment Workers Union," *New York History* 66 (January, 1985): 59-66.

2. *Labor Herald,* September, 1924, pp. 150-53.

3. Justice, Feb. 27, 1925.

4. *Ibid.,* May 1, 1925; *New York Times.* May 2,1925.

5. *New York Times,* June 7, 1925; Justice, Aug. 14, 1925; *Daily Worker,* June 19, 1925.

6. *Justice,* July 3, 1925; David Gurowsky, "Factional Disputes within the ILGWU, 1919-1928," Ph.D. dissertation, SUNY-Binghamton, 1978, p. 17; *Daily Worker,* June 1, 17, 18, 1925; William Z. Foster, "The Left Wing in the Needle Trades," *Workers, Monthly,* November, 1925, p. 2.

7. William Z. Foster, "Party Industrial Methods and Structure," *Workers' Monthly,* June,1925, p. 380.

8. Gurowsky, *op. cit.*, p. 168.

9. *Justice,* July 10, 1925; *Daily Worker,* July 11, 14, 1925; *New York Times,* July 11, 1925.

10. *Daily Worker.* Aug. 17, 1925; Justice, Aug. 21, 1925.

11. *Women's Wear,* Aug. 19, 1925; *Daily Worker,* Aug. 22, 1925.

12. Irving Howe and Lewis Closer, *The American Communist Party: A Critical History,* New York, 1962, p. 247; David M. Schneider, *op. cit.,* p. 93; Benjamin Stolberg, *Tailors' Progress: The Story of a Famous Union and the Men Who Made It.* Garden City, New York, 1944, pp. 128-29.

13. Nadel, "Reds Versus Pinks," p. 63.

14. For the full text of the agreement, *see* ILGWU Convention Report, 1925, pp. 53-54; *Justice,* Sept. 25, 1925, pp. 1-2.

15. Gurowsky, *op. cit.,* p. 188; Justice, Sept. 4, 1925; *New York Times,* Aug. 31, 1925.

16. Nadel, "Communists and the Needle Trades," p. 31.

17. Proceedings of the ILGWU Convention, 1925, pp. 53-54; *Women's Wear,* Sept. 22, 25, 1925.

18. *Daily Worker,* Dec. 1, 15, 1925; Jack Hardy, *The Clothing Workers,* New York, 1935, p. 42; William Z. Foster, *History of the Communist Party of the United States,* New York, 1952, pp. 253-54.

19. Proceedings of the ILGWU Convention, 1925, pp. 281-88.

20. *Ibid.,* pp. 288-89, 308-11.

21. William F. Dunne, "The ILGWU Convention," *Workers' Monthly,* February, 1926, pp. 174-77; Theodore Draper, *American Communism and Soviet Russia: The Formative Period,* New York, 1960, p. 222.

22. Proceedings of the ILGWU Convention, 1925, pp. 318-33; 339-44; Fannia Cohn to Florence C. Thorne, June 24, 1926, Fannia Cohn Papers, New York Public Library; Gurowsky, *op. cit.,* p. 216.

23. *Daily Worker,* Nov. 19, 1925; *Justice,* Nov. 6, 1925, Jan. 15, Feb. 5, 1926.

24. Gurowsky, *op. cit.,* pp. 221-22.

25. Hardy, *op. cit.,* p. 44.

26. *Justice,* Jan. 8, 15, 1926.

27. *Ibid.,* June 4, 11, 1925; *New York Times,* May 21, June 9, 1926; *Daily Worker,* June 14, 1926.

28. *New York Times,* June 30, 1926; *Women's Wear,* June 30, 1926; *Daily Worker,* July 2, 1926.

29. Philip S. Foner, *Women and the American Labor Movement: From World War I to the Present*. New York, 1980, p. 170.

30. *Daily Worker*, July 7, 1926.

31. *Ibid.*; *News Record*, July 5, 1926; *Women's Wear*, July 6, 1926.

32. *New York Times*, July 10, 1926; *Daily Worker*, July 8, 1926.

33. *New York Times*, Sept. 21, 1926; *Justice*, Sept. 24, 1926; Gurowsky *op. cit.*, p. 241.

34. *Daily Worker*, Sept. 21, 1926.

35. *Justice*, Oct. 1, 5, 1926; *Daily Worker*, Aug. 7, 1926.

36. Benjamin Gitlow, *I Confess: The Truth About American*, New York, 1939, pp. 31-32.

37. Irving Howe and Lewis Closer, the *American Communist Party: A Critical History*, New York, 1962, p. 250.

38. *Daily Worker* Nov. 17, 1926; *Justice*, Nov, 19, 1926.

39. Gurowsky, *op. cit.*, p. 246.

40. *New York Times*, Nov. 13, 1926; *Women's Wear*, Nov. 13, 1926.

41. *Women's Wear*, Nov. 13, 1926.

42. *Justice*, July 18, 1926; Nadel, "Reds Versus Pinks," p. 66n.

43. *Ibid.*, Dec. 2, 1926; Proceedings of the ILGWU Convention, 1928, pp. 83-89.

44. *Women's Wear*, Dec. 3, 1926; *Daily Worker*. Dec. 4, 1926.

45. *Women's Wear*, Dec. 9, 1926; *Justice*, Dec. 10, 1926.

46. *Justice*, Dec. 34, 1926; *Daily Worker*, Dec. 22, 1926.

47. *Justice*, Dec. 24, 1926; *Women's Wear*, Dec. 31, 1926; *American Labor Year Book*, 1927, pp. 107-09.

48. *New York Times*, Dec. 19, 1926; *Daily Worker*, Dec. 19, 1926; Melech Epstein, *Jewish Labor in the U.S.A.: An Industrial, Political, and Cultural History of the Jewish Labor Movement*, (New York, 1950-1953) 2: 149-51.

49. Epstein, *op. cit.*, 2: 148-49.

50. *Justice*, Jan. 14, 1927.

51. *Ibid.*, Jan. 28, 1927.

52. Margaret Larkin, "The Left Wing in the Garment Unions," *Daily Worker*, June 6, 1927.

53. Daniel Bell Papers, Tamiment Institute Library, New York

54. *Ibid.*

55. *Ibid.*

CHAPTER 5: THE LADIES' GARMENT WORKERS: II

1. Jack Hardy, *The Clothing Workers*, New York, 1935, p. 50; Gurowsky, *op. cit.*, pp. 281-84.

2. *Justice*, Feb. 4, 1927; *Daily Worker*, Feb. 3, 1927; *New York Times*, 2, 1927.

3. *Justice*, Feb. 18, 1927.

4. Gurowsky, *op. cit.*, p. 287.

5. *Daily Worker*, Jan. 14, March 15, 18, 1927.

6. *Ibid.*, May 24, 1927; *Justice*, May 30, 1927.

7. Morris Sigman to Morris Siskind, March 26, 1927, YIVO Institute for Jewish Studies Archives, New York City, Box 3, folder 40; Gurowsky, *op. cit.*, p. 289.

8. *New York Times*, April 6, 1927.

9. *Daily Worker*, June 14, 1927; Proceedings of the ILGWU Convention, 1928, pp. 102-22; interviews with retired dressmakers and cloakmakers cited in Gurowsky, *op. cit.*, pp. 23-24.

10. Minutes of the Joint Board Cloak and Dressmakers' Union, November 16, 1927, original in possession of Henry Foner, microfilm copy in Tamiment Institute Library, New York University.

11. Statement of Joint Board Cloak & Dressmakers' Union in answer to Editorial which appeared in *The Day*, on Sunday, December 18, 1927, *ibid.*

12. *Ibid.*

13. *Ibid.*

14. *Jewish Daily Forward*, Dec. 30-31, 1927. 15. *Ibid.*

16. *Ibid.*, Jan. 30-31, 1928.

17. Philip S. Foner, *The Fur and Leather Workers Union*, p. 315n.

18. Fannia Cohn letter, August 25, 1928, Fannia Cohn Papers, Box 4, New York Public Library.

19. Gurowsky, *op. cit.*, pp. 317-18; *American Labor Year Book, 1928*, New York, 1929, p. 115.

20. *Daily Worker*, March 23, 28, 1928; *Justice*, March 23, May 4, 1928.

21. *Daily Worker*, May 8, 1927; Gurowsky, *op. cit.*, pp. 207-08.

22. To the Convention of the International Ladies Garment Workers Union, signed by Louis Hyman and J. Levine, Minutes of the Joint Board Cloak & Dressmakers' Union, *op. cit.*

23. Proceedings of the ILGWU Convention, 1928, pp. 8-9, 25, 37-39.

24. *Ibid.*, pp. 8-9, 146.

25. Foner, *Fur and Leather Workers Union*, p. 315.

26. *New York Times*, May 10, 12, 1928.

27. *Ibid.*, May 13, 14, 16, 1928.

28. *Daily Worker*, May 17, 1928.

29. Minutes of the Joint Board Cloak & Dressmakers' Union, May 10, 1928, *op. cit.*

30. *Ibid.*

31. *Ibid.*, May 9, 10, 1928.

32. Gurowsky, *op. cit.*, pp. 309-10.

33. *New York Times*. May 29, 1928; *Daily Worker*, May 30, 1928.

34. *New York Times*, June 3, 1928; Gurowsky, *op. cit.*, p. 322; "Statement on the Present Situation in the ILGWU," Daniel Bell Collection, Box 10, Tamiment Institute Library, New York University.

35. *Justice*, Dec. 14,1928.

36. *Daily Worker*, Dec. 13, 14, 1928.

37. *Freiheit*, Aug. 8, 1928; *Daily Worker*, Aug. 9, 1928; Women's Wear Daily, Dec. 29, 1928; Nadel, "Reds Versus Pinks," p. 70; Report of the National Agitation Committee of the Ladies Garment Workers to the First Convention for the Establishment of the New Union," New York, 1929.

38. *Justice*, May 25, June 8, 1928; Joel Seidman, *The Needle Trades*, New York, 1942, p. 67; Nadel, "Reds Versus Pinks," p. 70.

39. Nadel, "Reds Versus Pinks," p. 71.

CHAPTER 6: THE FUR WORKERS

1. The most extensive treatment of the 1926 fur strike can be found in Philip S. Foner, *The Fur and Leather Workers Union: A Story of Dramatic Struggle and Achievements*, 1950, pp. 179-244.

2. "Our Demands and their Significance," pamphlet issued by Joint Board Furriers Union, copy in International Fur Workers Union Archives(Hereinafter cited as IFWU Archives); Foner, *Fur and Leather Workers Union*, pp. 179-80.

3. Foner, *Fur and Leather Workers Union*, pp. 181-83.

4. *Jewish Morning Journal*, Jan. 25, 1926; Paul Abelson to O. Shachtman, January 25, 1926, IFWU Archives.

5. Foner, *Fur and Leather Workers Union*, p. 183.

6. *Ibid.*, p. 184.

7. *Ibid.*, p. 185; *Freiheit*, Feb. 4, 1926; *New York Times*, Feb. 4, 1926.

8. Foner, *Fur and Leather Workers Union*, pp. 185-86; *Freiheit*, Feb. 4, 1926; *New York Times*, Feb. 4, 1926; *Women's Wear Daily*, Feb.12-14, 1926.

9. Foner, *Fur and Leather Workers Union*, p. 186.

10. *Fur Age Weekly*, Feb. 1 1926; Foner, *Fur and Leather Workers Union*, pp. 186-87, Emphasis in original.

11. Foner, *Fur and Leather Workers Union*, pp. 187-88.

12. *Daily Worker*, Feb. 17, 1926; *Freiheit*, Feb. 17, 1926; *Freiheit*; Foner, *Fur and Leather Workers Union*, p. 189.

13. Clara Meltzer, "Women Workers Militant in Fur Industry Struggle, *Daily Worker*, April 6, 1926, Clippings in the American Civil Liberties Union Collection, State Clippings, vol. IV, 1926 (N.Y. - W.Va.), Princeton University Library.

14. Foner, *Fur and Leather Workers' Union*, pp. 194-195.

15. *Ibid.*

16. *Ibid.*, pp. 196-97.

17. *Ibid.*, pp. 197-98.

18. *Ibid.*, pp. 198-201.

19. *Ibid.*, pp. 204-07; Hugh Frayne to William Green, June 17, 1925; William Green to Morris Sigman, June 17,1925, American Federation of Labor Archives. Hereinafter cited as AFL Archives.

20. *Fur Age Weekly*, April 5, 1926; Foner, *Fur and Leather Workers Union*, p. 207.

21. *Freiheit*, April 15, 16, 1926; *The Fur Worker*, April , 1926; Foner, *Fur and Leather workers Union*, pp. 208-09.

22. Foner, *Fur and Leather Workers Union*, pp. 209-10.

23. *Women's Wear Daily*, April 17, 1926; Foner, *Fur and Leather Workers Union*, pp. 213-14.

24. *Daily Worker*, April 21-22, 1926; Foner, *Fur and Leather Workers Union*, pp, 216-18.

25. Foner, *Fur and Leather Workers Union*, pp. 230-34; *New York Times*, May 18, 20-23, 24, 1926.

26. Foner, *Fur and Leather Workers Union*, pp. 233-34.

27. *Ibid.*, p. 235; *Daily Worker*, May 29, 30, 1926.

28. Foner, *Fur and Leather Workers Union*, pp. 238-39.

29. *Ibid.*, pp. 239-41; *New York Times*, June 14, 1926.

30. Foner, *Fur and Leather Workers Union*, pp. 242-44; *New York Times*, June 15, 1926; *Daily Worker*, June 15, 1926.

31. Bert Cochran, *Labor and Communism: The Conflict That Shaped American Unions*, Princeton, N.J., 1977, pp. 41-42.

CHAPTER 7: THE FUR WORKERS: II

1. New York *World*, May 3, 1926.

2. Foner, *Fur and Leather Workers Union*, pp. 248-49.

3. William Green to Charles Stetsky, August 23, 1929, AFL Archives.

4. William Green to Ben Gold, July 19, 1926, AFL Archives; Foner, *Fur and Leather Workers Union*, pp. 248-49.

5. William Green to O. Shachtman, July 23, 1926, AFL Archives.

6. Foner, *Fur and Leather Workers Union*, pp. 249-51.

7. *Ibid.*, p. 252.

8. *Ibid.*, pp. 250-54; "Investigation by the American Federation of Labor into the 1926 Strike," pp. 4, 37-39, 66, copy in AFL Archives.

9. Foner, *Fur and Leather Workers Union*, p. 254.

10. "Investigation ... into 1926 Strike," pp. 139-84.

11. O. Shachtman to William Green, January 8, 1927, AFL Archives.

12. Foner, *Fur and Leather Workers Union*, p. 256.

13. *Ibid.*, p. 257.

14. *Ibid.*, p. 259; *Freiheit*, Feb. 18, 1927.

15. Foner, *Fur and Leather Workers Union*, pp. 260-61.

16. *Ibid.*, p. 261.

17. *Ibid.*, pp. 261-62; Ben Gold to Sub-Committee, GEB, February 1, 1927, IFWU Archives.

18. Foner, *Fur and Leather Workers Union*, pp. 261-62.

19. *Ibid.*, pp. 263-64.

20. Matthew Woll, Hugh Frayne, and Edward F. McGrady to William Green, May 7, 10, 1927, AFL Archives.

21. Foner, *Fur and Leather Workers Union*, pp. 265-66.

22. *Ibid.*, pp. 266-67.

23. Morris Sigman to ACLU, March 26, 30, 1927; Arthur Garfield Hayes to Morris Sigman, March 31, 1927, American Civil Liberties Union Papers, New York Public Library.

24. Foner, *Fur and Leather Workers Union*, pp. 267-68.

25. *Ibid.*, p. 269.

26. Matthew Woll, Hugh Frayne and Edward F. McGrady to William Green, May 10, 1927, AFL Archives.

27. Foner, *Fur and Leather Workers Union*, pp. 269-70

28. *Ibid.*, p. 270.

29. *Ibid.*, pp. 270-72.

30. *Ibid.*, pp. 273-74.

·1. *Ibid.*, pp. 273-74.

32. *Ibid.*, p. 276; *New York Times,* June 4, 5, 1927; *Daily Worker,* June 2, 4, 1927; *Freiheit,* June 1, 3, 1927.

33. Matthew Woll, Hugh Frayne, and Edward F. McGrady to Hon. Joseph A. Warren, May 31, June 10, 1927, AFL Archives; Foner, *Fur and Leather Workers Union,* pp. 277-78.

34. New York *Evening Post,* June 24, 1927; New York *Sun,* June 25, 1927; Foner, *Fur and Leather Workers Union,* pp. 279-80.

35. New York *Sun,* June 25-26, 1927; Foner, *Fur and Leather Workers Union,* pp. 281-83.

36. *Daily Worker,* June 14, 26, 1927; *Freiheit,* June 15, 22, 24, 25, 26, 1927; *New York Times,* June 23-26, 1927; Foner, *Fur and Leather Workers Union,* pp. 285-86.

37. Foner, *Fur and Leather Workers Union,* p. 286.

38. Norman Thomas to Forrest Bailey, June 28, 1927, ACLU Correspondence, American Civil Liberty Union Papers, New York Public Library; Foner, *Fur and Leather Workers Union,* pp. 286-87.

39. *New York Times,* June 25, 1927; Foner, *Fur and Leather Workers Union,* p. 287.

40 *Daily Worker,* July 15, 1927; Foner, *Fur and Leather Workers Union,* p. 288.

41. Foner, *Fur and Leather Workers Union,* p. 288.

42. Matthew Woll, Hugh Frayne, and Edward F. McGrady to William Green, May 7, 1927, AFL Archives; Foner, *Fur and Leather Workers Union,* pp. 289-90.

43. Matthew Woll, Hugh Frayne, and Edward F. McGrady to O. Shachtman, April 21, 1927, AFL Archives; Foner, *Fur and Leather Workers Union,* pp. 289-90.

44. Foner, *Fur and Leather Workers Union,* pp. 293-94.

45. "Report of the Proceedings of the Eighth Convention of the International Fur Workers Union, held at Washington, D.C., June 13 to 18,1927," pp. 1-2, 10, 11, 18-19, IFWU Archives.

46. Foner, *Fur and Leather Workers Union,* pp. 292-93,297.

47. "Report of the Proceeding of the Eight Convention...," pp. 62-68; Foner, *Fur and Leather Workers Union,* pp. 296-97.

48. "Report of the Proceedings of the Eighth Convention.... pp. 88-110; Foner, *Fur and Leather Workers Union,* p. 297.

49. Local 30 to Harry Begoon, May 14,1928; Harry Begoon to George Pearlman, June 5, 1928, IFWU Archives; Foner, *Fur and Leather Workers Union,* pp. 305-06.

50. Edward F. McGrady to A.I. Shiplacoff, July 6, 1928, IFWU Archives, AFL Archives.

51. Letter of A.I. Shiplacoff, July 11,1928, IFWU Archives; *Jewish Daily Forward,* July 15, 1928; Foner, *Fur and Leather Workers Union,* pp. 310-11.

52. Foner, *Fur and Leather Workers Union,* p. 312; *Freiheit,* March 8, June 27, 1928.

53. Nadel, "Communists and the Needle Trades," p. 82.

54. Foner, *Fur Workers,* pp. 220-320.

CHAPTER 8: THE MEN'S CLOTHING AND MILLINERY WORKERS

1. Daniel Bell Papers, Tamiment Institute Library, New York University.

2. Stanley Nadel, "The Communists and the Needle Trades, 1920 to 1928," MA thesis, Columbia University, 1973, p. 50.

3. *Daily Worker,* Aug. 16, 1924.

4. *Ibid.*, March 12, 1925.

5. Charles E. Zaretz, *The Amalgamated Clothing Workers of America: A Study in Progressive Trades Unionism,* New York, 1924, pp. 252-53; *Daily Worker,* May 22, 1928.

6. Steven Fraser, "Sidney Hillman and the Origins of the 'New Unionism,'" 1890-1933," unpublished Ph.D. dissertation, Rutgers University, 1983, p. 240.

7. Zaretz, *op. cit.*, pp. 252-53.

8. *Advance*, Dec. 5, 1924.

9. *Ibid.*, Dec. 5, 1924; Amalgamated Clothing Workers of America, Documentary History, Chicago, 1926, pp. 58-59.

10. Melech Epstein, *Jewish Labor in the U.S.A.: An Industrial, Political, and Cultural History of the Jewish Labor Movement* (New York, 1950-1953) 2:166; *Documentary History of the Amalgamated Clothing Workers of America, 1924-26*, p. 50. Epstein says it was for opposing production methods, while the *Documentary History* says that it was for fighting.

11. Epstein, *Jewish Labor in the U.S.A.*, 2:15-16; Zaretz, *op. cit.*, pp. 250-51.

12. *Documentary History of the ACWA, 1924-26*, pp. 50-51; Epstein, *op. cit.*, 2: 166-67; *Freiheit*, Jan. 9, 1925; Zaretz, *op. cit.*, pp. 252-54.

13. Earl R. Beckner, "The Trade Union Educational League and the American Labor Movement," *Journal of Political Economy* 33 (August, 1925): 425.

14. *Daily Worker*, March 27, 1925; *Freiheit*, March 27, 1925; *Advance*, March 27, April 3, 1925.

15. Zaretz, *op. cit.*, pp.185, 256-58; ACWA Ninth Biennial Convention, 1928-1930, Toronto, 1930, p. 6; *New York Times*, Dec. 17, 1926.

16. Sherna Gluck, "The Changing Nature of Women's Participation in the American Labor Movement, 1900-1940's: Case Studies from Oral History," Paper delivered at the Southwest Labor History Conference, March 5, 1977, copy in possession of the present writer. The material is based on interviews with Sarah Rosner.

17. *Daily Worker*, July 4, 1925.

18. R.R. in *Advance*, Feb. 4, 1927.

19. *Daily Worker*, July 12, 15, 1925.

20. *Ibid.*, July 18, Sept. 20, Oct. 14, 1925.

21. Memo from Jacob Potofsky to Sidney Hillman, 1925, ACWA Files, Amalgamated Clothing Workers of America Office; *Documentary History of the ACWA, 1924-26; Daily Worker*, Nov. 27, 1926.

22. Epstein, *op. cit.*, 2: 18.

23. *Daily Worker*, Dec. 16,1925.

24. *Ibid.*

25. *Daily Worker*, Nov. 27, 1926.

26. Epstein, *op. cit.*, 2: 168.

27. Matthew Josephson, Sidney Hillman: *Statesman of American Labor*, Garden City, New York, 1952, pp. 279-80.

28. *Advance*, Jan. 12, 1927.

29. *Ibid.*, Jan.19, 26, 1927. See also Theresa Wolfson, "Equal Rights in the Union," *Survey* 57 (Feb. 15, 1927): 29-30.

30. *Advance*, Sept. 3, 24, 1926, March 24, 1927.

31. Proceedings of the ACWA Convention, 1928, p. 273; Gluck, *op. cit.*, pp. 9-10.

32. *Daily News Record*, Dec. 9, 1926.

33. *Jewish Morning Freiheit*, Oct. 26, 1932. See also William Z. Foster, *American Trade Unionism: Principles and Organization, Strategy and Tactics*, New York, 1947, p. 151.

34. Minutes Central Executive Committee, TUEL, Aug. 5, 1926, Daniel Bell Papers, Tamiment Institute Library.

35. William F. Dunne, "The Left Wing at Two Conventions," *Workers Monthly*, February, 1926, p. 173.

36. *Documentary History of the Amalgamated Clothing Workers, 1926-28*, p. 8.

37. Fraser, *op. cit.*, p. 117.

38. *American Labor Year Book*, 1925 (New York, 1925, p. 7.

39. *Daily Worker*, Dec. 28, 1924, Dec. 29, 1925.

40. *Ibid.*, June 12, 14, 17, 1925; Oct. 13, 14, 1926.

41. *Ibid.*, Nov. 14, 1926, March 8, 1927.

42. *Ibid.*, Oct. 18, 20, 1926, April 22, 1927.

43. Proceedings of the United Hatters, Cap and Millinery Workers International Union, 1927, pp. 173-77; *Daily Worker*, May 13, 1927.

44. *Daily Worker,*, April 12, 20, Nov. 12, 1928, May 7, 1929; *New York Times*, April 20, 1929.
45. *Daily Worker*, May 7, 1929.
46. Donald B. Robinson, *Spotlight on a Union*, New York, 1948, pp. 19-97.
47. *Daily Worker*, May 8,1929.
48. Foster, *American Trade Unionism*, p. 151.
49. Melech Epstein, *Jewish Labor in the U.S.A.: An Industrial, Political, and Cultural History of the Jewish Labor Movement* (New York,1950-1953)1: 323-24.
50. Bert Cochran, *Labor and Communism: The Conflict That Shaped American Unions*, Princeton, N.J., 1977, p. 42.

CHAPTER 9: THE AUTO WORKERS

1. Joyce Shaw Peterson, *American Automobile Workers, 1900-1933*, Albany, N.Y., 1987, pp. 11-13.
2. *Ibid.*, p. 21.
3. *Ibid.*
4. *Ibid.*, pp. 27-28.
5. Joyce Shaw Peterson, "Auto Workers and Their Work, 1900-1933," *Labor History* 22 (Spring, 1984): 228.
6. Stanley B. Matthewson, *Restriction of Output Among Organized Workers*, Carbondale, Ill., 1984, p. 7.
7. Peterson, *op. cit.*, pp. 230-35.
8. *Ibid.*, p. 224.
9. Peterson, *American Automobile Workers*, pp. 110-11.
10. *Ibid.*
11. *Ibid.*, pp. 112-14.
12. *Ibid.*, p. 114.
13. Robert W. Dunn, *Labor and Automobiles*, New York, 1929, pp. 13-22, 186-87.
14. *Ibid.*
15. Dunn, *op. cit.*, pp. 201-04.
16. Roger R. Keeran, "Communist Influence in the Automobile Industry, 1920-1933: Paving the Way for an Industrial Union," *Labor History* 20 (Spring, 1979): 197-98; Roger Keeran, *The Communist Party and*

the *Auto Workers' Unions*, Bloomington, Indiana, 1980, pp. 74-78.
17. Vera Buch; "The Functioning of a Detroit Shop Nucleus, *Party Organizer*, July-August, 1928, pp. 14-15; Theodore Draper, *American Communism and Soviet Russia: The Formative Period*, New York, 1961, p. 193.
18. Rebecca Grecht, "Factory Newspapers," *Party Organizer*, December, 1927, p. 16; "Issuing Shop Papers," *Party Organizer*, February, 1930, pp. 109-10; Dunn, *op. cit.*, pp. 192-94.
19. *Ford Worker*, April, 1926. Copy in Archive of Labor and Urban Affairs, Wayne State University (hereinafter referred to as Wayne State).
20. *Dodge Worker*, August, 1926. Copy in Wayne State.
21. *Fisher Body Worker*, December, 1926, Copy in Wayne State.
22. *Ford Worker, April*, 1926. Copy in Wayne State University.
23. Keeran, "Communist Influence" p. 202.
24. *Ford Worker*, May, 1926.
25. *Dodge Worker*, January, 1927.
26. *Ibid.*, November, 1926.
27. *Ford Worker*, October, 1926.
28. *Ibid.*
29. *Ibid.*, November, 1926.
30. *Ibid.*, December, 1926.
31. Dunn, *op. cit.*, p. 194; Keeran, "Communist Influence," p. 202.
32. The Ford Worker," *Party Organizer*, April, 1927, pp. 9-10.
33. Frank Marquart, *An Auto Worker's Journal: The UAW From Crusade to One Party Union*, University Park and London, 1975, pp. 33-35.
34. Keeran, "Communist Influence..." pp. 207-08.
35. Dunn, *op. cit.*, pp. 197-99.
36. Keeran, "Communist Influence..." pp. 208-09.
37. *Ibid.*, p. 209.
38. *Auto Workers News*, May, June, 1927. Copy in Wayne State.
39. *Ibid.*, July, September, October, December, 1927; Keeran, "Communist Influence..." pp. 215-16.

40. *Auto Workers News*, May, June, October, December, 1927. Copy in Wayne State.

41. Irving Bernstein, *The Lean Years: A History of the American Worker, 1920-1933*, Boston, 1966, pp. 84, 97-107.

42. *Proceedings*, AFL Convention, 1926, pp. 40, 171-73; Keeran, "Communist Influence..." pp. 211-12.

43. Keeran, "Communist Influence..." p. 212.

44. William Green, "Communist Internationale," *American Federationist*, November, 1926, pp. 1305-06.

45. *American Federationist*, 34 (August, 1927): 914-15; James O. Morris, "The AFL in the 1920's: A Strategy of Defense," *Industrial and Labor Relations Review* 11 (July, 1958): 574-75.

46. Peterson, *op. cit.*, pp. 123-24.

47. Dunn, *op. cit.*, pp. 176-80.

48. William Green to Robert L. Cruden, November 12, 1928, William Green Papers, State Historical Society of Wisconsin.

49. Morris, *op. cit.*, p. 576.

50. *Ibid.*

51. Ben Lipschitz, "Who Will Organize the Auto Workers?" *Daily Worker*, Aug. 25, 1928.

52. Keeran, "Communist Influence..." p. 220.

53. Peterson, *op. cit.*, pp. 126-27.

54. John Manley, "Communists and Auto Workers: The struggle for Industrial Unionism in the Canadian Automobile Industry," *Labour/Le Travail* 17 (Spring, 1980): 113.

55. *Ibid.*, pp. 114-15.

56. Keeran, "Communist Influence..." p. 220.

57. *Auto Workers News*, March, June, October, 1928.

58. Bernstein, *op. cit.*, p. 301; Keeran, "Communist Influence..." p.223.

59. Quoted in Keeran, "Communist Influence..." p. 222.

60. Joyce Shaw Peterson, "Black Auto Workers in Detroit, 1910-1930," *Journal of Negro History*, 1979, p. 188.

61. Keeran, "Communist Influence..." p. 221.

62. Frank Marquart, quoted in Peterson, "American Automobile Workers, p. 128.

63. Keeran, "Communist Influence..." p. 225.

CHAPTER 10: THE TEXTILE WORKERS

1. *Labor Herald*, July, 1923, pp. 23-24.

2. Robert Dunn and Jack Hardy, Labor and Textiles; A Study of Cotton and Wool Manufacturing, New York, 1931, pp. 202-03.

3. *New York Times*, Jan. 10, March 12, April 14, May 15, 1925.

4. *Daily Worker*, July 18, 1925.

5. *Labor*, Nov. 14, 1925.

6. *Daily Worker*, March 18, 1925.

7. *Ibid.*, April 24, 1926.

8. *Ibid.*, Feb. 12, 1925. The article contains a detailed list of towns and names of mills in New England, the percentage wage cut, and the date instituted.

9. *Textile Worker*, March, 1925.

10. *Daily Worker*, Jan. 7, Feb. 7, March 18, June 6, 1925.

11. *Ibid.*, Aug. 27, 1925.

12. Martha Glaser, "Paterson 1924: The ACLU and Labor," *New Jersey History* 94 (Winter, 1976): 155-72.

13. *Daily Worker*, Aug. 14, 1924; *Workers' Monthly*, November, 1924, p. 14.

14. *Daily Worker*. Nov. 15, 1924, Sept. 12, 15, 1926.

15. *Survey*, 44 (June 3,1920); 121; Morris Schonbach, *Radicals and Visionaries: A History of Dissent in New Jersey*, Princeton N.J., 1964, p. 73; Michael Hollander, "Prelude to a Strike," *Proceedings of the New Jersey Historical Society* 79 (July, 1961): 161-63.

16. U.S. Department of Labor, *Women's Bureau, Bulletin* No. 37, Washington, D.C., pp. 363-64; American Civil Liberties Correspondence, 1926, Passaic, vol. I, Section I, American Civil Liberties Union Papers, New York Public Library

17. *Advance*, March, 1926.

18. U.S. Department of Labor, *Women's Bureau, Bulletin* No. 40, Washington, D.C., 1925, pp. 30-36.

19. *Labor*, Oct. 16, 1926.

20. *Daily Worker*, March 24, 1927; Paul L. Murphy, Hermit Hall, and David Klassen, *The Passaic Textile Strike of 1926*, Belmont, Cal., 1974, p. 83; Morton Siegel, "The Passaic Textile Strike of 1926," Ph.D, diss., Columbia University, 1952, p. 80.

21. Siegel, *op. cit.*, pp. 81-82.

22. William Hard, "They Must Have Espionage," *New Republic*, April 21, 1920; Robert W. Dunn, *Spying on Workers*, New York, 1932, pp. 3-5; *New York Times*, April 15, 1925; *Daily Worker*, March 24, 1927.

23. U.S. Department of Labor, Women's Bureau, Bulletin No. 41, Washington, D.C., 1926, p. 36.

24. Murphy, Hall, and Klassen, *op. cit.*, pp. 12-13.

25. Raymond H. Groff, "The Passaic Textile Strike of 1926," Master's thesis, Columbia University, 1927, pp. 10-11.

26. *Daily Worker*, Feb. 12, Aug. 27, 1925.

27. *American Labor World*, April, 1926, p. 29; Siegel, *op. cit.*, p. 134; Stephen R. Irwin, "Conflict Resolution and the Development of Law: The Passaic Textile Strike of 1926 and the New Jersey State Riot Act," pp. 48-50, senior thesis, 1976, Archives Rutgers University, New Brunswick, N.J.; Murphy, Hall, and Klassen, *op. cit.*, pp. 36-38.

28. Murphy, Hall, and Klassen, *op. cit.*, pp. 36-38; Siegel, *op. cit.*, p. 135

29. *New York Times*, Jan. 26, 1926.

30. *Ibid.*, Jan. 20-Feb.7, 1926.

31. *Ibid.*, Feb. 5, 1926.

32. Dee Garrison, *Mary Heaton Vorse.. The Life of an American Insurgent*, Philadelphia, 1989, pp. 197-98.

33. Siegel, *op. cit.*, p. 331. Copies of the Strike Bulletin may be found in the Mary Heaton Vorse Papers, Wayne State University, Reuther Library, Archives of Labor and Urban Affairs.

34. *New York Times*, Jan. 26, 30, Feb, 7, 8, 9, 20, 21, 23, 24, 1926; *Daily Worker*, Feb. 9, 21, 23, 24, March 10, 11, 1926; Groff, *op. cit.*, 1926; Mary Heaton Vorse, *The Passaic Textile Strike, 1925-1927*, p. 17; Rosalyn Baxandall, *Words on Fire: The Life and Writings of Elizabeth Gurley Flynn*, New Brunswick, N.J., pp.

35. *Daily Worker*, Sept. 12, 1925.

36. Albert Weisbord, *Passaic: The Story of a Struggle Against Starvation Wages and for the Right to Organize*, Chicago, 1926, p. 44; *Daily Worker*, Feb. 24, 1926; I. Wenzenweig, in *Advance*, March 15, 1926, p. 8.

37. *Textile Strike Bulletin*, May 7,1926, p. 1. Copy in New York Public Library.

38. *Ibid.*, May 21, 1926, p. 3.

39. *Daily Worker*, Sept. 24,1926.

40. *Chicago Journal*, Aug. 10, 1926; *Daily Worker*, Aug. 12, 1926; May 1, 1927; Vera Buch Weisbord, *A Radical Life*, Bloomington and London, 1977, pp. 118-19.

41. *Textile Strike Bulletin*, April 28, 1926, p. 2.

42. *Daily Worker*, Oct. 12, 1926.

43. *New York Times*, Sept. 20, 1926 *Daily Worker*, Sept. 24, Oct. 5, 1926.

44. *New York Times*, March 3, 4, 1926.

45. *Ibid.*, March 4, 1926; Weisbord, op cit., pp. 118-19.

46. *New York Times*, March 9, 19, 1926.

47. *Ibid.*, March 8, 1926.

48. *Ibid.*, April 15, 17, 19, 1926; Glaser, *op. cit.*, pp. 167-68; Michael H. Ebner, "Strikes and Society: Civil Behavior in Passaic, 1875-1926," *New Jersey History* 97 (Spring,1979): 8.

49. Gloria Garrett Samson, "Toward a New Social Order: The American Fund for Public Service: Clearinghouse for Radicalism in the 1920s," unpublished Ph.D. dissertation, University of Rochester, 1987, p. 239; *New York Times*, April 13, 15, 1920.

50. *New York Times*, April 10, 11, 12, 15, 22, 1926; *New Leader*, April 17, 1926; *Passaic Daily Herald*, April 14, 15, 22, 1926.

51. *Daily Worker,* July 27, 1926; *Passaic Daily News,* July 27, 1926.

52. *Daily Worker,* July 27, 1926.

53. *Ibid.,* July 31, 1926.

54. *Ibid.*

55. *Ibid.,* Oct. 30, 1926.

56. Murphy, Hall, and Klassen, *op. cit.,* p. 38; Ebner, "Strikes and Society," pp. 19-20.

57. Groff, *op. cit.,* pp. 18-19.

58. *Ibid.,* pp. 20, 22-25.

59. *Ibid.,* pp. 30-37; *Passaic Daily Herald,* April 17-18, 1926.

60. Philip S. Foner, *Fur and Leather Workers Union,* p. 242n.

61. William Z. Foster, *From Bryan to Stalin,* New York, 1937, p. 202.

62. Siegel, *op. cit.,* pp. 250-51; Groff, *op. cit.,* p. 32; it, *New York Times,* Aug. 1, 5, 13, 1926; *Daily Worker,* Aug. 14, 17, Sept. 3, 1926.

63. Groff, *op. cit.,* pp. 32-34; *Chicago Tribune,* Oct. 28, 1926.

64. *Passaic Daily News,* Sept.15, 17, 1926.

65. *New York Times,* Nov. 5, 1926; Siegel, *op. cit.,* p. 263.

66. *Passaic Daily News,* Nov. 12, 1926; *New York Times,* Nov.12, 13, 1926; *Daily Worker,* Nov. 13, 1926; Siegel, *op. cit.,* p. 263.

67. *Passaic Daily News,* Dec. 14, 1926; Siegel, *op. cit.,* p. 264.

68. *Passaic Daily News,* March 2, 1927; *New York Times,* March 1, 2, 1927; Siegel, *op. cit.,* p. 265.

69. Weisbord, *op. cit.,* p. 64; *Daily Worker,* March 2, 8, Nov. 13, 1927; Theresa Wolfson, "Trade Union Activities of Women," *Annals of the American Academy of Political and Social Science* 143 (May, 1929): 127.

70. Minutes, National Committee, TUEL, Dec. 17, 1927, Daniel Bell Collection, Tamiment Institute library, New York University.

71. Siegel, *op. cit.,* pp. 263-68; Albert Weisbord, *The Conquest of Power* (New York, 1937) 2:1115; Albert Weisbord, *Passaic Reviewed* (San Francisco, 1976), p. 112.

72. Bert Cochran, *Labor and Communism· The Conflict That Shaped American Unions,* Princeton, N.J., 1977, p. 32.

73. *Daily Worker,* Sept. 5, 1926.

74. *The Communist,* November, 1929, p. 611, Foster, *From Bryan to Stalin,* p. 202.

75. U.S. Department of Labor, *Women's Bureau Bulletin,* Number 41 (Washington, D.C., 1926), p. 36; Murphy, Hall and Klessen, *op. cit.,* pp. 12-14.

76. Robert W. Dunn papers, Univ. of Oregon, Special Collections.

CHAPTER 11: THE TEXTILE WORKERS: II

1. *Daily Worker,* Jan. 24, 1927.

2. *Ibid.,* Feb. 21, 22, 1927.

3. Michael W. Santos, "Community and Communism: The 1928 New Bedford Textile Strike," *Labor History,* 26 (Spring, 1985): 230.

4. New Bedford *Evening Standard,* April 18, 1928; *New York Times,* April 14, 1928, *Daily Worker,* May 14, 15, 1928.

5. Santos, *op. cit.,* pp. 237-38.

6. New Bedford *Evening Standard,* April 19, 20, 1928; *Daily Worker,* April 25, 1928.

7. *Ibid.,*; New Bedford *Evening Standard,* April 24, 25, 1928, Santos, *op. cit.,* p. 240.

8. Bedford *Evening Standard,* May 25, 1928, *New York Times,* May 25, July 10, 1928.

9. *New York Times,* July 10, 1928.

10. *Daily Worker,* May 16, 1928; New Bedford *Evening Standard,* May 25, 1928.

11. New Bedford *Evening Standard,* May 6, 1928.

12. *Ibid.,* May 9, 1928; "Women in Textile Organizing: An Interview with Sophie Melvin Gerson, by Anne Fishel," *Radical History Review* 4 (Summer, 1977): 116.

13. New Bedford *Evening Standard,* May 12, 1928.

14. *Ibid.,* May 9, 11, 1928.

15. *Ibid.,* May 27, 1928.

16. *Ibid.,* May 1, 2, 3, 5, 1928.

17. *Ibid.,* May 4, 1928.

18. *Daily Worker,* May 17, 1928.

19. New Bedford *Evening Standard,* May 10, 1928.

20. *Ibid.,* May 11, 24, 1928; *Daily Worker,* May 11, 24, 1928.

21. New Bedford *Evening Standard,* June 11, 14, 1928.

22. *Ibid.,* July 1, 1928.

23. *Daily Worker,* Aug. 25, 1928.

24. New Bedford *Evening Standard,* July 15, 1928.

25. *Ibid.,* July 16, 1928.

26. *Daily Worker,* July 14, 1928.

27. New Bedford *Evening Standard,* Aug. 1, 24, 1928.

28. *Daily Worker,* July 23, 1928.

29. *Ibid.,* June 25, 1928.

30. *Ibid.,* June 29, 1928.

31. New Bedford *Evening Standard,* Aug. 28, 1928.

32. *Daily Worker,* Sept. 27, 1928; New Bedford *Evening Standard,* Sept. 25, 1928.

33. New Bedford *Evening Standard,* Sept. 27, 28, 1928.

34. Robert Dunn and Jack Hardy, *Labor and Textiles: A Study of Cotton and Wool Manufacturing,* New York, 1931, p. 164.

35. *Daily Worker,* Oct. 1, 1928.

36. *Ibid.,* Oct. 2, 1928.

37. New Bedford *Evening Standard,* Oct. 7, 8, 1928; *New York Times,* Oct. 8, 1928.

38. *Labor Defender,* September, 1928, p. 266.

39. *Daily Worker,* Oct. 13, 1928.

40. William Z. Foster, "Organizing the Unorganized," *Labor Herald,* July, 1923, pp. 11-12.

CHAPTER 12: LABOR AND FASCISM

1. Quoted in Dorothy Gallagher, *All the Right Enemies—The Life and Murder of Carlo Tresca,* New Brunswick, N.J., 1988, pp. 98-99.

2. *New York Times,* Nov. 1-2, 1922.

3. "Fascist Propaganda in the United States," six-page typed manuscript, Girolamo Valenti Collection, Tamiment Institute Library; Vincent M. Lombardi, "Italian American Workers and the Response to Fascism," in George E. Pozzetti, ed., *Pane e laboro: The Italian American Working Class,* Toronto, 1980, pp. 141-57.

4. *Advance,* May 10, 1923.

5. Gallagher, *op. cit.,* p. 128.

6. John P. Diggins, *Mussolini and Fascism: The View From America,* Princeton, N.J., 1972, p. 188.

7. Philip V. Cannistraro, "Luigi Antonini and the Italian Anti-Fascist Movement in the United States, 1940-1943," *Journal of American Ethnic History* 5 (Fall 1983): 21.

8. *Ibid.,* p. 21.

9. Rudolph J. Vecoli, ed., *Italian-American Radicalism, Old World Origins and New World Development,* New York, 1973, pp. 99-101; Rudolph J. Vecoli, "Pane e Gustizia, A Brief History of the Italian-American Labor Movement," *La Parola de Popolo* 26 (September-October 1976): 55-61.

10. *Advance,* May 10, 1923.

11. *Labor Herald,* July, 1923, p. 29.

12. *Industrial Worker,* April 21, 1923.

13. Diggins, *op. cit.,* p. 120.

14. *Ibid.*

15. *Industrial Worker,* July 4, 1923.

16. *Nation,* April 25, 1923, pp. 502-03.

17. Diggins, *op. cit.,* p. 213.

18. *Ibid.,* p. 116.

19. *Proceedings,* AFL Convention, 1923, pp. 66, 175, 178.

20. Egisto Rossi to Samuel Gompers, July 16, 1923, Samuel Gompers Papers, State Historical Society of Wisconsin. The full text of Rossi's letter may be found in Ronald Radosh, "Corporatism, Liberal, and Fascist as seen by Samuel Gompers," *Studies on the Left* 3 (Summer 1963): 69-70.

21. Samuel Gompers, "An Analysis of Fascism," *American Federationist* 30 (November 1923): 927-30.

22. *Ibid.,* pp. 929-33.

23. Diggins, *op. cit.,* p. 172.

24. *See* "Industry's Manifest Destiny," Report of the Executive Council to the 1923 AFL Convention, *American Federationist* 30 (November

1923): 890-95; Samuel Gompers, "Labor in Europe and America— Idle Words vs. Practical Works," *ibid* (June 1923):461-67; Samuel Gompers, "Significant Movements in Europe," *ibid* (July 1924): 565-70.

25. *Proceedings,* AFL Convention, 1927, p. 268.

26. Diggins, *op. cit.,* p. 172.

27. *Ibid.*

28. William Green, "Fascism and the Worker," *American Federationist* 33 (February 1926): 219-20.

29. *Proceedings,* AFL Convention, 1927, pp. 261-62.

30. *Ibid.,* p. 262.

31. Diggins, *op. cit.,* p. 173.

32. *Ibid.*

33. *Ibid.*

34. See *Advance,* May 11, Sept. 7, 1923, April 7, 23, 30, June 25, July 6, Nov. 12, 1926.

35. Pellegrino Nazzato, "Fascist and Anti-Fascist Reaction in the United States to the Matteoti Murder," in Francisco Corduso, ed., *Studies in Italian Social History: Essays in Honor of Leonard Covello,* Totowa, N.J., 1975, p. 50.

36. *New York Times,* June 27, 1924; Nazzaro, *op. cit.,* pp. 51-52.

37. Nazzaro, *op. cit.,* p. 56.

38. "The Manifesto of the North American Anti-Fascist Alliance," *Labor History* 13 (Summer 1972): 418-26.

39. *Ibid.,* p. 449.

40. *New York Times,* Aug, 1, Sept. 3, 4, 5, 1926; Diggins, *op. cit.,* p. 114.

41. *Daily Worker,* Sept. 4, 1926.

42. Diggins, *op. cit.,* p. 114.

43. Cannistraro, *op. cit.,* pp. 22, 25-26; Diggins, *op. cit.,* p. 119.

44. Paul Avrich, *Sacco and Vanzetti: The Anarchist Background,* Princeton, N.J., 1991, p. 213. Even before the execution of Sacco and Vanzetti, in July, 1927, Calozero Greco and Donato Carillo, followers of Luigi Galleani, a leading anarchist who had emigrated to the United States from Italy, were accused of murdering two Italian Blackshirts in New York. Clarence Darrow, the celebrated attorney, agreed to take the case, not only because he "detested Mussolini and everything he stands for, but because he had seen in the Sacco Vanzetti affair how 'prejudice and passion' could result in a questionable verdict. Greco and Carillo were acquitted." (*Ibid.*)

45. *Ibid.,* pp. 213-14.

CHAPTER 13: THE BLACK WORKERS

1. Philip S. Foner, *Organized Labor and the Black Worker, 1619-1981,* New York, 1982, pp. 140-41, 151-54; Ira DeA. Reid, *Negro Membership in American Labor Unions,* New York, 1930, pp. 29-30.

2. James W. Ford, "Foster and Negro-Labor Unity," *Masses and Mainstream,* March, 1951, p. 21. See also Mark Solomon, "Red and Black: Negroes and Communism," Ph.D. dissertation, Harvard University, 1972, pp. 79-88; James S. Allen, editor, *Lenin on the United States: Selected Writings by V.I. Lenin,* New York, 1970, pp. 58-59; James S. Allen, "Lenin and the American Negro," *The Communist* 13 (1934): 53-61.

3. *Labor Herald,* July, 1924, p. 152.

4. *Ibid.,* p. 156.

5. *Ibid.,* p. 152.

6. *Ibid.,* pp. 160-61.

7. Ford, *op. cit.,* pp. 21-22.

8. *Opportunity,* October, 1924, p. 300.

9. *The Crisis,* December, 1921, p. 104.

10. For the history of the American Negro Labor Congress, See Philip S. Foner and James S. Allen, editors, *American Communism and Black Americans: A Documentary History, 1919-1929,* Philadelphia, 1987, pp. 107-30.

11. *Ibid.,* pp. 117-18.

12. *Constitution and Program of the American Negro Labor Congress,* Chicago, n.d., p. 3.

13. *Ibid.,* pp. 7-8.

14. *Ibid.,* p. 9.

15. *Workers Monthly,* December, 1925, pp. 65-74.
16. *Daily Worker,* Oct. 26, 1925
17. Reid, *op. cit.* p. 127.
18. Reprinted in *Literary Digest,* Nov. 21, 1925, p. 14.
19. Foner, *Organized Labor and the Black Worker,* p. 172.
20. *American Federationist* 30 (October, 1925):162.
21. Foner, *Organized Labor and the Black Worker,* p. 169.
22. *The Crisis,* July, 1922, p.132.
23. Herbert R. Northrup, "The Negro and the United Mine Workers," *Southern Economic Journal* 9 (April, 1943):314.
24. Abram L. Harris, Jr., "The Negro Worker in Pittsburgh," unpublished M.A. thesis, University of Pittsburgh, 1924, and *Opportunity,* July,1925, p. 195.
25. James T. Faing, "The Negro Miner in West Virginia," unpublished Ph.D. dissertation, Ohio State University, 1933, p. 342.
26. National Urban League, *Negro Membership in American Labor Unions,* New York, 1930, p. 70.
27. Linda Nyden, "Black Miners in Western Pennsylvania, 1925-1931: The NMU and the UMW," *Science & Society* 41 (Spring, 1977): 85-86.
28. National Urban League, *Negro Membership in American Labor Unions,* p. 68.
29. Minutes of National Executive Committee, Trade Union Educational League, November 25, 1927, Earl Browder Papers, George Arents Research Library, Syracuse University.
30. *Pittsburgh Courier,* April 7, 1928, p. 1.
31. *Ibid.,* p. 8.
32. *Labor Unity,* May 28, 1928; Nyden, *op. cit.,* p. 86.
33. *Pittsburgh Courier,* May 12, 1928, p. 3.
34. *United Mine Workers Journal,* Nov. 15,1928; Nyden, *op. cit.,* p. 87. *See also* Herbert Hill, "Myth-Making as Labor History: Herbert Gutman and the United Mine Workers of America," *International Journal of Politics, Culture and Society,* 2 (Winter 1988): 132-200.
35. *The Crisis,* Aug. 1924, pp. 53-54.
36. Reprinted in *Literary Digest,* Nov 21, 1925, p. 14.
37. *Proceedings,* AFL Convention, 1925, pp. 323-24.
38. Foner, *Organized Labor and the Black Worker,* p. 172.
39. *The Messenger,* November, 1926, p. 12; *Pittsburgh Courier,* reprinted in *Daily Worker,* Nov. 10, 1926.
40. *Daily Worker,* Feb. 5, 1927.
41. Foner, *Organized Labor and the Black Worker,* p. 177.
42. *Labor Age* 15 (March, 1926): 2.
43. Foner, *Organized Labor and the Black Worker,* p. 177.
44. *Ibid,* p. 178.
45. *Ibid.*
46. Gloria Garrett Samson, *op. cit.,* pp. 368-69.
47. Jervis Webster Anderson, *A. Philip Randolph: A Biographical Portrait,* New York, 1973, pp. 159, 168; Harris, *op. cit.,* pp. xi, 2; *Messenger,* September, 1922, p. 335.
48. Harris, *op. cit.,* p. 35.
49. Foner, *Organized Labor and the Black Worker,* p. 179.
50. *Black Worker,* August, 1936.
51. Foner, *op. cit.,* pp. 179-80; Harris, *op. cit.,* pp. 51-54.
52. Samson, *op. cit.,* p. 372. Sterling Spero and Abram Harris note that "the most striking shortcoming of Randolph's tactics was hunger for publicity," and the "notion that publicity was a good in itself which would in some mystical manner win victory for the porters." Randolph, they point out, "relished the attention he received as well as his growing reputation as the spokesman for all Black workers." (Sterling D. Spero and Abram L. Harris, *The Black Worker: The Negro and the Labor Movement,* New York, 1931, P. 398. See also Paul Pfeffer, "A. Philip Randolph: A Case Study in Black Leadership," Unpublished Ph.D. dissertation, 1980, pp. 86-89.

53. Harris, *op. cit.*, pp. 89-90.
54. Samson, *op. cit.*, p. 373.
55. Foner, *op. cit.*, p. 180.
56. Foner, *op. cit.*, pp. 181; Harris, *op. cit.*, 41-46.
57. Samson, *op. cit.*, p. 372.
58. *Ibid.*, p. 373.
59. *The Nation*, June 9, 1926, p. 9.
60. *Daily Worker*, Aug. 25, 1926; *The Nation* June 9, 1926, p. 9.
61. Quoted in A. Philip Randolph, "Story of the Porter," *Silver Jubilee Anniversary Folder*, Chicago, 1950, p. 9.
62. Foner, *op. cit.*, 181.
63. *Ibid*, p. 182.
64. *The Nation*, June 9, 1926, p. 3.
65. *The Messenger*, August, 1926, p. 223.
66. Foner, *op. cit.*, p. 182.
67. *Ibid.*
68. Harris, *op. cit.*, pp. 57-58; Foner, *op. cit.*, p. 183.
69. *Railway Age*, March 17, 1928, p. 18.
70. *New York Times*, June 7, 1926.
71. Quoted in A. Philip Randolph, "Story of the Porter," *Silver Jubilee Anniversary Folder*, Chicago, 1950, p. 9.
72. New York *Evening Journal*, March 15, 1928; Harris, *op. cit.*, pp. 104-08; Foner, *op. cit.*, p. 184.
73. *New York Times*, June 7, 1928.
74. *Ibid.*
75. *Ibid.*
76. *Ibid.*, June 8, 1928.
77. *Ibid.*
78. *Pittsburgh Courier*, June 16, 1928.
79. Communist leaflet quoted in *New Leader*, June 16, 1928; Foner, *op. cit.*, p. 184.
80. Harris, *op. cit.*, pp. 114-15.
81. Brailsford, R. Brazeal, *The Brotherhood of Sleeping Car Porters*, New York, 1946, pp. 86-88.
82. Harris, *op. cit.*, pp. 113-14.
83. *Ibid.*, pp. 115-16.
84. Foner, *op. cit.*, p. 185; *Messenger*, February, 1925, p. 89.
85. *Chicago Defender*, Aug. 20, 1927; Louisville *News*, Dec. 26, 1925.

86. *Proceedings* AFL Convention, 1929, pp. 137-38; Harris, *op. cit.*, pp. 153-54.
87. *Proceedings* AFL Convention, 1928, pp. 137-39.
88. *Ibid.*, pp. 384-85; *Proceedings* AFL Convention, 1929, pp. 137-38.
89. Harris, *op. cit.*, 155.
90. Foner, *Organized Labor and the Black Worker*, p. 186.
91. *Proceedings* AFL Convention, 1928, pp. 384-85.
92. Harris, *op. cit.*, p. 157.
93. *Ibid.*, pp. 157-53; *Opportunity* 8 (February, 1930): 56.
94. Harris, *op. cit.*, p. 158; *Opportunity* 7 (December, 1929): 381-82.
95. Harris, *op. cit.*, p. 159.
96. Foner, *Organized Labor and the Black Worker*, p. 186,
97. Philip Randolph to M.P. Webster, August 3, 1926, Brotherhood of Sleeping Car Porters papers, Chicago Historical Society.

CHAPTER 14: SACCO-VANZETTI

1. Statement of Frank P. Walsh, February 8, 1921; John Gilman to Frank P. Walsh, March 16, 1921; Frank P. Walsh to John Gilman, March 23, 1921, Frank P. Walsh Papers, New York Public Library.
2. Roberta Strauss Feuerlicht, *Justice Crucified: The Story of Sacco and Vanzetti*, New York, 1977, pp. 32-45; Brian Jackson, *The Black Flag: A Look at the Strange Case of Nicola Sacco and Bartolomeo Vanzetti*, London and New York, 1981, pp. 38-49.
3. Felix Frankfurter, *The Case of Sacco and Vanzetti*, New Tork, 1927, pp. 39-48.
4. *Ibid.*, pp. 59-64; Feuerlicht, *op. cit.*, pp. 122-29.
5. Frankfurter, *op. cit.*, pp. 122-23; Feuerlicht, *op. cit.*, pp. 136-38.
6. Eric Foner, "Sacco and Vanzetti: The Men and the Symbols," The *Nation*, Aug. 20, 1977, pp. 135-36.
7. Frankfurter, *op. cit.*, pp. 128-30; Feuerlicht, op cit., pp. 182-86.
8. Frankfurter, *op. cit.*, pp. 133-34.

9. Jackson, *op. cit.*, pp. 182-83; Feuerlicht, *op. cit.*, pp. 192-93.

10. *Advance*, Nov. 25, 1921.

11. *Ibid.*, Dec. 9, 1921.

12. *Ibid.*, Aug. 5, 1921.

13. *Ibid.*, June 2, 1922.

14. *Ibid.*

15. Art Shields, "The CPUSA Defends Its Class," *Daily World*, Sept. 24, 1977; *Labor Herald*, March, 1922, pp. 3-4.

16. *Daily Worker*, Dec. 10, 1924.

17. *Ibid.*, Dec. 27, 1924.

18. *Ibid.*, March 18-20, 1925.

19. *Labor Defender*, January, 1926, pp. 10-12.

20. Shields, *op. cit.*; Arthur Zipser, "Sacco and Vanzetti: Their Friends and Enemies," *Political Affairs* 57 (January, 1978): 39.

21. Shields, *op. cit.*

22. Frankfurter, *op. cit.*, pp. 64-66, 72-74, 112-16.

23. Quoted in Eric Foner, *op. cit.*, p. 136.

24. Feuerlicht, *op. cit.*, pp. 212-14.

25. Johnson, *op. cit.*, pp. 192-94; Frankfurter *op. cit.*, pp. 123-24.

26. Feuerlicht, *op. cit.*, pp. 136-37.

27. The Sacco Vanzetti Case: Transcript of the Record of the Trial of Nico Sacco and Bartolomeo Vanzetti in the courts of Massachusetts and Subsequent *Proceedings* 1920-27 (New York, 1928-29) 5: 489.

28. *Ibid.*, p. 4904.

29. Marion Denmam Frankfurter and Gardner Jackson, editors, *The Letters of Sacco and Vanzetti*, New York, 1928, p. 276.

30. William L. Patterson, "Lessons of the Sacco and Vanzetti Case," *Daily World*, Aug. 20, 1977.

31. Feuerlicht, *op. cit.*, pp. 220-21; Jackson, *op. cit.*, pp. 262-66.

32. Eric Foner, *op. cit.*, pp. 137-38.

33. Philip S. Foner, *Fur and Leather Workers Union*, pp. 144-45; *Daily Worker*, March 12, 1925, April 14, July 5, 8, Aug. 11, 12-14, 15, 21, 22, 23, 1927; *New York Times*, Aug. 20, 21, 22, 23, 1927; *Proceedings* AFL

Convention, 1924, p. 293; 1926, p. 212.

34. Daniel Bell Papers, Tamiment Institute Library, New York University.

35. *Daily Worker*, July 8, Aug. 11, 12-14, 15, 21-23, 1927; *New York Times*, Aug. 20-23, 1927.

36. *Industrial Solidarity*, March 23, 1927; Donald J. McClurg, "The Colorado Strike of 1927—Tactical Leadership of the IWW," *Labor History* 4 (winter 1963): 70.

37. *Industrial Solidarity*, July 27, 1927; McClurg, *op. cit.*, p. 71.

38. McClurg, *op. cit.*, pp. 71-72.

39. *Ibid.*, p.72.

40. *Ibid.*

41. *Ibid.*

42. *Ibid.*

43. Gary R. Mormino and George E. Pozetta, *The Immigrant World of Ybor City Italians and Their Latin Neighbors in Tampa, 1880-1980*, Urbana and Chicago, 1988, pp. 160-62.

44. Johannes Zelt, *Proletarian Internationalism in the Battle for Sacco and Vanzetti*, Berlin, German Democratic Republic, 1958, pp. 66-74, 82-87.

45. Rosario Joseph Toriello,"'Requests I Cannot Ignore,'—A New Perspective on the Role of Cardinal O'Connell in the Sacco-Vanzetti Case," *Catholic Historical Review* 64 (July, 1938): 50-52.

46. Frankfurter and Gardner, *op. cit.*, pp. 112-13.

47. *Ibid.*, pp. 104-05.

48. Eric Foner, *op. cit.*, p. 317-18.

49. G. Louis Joughin and John Demarest, *The Legacy of Sacco and Vanzetti*, New York, 1940, p. 13.

50. *Ibid.*, p. 84.

51. Alfred J. Kuzik, "The Sacco-Vanzetti Case and the Communists," *Nature, Science & Thought*, 2 (1969): 166-67.

52. *New York Times*, Aug. 17, 1977; Boston *Globe*, Aug. 17, 1977. Michael S. Dukakis's proclamation and the technical report compiled by the governor's chief legal counsel, Daniel A. Taylor, are reproduced

in the appendix of Upton Sinclair's *Boston: A Documentary Novel of the Sacco-Vanzetti Case*, Cambridge, 1978, pp. 757-99.

53. *Journal of American History* 54 (April 1986): 121-22.

CHAPTER 15: MARITIME AND AGRICULTURAL WORKERS

1. Bruce Nelson, *Workers at the Waterfront: Seamen, Longshoremen, and Unionism in the 1930s*, Urbana and Chicago, 1988, p. 76.
2. See minutes of November 20, 1925, Executive Committee, TUEL, Daniel Bell Papers, Tamiment Institute Library.
3. *Fighting Years: A Short History of the Marine Workers Industrial Union*, New York, n.d., pp. 2-3.
4. *Fighting Years*, p. 25; Bert Cochran, *Labor and Communism: the Conflict that Shaped American Unions*, Princeton, N.J., P. 43; Joseph Bruce Nelson, "Maritime and Working-Class Consciousness in the 1930s," Ph.D. dissertation University of California, Berkeley, 1982, pp. 66-70; Paul S. Taylor, *Mexican Labor in the United States: Imperial Valley*, University of California Publications in Economics, vol. 6, Berkeley, California, 1928, p. 9.
5. *Ibid.*, pp. 9, 29, 32; Linda C. Majka and Theo J. Majka, *Farm Workers, Agribusiness, and the State*, Philadelphia, 1982., 28-45.
6. Charles Wollenberg, "Huelga 1928 Style: The Imperial Valley Cantaloupe Strike," *Pacific Historical Review* 38 (February 1969): 47-48.
7. Paul S. Taylor, *Mexican Labor in the United States*, Berkeley, 1933, I, pp. 43-44.
8. Mexicans in California, Report of Governor C.C. Young's Mexican Fact-Finding Committee, San Francisco, 1930, p. 163.
9. Taylor, *Mexican Labor in the United States: Imperial Valley*, p. 48; James Gray, "The American Civil Liberties Union of Southern California and Imperial Valley Agricultural Disturbances, 1930, 1934, Ph.D.

dissertation, University of California, Los Angeles, p. 11.
10. Cletus E. Daniel, *Bitter Harvest: A History of California Farm Workers, 1870-1941*, Ithaca, N.Y., 1981, p. 110.
11. *Ibid.*
12. *Daily Worker*, May 26, 1928; Daniel, *op. cit.*, p. 386 n. 16.
13. *Mexicans in California*, pp. 135-36, Report of Dr. Louis Bloch.
14. *Ibid.*
15. *Ibid.*, pp. 140-41; Wollenberg, *op. cit.*, p. 50.
16. Mexicans in California, pp. 141-42, Report of Dr. Louis Bloch.
17. *Ibid.*, p. 139.
18. Gray, *op. cit.*, p. 15.
19. *Ibid.*
20. *Ibid.*, p. 16.
21. *Ibid.*, p. 17.
22. *Ibid.*
23. *Ibid.*
24. Wollenberg, *op. cit.*, p. 53.
25. *Ibid.*
26. Gray, *op. cit.*, pp. 17-18.
27. Wollenberg, *op. cit.*, pp. 55-56.
28. *Ibid.*, p. 56.
29. Gray, *op. cit.*, p. 18.
30. *Ibid.*; Wollenberg, *op. cit.*, p. 56.

CHAPTER 16: A NEW TRADE UNION POLICY

1. *Workers Monthly*, June, 1925, p. 35.
2. Earl R. Beckner, "The Trade Union Educational League and the American Labor Movement," *Journal of Political Economy* 13 (August, 1925):427-28.
3. *Ibid.*, p. 423; *Labor Herald*, July, 1924, pp. 151-54.
4. *Workers Monthly*, April, 1925, p. 253.
5. *Ibid.*, March, 1925, p. 228.
6. William Z. Foster, "The American Federation of Labor Convention," *Workers Monthly*, January, 1925, p. 107.
7. *Daily Worker*, Sept. 7, 1926.
8. *Ibid.*
9. *Ibid.*
10. *Workers Monthly*, September, 1925, p. 499

11. *New Republic*, Oct. 27, 1926; *Proceedings* AFL Convention, 1926, pp. 40, 171-73.
12. Roger R. Keeran, "Communist Influence..." *op. cit.*, pp. 212-14.
13. William F. Dunne, "Surrender Raised to a System," *Communist*, November, 1927, p. 417.
14. William Z. Foster, "Capitalist Efficiency 'Socialism,'" *ibid.*, March, 1928, pp. 169-71.
15. *Workers Monthly*, November, 1926, pp. 125-27.
16. A. Losovsky, "Results and Prospects of the United Front," *Communist International* 5 (March, 1928): 143-46.
17. "Resolution on Trade Union work," *Communist, July, 1928, pp. 392-93.*
18. *Ibid.*, pp. 391-92, 397-98.
19. William Z. Foster, "Old Unions and New Unions," *ibid.*, pp. 401-02.
20. Melvyn Dubofsky and Warren Van Tyne, *John L. Lewis: A Biography*, New York, 1977, p. 147; *Daily Worker*, July 23, Aug. 24, 1928.
21. *Coal Digger*, Oct. 1, 1928; Linda Nyden, "Black Miners in Western Pennsylvania, 1925-1931: The NMU and the UMW," *Science & Society* 41 (Spring, 1977):87-88; *Pittsburgh Courier*, Sept. 15, 1928; *Labor Defender*, October, 1928, p. 204; *The Nation* 127 (September 26, 1928): 282.
22. John J. Watt, "Launching the National Miners Union," *Labor Unity*, October, 1928, p. 5.
23. *Coal Digger*, Nov, 1, 1928.
24. *Daily Worker*, Sept. 14, 1928; *Opportunity* 6 (October, 1928): 311.
25. Philip S. Foner, *Organized Labor and the Black Worker*, pp. 194-95.
26. *Daily Worker*, July 16, 1928.
27. Albert Weisbord, "Mill Workers Must Build Union," *ibid.*, Aug. 23, 1928.
28. *Daily Worker*, Sept. 24, 1928
29. *Ibid.*, Sept. 24, 26, 27, 1928.
30. *New York Times*, March 9, April 19, 1929.
31. *Daily Worker*, Sept 24, 1928, March 9, 1929.
32. Sam Wiseman, "The Textile Workers Organize Their Union," *Labor Unity*, October, 1928, pp. 10-12; *Daily Workers*, Sept. 24, 1928.
33. *Daily Worker*, Aug. 6, 9, 13, 15, 1928; *Freiheit*, Aug. 8, 9, 10, 1928,
34. *Daily Worker*, Aug. 13, 14, 1928; *Freiheit*, Aug. 13, 14, 1928.
35. *Daily Worker*, Aug.16, 17, 1928; *Freiheit*, Aug. 16, 17, 1928; Philip S. Foner, *The Fur and Leather Workers Union*, p. 318.
36. Foner, *Fur and Leather Workers Union*, p. 318.
37. *Ibid.*, p. 319.
38. Report of the National Organization of the Ladies Garment Workers, to the First Convention for the Establishment of the New Union, December 28, to January 1, 1929, pp. 23-24, 58-59, 59-60; *Daily Worker*, Dec. 2831, 1928, Feb. 7, 1929; *Freiheit*, Dec. 28-31, 1928; Foner, *Fur and Leather Workers Union*, pp. 318-20; *Negro Champion*, Feb. 23, 1929.
39. *Daily Worker*, May 22, 1921.
40. David Gurowsky, "Factional Disputes Within the ILGWU, 1919-1928," Unpublished Ph.D. dissertation, State University of New York at Binghamton, 1978, p. 325.
41. Irving Howe and Lewis Closer, *The American Communist Party: A Critical History*, New York, 1957, p. 253.
42. Jack Barbash, *The Practice of Unionism*, New York, 1956, p. 122; Harvey A. Levenstein, *Communism, Anticommunism, and the CIO*, Westport, Conn., 1981, pp. 14-16; Bert Cochran, *Labor and Communism*, Princeton, N.J., 1978, pp. 18-20.
43. Theodore Draper, "Communists and Miners, 1928-1933," *Dissent* 19 (Spring 1972): 373-74.
44. *See* Joel Seidman, *The Needle Trades*, New York, 1942, pp. 188-90.
45. Leo Wolman, *Ebb and Flow in Trade Unionism*, New York, 1936, pp. 16, 33-34, 40-41, 112-19.
46. Irving Bernstein, *The New Deal Collective Bargaining Policy*, Berkeley and Los Angeles, 1950, pp 2-3

47. Lewis L. Lorwin, *The American Federation of Labor, History, Policies, and Prospects,* Washington, D.C., 1933, pp. 279-80.

48. Fraser M. Ottanelli, *The Communist Party of the United States: From the Depression to World War II,* New Brunswick, N.J., 1991. p. 21.

CHAPTER 17: REVOLT OF THE SOUTHERN TEXTILE WORKERS

1. Sinclair Lewis, *Cheap and Contented Labor: The Picture of a Southern Mill Town in 1929,* New York, 1929, pp. 3-25.

2. Broadus Mitchell, "The Present Situation in the Southern Textile Industry," *Harvard Business Review,* April, 1930, p. 302.

3. Robert Barry in New York *Evening World,* Sept. 20, 1929; "A Working Mother from Bessemer City," *Daily Worker.* Oct, 3, 1929.

4. F. Ray Marshall, *Labor in the South,* Cambridge, Mass., 1967, pp. 83-85; George Brown Tindall, *The Emergence of the New South, 1913-1945,* Baton Rouge, 1967, pp. 333-34; George S. Mitchell, *Textile Unionism in the South,* Chapel Hill, N. Car., 1931, p.52; Harley E. Tolley, "The Labor Movement in North Carolina, 1880-1922," *North Carolina Historical Review* 30 (July, 1953): 354-75.

5. Tindall, *op. cit.,* p. 344.

6. Elizabeth L. Otley, "Women and Children in Southern Industry," *Annals of the American Academy of Political and Social Science,* January, 1931, p. 164; James Starr, "Deplorable Conditions Among Textile Workers," *American Labor Legislation Review* 18 (March, 1928):42; William B. Spofford, "Marion, North Carolina," *Christian Century* 36 (Dec. 4, 1929): 1502.

7. Margaret Larkin, "Tragedy in North Carolina," *North American Review* 218 (December, 1929): 686, 690; *Daily Worker,* April 8, 1929.

8. Marion Bonner, "Behind the Southern Textile Strikes," *The Nation,* 129 (Oct. 2, 1929): 352.

9. Tom Tippett, *When Southern Labor Stirs,* New York, 1931, pp. 112-13.

10. *Ibid.,* pp. 113-15.

11. Irving Bernstein, *The Lean Years: A History of the American Worker, 1920-1933,* Boston, 1960, p.13; Mitchell, *op. cit.,* pp. 61-64.

12. Letter from United Textile worker to William Green, reproduced in AFL Executive Council Minutes, February 18-25, 1929, pp. 65-66, cited in Marshall, *op. cit.,* p. 105; *Labor,* Oct. 26, 1929. *See also* Weimar Jones, "Southern Labor and the Law," *Nation* 131 (July 2, 1930):14.

13. *Daily Worker,* April 1, 1929.

14. U.S. Congress, Senate, *Working Conditions of the Textile industry in North Carolina, South Carolina and Tennessee,* Hearings on Sen. Res. 49, Senate Committee on Manufactures, 71st Cong., 1st sess. (1929), pp. 47-48; James A. Hodges, "Challenge to the New South: The Great Textile Strike in Elizabethton, Tennessee, 1929," *Tennessee Historical Quarterly* 23 (December, 1964): 346.

15. *Labor,* March 30, May 18, 1929.

16. Tippett, *op. cit.,* pp. 60-61.

17. *Labor,* March 30, 1929.

18. Marshall, *op. cit.,* p. 106.

19. Tippett, *op. cit.,* pp. 64-65; "Elizabethton, Tennessee," *Nation* 128 (May 1, 1929): 527.

20. *New York Times,* April 16, May 5, 1929.

21. *Labor,* May 18, 1929.

22. Tippett, *op. cit.,* p. 70.

23. Bernstein, *op. cit.,* p. 19; Tippett, *op. cit.,* p. 72.

24. *Daily Worker,* May 24, 27, 1929; Tippett, *op. cit.,* p. 72; Jacquelyn Dowd Hall, "Disorderly Women: Gender and Labor Militancy in the Appalachian South," *Journal of American History* 73 (September, 1986): 368.

25. *Labor,* June 8, 1929; George Fort Milton, "The South Fights the Unions," *New Republic,* July 10, 1929, pp. 202-03.

26. *New York Times,* Sept. 12, 1929; Marshall, *op. cit.,* p. 106; Bernstein, *op. cit.,* pp. 19-20; *Proceedings,* AFL Convention, 1929, pp. 271-72;

Hodges, *op. cit.*, pp. 356-571 Hall, *op. cit.*, p. 380.

27. The Gastonia strike is the best-studied labor conflict in the history of the South. See Tom Tippett, *When Southern Labor Stirs*, New York, 1931, pp. 60-72; Liston Pope, *Millhands and Preachers: A Study of Gastonia*, New Haven, Conn., 1942; Bernstein, *Lean Years*, pp. 20-32; Robin Hidd, "The Loray Mill Strike," Unpublished MA thesis, University of North Carolina, 1932; Fred E. Beal, *Proletarian Journey*, New York, 1937, especially pp. 111-35. More recent accounts include Theodore Draper, "Gastonia Revisited," *Social Research* 38 (Spring, 1971); Philip S. Foner, *Women and the American Labor Movement: From World War I to the Present*, New York 1980, pp. 230-39; Dorsett Edmunds, Laurie Graybeal, Eileen Hanson, Ann Horne, Charlie Thomas and Judith Vaughan, *Lets Stand Together: The Story of Ella Mae Wiggins*, Charlotte, N.Car., 1979. The most important contemporary journalistic treatments are Wm. Dunne, "Gastonia: The Center of Class Struggle in the New South," *Communist* 8 (July, 1929); Dunne, *Gastonia: Citadel of the Class Struggle of the New South* (New York, 1929); Paul Blanshard, "Communism in Southern Mills," *Nation*, April 24, 1929, and Blanshard, "One Hundred Percent Americans on Strike," *The Nation*, May 8, 1929.

28. *Daily Worker*, Aug. 24, 1928; Liston Pope, *Millhands and Preachers*, *op. cit.*, p. 230; Bernstein, *op. cit.*, pp. 20-21.

29. Larkin, *op. cit.*, p. 687.

30. *Daily Workers* April 30, 1929.

31. Fred E. Beal, *Proletarian Journey*, New York, 1937, pp. 111-18; Theodore Draper, "Gastonia Revisted," *Social Research*, 38 (Spring, 1971): 9-11; Pope, *op. cit.*, p. 30; Tippett, *op. cit.*, p. 88; Vera Buch Weisbord, *A Radical Life*, Bloomington and London, pp. 179-80; William Dunne, *Gastonia: Citadel of the Class*

Struggle of the New South, New York, 1929, pp. 20-23.

32. *Daily Worker*. April 8, 1929.

33. *Ibid.*, April 1, 1919; Pope, *Millhands and Preachers*, p. 257; Weisbord, *op. cit.*, p. 180; Tippett, *op. cit.*, p. 76.

34. *Daily Worker*. April 10, 1929; Lahne, *op. cit.*, p. 217.

35. Pope, *op. cit.*, p. 258; *Daily Worker*, April 12, 1928.

36. Reprinted in *Daily Worker*, April 6, 1929.

37. *Ibid.*, April 12, 1929; Weisbord, *op. cit.*, pp. 191-92; Marshall, *Labor in the South*, p. 111; Tippett, *op. cit.*, pp. 88-89; Pope, *op. cit.*, p. 258.

38. Tippett, *op. cit.*, p. 87; Pope, *op. cit.*, p.258.

39. Beal, *op. cit.*, pp. 159-60; Lahne, *op. cit.*, p. 217; *Daily Worker*, May 28, 1920.

40. *Daily Worker*. April 19, 20, 21, 1929; *New York Times*, April 20, 21, 1929; Lahne, *op. cit.*, p. 217.

41. *Daily Worker*, Sept. 20, 1929; Dorsett Edmunds, Laurie Graybeal, Eileen Hanson, Ann Horne, Charlie Thomas and Judith Vaughan, *Lets Stand Together: The Story of Ella Mae Wiggins*, Charlotte, N.Car., 1979, pp. 30-36.

42. *Daily Worker*, Sept. 14, 1938.

43. *Ibid.*, Oct. 4, 1929.

44. Edmunds and others, *Stand Together*, p. 9; Weisbord, *op. cit.*, pp. 208-09; Otto Hill, "Gastonia and the Negro," *Labor Defender*, October, 1929, pp. 254-55; Cyril Briggs, "The Negro Question in the Southern Textile Strikes," *Communist* 8 (June, 1929): 324-25; Dunne, Gastonia: *Citadel of the Class Struggle*, p. 29; Draper, *op. cit.*, pp. 18-22.

45. Weisbord, *op. cit.*, p. 260.

46. Lahne, *op. cit.*, pp. 218.

47. Tippett, *op. cit.*, p. 97.

48. *New York Times*, June 8, 1929.

49. Margaret Larkin, "Ella Mae's Songs," *The Nation*, Oct. 9, 1929, p. 122.

50. *Daily Worker*, Aug. 7, 1929.

51. Reprinted in *Daily Worker*, Sept. 26, 1929.

52. *New York Times*, Sept. 8, 9, 1929.

53. *Ibid.*, Sept. 10, 11, 1929.
54. *Daily Worker*, Sept. 18,1929, Jan. 14, 1930.
55. *Ibid.*, Sept. 18, 1929; Garrison, *op. cit.*, p. 229
56. *Ibid.*, Sept. 18, 1929, Jan. 14, 1930; Edmunds and others, *Lets Stand Together*, pp. 88-92..
57. Quoted in Herbert J. Lahne, *The Cotton Mill Worker*, New York, 1944, p. 219.
58. *Daily Worker*, Oct. 24, 1929.
59. Lahne, *op. cit.*, pp. 218-19; Broadus Mitchell, *Textile Unionism in the South*, p. 76.
60. Marshall, *Labor in the South*, p. 109; Bernstein, *Lean Years*, p. 13; Lahne, *Cotton Mill Worker*, p. 219; Pope, *Millhands and Preachers*, p. 249.
61. *Daily Worker*, June 19, 1929.
62. *Daily Worker*, April 19, Sept. 23, 1929.
63. William Dunne, "Gastonia: The Center of Class Struggle in the New South," *Communist* 8 (July, 1929): 379. Emphasis in original.
64. *Daily Worker*, Sept. 23, 1929.
65. Pope, *op. cit.*, p. 244.
66. Bernstein, *Lean Years*, p. 22.
67. Paul Blanshard, "Communism in Southern Mills," *Nation*, April 24, 1929, pp. 122-24.
68. Marshall, *Labor in the South*, p. 117; Tippett, *op. cit.*, pp. 140-55; Marion Bonner, "Behind the Southern Textile Strikes," *Nation*, Oct. 2, 1929, p. 352.
69. Marshall, *Labor in the South*, pp. 117-18.
70. Tippett, *op. cit.*, pp. 142-75; Benjamin Stolberg, "Madness in Marion," *Nation*, Oct. 23, 1929, pp. 462-64; *Daily Worker*. Oct.4, 11, 18, 22, 29, 1929.
71. Lahne, *op. cit.*, p. 221.
72. *New York Times*, Oct. 5, 1929.
73. Samuel Yellen, *American Labor Struggles*, New York, 1936, p. 326.
74. *Daily Worker*, April 1, 1929.
75. *Handbook of American Trade-Unions*, *Bureau of Labor Statistics*, Bulletin No. 618, p. 614.

CHAPTER 18: THE AMERICAN TRADE UNION DELEGATION TO THE S0VIET UNION, 1927

1. "British Labor's Report on Russia," *Machinists' Monthly Journal*, 27 (May, 1925): 267-69.
2. *Ibid.*
3. *Proceedings*, AFL Convention, 1925, pp. 139-43; Simeon Larson, "Opposition to AFL Foreign Policy: A Labor Mission to Russia, 1927," *The Historian* 43 (May, 1981): 347-48.
4. *Proceedings*, AFL Convention, 1925, pp. 150-53; *American Federationist* 32 (February, 1925): 11-13; American Federation of Labor, Official Publicity Release; Larson, *op. cit.*, p. 348.
5. Larson, *op. cit.*, 349.
6. *New York Times*, Nov. 16, 1925.
7. *Ibid.*, Nov. 18, 1925.
8. William Green to All Organized Labor, December 24, 1925, William Green Papers, Manuscripts Division, State Historical Society of Wisconsin, Madison, Wisconsin. (Hereinafter cited as Green Papers.)
9. Larson, *op. cit.*, p. 349
10. Albert F. Coyle to William Green, June 10, 1926, Box 2, William Mitch Papers.
12. *Ibid.*
13. *Ibid.*
14. *Ibid.*
15. William Green to Albert Coyle, June 17, 1926, Box 2, Mitch Papers.
16. Albert Coyle to William Green, June 23, 1926, Box 2, Mitch Papers.
17. Statement of the Executive Council American Federation of Labor, Cincinnati, Ohio, June 28, 1926, Box 2, Mitch Papers; From the American Federation of Labor Information and Publicity Service, July 1, 1926, Green Papers.
18. Albert Coyle to William Green, July 2, 1926, Box 2, Mitch Papers.
19. Albert Coyle to William Green, July 3, 1926, Box 2, Mitch Papers.

20. William Green to Albert F. Coyle, July 22nd, 1926, Box 2, Mitch Papers; Larson, *op. cit.*, p. 350*n*.
21. *Labor Journal*, July 9, 1926; *New Leader*, July 17, 1926, 2; Larson, *op cit.*, 352.
22. *New York Times*, July 8, 1926, 43.
23. Larson, *op. cit.*, p. 353.
24. Albert F. Coyle to William Mitch, August 21, 1926, Box 2, Mitch Papers.
25. William Mitch to Albert F. Coyle, August 24, 1926, Box 2, Mitch Papers.
26. Albert F. Coyle to William Mitch, August 26, 1926, Box 2, Mitch Papers.
27. Albert F. Coyle to William Mitch, September 25, 1926, Box 2, Mitch Papers
28. Labor Mission Press Release, September 27, 1926, Box 2, Mitch Papers; Larson, *op. cit.*, p. 353.
29. Albert F. Coyle to William Mitch, September 25, 1926, Box 2, Mitch Papers
30. Larson, *op. cit.*, pp. 353-54, based on *Proceedings*, AFL Convention, 1926, pp. 262-79.
31. *Proceedings*, AFL Convention, 1926, pp. 264-65.
32. *Ibid.*, p. 272
33. *Ibid.*, pp. 273-76.
34. *Ibid.*, pp. 265-66; Larson, *op. cit.*, p. 354.
35. Larson, *op. cit.*, pp. 354-55.
36. *Proceedings*, AFL Convention, 1926, pp. 276-79.
37. Statement by William Green, May 28, 1927, in Green Papers.
38. Statement of the American Trade Union Delegation to Russia, n.d., Box 2, Mitch Papers.
39. *International Molders' Journal*, 63 (August, 1927): 479-81; Larson, *op. cit.*, pp. 355-56.
40. *American Photo Engraver*, 19 (August, 1927): 938-40; Larson, p. 356.
41. L.E. Sheppard to Alfred F. Coyle July 8, 1927, Box 2, Mitch Papers.
42. Wm. Mitch to William Green, July 20, 1927, Box 2, Mitch Papers.
43. Wm. Green to William Mitch, July 23, 1927, Box 2, Mitch Papers.
44. John Brophy diary, entry of August 17, 1927, Mullen Library, Manuscript Division, Catholic University of America, Washington, D.C.; Larson, *op. cit.*, p. 357.
45. *New York Times*, Aug. 25, 1926, 6.
46. AFL Weekly News Service, September 3, 1927; Larson, *op. cit.*, p. 357*n*.
47. Joseph Stalin, *Interview with Foreign Workers' Delegations*, New York, 1927, pp. 37, 40-42.
48. *Russia After Ten Years: Report of the American Trade Union Delegation to the Soviet Union*, New York, 1927.
49. *New York Times*, Sept. 28, 1927, 11.
50. Stuart Chase, Robert Dunn, and Rexford Guy Tugwell, eds., *Soviet Russia in the Second Decade*, New York, 1928
51. *Russia After Ten Years*, pp. 17-18
52. *Ibid.*, pp. 30-32.
53. *Ibid.*, pp. 32, 34.
54. *Ibid.*, pp. 19-20.
55. *Ibid.*, pp. 20-21.
56. *Ibid.*, pp. 75-77.
57. *Ibid.*, pp. 88-89.
58. Larson, *op. cit.*, p. 360.
59. *Russia After Ten Years*, p. 96.
60. Chase, Dunn, and Tugwell, *op. cit.* p. xii.
61. *Ibid.*, pp. 193-94
62. *Ibid.*, pp. 195-96.
63. *Ibid.*, p. 200.
64. *Ibid.*, pp. 213-14.
65. Larson, *op. cit.*, p 360
66. *Ibid.*, pp. 362-63.
67. Irving Bernstein, *The Lean Years* Boston, 1960; repr. ed. Boston, 1972, pp. 136-41

Index